DATA PROFILING AND INSURANCE LAW

This timely, expertly written monograph looks at the legal impact that the use of 'Big Data' will have on the provision – and substantive law – of insurance. Insurance companies are set to become some of the biggest consumers of big data which will enable them to profile prospective individual insureds at an increasingly granular level.

More particularly, the book explores how: (i) insurers gain access to information relevant to assessing risk and/or the pricing of premiums; (ii) the impact which that increased information will have on substantive insurance law (and in particular duties of good faith disclosure and fair presentation of risk); and (iii) the impact that insurers' new knowledge may have on individual and group access to insurance.

This raises several consequential legal questions: (i) To what extent is the use of big data analytics to profile risk compatible (at least in the EU) with the General Data Protection Regulation? (ii) Does insurers' ability to parse vast quantities of individual data about insureds invert the information asymmetry that has historically existed between insured and insurer such as to breathe life into insurers' duty of good faith disclosure? And (iii) by what means might legal challenges be brought against insurers both in relation to the use of big data and the consequences it may have on access to cover?

Written by a leading expert in the field, this book will both stimulate further debate and operate as a reference text for academics and practitioners who are faced with emerging legal problems arising from the increasing opportunities that big data offers to the insurance industry.

Data Profiling and Insurance Law

Brendan McGurk

•HART•
OXFORD • LONDON • NEW YORK • NEW DELHI • SYDNEY

HART PUBLISHING

Bloomsbury Publishing Plc

Kemp House, Chawley Park, Cumnor Hill, Oxford, OX2 9PH, UK

First published in Great Britain 2019

A catalogue record for this book is available from the British Library.

Library of Congress Cataloging-in-Publication data

Names: McGurk, Brendan, author.

Title: Data profiling and insurance law / Brendan McGurk.

Description: Oxford, UK ; Chicago, Illinois : Hart Publishing, 2019. | Includes bibliographical references and index.

Identifiers: LCCN 2018059531 (print) | LCCN 2018060295 (ebook) | ISBN 9781509920631 (EPub) | ISBN 9781509920617 (hardback)

Subjects: LCSH: Insurance law—England. | Big data. | Insurance—Statistical methods. | Data protection—Law and legislation—England. | Tort liability of insurance companies—England. | BISAC: LAW / Computer & Internet.

Classification: LCC KD1859 (ebook) | LCC KD1859 .M38 2019 (print) | DDC 346.42/0862—dc23

LC record available at https://lccn.loc.gov/2018059531

ISBN: HB: 978-1-50992-061-7
ePDF: 978-1-50992-062-4
ePub: 978-1-50992-063-1

Typeset by Compuscript Ltd, Shannon

To my father, John McGurk, my mother,
Paula McGurk, my wife Katharine Radice,
and our two sons Hugo and Toby.

ACKNOWLEDGEMENTS

The publication of this book is an appropriate moment to express my gratitude to a number of people who have helped me more than perhaps they realise. Throughout my education, I have been lucky enough to have been taught by some incredibly able and decent people, first at St Columb's College and then at university. I should like to thank in particular Michael Roulston, Willie Clifford, Sean McGinty, Father Eamon Martin (as he then was), the late Father John R Walsh, Martin McIlvene, Jack McAuley, Professor Christopher Forsyth, Professor Martin Dixon, Dr Nick Bamforth, Jeffrey Hackney, Professor Chris McCrudden, and Professor John Gardner. In my early years as a barrister, I learned a huge amount from many people, most especially Martin Chamberlain QC, Leigh-Ann Mulcahy QC, Ben Hubble QC and Philip Moser QC.

Specifically in relation to the production of this book, I am enormously grateful to Mark Cannon QC. In 2008, Mark asked me to co-write *Professional Indemnity Insurance*,[1] now in its second edition. Mark's advice taught me much about how best to aim for a clear structure in legal writing; the experience of working with him paved the way for this project. Mark very kindly read and commented on the insurance chapters in this book. I am very grateful to Gerry Facenna QC who read and commented on the data law aspects of the text. Any errors in the text are, of course, mine alone. I should also like to thank the team at Hart Publishing and in particular Roberta Bassi who read the original proposal and recommended the commissioning of the text, Julian Bates who copy-edited the manuscript, and Rosamund Jubber, Tom Adams and Rose Wood for the production and marketing of the book.

Finally, and most importantly, I would like to thank my wonderful family. I am grateful to my father, John McGurk and my mother Paula McGurk for all the opportunities they have given me. I am indebted to my wife and best friend Katharine Radice for her love, support and incisive editorial remarks on the structure of the book's introduction and conclusion. Last, but certainly not least, I must thank our two brilliant boys, Hugo and Toby, who have been so kind and understanding during the writing of this book. I am blessed to have the family that I do.

Brendan McGurk
Cambridge
8 December 2018

[1] M Cannon and B McGurk, *Professional Indemnity Insurance* 2nd edn (Oxford, OUP, 2016)

CONTENTS

PART II
BIG DATA AND THE PRINCIPLES OF INSURANCE LAW

PART IV
REMEDIES

PART V
CONCLUSIONS

TABLE OF CASES

United Kingdom

European Union

European Court of Human Rights

TABLE OF LEGISLATION

Australian Statutes

New Zealand Statutes

UK Statutes

UK Statutory Instruments

EU Legislation

EU Treaties

EU Secondary Legislation

International Treaties

Introduction

I. Scope and Structure of the Book

This book considers the impact that the use of big data and predictive analytics will have on the conduct of insurance business and the consequential impact on existing principles of insurance law. It then considers the extent to which the use of big data is governed by wider regulatory norms and asks how those norms might in turn shape the development of principles of insurance law. Finally, having identified the wider issues to which the use of big data by insurers give rise, the book considers the remedies available to insureds and the extent to which the common law may need to develop remedies that are specifically tailored to provide redress for the misuse of data by insurers. The book is therefore structured as follows:

1. Part 1 considers the nature of big data, its potential impact on the conduct of insurance business and the wider issues to which its use gives rise in the insurance industry. Specifically, chapter one considers how big data provides new sources of information and insight into individual risks and how predictive analytics will enable insurers to more accurately predict and thus price risk. Chapter two considers how regulators have assessed insurers' use of big data and predictive analytics to date and their likely use of those techniques in future. Chapter three considers the wider legal and regulatory issues to which the use of big data and predictive analytics give rise.
2. Part 2 considers the law relating to the terms by which the scope of cover might permissibly be customised and the basis for and requirements of the good faith duty of disclosure. In particular, chapter four considers how real-time data enables insurers to more precisely tailor the scope of cover, monitor the risk, and provide for in-policy variations to the cover in light of events occurring within the policy period. Chapter five considers the rationale for the duty of good faith disclosure as it applies to insureds and insurers. It considers the extent to which information asymmetries have historically justified the duty giving rise to the questions of whether, in an age of big data, it remains justified as applied to insureds, and is sufficiently developed when applied to insurers.
3. Part 3 considers the extent to which regulatory law might constrain the way in which insurers can collect and use data about insureds and how the common law duty of good faith might evolve in light of the content of those regulatory norms. Therefore, chapter six asks to what extent financial services, consumer and data law constrain the way in which insurers might make use of big data and predictive analytics such as to identify whether, and if so to what extent, insurance law might be deficient in how it regulates insurers' use of those techniques. Chapter seven considers whether it is permissible and indeed sensible for the common

law to identify wider regulatory principles such as to develop common law by analogy with those principles.
4. Part 4 – chapter eight – considers the remedies available to insureds for data-related breaches of regulatory law, equality law and competition law by insurers. It then considers the impact of those remedies on the availability and development of common law remedies for breaches of insurers' duty of good faith disclosure.

This book asks these questions from an English law perspective. English insurance law has recently undergone its most profound changes since the codification of the common law in the Marine Insurance Act 1906 (MIA 1906), with the entry into force of the Consumer Insurance (Disclosure and Representations) Act 2012 (CIDRA 2012) and the Insurance Act 2015 (IA 2015). However, the questions raised in this book are equally relevant to other jurisdictions, particularly those that continue to impose duties of disclosure on insureds and insurers and where those duties have been justified on the basis of the historical information asymmetry between insured and insurer.

II. Big Data's Impact on Insurance

The collection and processing of information about individual risks has, from the very beginnings of insurance business, informed insurers' underwriting decisions, pricing policies, claims handling and the detection and prevention of fraud. In a digital age, insurers continue to collect and process information in the form of data. Big data refers to the enormous datasets which insurers are now able to analyse and parse for information relevant to individual risks.[1] Big data not only provides insurers with access to a wealth of new data; it also provides new means by which insurers can develop enhanced predictive models by reference to increasingly granular datasets with a view to more accurately evaluating – and thus pricing – individual risks.

Take, for example, life insurance. Historically, actuaries would analyse life expectancy by reference to various risk factors and would model mortality rates for the purpose of pricing risk. They did so on the basis of information that was public, historical and aggregated: actuarial analysis was evidenced-based; correlations between risk factors and outcomes were verified by reference to historic loss data.[2] Smokers would thus pay a higher premium because public information indicated that a smoker's life expectancy would on average be shorter by some established period of time. The prospective insured would be asked whether or not he was a smoker. It was for the insured – who knew whether or not he smoked – to answer the question truthfully. Now, insurers may not even need to ask the question: a Facebook profile picture might provide the answer;

[1] Big data involves the processing of datasets so large and complex that they cannot be handled by traditional data processing software. To that extent, it entails a step change in the way insurers can analyse and model information relevant to risk. The fastest-growing commodity on earth is the data we are generating. New information is growing at 66% per year, which means the total stock of data is doubling every 18 months.

[2] EW Kopf, *The Early History of the Annuity* (New York, Lawrence, 1927) 248ff.

so too might purchasing information (where some retailers provide information on individual purchases); or repeated Google searches for 'smoker's cough' might give the game away; other information gleaned from the insured's browsing history might equally provide the answer. More distant still from the actuarial model of risk-writing is the profiling being undertaken which uses analytics to scan thousands of regions of the proposed life insured's face to look for clues about how quickly the person is ageing, their body mass index and whether they smoke.[3] Armed with this and other information from customers, insurers contend that this provides a far more accurate prediction of life expectancy than traditional methods can offer.[4] It has thus been said that

> [i]n the future, the creative sourcing of data and the distinctiveness of analytics methods will be much greater sources of competitive advantage in insurance. New sources of external data, new tools for underwriting risk, and behavior-influencing data monitoring are the key developments that are shaping up as game changers.[5]

This book adopts the concept of 'data profiling' to describe the way in which insurers will use big data and predictive analytics for the purposes of, in particular, underwriting. The General Data Protection Regulation (GDPR)[6] came into force on 25 May 2018 and defines 'profiling' as

> any form of automated processing of personal data consisting of using those data to evaluate certain personal aspects relating to a natural person, in particular to analyse or predict aspects concerning that natural person's performance at work, economic situation, health, personal preferences, interests, reliability, behaviour, location or movements.[7]

Insurers' use of automated processing tools such as algorithms for the assessment of risk thus involves 'profiling' so defined. In the context of insurance, data profiling becomes a byword for risk profiling.

III. Information Asymmetries and Principles of Insurance Law

The thesis of this book is that the ongoing transformation of insurance practice in the age of big data has a consequential impact on the principles of insurance law.

[3] US company Lapetus is one company undertaking such analysis. It is already the case that facial recognition technology is now enabling firms to provide automated diagnoses of rare genetic conditions such as Hajdu–Cheney syndrome far earlier than would otherwise be possible: David Carr, 'Quantified Self should be about health not ego', *Information Week*, 25 September 2014, https://www.informationweek.com/healthcare/patient-tools/quantified-self-should-be-about-health-not-ego-/a/d-id/1316069.

[4] https://www.ft.com/content/e07cee0c-3949-11e7-821a-6027b8a20f23. Alternatively, some insurers have developed a new health-risk model by blending best-in-class actuarial data with medical science, demographic trends, and government data. This forward- and backward-looking tool for modelling longevity risk captures data from traditional mortality tables and adds data on medical advances and emerging lifestyle trends such as less smoking, more exercise and healthier diets: https://www.mckinsey.com/industries/financial-services/our-insights/unleashing-the-value-of-advanced-analytics-in-insurance.

[5] McKinsey, 'Unleashing the value of advanced analytics in insurance' (August 2014): https://www.mckinsey.com/industries/financial-services/our-insights/unleashing-the-value-of-advanced-analytics-in-insurance.

[6] Regulation 2016/679/EU.

[7] GDPR Art 4(4).

The transformation arises from the fact that insurers have an unprecedented level of information about each prospective insured, and one that has the potential to, at the very least, 'level up' the information asymmetry that has traditionally characterised the relationship between insurer and insured and which has, at least in part, justified the duty of disclosure on the insured. This levelling-up of the information imbalance between insured and insurer raises two sets of issues in insurance law: (i) to what extent might insurers more precisely tailor the scope of cover; and (ii) what impact does this have on the duty of good faith disclosure?

A. Big Data and Customised Cover

Historically, insurers' knowledge and information about particular risks was limited. If big data enables insurers to have greater knowledge of and insight into matters material to the risk, questions arise as to what impact that will have on the terms on which risks might be underwritten. As regards terms, connected devices provide real-time data about individual risks, for example through telematics in motor vehicles or biometric information generated by wearable technology. If an insurer can in real-time identify how risky the conduct of an insured is, can insurers legally make increasing use of conditions and warranties to tailor or even suspend cover in response to real-time events?

B. Big Data and the Duty of Good Faith Disclosure

Insurance is, unusually, a contract of *uberrimae fides*, one of utmost good faith. The duty is owed mutually by the insured and the insurer and operates both before and after the contract has been entered into. The duty of good faith requires the disclosure of all matters material to the risk. Moreover, the vast majority of decided cases relate to whether the insured had discharged their duty of good faith, reflecting the fact that it was the insured who had the relevant knowledge about the risk. In the UK, the insured's duty of good faith – at least in consumer insurance – has recently been replaced by a duty to take reasonable care not to make a misrepresentation to insurers. The duty remains, albeit in modified form as a duty of fair presentation, in the context of non-consumer insurance. Big data's potential to eliminate information asymmetries as to the nature of the risk might suggest that the insured's duty of disclosure ought in principle to be abolished. That question is considered in the context of both consumer and non-consumer insurance.

The good faith duty of disclosure continues to apply to insurers both in the UK and beyond. However, the content of that duty has been the subject of relatively limited discussion in the cases. The use of big data gives rise to two sets of questions.

1. First, does the use of big data analytics in assessing and pricing risk breathe new life into the question of what the duty of good faith requires of insurers? In particular, does the common law duty require insurers, for example, to reveal the source

of the information used in underwriting and pricing? Does it require insurers to afford prospective insureds the opportunity to assess and, potentially, correct that information? Does it prohibit insurers relying on certain information at all if, for example, that information was originally created for some entirely different purpose? Can insurers have regard to wider datasets for the purposes of claims handling and fraud detection than for the purposes of underwriting and pricing the risk? How long can an individual's data be kept and to what extent must insurers monitor its continued accuracy? And in so far as the notion of good faith imports a sense of fair dealing, what does fairness require of insurers when they avail of these new sources of data and the techniques by which individual risks can now be modelled?

2. Second, to what extent might regulatory law provide an answer to these questions? In particular, does existing regulatory legislation permit insurers to use big data in underwriting and claims and if so, to what extent? Insurers are already constrained by four sets of regulatory laws: (i) regulatory law specifically directed at insurance contracts. In this regard, the book considers the impact of the Insurance Distribution Directive (Directive 2016/97/EU);[8] (ii) general financial services law, and in particular the obligations imposed on insurers by the Financial Conduct Authority's Handbook (FCA/the Handbook); (iii) consumer protection law, and in particular the obligations imposed by the Consumer Rights Act 2015 (CRA 2015); and (iv) data protection law and, in particular, the obligations imposed by the GDPR.

These two sets of questions are of course linked: the extent to which the law of insurance permits insurers to use big data to profile prospective risks and assess claims has not yet been considered in the case law given how recently these technologies have emerged. However, although these questions have not yet arisen at common law, if regulatory law provides a framework which determines the extent to which big data can or cannot be used in the transaction of insurance business, that raises the question of whether the content of insurance law should either be developed in parallel with the obligations of regulatory law or, by contrast, should not enter the fray at all, the relevant protection having been set out by regulatory law. The latter question of course assumes that regulatory law – in its various strands – provides a code that answers all the questions which might otherwise fall to be determined by reference to insurers' duty of good faith. It is of course true that the scope and contours of common law duties are shaped by regulatory norms that apply to the field of activity in question. But it is equally true that the common law may be curtailed if the regulatory code applicable to that field of activity is found to be comprehensive or exhaustive. However, if regulatory law does not provide a complete answer as to how insurers might make use of these technologies, there would be room for the common law of insurance to develop the insurers' duty of good faith to plug the gaps – an approach

[8] Which replaces the existing Insurance Mediation Directive 2002/92/EC.

in fact envisaged in the UK further to the reform of insurance law between 2012 and 2015. As McDonald-Eggers and Picken tantalisingly put it:

> Under the [Insurance Act] 2015 … the duty of utmost good faith has been severely curtailed with the result that, whilst there may remain a duty on the part of the insurer, there are no prescribed remedies or consequences for failure to observe that duty on the insurer's part. Where the duty of utmost good faith remains uncertain, it may be that we need to look elsewhere for inspiration, either to other jurisdictions or other areas of the law.[9]

This book argues that the duty of good faith continues to bind insurers and as a result of the developments in big data and the response of, in particular, data protection law, there are ready-made sources of inspiration for the content of the insurers' duty of good faith disclosure in a digital age.

IV. Remedies for Insurers' Misuse of Big Data

Assessing the interaction between insurance law and regulatory law leads to a third set of questions regarding the remedies available to insureds for insurers' misuse of data. The extent of any available remedies will be determined by the scope of the duties that bind insurers in relation to the use of big data in profiling risk or handling claims. It is argued that insofar as the common law should take its cue from the applicable regulatory provisions as regards the development of the duty of good faith, there is an open question as to how it should commensurately develop remedies for the breach of that expanded duty. In that regard the question again arises as to whether the existence of regulatory remedies for misuse of data either encourages or constrains the common law in the development of its own remedies for misuse of data in the context of underwriting or claims decisions.

However, the remedial question goes beyond the impact of remedies available for the breach of data-related regulatory law. Insofar as big data promises to facilitate more fine-grained profiling of each individual insured, certain individuals, or groups whose profiles exhibit new risk factors that have been correlated with insured loss, may be priced out of cover. Such profiling and pricing practices may be based on non-risk-related information (such as a customer's price sensitivity or propensity to switch providers)[10] giving rise to the prospect of price discrimination, the legality of which falls within the remit of consumer and competition law. But more sinister forms of risk profiling might be based directly or indirectly on the insured's protected characteristics such as sex, race or sexual orientation. The book considers the extent to which human rights and equality law can be relied upon against insurers who take underwriting decisions on the basis of protected characteristics or on the basis of data that operate as proxies for protected characteristics and/or which have a disproportionate impact on those with certain protected characteristics. These violations

[9] S MacDonald-Eggers and S Picken, *Good Faith and Insurance Contracts* (Oxford, Informa Law, 2018) 1.05.

[10] And which in turn might be a practice more likely to be visited upon vulnerable customers.

arise out of the use of data but are not per se data violations; rather the use of data is, as lawyers would put it, not the cause of, but rather the occasion on which such violations might occur.

V. Relationship between Social Change and Legal Principle

The legal analysis of market transactions must be informed by economic and social perspectives in order to ensure effective regulation.[11] If regulation of a particular market transaction is to be effective, legal analysis must not only seek to consider the impact of legal rules on that transaction, but to consider how the social and economic conditions in which those transactions occur may alter or even undermine the premises upon which existing legal regulation takes place. Commercial law seeks to provide a framework whereby those who enter into transactions in accordance with the customs and practices of their own industry are able to enforce those transactions in accordance with those norms and understandings. The law of insurance is no different having developed as a result of the common law's absorption of the law merchant.[12] Changes in commercial practice thus often require existing legal principles to evolve to accommodate those new practices; it is much rarer that changes in commercial practice require a wholesale change to the legal principles themselves. Teubner pointed to the risk of the 'regulatory trilemma': either a legal rule fails to have an impact on social practice, or they may subvert desirable social practices by impractical demands, or the law may lose the coherence of its own analytical framework by seeking to incorporate sociological and economic perspectives in its reasoning.[13] To this we may add the risk that the law may fail to retain the coherence of its own analytical framework by failing to incorporate sociological, economic – and technological – perspectives in its reasoning.

With big data analytics, the genie is out of the bottle. The insurance industry as a whole is not likely to go back to relying only on its traditional methods of assessing and pricing risk given the opportunities that big data affords. The rise of the Internet of Things and connected devices will generate an exponential rise in the amount of data about insureds, their homes and their lifestyles. Insurers will wish to have access to as much of that information as is consistent with law and the reputational risks to which the use of such data gives rise. Regulators have a careful line to tread: on the one hand, they will seek to regulate to ensure that the many and considerable benefits offered by the use of big data and predictive analytics are not stifled; but similarly, they will seek to ensure that big data is not used in a way that (i) violates individual insureds'

[11] H Collins, *The Law of Contract* 3rd edn (London, Butterworths, 1997) 2.
[12] See, generally, Guido Rossi, *Insurance in Elizabethan England* (Cambridge, Cambridge University Press, 2016); and Rossi, 'London 1426–1601: Marine Insurance and the Law Merchant' in Leonard (ed), *Marine Insurance: Origins and Institutions, 1300–1850* (Cambridge, Palgrave, 2016).
[13] G Teubner, 'After Legal Instrumentalism? Strategic Models of Post-Regulatory Law' in G Teubner (ed), *Dilemmas of Law in the Welfare State* (New York, De Gruyter, 1988), 299 at 309.

consumer, data and human rights or (ii) otherwise undermines the competitiveness of the market as a whole. And all of this has a significant bearing on the survival of the insured's duties of disclosure and the content of insurers' equivalent duties.

It is very early days. This book will raise more questions than it can sensibly answer. As industry practice settles down relative to regulatory requirements, the full impact of the use of big data will begin to emerge. This initial phase will generate the sorts of disputes the litigation of which will help to clarify the content of insurance law and what further regulatory responses might be needed. With the increased use of big data, regulatory law may move beyond imposing norms governing the conduct of the sale of insurance and may begin to have an impact on the substantive law of insurance itself. It will be imperative for insurance lawyers to become fully conversant with big data techniques and the regulatory and rights issues to which the use of big data give rise. This book is a contribution to that emerging discussion.

PART I

Big Data's Impact on the Provision and Regulation of Insurance

1

Big Data and Predictive Analytics

I. Big Data: Definition and Techniques

Before considering its impact on the insurance industry, it is necessary to consider what the term 'big data' means. Data is, in essence, digitised information. Big data has been defined as 'high-volume, high-velocity and high-variety information assets that demand cost-effective, innovative forms of information processing for enhanced insight and decision-making'.[1] Big data encompasses all types of information, not just that specific to an individual consumer. Mayer-Schonberger and Cukier explain that 'Big data refers to things one can do at a large scale that cannot be done at a smaller one, to extract new insights or create new forms of value, in ways that change markets, organisations, the relationship between citizens and governments and more'.[2] They go on to explain that 'Big data is not about trying to "teach" a computer to "think" like humans, instead it's about applying math to huge quantities of data in order to infer probabilities … [T]hese systems perform well because they are fed with lots of data on which to base their predictions'.[3] Greengard observes that big data 'centres on collecting storing, and using data-sets generated from both structured data (which resides in a database) and unstructured data (which exists outside a database), typically in the form of messaging streams, text documents, photos, video images, audio files and social media'.[4] Previously, the storage of large amounts of data required supercomputers and was prohibitively expensive. Now, as data storage and processing is so much cheaper and faster, it has become possible to record and analyse data in volumes and forms that was, until relatively recently, inconceivable. As technology historian George Dyson puts it, 'big data is what happened when the cost of storing information became less than the cost of throwing it away'.[5]

Big data identifies correlations, not causes. It works not by seeking to explain why certain variables give rise to certain outcomes but simply identifying the existence

[1] Gartner IT glossary, Big Data: http://www.gartner.com/it-glossary/big-data. Volume refers to the step change in the amount of available data; variety refers to the ability to combine different datasets and data sources; velocity refers both to the speed at which data is generated (including in real-time) and processed.

[2] V Mayer-Schonberger and K Cukier, *Big Data: The essential guide to work, life and learning in the age of insight* (London, John Murray, 2017) 6.

[3] ibid, 12.

[4] S Greengard, *The Internet of Things* (Cambridge, MA, MIT Press, 2015), 44.

[5] A Warner, George Dyson seminar media. The Long Now Foundation, 28 March 2013, http://blog.longnow.org/02013/03/28/george-dyson-seminar-media/.

of the correlation in the first place; big data analytics are not used to test particular hypotheses or identify particular causes in the manner of traditional scientific method. If a pattern reliably emerges from the detailed examination of datasets, that is enough to provide a basis for the operation of predictive analytics, a core part of big data's offering in the insurance industry. Analytics are divided between descriptive and predictive analytics. Descriptive analytics is designed to uncover and summarise patterns or features that exist in datasets. By contrast predictive analytics refers to the use of statistical models to generate new data. Predictive analytics use algorithms to analyse data in order to identify the likelihood of a certain event before it happens.[6] In the context of insurance, the algorithm will be trained to analyse large datasets to identify both good and bad risks; the likelihood of insured perils occurring and claims being made. Algorithms can already predict when a customer is ready to buy a certain product, a car needs servicing or a person is at risk of disease.[7] But in being focussed on correlation, not cause, the use of predictive analytics gives rise to its own risks.

Algorithms are designed by reducing a series of steps into code. Those steps, so encoded, embody a process whereby the algorithms make sense of the data which they have trawled. But because the steps in that process are determined, at least in the first instance, by humans, the coding is laced with value choices: the analysis of data is not value-neutral.[8] The Financial Services Users Group (FSUG)[9] makes the point clearly:

> Even as the public gradually becomes more familiar with the way platforms work with data, and even with more pointed data scrutiny, it is still a common belief that data and algorithms

[6] The FTC compares predictive credit analysis with traditional credit analysis as follows: 'Under traditional credit scoring models, companies compare known credit characteristics of a consumer – such as past late payments – with historical data that shows how people with the same credit characteristics performed over time in meeting their credit obligations. Similarly, predictive analytics products may compare a known characteristic of a consumer to other consumers with the same characteristic to predict whether that consumer will meet his or her credit obligations. The difference is that, rather than comparing a traditional credit characteristic, such as debt payment history, these products may use non-traditional characteristics – such as a consumer's zip code, social media usage, or shopping history – to create a report about the creditworthiness of consumers that share those non-traditional characteristics, which a company can then use to make decisions about whether that consumer is a good credit risk.' Federal Trade Commission (FTC), 'Big Data: A Tool for Inclusion or Exclusion?' January 2016, pp 15–16: https://www.ftc.gov/system/files/documents/reports/big-data-tool-inclusion-or-exclusion-understanding-issues/160106big-data-rpt.pdf, 15–16. The very same approach can be used by insurers.

[7] 'The world's most valuable resources', *The Economist*, 6 May 2017.

[8] Professor Latanya Sweeney of Harvard University undertook a study that found that users with African-American names were often being targeted with Google adverts that suggested that they had arrest records that they might wish to have deleted. That targeting by the algorithm reflected the values inherent in its design. Similarly, Facebook's algorithms determine what articles we see in our newsfeed. Of the millions of things that might be pushed in the direction of a particular Facebook user, the algorithms decide what that user will in fact see, largely through how that user's interests and preferences have been profiled by the algorithms.

[9] The FSUG is an expert group set up by the European Commission whose objective is 'to secure high quality expert input to the Commission's financial services initiatives from representatives of financial services users and from individual financial services experts'. It is mandated, inter alia, to proactively seek to identify key financial services issues which affect users of financial services. Its report from which the above quotation is taken (p 6) is entitled 'Assessment of current and future impact of Big Data on Financial Services' and is dated June 2016: https://ec.europa.eu/info/sites/info/files/file_import/1606-big-data-on-financial-services_en_0.pdf.

> systematically and impartially uncover genuine patterns of user activity. Big data and algorithms cannot and do not work without some form of human intervention/supervision. In fact, algorithms just do what they are programmed to do very quickly and with a vast amount of data. Algorithms identify patterns in data, but they cannot operate a judgment on that data. In the end, people are behind the algorithms because they produce the activity being measured, they design the algorithms and set their evaluative criteria, they decide what counts as a trend, they name and summarize them, etc. In the end these people who programmed the algorithms employ their own human judgment in its design, clouding such reality by assuming algorithms provide analytical certainty. But who are the people behind the algorithms and who gives them instructions? They are the holders of an incredible power in dictating what is and is not displayed, what is and is not presented, the logics, etc ... This process is far from being neutral and there is always a strong human bias, which in this case is the financial services industry bias and/or interests.[10]

The next stage in predictive analytics involves machine learning, a subset of Artificial Intelligence (AI).[11] Machine learning relies on algorithms that are designed to improve how they evaluate data over time.[12] Machine learning can be separated into two types of learning: supervised and unsupervised. In supervised learning, algorithms are developed based on labelled datasets. In this sense, the algorithms have been trained how to map from input to output by the provision of data with 'correct' values already assigned to them. This initial 'training' phase creates models of the world on which predictions can then be made in the second 'prediction' phase, the phase of most interest to insurers seeking to model risk.[13] Conversely, in unsupervised learning the algorithms are not trained and are instead left to find regularities in input data without any instructions as to what to look for.[14] As the Information Commissioner notes, in both cases, it is the ability of the algorithms to change their output based on experience that gives machine learning its power.[15] Algorithms search through and analyse

[10] See Cathy O'Neill, *Weapons of Math Destruction: How Big Data Increases Inequality and Threatens Democracy* (London, Penguin Random House, 2016), who demonstrates that algorithms can accentuate human biases. See also: Kate Crawford, 'The Hidden Biases in Big Data', *Harvard Business Review*, 2013; and 'Franken-Algorithms: the deadly consequences of unpredictable code', *The Guardian*, 30 August 2018. Problems include the accuracy of the data in datasets, the completeness of the data, and its representativeness. These are discussed in ch 3 below. A stark example of the biases that can be built into algorithms can be seen if one Googles 'racist soap dispenser'. There have thus been calls for 'algorithmic accountability'. 'In essence, this is about being able to check that the algorithms used and developed by machine learning systems are actually doing what we think they're doing and aren't producing discriminatory, erroneous or unjustified results': see Hemant Taneja, 'The need for algorithmic accountability', *TechCrunch*, 8 September 2016, https://techcrunch.com/2016/09/08/the-need-for-algorithmic-accountability/.

[11] The Government Office for Science defines AI as 'the analysis of data to model some aspect of the world. Inferences from these models are then used to predict and anticipate possible future events.' Government Office for Science, 'Artificial Intelligence: Opportunities and Implication for the Future of Decision-making', 9 November 2016.

[12] Machine learning has been defined as 'the set of techniques and tools that allow computers to "think" by creating mathematical algorithms based on accumulated data': Deb Landau, 'Artificial Intelligence and Machine Learning: How Computers Learn', *iQ*, 17 August 2016, https://iq.intel.com/artificial-intelligence-and-machine-learning/.

[13] By definition, the outcome of this initial 'discovery' phase of data processing is uncertain and has been described as 'unpredictability by design': John Edwards and Said Ihrai, 'Communique on the 38th International Conference of Data Protection and Privacy Commissioners', ICDPPC, 18 October 2016.

[14] Ethem Alpaydin, *Introduction to Machine Learning* (Cambridge, MA, MIT Press, 2014).

[15] Information Commissioner, 'Big Data, artificial intelligence, machine learning and data protection', 4 September 2017 (ICO 2017), https://ico.org.uk/media/for-organisations/documents/2013559/big-data-ai-ml-and-data-protection.pdf.

data, assimilating the lessons of previous searches to more precisely undertake the next round of searching and analysis.[16] Increasing the size of the data enables the algorithms to refine their analysis of the correlations identified. Having learned from the new data and refined the correlations, the algorithms are then able to fine tune their predictive power as well as making automated decisions, such as determining an applicant's eligibility for insurance. Machine learning already excels in spotting unusual patterns of transactions which can indicate fraud. Startups such as Shift Technology are already offering such services to insurers.

II. The Nature, Collection, Sources and Aggregation of Data

A. Types of Data

The Information Commissioner distinguishes between four types of data which may be categorised based on the way in which that data is collected or generated:[17]

1. 'Provided data' is data consciously given by individuals, e.g. when filling in an online form;
2. 'Observed data' is data that is recorded automatically, e.g. by online cookies, geo-location data or CCTV linked to facial recognition technology;
3. 'Described data' is data that is produced in a relatively simple fashion, e.g. calculating profit on an individual insured which is calculated by comparing premium income received against payment of claims; and
4. 'Inferred data' is data produced by considering, for example, how the presence of certain identified risk factors might enable an insurer to predict the likelihood of future behaviours or outcomes. Inferred data is based on probabilities and is therefore less certain than derived data.

B. Collection of Data: First Party or Third Party

Businesses collect personal data[18] directly from consumers as first parties. Data provided directly by consumers to first parties is often likely to be the most detailed and accurate form of consumer data. In the insurance context, insurers receive applications or

[16] See Franklin Foer, 'World Without Mind: The Existential Threat of Big Tech' (London, Jonathan Cape, 2017), 67–71.

[17] ICO 2017, 12–13.

[18] Personal data is defined in Art 4(1) of the General Data Protection Regulation as 'any information relating to an identified or identifiable natural person ("data subject"); an identifiable natural person is one who can be identified, directly or indirectly, in particular by reference to an identifier such as a name, an identification number, location data, an online identifier or to one or more factors specific to the physical, physiological, genetic, mental, economic, cultural or social identity of that natural person.'

proposal forms for insurance directly from prospective insureds (or their brokers).[19] Taking motor insurance as an example, the information provided directly by the insured in seeking a quotation falls into three broad categories: (i) information about the insured (e.g. the driver for a motor policy: such details will include, for example, date of birth, occupation, no claims bonus (NCB), claims and convictions record, home ownership, annual mileage); (ii) information about the vehicle (e.g. make, model, value, transmission, security devices, modifications, year, colour); and (iii) information about the location (e.g. address, whether the vehicle is kept on the road, on a driveway or in a garage). That information is known to the insured and, barring transcription errors or conscious fraud, is likely to be correct and in any event objectively verifiable.

The CMA's research into the commercial use of consumer data noted how the timing and frequency of interactions between businesses and consumers varied between sectors. In the motor insurance sector, the (erstwhile) annual nature of most cover means that insurers typically collect data from actual and potential customers as a snapshot once a year, close to renewal (unless a claim is made or policy details are changed). While historic data is important to the development of predictive models of risk, annual data on individuals can degrade in value even within a year.[20] However, as insurance is increasingly provided on a pay as you go basis (Pay-As-You-Drive in motor insurance; Pay-As-You-Live for life and health insurance), the frequency of direct data collection will increase.

Third parties with no direct relationship with a potential insured may also collect data on that individual. Such data may be observed, derived or inferred. Third parties collect data from and about consumers in various ways. For example, a business may acquire data from a first party or another third party through purchase, licensing or exchange. Third parties may collect and analyse the data themselves or they may conduct analysis for other firms that may lack the required technical resources and skills. As the CMA notes, in practice there is a substantial amount of data sharing occurring between firms – for instance in support of first party service delivery. For example, first parties may commission third parties to gather data on their behalf and to pursue their own commercial interests (such as advertising and product development) by, for example, (i) enabling third parties to embed and control cookies on the first party's website to track user visits to the site (on cookies, see further below); (ii) commissioning surveys and other market research; and (iii) using specialist data collection tools, such as 'black box' telematics devices.[21]

C. Sources of Data

Insurers and third party data collectors have access to internal and external sources of information on insureds and prospective insureds. Internal sources of information

[19] More generally, retailers collect electronic Point of Sale (ePOS) data which, combined with loyalty card data on the individual purchasers, can provide rich information on their transactional preferences and even personal circumstances.

[20] CMA, Commercial Use of Consumer Data, June 2015.

[21] ibid, para 2.34.

on insureds will include data held in paper files from legacy systems, and their newer generation of electronic databases. In addition, there are several external sources of information that can be aggregated to enable algorithms to identify good and bad risks. Those sources are public and private and may be obtained offline or online.

i. Public Sources of Data

Public sources of information that may be relevant to insurers to enable them to profile prospective insureds in detail include the land registry, court and insolvency records, Companies House, the electoral roll,[22] and census information. In addition, the release of previously unavailable or inaccessible public-sector data has greatly expanded potential sources of third-party data. The US and UK Governments and the European Union have recently launched 'open data' websites to make available very substantial amounts of government statistics, including health, education, worker safety and energy data, amongst others.[23] Further, insurers will routinely search databases available to insurers, principally as a means of cross-checking information and preventing fraud.[24]

ii. Private Sources of Data

Private sources of information may be obtained offline and online. Insurers can gain access to proprietary data, meaning data acquired from connected companies. That data will have been provided by the insured to that connected company on the basis that the company may share it with other connected companies. A further category of offline information is purchasing information. Some retailers share information about purchases made by people, including item description, price and the person's name. In addition, loyalty cards provide a wealth of consumer data on individual purchasing habits and preferences.

The following seven sources of online information can be identified as central to the future of data – and risk – profiling in insurance: (i) web browsing activity; (ii) online purchasing information; (iii) geo-location data; (iv) the Internet of Things; (v) self-tracking devices; (vi) social networking platforms; and (vii) third parties gathering private information from a range of other sources.[25]

[22] Credit reference agencies are able to buy the full version of the electoral register (which can include names, addresses, national insurance numbers, nationality and age), while other businesses can buy the open (edited) register from which individuals can opt to have their personal details removed. Such data is typically non-rivalrous, in the sense that access to it by one party does not restrict the ability of other parties to access it.

[23] See https://data.gov.uk/, which invites users to 'find data published by central government, local authorities and public bodies to help you build products and services'. The categories of open source data which can be searched through include: (i) crime and justice; (ii) education; (iii) health; (iv) mapping; and (v) transport.

[24] Discussed in more detail in ch 2.

[25] The CMA divides the sources of consumer data into (i) data that consumers offer voluntarily ('declared data') – eg when transacting or registering for a service; (ii) data consumers generate and supply passively ('observed data') – eg on social media, or when online browsing activity is tracked; and (iii) data generated by first and third parties as a result of analysis or in combination with other data. See Commercial Use of Consumer Data, June 2015.

a. Web Browsing/Aggregated Search Engine Data

Analysing a person's browsing history is facilitated by cookies. Cookies are small bits of text that are downloaded to a browser as a person surfs the web. Their purpose is to carry bits of useful information about that person's interaction with the website that uses them. Cookies generally do not contain any information that would identify a person. Usually they contain a string of text or a 'unique identifier'. This acts like a label. When a website sees the string of text it set in a cookie, it knows that it was the person with the unique identifier number who has visited the site previously. Cookies are thus used to (i) help remember a web user's preferences on a site; (ii) to understand how web users are using the site; and (iii) for logging in to a service or to make sure the user is logged in securely.[26] Cookies were thus originally designed to be helpful to users. However, companies subsequently realised that they could set their own cookies on pages belonging to other sites, albeit with that site's permission and by paying a fee. In this way, the third-party cookie was born. These third-party cookies enabled third parties (such as advertising networks and analytical companies) to track users and their behaviours across multiple sites that use the same third-party cookies and to better evaluate users' preferences for the purpose of more targeted advertising and the personalisation of offers.[27] As Schneier points out,

> Enterprises like DoubleClick (purchased by Google in 2007) started tracking web users across many different sites. This is when ads started following users around the web. Research a particular car or vacation destination or medical condition and for weeks you'll see ads for that car or city or a related pharmaceutical on every commercial Internet site you visit.[28]

The CMA raised concerns over the use of cookies in its Commercial use of Consumer Data report of June 2015. These concerns were that: (i) cookies and similar technology (such as beacons) can collect a large amount of data which are not necessary for the provision of the service requested; (ii) the acceptance of non-essential cookies is bundled with the acceptance of essential cookies which is an unfair condition of access; and (iii) some websites will not work properly if cookies are disabled. It noted that many websites load multiple third-party cookies serving differing purposes onto a user's computer each time they visit.[29] In 2014, the Information Commissioner in the UK led an international study looking at the use of cookies on 478 websites, which

[26] https://www.theguardian.com/technology/2012/apr/23/cookies-and-web-tracking-intro.

[27] As Antonio Garcia Martinez explains: 'When you load a page in your browser, everything you see (and most of the things you don't) is not from the company whose ".com" address you've entered. The way the modern web works, different elements come from different places. Every element you load … touches your browser and is allowed to read data in the form of what's known as cookies': *Chaos Monkeys* (London, Ebury Press, 2016), 6.

[28] Bruce Schneier, 'Data and Goliath: The Hidden Battles to Collect your Data and Control your World' (New York, Norton, 2015), 56. He points out that it is no different on your smartphone since the apps you download can often track users in the same way. Other examples of third party cookies include (i) Google Analytics, which is used to measure website activity and performance for search engine optimisation and marketing purposes; (ii) Criteo and Struq, which are used to gather information to support re-targeting advertising; (iii) web-traffic measurement companies such as Hitwise, which allows clients to analyse search traffic (eg on Google) to learn about their consumers' preferences; and (iv) Quantcast, which similarly measures online traffic to individual websites to help them understand more about who their visitors are and how they use the hosts' websites.

[29] CMA, Commercial Use of Consumer Data, June 2015, paras 5.60–5.61.

found that UK websites placed the highest number of cookies, averaging 44 cookies during a person's first visit. Ten of the 84 UK sites examined set more than 100 cookies on the site. The Information Commissioner further noted that 70% were third-party cookies and that 86% were persistent cookies.[30] The Information Commissioner has recognised that, in practical terms, obtaining informed consent for third party cookies on a publisher website is particularly challenging because the third party (which sets the cookie) has no direct interface with the user (since the cookie, which may be set when the user visits the publisher website, may not be visible on the screen).[31]

Companies can also analyse the traffic to and use of their own websites by individuals. Amazon tracks consumers' shopping preferences. Google knows everything about users' browsing history and habits (and knows they do not lie to their search engine about their interests and concerns). When web users enter a search term into Google, it holds an instantaneous auction; Google then considers bids and estimates the likelihood of a click and sells to the bidder whose offer is likely to make most money (the product of multiplying the price per click by the number of clicks). It then displays the bidder's associated advert that the bidder has created and uploaded to Google for the search term originally entered. Google refines its list of keywords over time as it is better able to understand which search terms/keywords are most likely to be clicked on; those keywords are those which advertisers have to pay the most if they are to succeed in having their goods and services displayed once that search term is run.[32] And Twitter and Facebook between them identify where we are, who we are with, how we are feeling and what we are doing. The computers we use therefore constantly produce personal data about what we read, search for, watch and listen to.

b. Purchasing Information

As more purchasing takes place online, more data becomes available via online transactions, data that is available both to sellers and intermediaries:

- As regards sellers, most consumer data is generated as a result of consumers purchasing goods and services. What we buy also tells stories. Our grocery shopping might provide a clear indication of the purchaser's ethnicity; or whether they are vegan, vegetarian or have other dietary requirements; or their drinking habits. Our pharmacy shopping might give a clear indication as to our current state of health. Widen the range of purchases and one can identify a person's age, gender and religion amongst other things.

[30] ICO, *Article 29 Cookie Sweep Results*, February 2015, https://ico.org.uk/media/about-the-ico/documents/1043274/a29-cookie-sweep-combined-analysis-report.pdf.

[31] Since 2011, website publishers in the UK and the rest of Europe are required to set out their policies on the use of cookies, data collection, data use and data sharing on their websites, in accordance with revisions to the ePrivacy directive. In order to place and process cookies, websites must either obtain explicit consent or satisfy themselves (and the Information Commissioner's Office) that users have been properly informed about these devices so that consent can be presumed (eg by their continuing to use the service). Most websites do so through pop-up windows on the home page, explaining that they use cookies and that continued use of the site implies consent for them to do so.

[32] The top 10 costliest keyword searches include the term 'insurance': Garcia Martinez, *Chaos Monkeys* (London, Ebury Press, 2016), 82.

- As regards intermediaries, the larger banks and card issuers like Visa and MasterCard find themselves between banks and merchants in the course of billions of individual transactions. It has thus been pointed out that 'By serving many banks and merchants, they can see more transactions over their networks and use them to make inferences about consumer behaviour. Their business model shifts from simply processing payments to collecting data. The question then is what they do with it. MasterCard could licence the data to third parties who would extract the value … but the company prefers to do the analysis itself. A division called MasterCard Advisors aggregates and analyses 65 billion transactions from 1.5 billion cardholders in 210 countries in order to divine business and consumer trends. Then it sells that information to others.'[33] And most obviously, with the rise of new means of digital payment (e.g. via our phones) we again leave a digital trail of what we purchased and how much we paid.

c. Geo-location Data

Another important source of private information is the constant stream of geo-location data produced by a smart phone merely as a result of having that phone turned on. As has been pointed out, mobile phones permit a very intimate form of surveillance. It:

> tracks where you live and where you work. It tracks where you like to spend your weekends and evenings. It tracks how often you go to church (and which church), how much time you spend in a bar and whether you speed when you drive. It tracks – since it knows about all the other phones in your area – whom you spend your days with, whom you met for lunch, and whom you sleep with. The accumulated data can probably paint a better picture of how you spend your time than you can, because it doesn't have to rely on human memory. In 2012 researchers were able to use this data to predict where people would be 24 hours later, to within 20 meters.[34]

In 2014 a Stanford University study examined the phone metadata of 500 volunteers over several months. The personal nature of what even the metadata revealed was surprising. One participant was identified as having spoken at length to cardiologists at a major medical centre, talked briefly with a medical laboratory, received calls from a pharmacy and placed short calls to a home reporting hotline for a medical device used to monitor cardiac arrhythmias.[35] All of which would be highly material to a prospective life insurer. Mobile phone companies have recognised the value of geo-location data and sell that information to data brokers.[36]

[33] Mayer-Schonberger and Cukier, *Big Data*, 127.

[34] Bruce Schneier, 'Data and Goliath: The Hidden Battles to Collect your Data and Control your World' (New York, Norton, 2015), 1–2.

[35] Jonathan Mayer and Patrick Mutchler, 'MetaPhone: The sensitivity of telephone metadata', March 2014, Web Policy, http://webpolicy.org/2014/03/12/metaphone-the-sensitivity-of-telephone-metadata. And as Schneier points out, 'data is content and metadata is context. Metadata can be much more revealing than data, especially when collected in the Aggregate': above n 34, p 26.

[36] Companies like Sense Networks specialise in using this data to build personal profiles of individuals.

d. The Internet of Things

Sensor technology and miniaturisation means that physical objects can now be connected to and monitored by the internet. That has created the Internet of Things (IoT). Physical objects generate information that sensors can now record and transmit to computers and to other objects. That data can in turn be stored and analysed. 'By tagging objects and imbuing them with internet connectivity it's suddenly possible not only to track the objects and collect new types of data but also combine these data to generate a greater level of information and knowledge.'[37] Every object has a Unique Identification Number and an Internet Protocol address. These objects can be connected via the internet by way of, amongst other means, satellites, cellular networks, Wi-Fi and Bluetooth. As Greengard explains:

> A key tool that makes it possible to bring physical devices into the digital realm is [Radio Frequency Identification] RFID.[38] The technology relies on microchips that pull data from sensors built into the machines or chips that reside on or in a device. RFID uses both 'active tags' with a power source – often battery – and 'passive tags' that do not require a battery or other power source. Both allow nearby RFID readers to collect and exchange data with computers. When an RFID chip is within range of the reader, it automatically sends a signal and data to a computer.
>
> Passive RFID is particularly compelling because it doesn't require a power source, the tags can function for twenty years or longer, and they cost only a few cents each. A passive tag pulls the necessary power from a nearby reader.[39]

The IoT is likely to expand rapidly because objects that are essentially physical, non-digital objects (e.g. a medical device,[40] a car's engine, a body part[41]) can be connected to other physical objects as well as digital devices, including computers and software applications. A May 2015 study on the rise and impact of the smart product economy found that 46% of businesses reported that smart products were already bringing them information about their customers that was previously not possible or cost-effective to acquire.[42] Ofcom reported in 2015 that over 40 million devices are already connected via the IoT in the UK, and this is forecast to grow so that by 2022 there could be

[37] Samuel Greengard, *The Internet of Things* (Cambridge, MA, MIT Press, 2015).

[38] RFID readers are what allow you to track your friends' progress in the marathon in real time. It is the same technology that tracks baggage in airports, allows for data to be embedded in biometric passports and allows you to find chip-enabled golf balls when they have been shanked into the deep rough.

[39] Samuel Greengard, *The Internet of Things* (Cambridge, MA, MIT Press, 2015), 17. IoT devices that operate within wireless networks can transmit data to mobile network base stations or network access points but to do so will need access to appropriate spectrum bands to meet different capacity and coverage requirements. See Ofcom's Promoting Investment and Innovation in the Internet of Things, January 2015, section 5.

[40] Blood pressure monitors, blood sugar monitors and in-home medication dispensing systems can now all be connected to the internet allowing for reminders to be issued, accurate doses to be calibrated and to alert healthcare professionals if a problem arises.

[41] It is expected that within the next two decades RFID sensors and other devices may be implanted in the human body or placed on the body to gather and transmit real-time data about, for example, blood pressure, blood sugar, heart-rate and other vital signs. Such data could also communicate with other devices designed to automatically dispense medicines or insulin as and when needed and in the doses more specifically determined by the data at that point in time.

[42] The study was by Cognizant and the Economist Intelligence Unit: https://www.cognizant.com/whitepapers/the-rise-of-the-smart-product-economy-codex1249.pdf.

369 million devices and more than a billion data transactions a day.[43] Ofcom noted that these connections have the potential to deliver benefits across multiple sectors including the health and motoring sectors.[44] Ofcom noted that a common framework that allows consumers easily and transparently to authorise the conditions under which data collected by their devices is used and shared by others will be critical to the future development of the IoT.[45]

Ofcom, in discussing the potential future benefits brought by the IoT, gave the following sectoral examples of relevance to insurers:

- **Healthcare:** Devices that monitor fitness and activity levels can help to prevent illness and encourage a healthy lifestyle. For the unwell, the IoT could enable a patient's condition to be monitored and managed remotely, allowing them to recover at home, rather than in hospital. This has the potential both to reduce healthcare costs and to improve the medical treatment and care of patients. Monitoring fitness and activity is of enormous relevance to health and life insurers: in September 2018, the largest life insurer in the United States, John Hancock, announced that activity tracking would be made compulsory for all of its life insurance products.[46] Other life insurers are bound to follow suit.
- **Transport:** Connecting vehicles to the internet could enable them to be tracked and have the performance of their engine and other mechanical components remotely monitored. This data could also be used for analysis to improve vehicle design over time. Connected vehicles should be better able to avoid accidents by detecting and monitoring the presence of other road users, and tracking information can also be used to improve traffic flow.[47]

The best known example of data from the IoT being relied upon by insurers is telematics data from vehicles: black-box recorders gather real-time information on the location of the car, speed, rates of acceleration and deceleration, cornering, mileage, tyre pressure and (increasingly) wear and tear. Much of this will assist in calculating premium on renewal and can assist in determining where fault lies in the context of claims following accidents. Home telematics products have also come onto the market, some of which – such as connected smoke alarms, connected carbon monoxide detectors, connected water leak detectors, and smart locks on doors and windows – are relevant to home and

[43] Ofcom M2M Application Characteristics and their Implications for Spectrum, May 2014.

[44] Ofcom, Promoting Investment and Innovation in the Internet of Things – summary of responses and next steps, January 2015. That report was principally focussed on the spectrum demands the increasing number of connected objects will make, the security and resilience of networks used to transmit and store IoT data and the privacy issues to which the IoT gives rise.

[45] ibid, para 1.4.4.

[46] In its press release it stated: 'Starting today, in a departure from the traditional life insurance business model, all John Hancock life insurance policies will come with Vitality – a behavior change platform that rewards customers for the everyday steps they take to live longer, healthier lives. Built on the convergence of behavioral economics and consumer technology, John Hancock Vitality policies incentivize healthier choices linked to physical activity, nutrition and mindfulness.'

[47] Ofcom, Promoting investment and innovation in the Internet of Things, para 2.1. See also Government Office for Science, The Internet of Things: making the most of the Second Digital Revolution – A report by the UK Government Chief Scientific Adviser, December 2014.

contents insurers.[48] Some insurers will now offer discounts for homes with qualifying monitoring systems.

e. Self-tracking Devices[49]

Society increasingly uses self-tracking devices or devices otherwise connected to the internet to monitor various aspects of our well-being, including diet, weight, sleep and exercise. Self-tracking devices are thus a sub-set of the IoT, being physical objects connected to the internet and that provide data. However, these physical objects warrant separate consideration because self-tracking does not just generate data about an object, but sensitive data about a person. Unlike traditional forms of self-tracking (like keeping diaries), these devices leave a digital trail, creating data that can be aggregated and sold. Apps enable us to immediately identify and log the foods we consume; internet-enabled scales record and track our weight over time; wristbands and smart watches allow us to track and record our sleep, and the amount and quality of the exercise we take.[50]

However, trackers may reveal more information than was originally intended, too. For example, accelerometer data in wristbands that track steps and speed can, subject to a different algorithm, reveal the possible presence of Parkinson's disease.[51] The combined use of these devices and apps provides a comprehensive picture of our daily activity and diet, information of significant value to life and health insurers. Many companies providing self-tracking technology provide these products on terms that mean the data generated by use of tracking devices is theirs to sell (or at least gives them a right to sell).[52] As Kevin Kelly puts it, 'massive tracking and total surveillance is here to stay'.[53] And the ubiquity and inevitability of tracking will be accelerated as the number of devices connected to the IoT continues to rise.

f. Social Media

Data is a by-product of our interaction with social media networks like Facebook, Twitter, Instagram and WhatsApp. These platforms do not merely transfer data between users: they create data records of users' interactions with each other. Facebook initially used data they collected from users to enable their paying customers – companies

[48] Insurers confirmed to the FCA that they use information from connected devices: see the FCA's Feedback Statement, para 2.17: https://www.fca.org.uk/publication/feedback/fs16-05.pdf.

[49] See generally Gina Neff and Dawn Nafus, *Self Tracking* (Cambridge, MA, MIT Press, 2016).

[50] In 2014 funding for digital health companies exceeded $4.1 billion. Digital health funding is growing at a faster rate than venture capital funding in general. The top areas for funding within digital health are analytics and big data, healthcare consumer engagement, digital medical devices, telemedicine, personalised medicine and population health management: Malay Gandhi and Teresa Wang, 'Rock Health Digital Health Funding Year in Review 2014', 1 January 2015, http://www.slideshare.net/RockHealth/rock-health-2014-year-in-review-funding-1.

[51] Neff and Nafus, *Self Tracking*, 49.

[52] The FCA's Feedback Statement of September 2016 confirmed the use of self-tracking devices – referred to by the FCA as 'connected devices, a subset of objects within the internet of things': see para 2.17.

[53] Kevin Kelly, *The Inevitable: Understanding the 12 Technological Forces that that will Shape our Future* (New York, Penguin, 2016) 5.

seeking to advertise their products – to target Facebook users. In 2012 it was proposed that Facebook's social plugins – 'Likes' and 'Shares'[54] – would operate as all-seeing eyes that would hoover up users' browsing behaviour. As Garcia Martinez explains,

> [t]he popularity of Facebook's Like and Share buttons meant Facebook was on … half the Web in a mature market like the United States. As you browse the Web far and wide, from shoe shopping … [to] reading [the New York Times], Facebook sees you everywhere … Facebook's terms of service had so far prohibited the use of the resulting data for commercial purposes, but [a proposal made in April 2012] suggested lifting that self-imposed restriction.

He refers to two more radical proposals made and implemented at the same time:

> The Plan was to join the Facebook Ads experience to data generated completely outside Facebook. Thus far, all ads on Facebook used FB-only data, but this proposal would involve tapping into "external" data like browsing history, online shopping and offline purchases in physical shops. Historically, Facebook had been a walled garden, in which advertisers could not use their data in Facebook or Facebook data elsewhere. From the data perspective, it was as if Facebook was absent from the internet ecosystem … [W]e were proposing to bridge that divide.[55]

In 2012 Google announced that it would link a user's search data with data from Gmail, YouTube, GooglePlus etc into one larger dataset about that user. However, in recent years they have discovered that data can be turned into any number of AI or cognitive services including translation, visual recognition and assessing someone's personality by sifting through their writings – all of which can be sold to other firms such as insurers – for use in their own products. The more users write comments, 'like' posts and otherwise engage with Facebook, the more it learns about users and the better targeted the adverts on newsfeed become.[56]

Twitter sells data on people's thoughts, moods and interactions to data aggregators Datasift and Gnip Online: they run surveys designed to get people to describe their lifestyles and health conditions. Increasingly, they gather online information, including from social networking sites such as Facebook, Twitter and Instagram. Acxiom Corp, one of the biggest data firms, was already gathering 'public' information from social networking sites in 2010. Information once gathered and sold to advertisers and marketers seeking to better target their products is now being sold to insurers to enable them to better assess risk. In other words, information collected for one purpose is at risk of being repackaged and sold for entirely different purposes.

Apps also generate large amounts of personal data. Indeed, many apps have been designed for the principal purpose of gathering and re-selling data, reflecting the old adage that if the user is not paying, the user is not the customer. Consumers can log in to websites and apps via social media platforms, providing the app developer with personal data that the social media platform holds on the user. For example, if a user logs into an app using their Facebook login, their public profile information

[54] Which operate as glorified cookies.
[55] Antonio Garcia Martinez, *Chaos Monkeys*, 6–7.
[56] Similarly, the more people search on Google, the better its search results become.

(including the name of the user, their Facebook link, profile picture, location and time zone) is provided by default to the app developers.

Big data has given rise to a new form of data broking intermediary. In 2014, the role of data brokers was investigated in the US by the Federal Trade Commission (FTC), whose findings were published in a report.[57] The FTC observed that:

> [d]ata brokers acquire a vast array of detailed and specific information about consumers; analyse it to make inferences about consumers, some of which may be considered sensitive; and share the information with clients in a range of industries. All of this activity takes place behind the scenes, without consumers' knowledge.[58]

It considered, amongst other things, data brokers' role in collecting information that was provided by consumers for one purpose but is then compiled and analysed for very different purposes. Similarly, Dot.Econ noted in 2015 that there was a growing number of companies that specialise in data collection and data processing, including personal data, without necessarily having any direct interactions with consumers. Business models are developing based on data enrichment activities and aggregating consumer data in new and different ways. Some companies now specialise in scraping and indexing information available on the internet, in particular on social media websites, to gather comments or messages linked to its commercial client's name, brand or products.[59]

g. Third-party Data Gathering: Miscellaneous Sources

A range of third parties gather data from a range of other sources:

- credit reference agencies, who collect information from lenders on how people manage repayment commitments:[60] credit information is routinely used by insurers before completing a contract of insurance and has also been used to profile those insureds who might be more likely to make claims on their policies. In the mid-1990s, data professionals found that certain factors in individual credit histories were strong indicators that those individuals might be more likely to make claims on their car- and home-insurance policies. Today, most car and home insurers use people's credit reports or credit history to price their policies;
- price comparison websites (PCWs) can collect information provided by consumers looking for quotations, and details of the contract in fact entered into. PCWs share information about, for example, drivers, vehicles and locations securely and simultaneously with insurers. Two key implications of this for insurers are that (i) insurers who operate on PCWs receive information about more consumers than

[57] 'Data Brokers: A Call for Transparency and Accountability', https://www.ftc.gov/system/files/documents/reports/data-brokers-call-transparency-accountability-report-federal-trade-commission-may-2014/140527databrokerreport.pdf.

[58] ibid, vii.

[59] Dot.Econ, 12.

[60] Frank Pasquale, *The Black Box Society* (Cambridge, MA, Harvard University Press, 2015), who refers to the case of a couple who used a credit card to access mental health services only to subsequently discover that this had a negative impact on their credit score.

they otherwise would, although only a fraction are converted to sales; and (ii) some insurers receive more information per consumer than they might otherwise have requested.[61]

These sources of data are not hermetically sealed. Most activity-tracking apps (think of Fitbit and Strava) have social features in that they encourage individual self-trackers to invite friends and family to join to compete or support and offer sharing and messaging tools. The way in which one invites friends and family to participate will often be through social media such as Facebook. Moreover, companies are also seeking to correlate online and offline behaviour: Facebook, for example, entered into a partnering arrangement with data brokers Acxiom and Epsilon to match a person's online profile and their in-store purchases.[62] Nor are these sources of data exhaustive. The much reduced cost of sequencing and analysing DNA means that genetics will open up a new vista for the harvesting of what is some of our most highly sensitive data. The genetics' testing company 23andMe offers a comprehensive understanding of ancestry, traits and health through analysis of an individual DNA sample. It hopes to use this information to identify genes associated with disease leading to new and profitable cures. While customers have to pay a fee for the service, 23andMe share that data with other biotech companies.[63]

As noted above, insurers can either obtain and analyse information from all of the above sources or outsource those tasks to third-party data brokers. The CMA's research on the commercial use of consumer data commented as follows:

> motor insurers generally prefer to carry out the complex analysis underpinning their predictive risk modelling in-house. However, they have a strong incentive to collect more and more detailed information, because more accurate risk assessments can confer substantial commercial advantages. They may therefore seek to draw in external datasets (such as credit ratings and shopping records) to give themselves a competitive edge.[64]

III. How Big Data is Transforming Insurance Business

A. Changes in the Way Insurance is Sold and Distributed

Historically insurance cover was obtained through a broker. Over time, consumer insurance became available to purchase directly through bricks and mortar establishments

[61] In that regard, Dot.Econ noted that PCWs must collect data if it is required by *any* of the participating providers in order to produce quotes, meaning that the range of information being collected from each consumer may have expanded due to PCWs.

[62] Cotton Delo, 'Facebook to partner with Acxiom, Epsilon to match store purchases with user profiles', *Advertising Age*, 22 February 2013.

[63] In 2014, 23andMe entered into a $60 million deal that gave Genentech (a biotech company and subsidiary of pharmaceutical giant Roche) access to the data extracted from the test results from 23andMe customers; Matthew Harper, 'Surprise! With $60 million Genentech Deal, 23andMe has a Business Plan', *Forbes Magazine*, 6 January 2015, http://www.forbes.com/sites/matthewharper/2015/01/06/surprise-with-60-million-genentech-deal-23andme-has-a-business-plan/.

[64] DotEcon, 15 June 2015. That report focussed on motor insurers specifically, rather than general insurance providers more generally. The observation is likely to be true of the approach taken by general insurers to a wider set of consumer risks.

and, with the rise of the internet, via direct online sales channels. PCWs have since come to the fore, aggregating all available policies from participating insurers relative to the insured's requirements. Yet consumers have found PCWs time-consuming and lacking transparency. In 2017, the UK's Competition and Markets Authority undertook a market study into the use of PCWs. While that study found that PCWs provided a range of benefits to consumers, a market investigation was subsequently opened in relation to certain of the practices of the largest PCW.[65] Increasingly, consumers can purchase insurance directly, through smartphones that enable cover to be purchased at any time. Partly as a result of profiling, consumers are likely to be offered policies that are customised to their own particular needs. As European Insurance Regulator EIOPA puts it, 'the greater availability of customer data [enables] the development of more personalised products and services adapted to the needs and demands of consumers'.[66] These direct, disintermediated sales through the internet or smartphone apps benefit from simplified processes and reduce distribution costs.

Whether insurance is effected through intermediaries or insurers directly, providers will be able to provide quotations for insurance without the need to ask consumers the range of questions that were traditionally asked of prospective insureds. An example of this is how Aviva prices its car insurance. Previously a prospective insured would answer questions about the type of car, the place at which it would be kept and the insured's driving history. However, Aviva has found a significant statistical link between the purchase of life insurance policies and safer driving. Life insurance policyholders therefore benefit from lower premiums.

As insurers increasingly rely on more external information about the risk, complex proposal forms will become a thing of the past. Insurers are presenting this as a benefit to insureds, particularly small and medium sized enterprises, who are saved from having to spend time filling out forms and providing detailed data.[67] If insurers, through data mining, are presenting their understanding of the risk to the insured via the insured's broker, the role of the broker and the insured becomes one of validation, not presentation.

B. Changes in How Risk is Assessed and Priced

Most importantly to this book is the way in which insurers will in future be able to assess risk. Data profiling is at the heart of risk assessment in the age of big data. Insurers have a significant incentive to use predictive analytics since even a marginal improvement in risk modelling can give rise to a competitive advantage. As Baker notes, '[a]n insurer that discovers a new way to identify and exclude high risks improves

[65] https://www.gov.uk/cma-cases/price-comparison-website-use-of-most-favoured-nation-clauses.

[66] EIOPA InsurTech Roundtable: 'How technology and data are reshaping the insurance landscape', summary of roundtable on 28 April 2017, published on 5 July 2017 https://eiopa.europa.eu/Publications/Reports/08.0_EIOPA-BoS17-165_EIOPA_InsurTech_Roundtable_summary.pdf.

[67] Mining rich data – and using it effectively', *The Telegraph*, 21 March 2018 https://www.telegraph.co.uk/business/risk-insights/mining-rich-data/.

its competitive position in two ways: it lowers its average risk and, assuming the people it rejects go elsewhere, it increases the average risk of its competitors'.[68] Two refinements may be made to this point: First, if insurers accept risks albeit on the basis of a much higher premium than would have been offered on a standard, aggregated assessment, then the additional premium also offers a competitive advantage over similar risks insured by competitors on standard, aggregated models. Second, an insurer with better predictive models may be able to proactively 'cherry-pick' low-risk individuals that its competitors have failed to identify as such.

In relation to underwriting and pricing, the use of big data and predictive analytics in insurance enables more granular segmentation of risks, increases the effectiveness of risk identification, and also allows for pricing that is more risk-sensitive. This reduces underwriting costs and in turn reduces both the premium and the degree of uncertainty in relation to the risk to be insured, thus providing for greater resilience within the underwriting process. Combining the above sources of data makes it possible for insurers to establish a prospective insured's risk profile. Predictive analytics is deployed over the relevant datasets to identify indicators of risk that are particular to that individual and not dependent on that person's membership of a wider class (by virtue of sex, age, or other group characteristics). Algorithms are now available to insurers to identify which prospective insureds would be a good bet and which should be avoided. Whereas basic profiling in insurance is not a new phenomenon, big data enables profiling to take place at an increasingly atomised level, by modelling how a wider range of individual factors enables risk to be more accurately assessed and priced.

The problem is that prediction of future behaviour is a matter of probability not certainty. The algorithms still cannot say whether an insured peril will or will not occur: if they could, we would no longer inhabit the world of insurance because one cannot insure against events that are certain to happen, unless there remains residual uncertainty over the time at which that event might occur (as with time of death for the purposes of life insurance). But while future behaviour is a matter of likelihood, decisions on whether to provide cover and if so on what terms then turn on the reliability of the data and the analytics used to calculate the probability of the insured event occurring and/or the prospective insured making claims on the policy. Because predictive analytics operates by reference to correlation and not causality, there is a risk of prospectively punishing people for their propensities and not their actions.[69] But in the context of insurance, that is precisely what insurers must do: absent an obligation on insurers to provide insurance, they must decide by reference to all information available whether to offer cover to the individual applicant. Moreover, there is also a concern that modelling risk on the basis of correlations means that individual risk factors may yet mean that individual risk is assessed by reference to an actuarially unproven link between a risk factor or propensity and the incidence of insured loss.

[68] Tom Baker, 'Containing the Promise of Insurance: Adverse Selection and Risk Classification', June 2002, http://ssrn.com/abstract=322581.

[69] As Mayer-Schonberger and Cukier put it: *Big Data*, 170.

C. Changes in the Nature of the Claims Process/Detection of Fraud

Claims handling is likely to benefit significantly from big data, with the data relevant to claims capable of being analysed for any unusual features instantaneously. There will be millions of documents in archives covering thousands of similar claims. Many of those claims will have been paid but some will not. Machine learning will enable algorithms to review the claims datasets and understand the features of those claims that were paid and the features of those that were not and which call for further investigation. The data from these claims can be used to drive better claims decision making. The process will thus involve the comparison of each new claim with all similar past claims: that will yield immediate information on whether insurers have paid out on similar claims in the past, if so, what they have paid, how much they have reserved and what factors triggered further investigations. This is likely to lead to claims being paid much more efficiently. For the insurer or adjuster it would ensure that their skills were deployed on claims that had genuine reasons for further investigation.

As to fraudulent claims, insurers are already using big data to improve fraud detection and criminal activity through data management and predictive modelling. Already by 2013, research suggested that most insurers in Europe and Latin America used, or planned to use, fraud modelling or predictive analytics techniques to detect fraud. Predictive models may be built using an insurance provider's historical data, identifying common patterns in known fraudulent cases. These insights can be used to predict the likelihood of fraud in future claims received and, through an automated process, to identify suspicious claims that warrant in-depth investigation early in the claims process. This will be facilitated further by the data acquired from connected devices (e.g. real-time data can establish the circumstances of a road traffic accident).[70]

Predictive modelling can match the variables in every claim against the profiles of past claims which were fraudulent so that when there is a match, the claim is flagged for further investigation. These matches could also involve the behaviour of the person making a claim, the network of people that the claimant associates with (as discerned from social media, credit reference agencies etc) and partner agencies involved in the claim (e.g. vehicle repair shops who may have, for example been involved in previous exaggerated claims). These complicated matches might be missed by a human; however, they are readily detectable by big data analysis.[71] Additionally, various databases, such as the CUE database and the CIFAS National Database,[72] are commonly accessed by insurance providers in order to establish whether any claims information links the individual or the vehicle to previous cases of fraudulent activity.

[70] Accenture, 2013, 'How to effectively fight insurance fraud', Figure 1, http://www.accenture.com/SiteCollectionDocuments/PDF/Accenture-How-Effectively-Fight-Insurance-Fraud.pdf.

[71] 'Top 7 Big Data Use Cases in Insurance Industry', Exastax, 13 April 2017, https://www.exastax.com/big-data/top-7-big-data-use-cases-in-insurance-industry/.

[72] Which are discussed in more detail in ch 2.

Social media data is already being used by some insurers to combat claims fraud.[73] However, insurers may not – and may permissibly not – allude to the fact that they refer to social media to prevent fraud. There is evidence that some insurers have discussed the issue with the Information Commissioner and have decided not to divulge substantial details about its approach to fraud detection for fear that by doing so it could make it easier for fraudsters to escape detection.[74] Other possibilities are that social media might be used to confirm suspicions about fronting (where a high-risk driver, e.g. a young driver, is in reality the main driver of the vehicle but is only stated as a named driver in order to reduce the premium), or that information on social media might contradict a claimant's account of an accident (e.g. where photographic or video evidence is found).[75]

The ABI estimates that the general insurance industry invests £200 million per year in fraud detection and that fraud adds £50 to the average general insurance premium in the UK;[76] thus there is a clear commercial benefit to reducing fraud, while consumers also stand to benefit as long as some proportion of any savings is passed on through lower premiums.

D. Changes to the Structure and Role of the Market

The techniques of big data in the insurance sector have given rise to the concept of InsurTech, a subset of Fintech, which refers to the use of technological innovations designed to reduce cost and improve efficiency in the provision of insurance services. The technology is also giving rise to insurance startups who are seeking to use the technology to disrupt traditional underwriting models. This is leading to significant changes in the structure of the market, on both the supply side and the demand side.

i. Supply-side Changes

Four big changes to the supply side of the market are (i) the rise of on-demand or usage-based insurance (UBI) (where providers are often startups); (ii) the rise of peer-to-peer insurance (where providers are again often startups); (iii) the role of partnering between insurers and tech firms; and (iv) the potential impact of Blockchain technology.

a. Usage-based Insurance

Consumers typically purchase insurance cover for cars and household contents annually for a 12-month period. But some motorists make only occasional use of their cars

[73] Dot.Econ, 54. And see, eg, https://www.smdiscover.com/insurance-claims-adjustmentby-referencing-social-media-content/.

[74] Dot.Econ, 57.

[75] See, eg, 'Investigators combing social media to expose insurance scams', CBS, February 2015, http://www.cbsnews.com/news/investigators-combingsocial-media-to-expose-insurance-scams/.

[76] https://www.abi.org.uk/Insurance-and-savings/Topics-and-issues/Fraud.

and end up paying over the odds to insure vehicles that spend most of the time in the garage. Consumers may wish – and be offered – the opportunity to purchase cover for much smaller and specific periods. As EIOPA again notes, the availability of more personalised products is reflected 'for instance [in] the case of new on-demand / just-in-time insurance products, where consumers are offered the possibility to purchase tailored insurance policies only for the period without being obliged to subscribe to longer term plans'.[77]

As its name suggests, UBI is the provision of insurance as and when it is needed. Indeed, policies may be designed to enable policyholders to switch their insurance on and off enabling motorists to pay lower premiums, or, alternatively, the policy will switch itself off automatically once the vehicle has been idle for more than a certain period of time.[78] Surveys conducted on motor insurers have revealed that nearly half of the respondents were not yet prepared to provide UBI. The market will thus be split between those insurers who do offer such cover and those who do not, with those drivers who choose to be monitored representing a separate class of drivers who are underwritten in a different way, supplementing at first and perhaps later supplanting traditional pricing factors. It is conceivable that those who refuse to be monitored (a diminishing number over time) will constitute more of a specialty market for traditional insurers.[79]

UBI for motor insurance is facilitated by telematics. In the early stages of telematics, first-movers have sought to attract customers by offering discounted coverage. In a sense, this is a win-win: insurers get access to new and increasingly large datasets to improve their predictive analytics while insureds benefit from lower premiums. However, once there is 'saturation' – that is, as market adoption of all policyholders who are likely to opt into telematics nears completion – usage-based insurers will have to differentiate their offerings. Deloitte suggests that to do so, insurers will have to offer more value-added, telematics-based services such as providing incentives for behaviour that prevents losses, thereby generating value for insureds and carriers throughout the policy year. This would make insurance more of a proactive, prevention-driven engagement, rather than a reactive, price-driven commodity. The goal then will be to create value for both insurer and insured while engendering greater loyalty at renewal.[80]

More fundamental are the consequences of real-time analytics on the way cover is provided. Take, for example, telematics-based motor insurance where data is provided to insurers who will know in real time that an insured is breaching the terms of cover (eg by doing 50 mph in a 30 mph zone) such as to contractually entitle the

[77] EIOPA InsurTech Roundtable: 'How technology and data are reshaping the insurance landscape', summary of roundtable on 28 April 2017, published on 5 July 2017 https://eiopa.europa.eu/Publications/Reports/08.0_EIOPA-BoS17-165_EIOPA_InsurTech_Roundtable_summary.pdf.

[78] Cuvva in the UK and Metromile in the United States are already offering car insurance on that more tailored – pay-as-you-go – basis. Cuvva offers rates by the hour (based simply on the car's registration, the insured's date of birth and the starting position of the vehicle) and the accompanying app indicates when the cover starts and how long is left.

[79] See Deloitte's 'overcoming speed bumps on the road to telematics': https://www2.deloitte.com/content/dam/insights/us/articles/telematics-in-auto-insurance/DUP-695_Telematics-in-the-Insurance-Industry_vFINAL.pdf.

[80] ibid.

insurer to treat the insured as outside the scope of cover for, at least, the period of the breach. Or real-time driving data may permit an insurer to introduce new prospective exclusions over the term of the policy. These issues are considered further from an insurance law perspective in chapter four.

b. Peer-to-peer Insurance

A number of insurance startups have adopted a peer-to-peer insurance model. The definition of peer-to-peer (P2P) insurance implies a pooling of peer groups. The size of the group depends on the type of insurance and the expected benefits to be generated. However, the definition of P2P insurance is sometimes misleading, since its difference from traditional mutual insurance is not always evident and it does not work as a two-sided platform like other peer-to-peer models. P2P insurance can be provided either directly through an insurer or through a broker/intermediary.[81]

Key to the success of the model is the relationship between the group of customers: the closer the attachments between members of the group, the less likely it is that claims are made. P2P insurance may lead to more responsible behaviour from consumers, including reduced fraud, and improved risk management, because the participants will form smaller groups of people for whom there is potentially greater downside by engaging in the behaviour insured against insofar as it amounts to a breach of trust and harms the other members of the insured pool. Friendsurance is a P2P insurer that has sought to bring together customers who have been claim-free year after year. Friendsurance connects groups of customers and provides a yearly cash-back when that group remains claims-free, with the cash-back reducing as the number of claims made within the group increases. Even if the value of claims made by the group is greater than the amount of the premium that the group has paid, insured members of the group never pay more than the premium they originally paid.[82] Lemonade is another P2P insurer which offers groups of customers' homeowners and renters' insurance. It is using machine-learning both to sell insurance policies and to manage claims.[83] It takes a fixed fee on a monthly debit, pays for reinsuring the risk, and uses the balance to pay claims with the unallocated balance being given to the group's charitable causes. A further unique selling point is, by contrast with traditional insurers, the promise to pay claims within three days.[84] So Sure insures

[81] Currently P2P insurance needs to be provided in co-operation with a licensed insurance undertaking: https://eiopa.europa.eu/Publications/Letters/EIOPA%20response%20to%20EC%20FinTech%20consultation%20.pdf.

[82] P2P insurance might superficially look like mutual insurance. However, while some P2P arrangements may operate on a not-for-profit basis (as do mutuals), the fact that the premium is fixed from the outset such that no further 'calls' for further income might be made from members of the P2P pool is what differentiates it from mutual insurance.

[83] 'Unshackled Algorithms', *The Economist*, 27 May 2017.

[84] A very early UK P2P insurance startup, Guevara, has since collapsed. Guevara was a car insurer which allowed customers to pool their premiums in order to lower the collective premium and then refund unclaimed capital to the group. It may have failed in part because customers of motor insurance look for more established insurers and where claims at the back end are more costly than other forms of personal property insurance: https://www.globaldata.com/guevaras-collapse-industry-ready-p2p-insurance/.

mobile phones and also provides rewards when the insured looks after the phone and additionally returns 80% of the insured's premium if no claim is made in the policy period.[85]

c. Partnering Arrangements

Although the impact of digital technologies has taken longer in the insurance sector,[86] leading insurers are investing billions in these technologies.[87] Axa, Aviva and Allianz have all launched venture arms to back young InsurTech companies. And insurers such as Swiss Re, Scottish Widows and LV= were sponsors of Startupbootcamp InsurTech.[88] The Joint Committee of Supervisory Authorities further observes that 'financial institutions' growing interest in the use of big data may also be partially attributable to the potential threat posed by (non-financial) technology companies which have considerable amounts of data that offer valuable insights into their users'. They consider that it

> is entirely plausible that tech firms would expand into broader financial services, leveraging their own technical expertise, innovative and integrated platforms, extensive consumer data or loyalty among millennials and digital natives. Many financial incumbents understand this reality and are well aware that Big Data related technologies are a potential threat as well as an opportunity for their sector.[89]

This may explain the rise in the number of partnering arrangements between existing insurers and tech firms who have much larger datasets that could be used to generate profit in the insurance market. Incumbent insurers have recognised the benefits of collaborating with technology companies to provide services that interface directly with clients and have been seeking to increase their engagement with the startup world.

Many insurance undertakings have started to embark on ambitious digital transformation projects to upgrade their technology capabilities along the insurance value chain, often in collaboration with InsurTech startups. This can take place via different frameworks, such as the sponsorship of startup accelerators, digital labs or venture capital funding. This may mitigate the disruptive impacts of insurance start-ups or potential market entry by existing BigTech and FinTech firms. And as EIOPA

[85] EIOPA suggests that the changes to date would more accurately be described as reshaping the insurance landscape rather than disrupting it. See its response to the Commission's Public Consultation on FinTech, 16 June 2017: https://eiopa.europa.eu/Publications/Letters/EIOPA%20response%20to%20EC%20FinTech%20consultation%20.pdf.

[86] The so-called digital delay may be attributed in part to the heavy regulation of the insurance industry which creates higher barriers to startup entry. It might also be due to legacy issues. As EIOPA observed: 'The scale and complexity of core processes in combination with a reliance on outdated hardware and manual processes, in some cases established since decades, mean that the implementation of new technologies and processes is difficult and risky. InsurTech start-ups do not face such problems.' Roundtable Summary, 28 April 2017: https://eiopa.europa.eu/Publications/Reports/08.0_EIOPA-BoS17-165_EIOPA_InsurTech_Roundtable_summary.pdf.

[87] 'Insurance and the big data technology revolution', *Financial Times*, 24 February 2017.

[88] https://www.fnlondon.com/articles/insurance-industry-gets-digital-20160505.

[89] Joint Committee of the European Supervisory Authorities, Joint Committee Discussion Paper on the use of Big Data by Financial Institutions, 2016, para 75; and see 'Digitizing Intelligence: AI, Robots and the Future of Finance', 3 March 2016.

further notes, partnering may be the more likely short-term solution for the further reason that:

> [s]oft skills such as the possession of a tech and data-savvy workforce represent one of the key competitive advantages of Insurtech start-ups, this being particularly relevant at a time when customer's digital data is a highly valued commodity. Yet incumbents possess large customer bases and economies of scale arising from their established balance sheets and existing business. Furthermore, incumbents' experience in underwriting and regulatory experience is also an important added value, particularly given the detailed regulatory framework under which insurance is conducted.[90]

d. Blockchain

Blockchain is a type of distributed ledger technology. It is characterised as a digital, chronologically updated, distributed and cryptographically sealed ledger of transactions. Blockchain technology could have the potential to significantly disrupt the insurance sector not least because it has the capacity to render intermediaries redundant as all relevant risk-related data would be stored in a single distributed database. Formerly, a highly fragmented network of insurance brokers meant that clients who had insurance policies with different insurers (arranged by different brokers) had no efficient way to manage all of their policies in one place. Blockchain enables a complete record of all cover with all insurers to be kept. Swiss startup Knip provides an app that helps aggregate all of a user's insurance policies in one place, and suggests new products based on potential gaps in a client's coverage. Similarly, startup FinanceFox provides a tool for users to manage all their policies in one app. The app also enables users to engage with personal consultants. Brokers can use the app to bring clients on to the service.[91] In the same way, it could also be used for improving the recognition of claims history statements (which are used to calculate no-claims bonuses).

Blockchain could also be used to underpin smart contracts where, upon the occurrence of some contingency, some further contractual action is automatically executed (eg the suspension of cover or the imposition of an endorsement). Smart contracts could be used in relation to catastrophe cover. EIOPA gives the example of a hurricane in a certain location, where the smart contract could pay out automatically without the need for formally submitting a claim. Smart contracts could also be used in travel insurance. Here, if a flight is cancelled or delayed, a payment would be made automatically to the customer.[92]

Further, Blockchain will assist in tackling fraud by creating an international, cross-industry database that can be used to detect identity fraud, and to check claims history and police reports. Individual insurance contracts and all claims made on those contracts could be recorded on to the Blockchain, ensuring that only valid claims are made and ensuring that multiple claims for a single peril are rejected.[93]

[90] https://eiopa.europa.eu/Publications/Reports/08.0_EIOPA-BoS17-165_EIOPA_InsurTech_Roundtable_summary.pdf, p 6.

[91] https://www.fnlondon.com/articles/insurance-industry-gets-digital-20160505.

[92] EIOPA Roundtable April 2017, p 10.

[93] https://www.pwc.com/gx/en/financial-services/pdf/how-blockchain-tecnology-might-transform-insurance.pdf.

Use of Blockchain technology in insurance is currently limited but it is considered to have significant potential in the sector.

ii. Demand-side Changes

The FSUG has observed[94] that:

> Consumer's individual risk beliefs and their willingness-to-pay based on those beliefs directly affect their take-up of insurance products and also influence the insurance market and development of "new" insurance products. Increased predictability could directly affect consumer's risk beliefs and willingness-to-pay as they would have a better understanding/knowledge of their individual risk and therefore whether it is "worth" to take out an insurance policy or not based on their risk.[95]

It further observes that:

> Through access to their data and algorithms, users could consult their probability of having a car accident based on their driving behaviour, the probability of having an accident during vacation based on their activities and the country they go to, the probability of developing a disease based on their diet etc … The 'end result' could be two-fold: the end of insurance (since only consumers who have a high risk would consider paying for an insurance) and/or a drastic homogenization of consumer behaviour or cheating their data to get the best deal (modifying driving behaviour, eating better, choosing 'safe' travel destinations and activities). In the latter case, even if the effect seems positive, shaping consumer behaviour in such a manner might go too far.[96]

IV. Conclusions

Plainly big data in insurance offers very significant advantages. Predictive analytics not only allows insureds who are lower risks to avail of lower premiums than the aggregated premiums they were previously charged; it also enables insurers to incentivise less risky behaviour to the benefit of both the insured (who will suffer less insured loss), insurers (whose claims bill will be reduced) and society as a whole (because prevention is better than cure). It is of course true that, historically, the insurance industry helped eliminate certain risks. For example, insurers had a role in founding the first fire departments, building codes and vehicle safety testing. Insurance today has the capacity to increasingly shape the choices we make. Insurers now reward individuals for being more active and maintaining a healthier lifestyle. Real-time monitoring and feedback of driving or lifestyle behaviour reveals risk (and price)-increasing behaviour

[94] Paper on the Assessment of current and future impact of Big Data on Financial Services, June 2016, p 5 https://ec.europa.eu/info/sites/info/files/file_import/1606-big-data-on-financial-services_en_0.pdf.

[95] The problem of 'adverse selection' in insurance and the way in which this is accentuated by an insured's knowledge of their own relative risk – and thus the extent to which insurance offers value in relation to that degree of risk – is considered in more detail in ch 3.

[96] Above n 94, p 10.

more quickly, enabling the insured to take corrective steps.[97] Big data has the power to enable the basic model of insurance to evolve from ex post facto protection to ex ante prediction and prevention. And so it has been said that:

> arguably the greatest societal benefits come from the potential to reduce risks through better data and new digital technologies. The ubiquitous availability of vast amounts of data and the ability to analyse it allow for individual and dynamic risk assessment and a continuous feedback loop to policyholders, with no or limited human interaction. By providing risk insights to policyholders, such 'digital monitoring' encourages behavioural change to reduce risks. Moreover, new data sources allow for the implementation of advanced risk management systems that use predictive analytics as a basis for early intervention[98] and risk prevention. Ultimately, these technologies allow the role of insurance to evolve from pure risk protection towards predicting and preventing risks.[99]

As the Association of British Insurers notes, by way of example,

> [t]he availability of extremely sensitive and hyperlocal weather information means that insurers can increasingly predict flooding and storm damage, and give valuable advance warning to customers of potential damage. Insurers can also provide advice on how to minimise this damage, and use the warning period to prepare.

Similarly it observes that insurers can analyse driving data to identify the steps you could take to become a safer driver, and with data from wearables, proactively monitor health: by understanding trends and patterns from millions of customers, insurers can identify when an insured's data suggests that they might be at risk of a health-related incident.[100]

But big data's use in insurance also creates a range of potential problems. Risk profiles may be inaccurately modelled if a particular correlation has no predictive value in relation to a particular individual; the data used to profile an individual may be inaccurate and, worse, may not be known to the insured who may have no opportunity to correct the basis upon which their premium is calculated; those who previously benefited from the premium charged of insureds within wider risk pools may pay more, or be excluded from cover. And indeed profiling may take place, consciously or unconsciously, on more insidious grounds, something that insureds may again be unaware of unless insurers are required to disclose the basis on which the price and scope of the proposed cover is to be written. It is very early days; the technologies are rapidly developing and there is no uniformity in practice across the sector. In those circumstances, the assessment of the impact of big data will fall, in the first instance, to those regulators with responsibility for the conduct of insurance business. It is to those early assessments that chapter two turns.

[97] Because big data has the ability to identify and potentially penalise risky behaviour, some motor insurers have called for telematics devices to be made compulsory for drivers under the age of 25 (the highest-risk group of motorists).

[98] eg the real-time analysis of data will enable the creation of early warning systems that will allow timely preventative measures to be taken to avoid insured loss.

[99] The Geneva Association, 'Big Data and Insurance: Implications for Innovation, Competition and Privacy', March 2018, https://www.genevaassociation.org/sites/default/files/research-topics-document-type/pdf_public/big_data_and_insurance_-_implications_for_innovation_competition_and_privacy.pdf.

[100] Association of British Insurers, 'How data makes insurance work better for you', September 2015.

2

Regulatory Assessment of the Use of Big Data by Insurers

The previous chapter considered how big data was beginning to impact on the insurance industry, both in terms of the evolution in risk evaluation and the impact on the wider market. This chapter considers how UK and EU insurance regulators have assessed the use of big data and predictive analytics in insurance business.

I. Regulatory Assessment by UK Regulators

A. CMA's Report on the Commercial Use of Consumer Data 2015

In June 2015, following a call for information,[1] the Competition and Markets Authority (CMA) published a report entitled 'Commercial use of consumer data' (the CMA Report).[2] Specifically, it sought to understand how consumer data was being collected and used commercially. The CMA observed that the collection and commercial use of consumer data had become widespread in the UK, being carried out by a large number of firms across a wide range of sectors.[3] One of its illustrative case studies was the collection and use of data in the motor insurance market. What follows relates to their analysis of data use and collection specifically by UK motor insurers. In that regard the CMA commissioned research into how motor insurers were collecting and using personal data. It published its research in June 2015 (the CMA Research).[4] The CMA did not have or exercise any compulsory information-gathering powers.[5] However, it noted that there was a large body of research and well-documented

[1] https://assets.publishing.service.gov.uk/government/uploads/system/uploads/attachment_data/file/398283/Consumer_Data_-_CFI.pdf.

[2] https://assets.publishing.service.gov.uk/government/uploads/system/uploads/attachment_data/file/435817/The_commercial_use_of_consumer_data.pdf.

[3] ibid, para 1.1.

[4] https://assets.publishing.service.gov.uk/government/uploads/system/uploads/attachment_data/file/435777/The_Commercial_Use_of_Consumer_Data_-_DotEcon_and_Analysys_Mason.pdf.

[5] No consumer, competition or information regulator has used information-gathering powers to require undertakings to provide responses as regards the collection and use of personal data in the general insurance market.

evidence of commercial practices within the motor insurance sector. It stated: 'As a result, we have reasonable confidence that the full breadth of issues for consumer data in the motor insurance sector has been explored.' The CMA's Report is therefore not a comprehensive overview of data practices within the wider general insurance sector. However, it provides one of the first clear snapshots of insurers' collection and use of personal data in the UK.

Motor (and other general) insurers usually collect data directly from existing and would-be customers infrequently, namely once a year at or near the time of seeking cover or renewal and additionally in the event that a claim is made. That data includes personal (being individual, location and vehicle-specific data) and behavioural information (being, principally, information about previous claims). That information can become dated, even within the policy period (subject of course to obligations to provide insurers with updated information on those matters). However, that information aggregated over many years can provide a more detailed picture of the risk that that person presents.

The research indicates that while much of the data about a driver or vehicle is provided directly by the insured at point of quote or renewal, insurers

> enrich the data with additional information, either held internally or obtained from a third party. In order to evaluate risk, insurers rely on predictive models that are built and continually refined through a resource-intensive process of data analysis to establish correlations between particular variables and risk. Insurers usually carry out such analysis in-house.[6]

Consumer data is used both in support of the risk evaluation – and pricing – process and to detect mistakes or possible instances of fraud in relation to claims. The insured's declared information can be cross-checked against the various databases to which insurers have access and which are referred to below.

More specifically, the research found that in addition to information provided directly by insureds, the sector was undergoing a process of change, with insurers seeking to collect more data as enabling technologies have developed. 'A clear example is the use of telematics devices and smartphone applications (apps) to collect driving data.' In that regard, a global survey of insurance CEOs by PricewaterhouseCoopers (PwC) in 2014 found that 'analytics and data are insurance CEOs' top transformational priority'.[7] However, the report observed that 'the process of seeking out greater data sources and integrating big data into insurers' business processes may still be in its infancy: responses from those insurers interviewed indicated that the impact on firms' operations and processes thus far is relatively limited.'[8] It was noted that 'the role of "big data" in the industry has been emphasised by third-party data and analytics providers with an interest in selling their services'.

In relation to data collected through third parties, the report described how additional data can be grouped within the following three categories: (i) additional

[6] CMA Research, p 13.
[7] PwC, 2014, 'Doing more with more: How P&C insurers are creating an information advantage with 3rd party data', http://www.pwc.com/en_US/us/insurance/publications/assets/pwc-third-partydata-insurance.pdf.
[8] CMA Research, pp 29–30.

information about the driver; (ii) additional information about the vehicle; and (iii) additional information about location.

i. Sources of Additional Driver Information

The following insurance-specific databases are used by UK insurers in order to ascertain or verify information about the driver/insured:

- The Claims and Underwriting Exchange (CUE), which contains records for previous motor, home and personal injury claims. CUE is administered by the Motor Insurers' Bureau (MIB). Specifically, it is a central database of motor, home and personal injury/industrial illness incidents reported to insurance companies which may or may not have given rise to a claim. CUE was established in 1994 to help fight insurance fraud. By enabling insurers (and brokers)[9] to access details of incidents, it makes it harder to successfully commit claims fraud or misrepresent claims history.[10]
- The Insurance Fraud Register (IFR): this was founded in 2013 and is funded by the Association of British Insurers (ABI) under the auspices of the Insurance Fraud Bureau. It contains a list of all persons who have been convicted of insurance fraud. The IFR is available to all insurers within the UK and can be accessed by their underwriting and claims departments when deciding whether to accept a risk or when processing a claim.
- The MyLicence database, which came into force in 2014, enables insurers to obtain licence details directly from the Driver and Vehicle Licensing Agency (DVLA).[11] The MyLicence programme is a joint initiative of the DVLA, the Department for Transport, and the insurance industry, represented by the ABI and the MIB. Insurers use MyLicence to access a prospective insured's driving licence number (DLN) to be able to quickly request that person's driving record and thus to make an offer of insurance based on accurate information. The scheme eliminates the risk of insureds providing insurers with mistaken information and is a means of preventing fraud. Currently, drivers are required to answer a series of questions about their entitlement to drive, penalty points and convictions. Those who provide their DLN to MyLicence enable insurers to access these details immediately. Insurers are not entitled to any other information, including medical information, home address or the driver's photograph. The site states: 'When you request a quote, or multiple quotes, the insurer will be provided with the DVLA data. However, insurers can only keep this information while the quote is valid; approximately 30 days. After the quote expires, the insurer can anonymise the information and use it for analysis

[9] The data on the database is available to individual consumers upon specific request.

[10] The CMA Research noted that there was some evidence that incidents may be logged in the database even when a claim is not ultimately made, and that allegedly insurers may take these past incidents into account when setting premiums. CMA Research, p 56.

[11] Before this was launched, firms were unable to check licence details (eg type of licence, date issued, any driving convictions or points) at the point of quoting for policies, and so had to 'price in' the risk that the information disclosed by the licensee was incorrect, either due to mistakes or due to deliberate fraudulent behaviour: *The Guardian*, January 2014, 'Car insurance premiums may fall as driving licence records go online', http://www.theguardian.com/uk-news/2014/jan/09/carinsurance-premiums-licence-records-online.

purposes (in which you are unidentifiable), after which it will be deleted. Once you have purchased a policy, the insurer or broker you have purchased the policy from will retain the data in order to administer the policy.'

- The Insurance Fraud Investigators Group (IFRG) is another member organisation that facilitates the sharing of fraud-related information, covering the majority of the insurance industry.
- The National Fraud Database, which is managed by the Credit Industry Fraud Avoidance System (CIFAS) to check for links to confirmed cases of fraud. Insurance providers are amongst those contributing data to the database.[12]
- The No Claims Discount database: this database is again administered by the MIB. It is an online service that replaces the need for motor insurers and insureds to manually exchange papers about an insured's no claims discount data.
- The Motor Insurance Database (MID): this is a national database which shows the insurance status of each registered vehicle in the UK. In particular, it reveals whether the vehicle is insured and the identity of its insurer. The MID works with the DVLA and the police to address uninsured driving. It is not only open to insurers and brokers but all members of the public.
- The Motor Insurance Anti-Fraud and Theft Register (MIAFTR): This is a record of all vehicles declared 'write-offs' due to an accident or which have been stolen and not recovered. Again it is used to prevent fraudulent claims. MIAFTR can be accessed by claims departments of insurers when processing claims and is used as part of their standard fraud checks whenever a claim has been notified.

Crime and road accident data can provide further information about vehicle location. In addition, companies such as Experian and Callcredit have built geo-demographic segmentation systems which classify consumers into different consumer types, for example at postcode level or at household level. This is not information that relates to the specific risk presented by a specific insured but such aggregated information enables insurers to make inferences about levels of risk.[13]

These various sources of information are, strictly speaking, databases. They do not involve the analysis of vast datasets. They are relatively small and structured databases that are amenable to ordinary software processing. That notwithstanding, this wider range of risk and claims-related information is being increasingly used by general insurers. As the data in these databases expands, so too does the breadth of the information held on more and more insureds.[14]

[12] https://www.cifas.org.uk/services/national-fraud-database. The National Fraud Database enables member organisations from across the public and private sectors to share data and intelligence with each other in real time and online.

[13] The Joint Committee of the European Supervisory Authorities similarly observed, in the context of flood insurance, that 'traditional risk segmentations based on zip-codes may progressively be substituted in some areas by satellite images or heat maps, allowing more accurate determinations of which real estate properties are more prone to be affected by floods and which ones are not. The latter may therefore be offered insurance coverage at conditions which in the past could not have been possible'. See p 21 of its Discussion Paper on the use of Big Data by Financial Institutions, discussed below at section II, pp 49–52.

[14] The ABI has noted insurers' increasing use of databases to provide information about the risk to be insured: 'insurers in the future might be able to access existing databases with your permission in order to

ii. Use of Algorithms/Predictive Analytics

The CMA's research found that insurers used the above databases for cross-checking, real-time verification and risk assessment. In respect of policies supplied through brokers, quotes were generated using software platforms provided by third-party firms which apply risk-prediction models based on algorithms supplied and periodically updated by insurers.[15] These algorithms tended to be static algorithms which did not necessarily use additional third party or real-time data to supplement information provided by the insured.

The principal source of real-time data enrichment for motor policies came from the use of telematics devices installed in cars to collect information on a range of driving variables. Smartphone apps were also being used to collect such data (although these can be less reliable because they are capable of being switched off). As at mid-2015, the CMA noted that 'In the UK, black box policies have been marketed primarily at young drivers, a high-risk segment who typically face high premiums because of their age and inexperience, and who may be able to achieve substantial savings with such policies.' It noted that different business models have been built on the collection of driving data: some policies collected telematics data continuously but some providers might only collect data for a fixed period, such as 200 miles. The analysis of that data then gives rise to driving scores for individuals whereby premiums can be adjusted upwards or downwards according to those scores or, depending again on the business model, a downward only adjustment to encourage uptake. The number of providers of telematics policies and the uptake of such policies increased by 200 per cent between 2011 and 2013[16] although there was, at the time, uncertainty over the extent to which the rate of uptake would continue. Car manufacturers are increasingly building cars with telematics capabilities, something which should facilitate the continued uptake of such cover.[17]

pre-populate information in your application. For example, you can now enter your car license plate information to automatically provide details about your vehicle's engine size, number of doors etc. However, in the future, that could be extended to any number of areas – you might enter your postcode and house number and information about your home's number of bedrooms, types of locks and roof construction would be automatically provided.' 'How data makes insurance work better for you', September 2015, see https://www.abi.org.uk/globalassets/sitecore/files/documents/publications/public/2015/data/how-data-makes-insurance-work-better-for-you.pdf.

[15] CMA Research, p 36, see https://assets.publishing.service.gov.uk/government/uploads/system/uploads/attachment_data/file/435777/The_Commercial_Use_of_Consumer_Data_-_DotEcon_and_Analysys_Mason.pdf.

[16] British Insurance Brokers' Association, Research on Telematics Market, 2014.

[17] Indeed, the report observed that manufacturers themselves may come to play an important role in the data collection process in the future: See Computerworld UK, August 2014, 'BMW to install usage-based insurance telematics into cars', http://www.computerworlduk.com/news/itbusiness/3534379/bmw-to-install-usage-based-insurance-telematics-into-cars/; Moneysupermarket, 21 March 2013, 'Telematics: The future of driving?', http://www.moneysupermarket.com/c/news/telematics-the-future-ofdriving/0017203/; Pinsent Masons, 22 January 2015, 'Telematics insurance, market disruption and control of data' http://www.outlaw.com/en/articles/2015/january/telematics-insurance-market-disruption-andcontrol-of-data-/. See also Deloitte's 'Overcoming speed bumps on the road to telematics', April 2014 which notes three categories of driver: those keen to take up telematics; those who would consider it depending on impact on premium; and those (nearly half) who would not wish to have their driving monitored under any circumstances. Age was the biggest differentiator amongst constituents of the three groups, with youngest drivers being most keen.

Telematics policies were, at that stage, being offered on a wholly opt-in basis and the ABI offered guidance (in the form of voluntary good practice) to insurers in relation to the provision of such policies. Good practice included obtaining explicit consent, presenting customers with clear and comprehensive information about how the data would be collected and used and clarifying who would have rights of access to it. Moreover, the guidance provided that data should not be recorded unless it is necessary for the purposes it is being used for, as declared to the customer.[18]

The CMA Report makes clear that notwithstanding insurers were at the early stages of using new datasets relevant to risk evaluation, many (albeit not all) were keen to enhance their predictive analytics capabilities by increasing the use of external data in underwriting, pricing and claims.[19] By August 2014, Lloyds of London had already observed that with the vast treasure trove of data created, inter alia, by the IoT, insurers were 'pushing hard to analyse it effectively and then apply the findings to their businesses'.[20] The CMA noted that one way to test the value or utility of new data sources was to take that additional data and correlate it against past insurance losses: positive correlations would indicate that such data can improve the assessment of risk. There were a number of such additional sources that insurers were either already using or were contemplating the use of.

Credit ratings and financial information: the CMA Report noted that 'an individual's credit scores and history are typically used [by insurers] when the individual opts to pay for insurance in instalments, as insurers seek to establish the individual's likelihood of keeping up with monthly payments and set the interest rate accordingly'. However, this information might be valuable as part of individual risk assessments more generally: empirical evidence has established that people who pay their bills on time are also safer drivers.[21] What was harder to discern empirically was the extent to which insurers are in fact referring to credit and financial information and for what specific purpose. Terms and conditions are often couched in language that gives insurers the power to conduct credit reference checks in certain circumstances. This gives rise to an important distinction between risk and non-risk-related information: risk-related information is information that bears on the nature of the risk proposed and will affect the terms on which cover is offered. Non-risk-related information can include things such as price sensitivity and credit history, which can be used to increase the price of cover for those who appear less risk sensitive or are less likely to 'switch' providers.

[18] ABI, April 2013, '"Pay How You Drive" Motor Insurance'; and ABI, April 2013, 'Selling Telematics Motor Insurance Policies', https://www.abi.org.uk/News/Newsreleases/2013/05/The-ABI-and-BIBA-publishes-consumer-guide.

[19] Aviva, 2014, Annual report and accounts 2013, https://www.aviva.com/library/2013ar/pdf/Strategic_report/Market_context.pdf.

[20] https://www.lloyds.com/news-and-risk-insight/news/market-news/industry-news-2014/a-treasure-trove-of-big-data.

[21] R Clarke and A Libarikian, "Unleashing the value of advanced analytics in insurance" (McKinsey & Company, 2014), http://www.mckinsey.com/insights/financial_services/unleashing_the_value_of_advanced_analytics_in_insurance p 43; and see *Telegraph*, July 2014, 'Thrifty drivers could save on insurance premiums', http://www.telegraph.co.uk/finance/personalfinance/10963992/Thrifty-driverscould-save-on-insurance-premiums.html.

Information as to credit history can constitute both risk- and non-risk-related information: if insurers are using credit history information as a means of assessing risk on the basis that on-time payers are likely to be better risks then the information may properly be regarded as risk-related information. Moreover, if credit history and financial status data is being relied upon to assess ability to pay, that would appear to be an unobjectionable use of such data. But if it is being used to ascertain willingness to pay in pursuit of policies of price optimisation/discrimination, that is likely to be more controversial.[22] As at mid-2015, the CMA Report noted that financial data was primarily being used for identity verification and setting of the APR for payment by instalments rather than being used in risk assessment. However, it was noted that Scottish Widows, Lloyds' insurance arm, was using data that it held on its customers who also bank with Lloyds, to identify individuals who are expected to be relatively safe drivers (ie using the financial information for risk-assessment purposes).

Shopping data: Grocery retailers who also provide insurance, such as Sainsburys, Tesco and the Co-Op were all reported to be using grocery purchasing data (available through loyalty card schemes) for risk-related purposes. Tesco was reported to have offered discounts of as much as 40 per cent on home and car insurance to those it considers present less risk based on their shopping habits.[23]

Social media: The CMA Research noted that data derived from social media has been reportedly used by life insurance providers.[24] But other insurers were denying the use of social media, even in the context of claims.[25] It thus concluded:

> In the context of the UK motor insurance sector, there is little tangible evidence to indicate that social media data is currently being used in this way, but the situation could change in the future. One insurer told us that it has conducted some research in this area, finding some evidence of social media information having predictive value for risk. However, at present it is not making use of any social media information in this way.[26]

It is possible that motor insurers' use of profiling through social media is slower given that telematics-enabled analytics are likely to provide a more accurate picture of the riskiness of an individual driver than posts he or she has placed on Facebook.

As to the use of data derived from social media in the context of claims, the CMA Research noted that in 2013 the Direct Line Group completed a claims transformation programme in its motor and home insurance business, 'including the use of social

[22] Financial Times, 1 February 2015, 'Insurers warned to use "big data" responsibly', http://www.ft.com/cms/s/0/08f6049c-a7cd-11e4-8e78-00144feab7de.html.

[23] https://www.telegraph.co.uk/finance/personalfinance/10963992/Thrifty-drivers-could-save-on-insurance-premiums.html.

[24] See eg BBC, November 2013, 'How big data is changing the cost of insurance', http://www.bbc.co.uk/news/business-24941415; and see Celent, 'Using Social Data in Claims and Underwriting', October 2011, https://www.celent.com/insights/186911113.

[25] Financial Times Adviser, November 2014, 'Protection providers deny social media snooping', https://www.ftadviser.com/2014/11/10/insurance/health-and-protection/protection-providers-deny-social-media-snooping-GX8FaIt76YFF5bLsVyDjoM/article.html.

[26] CMA Research, June 2015, p 47, see https://assets.publishing.service.gov.uk/government/uploads/system/uploads/attachment_data/file/435777/The_Commercial_Use_of_Consumer_Data_-_DotEcon_and_Analysys_Mason.pdf.

networking techniques to combat fraud'.[27] It also noted that Tesco's car insurance policy stated: 'We may research, collect and use data about you from publicly available sources including social media and networking sites. We may use this data for the purposes of fraud detection and prevention.'[28] One insurer gave the following example of how social media may be used in practice: in a claim that involved several passengers in an alleged collision who, between them, claimed a total sum in excess of £100,000, the insurer was able to use information from Facebook to establish that the drivers of the two vehicles, as well as some of the passengers, were known to each other. Ultimately this helped to prove that the accident was staged.[29] As to the use of predictive analytics in detecting fraud, the report stated that evidence from stakeholder interviews did not suggest that the use of similar third-party technologies is particularly widespread at present in the UK.[30]

Telematics data: the CMA noted that the biggest impact of big data was in relation to the use of telematics. Telematics provides data directly related to individual driving behaviour, and enables more granular assessment of risk as compared with the proxy data on gender, age and previous claims traditionally used by insurers. The CMA Research noted that

> [s]takeholder interviews suggest that the analysis and interpretation of telematics data is an area that is in evolution, with some telematics policies currently relying on fairly basic techniques and rudimentary driving scores that do not necessarily provide a full and accurate picture of driving behaviour for all drivers.[31]

The report noted that one reason why the development of sophisticated analytical models may be taking some time is that it can be difficult to build sufficiently accurate models until data from a large number of policyholders has been collected. Deloitte predicts that '[i]nsurers will need to collect a substantial volume of such data to achieve a critical mass in order to identify potential correlations and create predictive models that produce reliable underwriting and pricing decisions'.[32] It noted that

> [m]any UBI programs today provide a discount based only on participation rather than on actual performance, as carriers look to collect a critical mass of data and determine how to effectively leverage it for predictive modeling purposes. Conceptually a portion of this discount is an incentive to sign up for a UBI program, as well as the cost of purchasing the consumer's telematics data – a quid pro quo to compensate the buyer for allowing their driving to be monitored, thus providing valuable information to the insurer.[33]

But as insurers build large, statistically and actuarially credible UBI datasets, price cuts will be earned on the basis of actual driving behaviours and the correlations to losses

[27] Direct Line Group, 2013, Annual Report & Accounts 2013, http://ara2013.directlinegroup.com/downloads/pdf/direct_line_group_2013_annual_report_and_accounts.pdf.
[28] See https://www.tescobank.com/assets/sections/carins/pdf/data-processinginformation.pdf.
[29] CMA Research, June 2015, p 57, see https://assets.publishing.service.gov.uk/government/uploads/system/uploads/attachment_data/file/435777/The_Commercial_Use_of_Consumer_Data_-_DotEcon_and_Analysys_Mason.pdf.
[30] ibid, p 58.
[31] ibid, p 48.
[32] Deloitte Center for Financial Services, 21 April 2014, 'Overcoming speed bumps on the road to telematics', http://dupress.com/articles/telematics-in-auto-insurance/.
[33] ibid.

that carriers discover during this early phase of telematics. As the market matures, it is likely that some insurers will defer the discount to the end of the first policy term rather than offering it at inception.[34]

In September 2015, and following the CMA's Report, the ABI issued its first major publication on the impact of big data.[35] The paper observed that at that point in time, insurance had not seen the same rate of transformation as some other industries. However, it noted that big data was having an impact in two ways. First, it enabled more evidence-based decisions and a better understanding of the customer. Second, it was improving insurers' ability to understand risk and the likely incidence of insured loss. In the same month, the ABI held its inaugural Data Conference, acknowledging that 'In the digital world, data is increasingly a critical asset for insurers looking to offer their customers the right products, at the right prices and in the right ways'.[36] The ABI noted that big data was increasingly allowing insurers to access new information about potential customers that influenced pricing and underwriting decisions. 'This is often despite that information having been created for a different purpose, or as a by-product of daily life. Examples are information on social media platforms, loyalty card information from supermarkets or information from health tracking devices.'[37] The ABI also noted how big data enabled real-time pricing giving rise to the prospect of premium being adjusted and notified automatically upon the occurrence of certain behaviours (eg speeding) which insurers can monitor in real time. The ABI noted that '[i]n the future, this could mean your change in behaviour resulting in savings straight away, with you getting the satisfaction of seeing the direct impact of your choices'.[38]

B. The FCA's Feedback Statement 2016

In November 2015, the Financial Conduct Authority (FCA) announced that it wanted to better understand the way in which retail insurers were using big data and how this affected consumer outcomes and competition in the general insurance sector.[39] It is important to note that the FCA's remit is to pursue consumer and competition objectives: it is not a privacy regulator, a role that falls to the Information Commissioner's Office (ICO).

Following responses from the industry and other regulators, the FCA published a Feedback Statement in September 2016.[40] The FCA reported that most insurers

[34] By March 2018, the Geneva Association observed that telematics insurance often provided an upfront premium discount and a cash-back discount at the end of the contractual period, depending on the risk score: 'Big data and Insurance: Implications for Innovation, Competition and Privacy', March 2018, p 30.

[35] ABI, 'How Big Data Makes Insurance Work Better for You', September 2015 https://www.abi.org.uk/globalassets/sitecore/files/documents/publications/public/2015/data/how-data-makes-insurance-work-better-for-you.pdf.

[36] https://www.abi.org.uk/Events/2015/ABI-Data-Conference.

[37] https://www.abi.org.uk/globalassets/sitecore/files/documents/events/2015/event-agenda data-conference.pdf.

[38] ibid.

[39] https://www.fca.org.uk/publication/consultation/big-data-call-for-inputs.pdf. Specifically, the FCA focussed its attention on motor insurance and home and contents insurance.

[40] https://www.fca.org.uk/publication/feedback/fs16-05.pdf.

were still relying on traditional generalised linear models (GLMs) to assess and price risk.[41] However, the FCA went on to note that a small number of insurers had indicated that they used other analytical techniques to create the inputs for their GLMs. It observed that

> [o]ne insurer told us they use techniques such as decision tree analytics, which is a method of segmenting data based on a series of attributes and values that form a 'decision tree'. Other firms mentioned using non-linear techniques e.g. machine learning techniques (which involves developing computer algorithms that can grow and change with new data).[42]

The FCA then examined how big data is used in the lifecycle of insurance products as follows.

i. Product Design

The FCA noted the impact of telematics on the design of motor insurance policies. In particular, telematics enabled insurers to adjust pricing and offer rewards for good driving. Other insurers were beginning to offer UBI or on-demand cover as discussed in chapter one. As regards home insurance, it noted that home telematics devices were not yet having an impact on insurance pricing, but that firms were 'starting to explore how they might link smart home data to insurance premiums in the future'.[43]

ii. Underwriting

The FCA distinguished between two key factors that impacted on the pricing of policies. As noted above, the first might broadly be referred to as risk-related pricing (factors that bear on the nature of the risk itself), the second non-risk-related pricing (factors that relate to things like the insured's price sensitivity or willingness to switch provider).

The FCA found that most retail insurers that responded confirmed that they used a much wider range of third party data sources in underwriting and pricing compared to five years ago. This was said to increase the accuracy of models both in predicting an insurance event occurring and a claim being made, each of which enhanced pricing accuracy. However, as regards social media, the FCA observed as follows:

> We heard speculation that the use of social media data will become prevalent in underwriting. Despite this, we did not encounter examples of firms using social media data in underwriting or pricing and most firms said they had no plans to do so in the next five years.[44]

[41] Feedback Statement, para 2.20.

[42] ibid, para 2.21.

[43] ibid, para 3.8. The ABI in September 2015 had noted that 'Connected devices in the home such as "smart" boilers, thermostats, locks and smoke detectors monitor your home, making sure that crucial appliances are regularly serviced, and the house is well maintained. The data collected can be used to warn you of potential faults with your appliances, or remind you to, for example, turn the thermostat up if there is due to be cold weather, in order to avoid frozen pipes. Your insurance price is based on how conscientiously you care for your house, rather than the average homeowner.'

[44] The FCA of course only had responses from a subset of insurers, including from Admiral, Aegeas and AXA. It is not clear whether this observation can be assumed to apply to the balance of those insurers who did not respond.

> There appears to be an additional consideration among firms that this use of data would lead to reputational damage because of consumer disquiet. However ... social media data are being used in claims handling.[45]

Notwithstanding that the FCA recorded that most firms did not intend to use social media data in underwriting, in November 2016 – just two months after the FCA published its Feedback Statement – the motor insurer Admiral announced the proposed launch of a new insurance product aimed at young drivers. The product, called Firstcarquote, proposed to use the Facebook profiles of their prospective insureds to determine their risk profile and, ultimately, the price of cover. A personality profile would be established from a person's posts and 'likes'.[46] Those exhibiting personality traits linked to safe driving would be offered a discount of up to £350 a year. However, the product was pulled at the last minute since Facebook considered that the proposed use of that data violated its platform policy then in force.[47] But this case did not mark the end to Admiral's interest in profiling prospective customers. Firstcarquote was subsequently relaunched requiring insureds to 'login via Facebook' and a personality quiz replaced the proposed analysis of Facebook posts, which enabled a comparable form of risk profiling to be undertaken.

That example reflected the FCA's further observation that insurers'

> appetites to use innovative forms of personal data varied across the industry. For example, we spoke to insurance providers that are more receptive to utilising new sources of personal data, such as obtaining consumers' consent to analyse social media accounts and the connections between members. We also spoke to some insurance firms who are utilising new types of data in pricing, for example, using behavioural factors from retailers to build a better profile of customers in order to offer discounts.[48]

Insurers appeared to want to make more use of these sources of data without falling foul of regulations and that appeared to drive several respondents to request that the FCA introduce guidelines on the ethical use of data.[49]

iii. *Pricing Practices*

Price discrimination (or optimisation) is defined as the sale of different units of the same product at price differentials that do not correspond to any cost difference. The most common form is the sale of identical products to different customers at different prices.

[45] The FCA also noted that some insurers thought using social media data would be viewed as unreasonably invasive by consumers or would not be easy to validate to a sufficient degree to be used in risk pricing: Feedback Statement, paras 5.11–5.12.

[46] For example, Facebook users who write in short, concise sentences, use lists, and arrange to meet friends at a set time and place, rather than just 'tonight', would be identified as conscientious. In contrast, those who frequently use exclamation marks and phrases such as 'always' or 'never' rather than 'maybe' could be overconfident.

[47] The May 2016 version of this policy contained clause 3.15, which stated: 'Don't use data obtained from Facebook to make decisions about eligibility, including whether to approve or reject an application or how much interest to charge on a loan.'

[48] Feedback Statement, para 5.14.

[49] ibid, para 5.10.

Charging customers different prices that reflect different costs is not discriminatory. Insurers may charge different prices for the very same policy (being a product that has the same cover, exclusions and excess) supplied to two insureds whose risk profile is identical. The difference in pricing is thus due to non-risk-related factors such as the insured's price sensitivity or willingness to switch provider on renewal. The question is whether this is problematic.[50] The FCA observes:

> … there may be instances where such pricing practices raise concerns. For example, we may have consumer protection concerns, if those who face higher prices tend to be vulnerable or older consumers. There may also be competition concerns, for example if pricing for reasons other than cost and risk creates barriers to entry or (at an extreme) forces other firms to exit the market.[51]
>
> (…)
>
> Furthermore, in previous work on renewals in [General Insurance], we came across examples of pricing practices where the evidence suggested that the length of time a customer has a policy may be a key factor in persistent high prices, rather than the underlying risk or cost. This may amount to a form of price discrimination.[52]

The FCA observed that insurers responding to the Call for Inputs provided little detail on the issue of pricing practices and in particular pricing for reasons other than risk and cost. In its assessment, the FCA stated that it was its expectation that the increasing availability of data – including behavioural data – coupled with the growing sophistication of analytical tools will enable firms to more effectively develop these pricing practices in the future. In essence the FCA indicated that a more detailed analysis would be required to assess whether particular forms of price discrimination within different sectors of retail insurance would undermine consumer protection (particularly with vulnerable customers) and competition objectives.[53]

iv. Marketing, Distribution and Sales

Perhaps unsurprisingly, the FCA found that big data was being used to target customers more effectively. Insurers confirmed that they use aggregated search engine data to analyse potential groups of consumers who may have specific insurance needs.

[50] The National Association of Insurance Commissioners (NAIC) is a US regulator created and governed by insurance regulators from all 50 states. In its 2015 paper on the subject, the NAIC recommended that consideration of the following factors is inconsistent with the statutory requirements that rates shall not be unfairly discriminatory: price elasticity of demand; propensity to shop for insurance; retention adjustment at an individual level; and a policyholder's propensity to ask questions or file complaints: www.naic.org/documents/committees_c_catf_related_price_optimization_white_paper.pdf, p 16.

[51] See also the FCA's Occasional Paper No. 22 on price discrimination and cross-subsidy in financial services: September 2016, https://www.fca.org.uk/publication/occasional-papers/op16-22.pdf.

[52] FCA's Occasional Paper No. 22 on price discrimination and cross-subsidy in financial services, paras 3.35 and 3.37.

[53] The FCA's statutory framework consists of an over-arching strategic objective to ensure that markets function well and three operational objectives: (i) to protect and promote market integrity; (ii) to secure an appropriate degree of consumer protection; (iii) to promote competition in the interests of consumers. Underpinning that is a competition duty which broadly requires the FCA to take as pro-competitive an approach to its regulatory activities as it can. See https://www.fca.org.uk/about/the-fca.

By looking at what consumers are searching for, firms are better able to understand their requirements and meet their needs. Consumer profiles were also being evaluated by analytics firms to sell add-on products[54] or to facilitate cross-selling (eg customers seeking motor insurance might be offered home insurance products for which their profile indicates an eligibility).

In relation to distribution and sales of insurance products it was found that insurers are increasingly using external data sources of the type described at page 38 above in section I.a.i to verify consumer information during the sales process. Important for these purposes was the observation that a significant number of insurers have commented that, in the near future, big data should make it even easier for consumers to obtain quotes where automation will reduce the amount of information consumers have to provide to insurers to get a quote. Data fields in proposals/applications could be pre-populated from data sourced automatically and reliably from other databases holding information about a consumer, their car or their house.[55]

v. Claims Handling

Insurers were also found to be using big data to assist with claims verification, particularly through the use of devices connected to the internet. Given the real-time recording of speed and location, telematics devices can provide a wealth of information surrounding an accident and may even indicate where fault lies. Some insurers also indicated that they were using social media to verify claims, detect fraudulent claimants and identify suspected fraud rings, all of which should lead to a lower premium for customers. In addition, information generated by telematics devices can also reduce the burden on the consumer in presenting their claim. Reports from telematics devices are likely to make form-filling a thing of the past, saving time and money for both insured and insurer. The FCA noted that potential future developments in claims handling include using mobile apps to submit claims, online claims portals and more digitised claims processes. Insurers generally believe such initiatives will make the claims process more efficient for consumers.

Given the largely positive findings, the FCA decided not to launch a full-scale market study into the use of big data in the retail insurance sector.

[54] General Insurance add-ons include, for example, travel insurance offered alongside a holiday or GAP insurance with a new car. The FCA published a market study on general insurance add-ons in March 2014.

[55] Feedback Statement; ABI, How Data Makes Insurance Work Better for You, https://www.abi.org.uk/globalassets/sitecore/files/documents/publications/public/2015/data/how-data-makes-insurance-work-better-for-you.pdf, para 3.37. The ABI also noted that this was another area where big data was making a real difference; in relation to obtaining quotes for cover, it noted that: 'Instead of asking you all over again, insurers in the future might be able to access existing databases with your permission in order to pre-populate information in your application. For example, you can now enter your car license plate information to automatically provide details about your vehicle's engine size, number of doors etc. However, in the future, that could be extended to any number of areas – you might enter your postcode and house number and information about your home's number of bedrooms, types of locks and roof construction would be automatically provided.' ibid, p 13.

C. The FCA and ICO's Forum on the Use of Big Data 2016

On 17 January 2017, the FCA and ICO issued a summary of the forum on the use of data in retail general insurance.[56] Three main topics were covered: (i) use of social media; (ii) obtaining consent and transparency of data; and (iii) data protection risks.

Regarding social media, it was noted that insurers were still unsure as to whether using social media data for pricing cover would be effective, as they did not know which data would actually be of use. Without being able to test whether the data are valuable for pricing, insurers were reticent about using it (although it was envisaged that use of social media data may yet become the norm). If such data could be useful, the issue then would be how to communicate with consumers as regards the use of that data. It was clear that the coming into force of the GDPR presented a number of issues to insurers including what data insurers could consider in making a quote and the requirements relating to consumer consent. Insurers also revealed that when using data from a wider array of sources, they did not always seek to rely on consent to legitimise processing of consumer data, as consent could be difficult to obtain and could be withdrawn at any time. 'Legitimate interest' and 'necessity for contract' were commonly used alternative justifications for processing under the Data Protection Act 1998 (DPA).[57]

The forum also addressed the issue of inaccurate data and noted that some participants discussed the effort that had already been put into detecting and correcting inaccurate data, but felt they could not catch every error. It was noted that avenues for consumers to check their own data (beyond subject access requests under the DPA) already existed for some databases (eg from the DVLA) but that consumers may not be aware of these means of checking data accuracy.

II. Regulatory Assessment by EU Regulators

The European System of Financial Supervision (ESFS) was introduced in 2010, following the global financial crisis, and consists of the European Systemic Risk Board (ESRB) and three supervisory authorities (ESAs), namely: (i) the European Banking Authority (EBA); (ii) the European Securities and Markets Authority (ESMA); and (iii) the European Insurance and Occupational Pensions Authority (EIOPA).[58] The ESFA is a decentralised, multi-layered system of micro- and macro-prudential authorities established by the European institutions in order to ensure consistent and coherent financial supervision in the EU. The relationship between the ESRB, the ESAs and national competent authorities can be represented as follows:[59]

[56] https://ico.org.uk/media/2013444/fca-ico-big-data-forum-20170116-summary.pdf.

[57] The bases for lawful processing are discussed in ch 7 below.

[58] Both the ESRB and the three ESAs began operating in 2011 following the adoption of a package of legislative acts by which they were founded and empowered. EIOPA was established under Regulation 1094/2010.

[59] The diagram is taken from ESMA's website: https://www.esma.europa.eu/about-esma/governance/european-supervisory-framework.

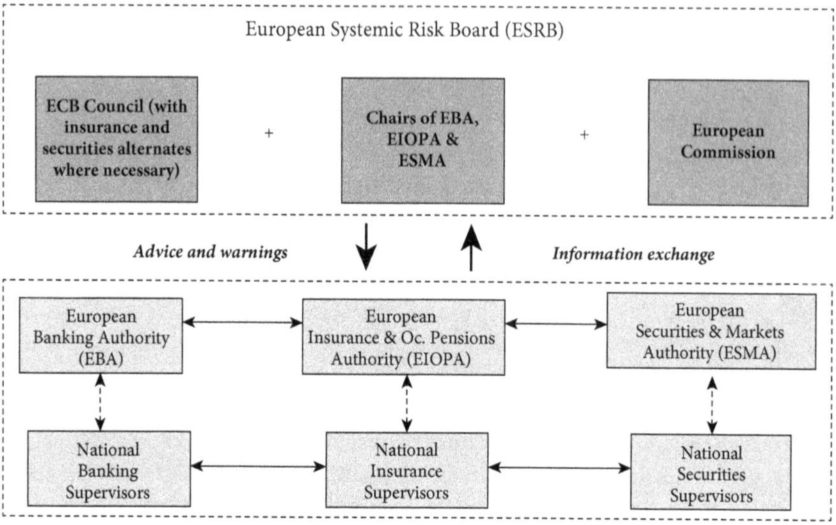

The main objective of the ESFS is to ensure that the rules applicable to the financial sector are adequately implemented in order to preserve financial stability and to promote confidence in the financial system as a whole, and provide sufficient protection for financial consumers. While national supervisory authorities (which, for insurers in the UK, means the Prudential Regulation Authority in relation to financial safety and soundness (prudential and capital requirements) and the FCA for conduct of business) remain in charge of supervising individual financial institutions, the objective of the ESAs is to improve the functioning of the internal market by ensuring appropriate, efficient and harmonised European regulation and supervision.[60] Along with the two other European Supervisory Authorities, EBA and ESMA, EIOPA forms part of the Joint Committee which works to ensure cross-sectoral consistency and joint positions in the area of supervision of financial conglomerates and on other cross-sectoral issues. The ESAs, within the Joint Committee, explore and monitor potential emerging risks for consumers and financial markets participants as well as new and existing financial activities and to adopt measures, where needed, with a view to promoting consumer protection and the safety and soundness of markets and convergence in regulatory practices.

In December 2016, the Joint Committee published its Discussion Paper on the use of big data by financial institutions. It stated that in monitoring consumer protection developments and financial innovations, the ESAs had noted the continued increase in the use of big data in the banking, insurance and securities sectors across different EU Member States. The Discussion Paper sought feedback on the ESAs assessment of the relative benefits and risks linked to the use of big data by financial institutions. The Joint Committee's final report was published on 15 March 2018. It is perhaps regrettable that only 10 of the 68 respondents were from the insurance sector and to that extent the

[60] On 20 September 2017, the EU Commission released a Draft Regulation to review and enhance the powers of the ESAs.

general comments and conclusions again cannot be taken as being representative of big data use across that sector.[61] As with the domestic reports considered above, this was an informal/voluntary study, not a market investigation and thus did not have the benefit of powers to call for compulsory responses.

The final report noted that for certain respondents the main areas of application of big data observed concerned the improvement in understanding consumers' preferences. Based on improved information (for instance from personal devices/online data, etc) product/service providers strengthen the feedback loop between them and consumers. This may lead to increased personalisation of products and services as well as more accurate consumer profile/risk assessments. Several respondents mentioned further examples of the use of big data:

> increasing sales of pay as you drive or pay as you live insurance (also-known as usage-based insurance'); increased personalisation of risk assessment; credit scoring using broad ranges of data; fraud management; increased use of robo-advice. Certain respondents also saw potential in the areas of claims handling, fraud detection, pricing, risk selection and underwriting.[62]

As to the type and sources of IT tools, the report noted that a 'few' banking and insurance respondents mentioned that most data stems from internal sources and, in comparison, data from external sources would play a minor role. Some insurance respondents noted that the very nature of the industry required the processing of large amounts of data; a few also noted the recent increase of the use of external data sources. Other respondents provided examples of different types of data they use: credit history, behavioural data, consumer habit data, statistical data and data found in broader networks, both individual as well as aggregated data. However, some respondents also noted that they collected data on online behaviour and geolocation data that went beyond the range of data strictly required to provide usual financial services.

The report considered a range of other regulatory laws and considered that the fact that some of those laws (in particular the Insurance Distribution Directive (IDD) and the GDPR) had not yet come into force or had only recently come into effect meant that it was prudent to monitor the effect of those laws on the use of big data made by financial firms once those laws bedded in. In that regard, the report stated:

> In this Final Report, the ESAs highlight the relevance of a number of existing requirements in the sectorial financial legislation as well as in other relevant areas (such as data protection, cyber security and consumer protection). The ESAs believe that the legislative requirements existing in these areas constitute an already quite solid framework to mitigate the risks identified in the context of this work. The ESAs also note that this framework will be further strengthened with the entry into application of several key pieces of legislation in the financial sector (e.g. IDD, MIFID II,[63] PSD2[64]) as well as in the data protection sector (notably, GDPR).

[61] The list of respondents and their responses is here: https://www.esma.europa.eu/press-news/consultations/joint-committee-discussion-paper-use-big-data-financial-institutions.

[62] Joint Committee of the European Supervisory Authorities, Final Report on Big Data, 15 March 2018 https://www.esma.europa.eu/sites/default/files/library/jc-2018-04_joint_committee_final_report_on_big_data.pdf, para 23.

[63] Directive 2014/65/EU on Markets in Financial Instruments (the Second Markets in Financial Instruments Directive).

[64] Directive 2015/2366 on Payment Services in the Internal Market (the Second Payment Services Directive).

> The ESAs will monitor how and to which extent these additional requirements will contribute to mitigate further the risks identified in the context of this work.
>
> The ESAs consequently consider that a legislative intervention at this point would be premature, given that some key pieces of legislation are yet to be implemented or have just entered into application. However, the ESAs believe that it is very important for supervisors across various policy areas to coordinate better to ensure that these requirements are effectively complied with.[65]

In April 2018, EIOPA announced the establishment of the InsurTech Task Force which would undertake a thematic review on the use of big data by insurance undertakings and intermediaries.[66] EIOPA's call for evidence on the use of big data was announced on 6 July 2018 and stated that the purpose of the thematic review would be to gather empirical evidence on the use of big data by insurance undertakings and intermediaries along the whole insurance value chain, that is, in pricing and underwriting, in product development, in claims management, as well as in sales and marketing. The review will specifically focus on the motor and health insurance markets and EIOPA proposes to publish the key findings in the first quarter of 2019.[67]

III. Conclusions

It seems clear from the reviews undertaken by the CMA and the FCA that the use of big data by insurers is in its very early stages. Neither of their reports was based on a market investigation and the responses received from insurers cannot be taken to be representative of industry practice. However, it is clear that insurers want to avail of these technologies. In light of the survey of data sources and how that data might be used by insurers, it is necessary to turn and consider in more detail the potential legal issues to which those uses give rise.

[65] Joint Committee of the European Supervisory Authorities, Final Report on Big Data, 15 March 2018, paras 17–18.

[66] https://eiopa.europa.eu/Publications/Administrative/InsuTech%20Task%20Force%20Mandate%20-%20BoS.pdf.

[67] The press release is here: https://eiopa.europa.eu/Publications/Press%20Releases/EIOPA%20seeks%20evidence%20on%20the%20use%20of%20Big%20Data.pdf.

3

Emerging Themes and Issues

Several themes and issues emerge from the first two chapters which might be categorised as follows: (i) insurers' access to certain types of data, and the nature and quality of the data upon which they might seek to rely in making insurance decisions; (ii) the implications of the use to which that data is put, both for the assessment of risk and the concept of risk-pooling generally; and (iii) insureds' access to insurance, which considers the potential for insurers to discriminate against insureds and/or deny cover for reasons over which the insured has no choice or control.

I. Transparency and Privacy Concerns

If insurers' access to data is such that their knowledge of an individual risk might in many respects be as extensive as that of the insured, a range of questions arise as to the insured's rights to know what information is held about them and how that information is sought to be relied upon in assessing: (i) the risk as reflected in the terms of cover offered (if offered at all); and (ii) any claim that has been made. As Schneier observes, '[f]or personal data, transparency is … straightforward: people should be entitled to know data is being collected about them, what data is being archived about them and how data about them is being used – and by whom.'[1]

A. The Right to Know What Information is Held and to Determine its Accuracy

It is only through increased transparency from insurers who profile an individual risk on the basis of various online and offline sources that an insured might be able to

[1] B Schneier, *Data and Goliath: The Hidden Battles to Collect Your Data and Control Your World*, (New York, WW Norton & Co, 2015), 186. See also K Kelly, *The Inevitable: Understanding the 12 Technological Forces that will Shape our Future* (New York, Penguin, 2016), 260–63: 'Ubiquitous surveillance is inevitable. Since we cannot stop the system from tracking, we can only make the relationships more symmetrical … If symmetry can be restored so we can track who is tracking, if we can hold the trackers accountable by law … and responsible for accuracy, and if we can make the benefits obvious and relevant, then I suspect the expansion of tracking will be accepted.' The implication is that individual insureds will accept tracking and profiling to a greater extent if they know what information is held about them, how it is used and have an opportunity to correct it where it is wrong.

establish that the underwriting assessment has been made on an incorrect basis. The right to be told the reasons for decisions in other areas of the law is often expressly justified to facilitate legal challenges insofar as those reasons may reveal errors in the decision-making process. In public law, the right to reasons has often been justified on the basis that a claimant could not otherwise bring a claim for judicial review unless he is given sufficient information about the basis of the decision such as to enable him to identify whether any public law errors have been made.[2] Similarly in procurement law, the right of a disappointed bidder to reasons as to why its bid failed is expressly justified on the basis that the bidder and the reviewing court must be able to assess whether the awarding authority made an error in selecting the preferred bidder.[3]

Previously, when underwriters assessed individual risks by reference to historic loss data pertaining to a limited number of risk factors, the information relied upon, particularly in consumer insurance, was limited and straightforwardly verifiable. Individual insureds would provide information by way of an application or proposal on which insurers would rely. It will be unusual for an issue as to the accuracy of a person's age, sex, postcode or claims history to arise (particularly as a result of the claims databases that have emerged over the past 20 years).

B. The Problems of Correlation and Context

As insurers obtain more information from third-party sources and as profiling will increasingly rely on inferences drawn from that information, the risk of making underwriting decisions on an incorrect basis accordingly increases. That gives rise to the twin problems of correlation and context.

As to the problem of correlation, chapter one made the point that predictive analytics operate by identifying correlations, not causes. The Council of Europe Recommendation CM/Rec (2010)132 explains that profiling may involve three distinct stages: (i) data collection; (ii) automated analysis to identify correlations; and (iii) applying the correlation to an individual to identify characteristics of present or future behaviour.[4] It is plain that showing a correlation between A and B does not entail that

[2] See the recent discussion of the Court of Appeal in In *Oakley v South Cambridgeshire District Council* [2017] EWCA Civ 71.

[3] See eg Case 272/06 *Evropaiki Dynamiki [2008] ECR-II 00169* at [27]; and in Case 447/10 *Evropaiki Dynamiki* at [92] the Court said: 'The corollary of the discretion enjoyed by the Court of Justice in the area of public procurement is a statement of reasons that sets out the matters of fact and law upon which the Court of Justice based its assessment. It is only in the light of those matters that an applicant is genuinely in a position to understand the reasons why those scores were awarded. Only such a statement of reasons therefore enables him to assert his rights and the General Court to exercise its power of review.' See also *Healthcare at Home Limited v The Common Services Agency* [2014] UKSC 49; [2014] 4 ALL ER 210 at [17]; these authorities were recently discussed and applied by Stuart-Smith J in *Lancashire Care NHS Foundation Trust & Anor v Lancashire County Council* [2018] EWHC 1589 (TCC), who observed: 'It is no accident that each of these statements of principle refers to the need to provide "reasons" and "reasoning". With one possible exception, that is not the same as providing a list of factors that were taken into account.'

[4] Council of Europe, 'The protection of individuals with regard to automatic processing of personal data in the context of profiling', Recommendation CM/Rec(2010)13 and explanatory memorandum, 23 November 2010, https://www.coe.int/t/dghl/standardsetting/cdcj/CDCJ%20Recommendations/CMRec(2010)13E_Profiling.pdf.

A caused B (or vice versa). As the FTC notes, if companies use correlations to make decisions about people without understanding the underlying reasons for the correlations, those decisions might be faulty and could lead to unintended consequences or harm for consumers and companies.[5] Predictive analytics can operate by comparing a known characteristic of a consumer to other consumers with the same characteristic in order to predict whether that consumer will meet, for example, his or her credit obligations, or be regarded as a greater (eg motor) risk. The difference is that, rather than using traditional risk characteristics, predictive analytics may use non-traditional characteristics – such as social media usage, or shopping history – in order to make decisions about whether insureds who exhibit those characteristics are a good credit or insurance risk. In insurance, the risk pool has historically been segmented according to risk factors that have been actuarially established, in the aggregate, to indicate greater levels of risk (young male drivers being far more risky than older female drivers, for example). But there may be no equivalent actuarial data to show that those who use social media in a certain way or who have certain shopping habits are – in the aggregate – a higher risk group for those reasons. The fact that there may be a correlation between those non-traditional factors and the level of risk does not entail that individuals exhibiting those characteristics present an objectively greater risk. Indeed, by comparing prospective insureds in this way, far from reflecting the ideal of generating an individualised risk profile, some insureds may find that their premiums are tied to that of others because of a shared characteristic that may not in fact be causative of a higher level of risk, either individually or in the aggregate. The problem of correlation therefore not only goes to the accuracy of risk profiling, but also raises issues for how risk is being modelled by these new group-based or aggregated methods. The latter is important as big data is often justified as capable of more accurately identifying which individual insureds are better risks as compared with traditional actuarial pricing for someone of his age or sex etc.[6] If correlation wrongly leads to risk profiling because of shared characteristics with others, then there is a risk that individuals who are good risks will pay higher premiums because of their membership of groups that have been constituted solely because big data has identified a correlation between the relevant characteristic and insured loss.[7]

[5] Federal Trade Commission (FTC), Big Data: A Tool for Inclusion or exclusion? Understanding the Issues, January 2016, https://www.ftc.gov/system/files/documents/reports/big-data-tool-inclusion-or-exclusion-understanding-issues/160106big-data-rpt.pdf, 9.

[6] One way in which insurers have sought to ensure the data is more robust arises out of Aviva's life insurance modelling. In 2010, Aviva used credit reports and consumer-marketing data as proxies for the analysis of blood and urine samples. It did so not in respect of existing applicants but applicants that had already been assessed in accordance with traditional underwriting methods. The new methodology was designed to assess to what extent the proxy information could replicate the underwriting decisions reached by traditional methods, albeit more quickly and cost-effectively. Other insurance firms such as Prudential and AIG have examined similar initiatives. Scism and Maremont, 'Insurers test data profiles to identify risky clients', 19 November 2010: https://www.wsj.com/articles/SB10001424052748704648604575620750998072986; and see also 'Inside Deloitte's Life-insurance Assessment Technology', https://www.wsj.com/articles/SB10001424052748704104104575622531084755588.

[7] The FTC gives the following example in the credit context: 'Participants raised concerns that big data can lead to decision-making based on the actions of others with whom consumers share some characteristics.

In addition, there is the problem of context: if insurers hold information but that information is taken out of context, insurers – or the algorithms they deploy – might draw incorrect inferences about the insured from the data. For example, the research on telematics motor insurance accompanying the CMA's Report on the Commercial Use of Consumer Data observed that the analytical process involved in deriving accurate and fair insights about an insured's driving from telematics data is complex. For example, in a claims context, data collected about a driver's speed at a particular time may need to be contextualised in various ways, for example by taking into account not only the applicable speed limit at that location but also assessing such factors as the traffic, weather and road conditions.[8] Just because the insured was involved in a crash and there was ice on the road does not mean the insured was at fault: insurers need to consider the speed the insured was driving and the condition of the road in order to assess causation accurately. The more data sources that are merged (eg mapping data, meteorological data and driving data), the better the overall picture that insurers will have but the greater the need for certain safeguards to be put in place to ensure that correct inferences are being drawn from the data.

Insurers are not, of course, public authorities and are not amenable to judicial review. Short of any contractual right to know what information is held on an insured or what use has been made of that information, the question is whether insurers come under some other obligation to inform insureds as to the information they hold and how they have used (or will use) that information. There are two candidates. First, does the common law duty of good faith as it applies to insurers require them to inform insureds of what information they hold such as to enable them to correct any inaccuracies in that information? Second, does any regulatory norm impose similar obligations on insurers? Those questions are explored in chapters five and six respectively.

C. The Problem of Opacity

There are a number of difficulties in relation to an insured's ability to know what data is held about him or her and, more importantly, to understand how it has been used in relation to any underwriting or claims decisions. The Information Commissioner points to the opacity of processing personal data through algorithms:[9]

> The current 'state of the art' in machine learning … involves feeding vast quantities of data through non-linear neural networks that classify the data based on the outputs from each

Several commenters explained that some credit card companies have lowered a customer's credit limit, not based on the customer's payment history, but rather based on analysis of other customers with a poor repayment history that had shopped at the same establishments where the customer had shopped. Indeed, one credit card company settled FTC allegations that it failed to disclose its practice of rating consumers as having a greater credit risk because they used their cards to pay for marriage counselling, therapy, or tire-repair services, based on its experiences with other consumers and their repayment histories. Using this type of a statistical model might reduce the cost of credit for some individuals, but may also result in some creditworthy consumers being denied or charged more for credit than they might otherwise have been charged,' see above, pp 9–10.

[8] ibid, 47.

[9] ICO, 'Big Data, Artificial Intelligence, Machine Learning and Data Protection', September 2017: https://ico.org.uk/media/for-organisations/documents/2013559/big-data-ai-ml-and-data-protection.pdf.

> successive layer.[10] The complexity of the processing of data through such massive networks creates a 'black box' effect.[11] This causes an inevitable opacity that makes it very difficult to understand the reasons for decisions made as a result of deep learning … This lack of human comprehension of decision-making rationale is one of the stark differentials between big data analytics and more traditional methods of data analysis.[12]

It will be nigh on impossible for insureds to trace the precise reason for underwriting decisions where insurers are applying predictive analytics to extremely wide datasets. Indeed, insurers and those who programmed these algorithms may find it difficult to unravel and explain their decisions themselves. It has thus been observed that in these scenarios, there is a risk that big data predictions and the algorithms and datasets behind them will become black boxes that offer us no accountability, traceability or confidence. Moreover, if algorithms operate in a way that makes it unclear why someone's premiums are high, the insured will not be able to identify which behaviours he must change or improve in order to benefit from lower premiums: algorithms operating in that way would fail to incentivise socially better (and less risky) behaviours. To prevent this, big data will require monitoring and transparency and will require insurers to have sufficient comprehension of how their algorithms work in order to be able to explain to insureds the basis upon which they have made underwriting or claims decisions.

D. The Problem of Data Minimisation and Repurposing

As will be apparent, big data operates by trawling and analysing an enormous amount of information about individuals, much of which would never be considered by underwriters writing risks on a more traditional basis. But with predictive analytics, all available information about an individual may be combined in order to build a profile from which decisions about risk might be made. In a public or governmental setting, high-profile challenges have been successfully brought against surveillance that casts the net equally wide. The Court of Appeal has ruled that the Data Retention and Investigatory Powers Act 2014 was incompatible with EU law to the extent that, for the purposes of the prevention, investigation, detection and prosecution of criminal offences, it permitted

[10] B Marr, 'What Is The Difference Between Deep Learning, Machine Learning and AI?' *Forbes*, 8 December 2016: http://www.forbes.com/sites/bernardmarr/2016/12/08/what-is-the-difference-betweendeep-learning-machine-learning-and-ai/#f7b7b5a6457f.

[11] The Information Commissioner made the same point in its response to the FCA's call for inputs when she observed: 'Another issue from the consumer perspective is that, as a result of the substantial technical complexity in using telematics data, it is inherently difficult for insurance providers to give full transparency to their customers with respect to how their data is being used to assess driving performance (notwithstanding the fact that, as mentioned above, they may not wish to grant such transparency). While consumers who opt in to telematics policies should have a high-level understanding of the fact that their driving speed, braking patterns and so on are being taken into account in order to produce driving scores, the analytical processes that achieve this in practice effectively take place "behind the scenes". Some form of common standards for telematics data collection and use in risk assessment may eventually emerge in the sector. Thus, the future use of telematics data for risk evaluation may evolve towards greater transparency and standardisation.

[12] ICO, 'Big Data, Artificial Intelligence, Machine Learning and Data Protection', September 2017: https://ico.org.uk/media/for-organisations/documents/2013559/big-data-ai-ml-and-data-protection.pdf.

access to retained data (a) where the object pursued by that access was not restricted solely to fighting serious crime; or (b) where access was not subject to prior review by a court or an independent administrative authority.[13]

The question arises as to whether, if it is unlawful for government to access and analyse confidential personal phone and web browsing records that were not restricted to the particular purpose of investigating serious crime, and which authorised their own access to that information without consent or adequate oversight, should similar principles not apply to commercial entities that extract and analyse equally wide (and often, equally irrelevant) categories of personal information for the purpose of making important decisions about the services to which those individuals seek access?

The principle of data minimisation overlaps with the risk of repurposing of data, which arises where data initially collected with the consent of the data subject for purpose A is used (whether by the same or a separate undertaking) for purpose B. The Information Commissioner describes the issue as follows:

> [A] further feature of big data analytics is the use of data for a purpose different from that for which it was originally collected, and the data may have been supplied by a different organisation. This is because the analytics is able to mine data for new insights and find correlations between apparently disparate datasets.[14]

The problem of repurposing of data use reflects a deeper issue as to the ownership of data. The ownership and fate of personal data produced by or about someone via a social media platform or a self-tracking device will in the first instance be determined by the terms and conditions of the platform or manufacturer. Data – whether personal or not – can be assigned in the same way as other intellectual or informational goods. Such terms and conditions may deem the creation or publication of data to belong to the platform or manufacturer and thus is capable of being sold to third parties. The question is whether regulatory law requires personal data to be treated (and traded) differently, notwithstanding the terms and conditions by which such data may become the property of the platform or manufacturer in the first instance.[15]

[13] *Secretary of State for the Home Department v Watson* [2018] EWCA Civ 70. The case was decided following a reference to the CJEU in *Tele2 Sverige AB v Post- och telestyrelsen* (C-203/15) EU:C:2016:970, [2017] QB 771 which held that Art 15(1) of the Directive on privacy and electronic communications (Directive 2002/58) precluded national legislation which, for the purpose of fighting crime, provided for general and indiscriminate retention of all traffic and location data of all subscribers and registered users relating to all means of electronic communication. Paragraph 2 of the dispositive provided that Art 15(1) precluded national legislation governing the protection and security of traffic and location data and, in particular, access of the competent national authorities to the retained data, where the objective pursued by that access, in the context of fighting crime, was not restricted solely to fighting serious crime, where access was not subject to prior review of a court or an independent administrative authority, and where there was no requirement that the data concerned should be retained within the EU. See also *R (on the application of Liberty) v Secretary of State for the Home Department* [2018] EWHC 975 (Admin), which considered a wider-ranging challenge to the Investigatory Powers Act 2016.

[14] ibid, para 18, which goes on to observe that: 'Companies such as DataSift take data from Twitter (via Twitter's GNIP service), Facebook and other social media and make it available for analysis for marketing and other purposes.'

[15] As there is no generally applicable federal data or privacy laws in the United States, the problem is more pronounced there. There are a limited number of Federal Acts that do, however, provide some limited data and privacy protection (e.g. (i) the Fair Credit Reporting Act (where companies using consumer reports have to notify a prospective insured if that person has been denied on the basis of what was contained in

E. The Problem of Out-dated Data: A Right to Delete?

Part of the problem of analysing data in a decontextualised manner is that it considers an individual risk in a single snapshot, albeit by reference to all available (if not necessarily relevant) historical data. Certain data that an algorithm finds particularly salient for the purpose of an underwriting decision might concern events a long time in the past. The law allows individuals to move on, most obviously in relation to spent convictions. The Rehabilitation of Offenders Act 1974[16] is intended to improve the chances of people with convictions being fully rehabilitated into society by removing some of the barriers that they face in accessing employment and services. It provides that after a specific period of time has passed (which varies according to the disposal or sentence received), cautions and convictions are regarded as 'spent'. Once a caution or conviction becomes spent, an individual is treated as rehabilitated with regard to that offence, and they don't have to declare it for most purposes, for example when applying for employment or insurance.[17] Moreover, there will be few prospective insureds who have not done things that they have come to regret. In a pre-internet world, and, more particularly, in a pre-social media world, those things were not recorded and will have been forgotten. Now, every indiscretion captured on a smartphone or posted on a social media platform creates a digital record and in principle remains accessible forever. That fact has the potential to prevent people from moving on, particularly if such indiscretions are relied upon by those who would profile applicants for employment or insurance purposes. One should have the right to be able to move on, unconstrained not just by criminal wrongs that are deemed spent but, *a fortiori*, non-criminal indiscretions that may reflect our historic risk-taking selves but which no longer hold true.[18]

The right to move on is an aspect of the need to contextualise data but raises the prospect that individuals should be entitled not just to correct the inaccuracy of data held about them, but to have that data deleted. In *Google Spain SL and Google Inc v Agencia Espanola de Proteccion de Datos & Mario Costeja Gonazalez*,[19] the CJEU affirmed the existence under EU law of a right to have personal data deleted from search engines, giving rise to the right to be forgotten.[20] This again raises the question as to whether insurers are obliged, under the duty of good faith at common law, to treat personal data in the same way, whether by reference to regulatory obligations or in any event. This is considered in chapters six and seven below.

a consumer report and must further notify them where they charge higher premiums on the basis of such reports: In each case consumers are entitled to check their consumer reports and correct any inaccuracies); (ii) some protection is also afforded by the Federal Trade Commission Act and the Genetic Information Non-discrimination Act (GINA) (albeit in relation to the latter, those protections only extend to health insurance and employment discrimination)).

[16] Which was amended by Legal Aid, Sentencing and Punishment of Offenders Act 2012 (LASPO 2012).

[17] s 4(2) entails that any question about a conviction that is spent is permitted to be treated as a question about an unspent conviction.

[18] As Schneier observes: 'the situation is exacerbated by the fact that we are generating so much data and storing it indefinitely. Those fishing expeditions can go into the past, finding things you might have done 10, 15 or 20 years ago … and counting. Today's adults were able to move beyond their youthful indiscretions; today's young people will not have that freedom. Their entire histories will be on the permanent record.' B Schneier, *Data and Goliath*, above n 1, 109.

[19] Case C-131/12, 13 May 2014.

[20] The case is discussed in more detail in ch 6, section III.A.iv.e, 'The Right to Erasure'.

II. Information Asymmetries, Adverse Selection and Segmentation of Risk Pools

A. Information Asymmetry and Adverse Selection

Economists in the 1960s and 1970s showed how the existence of an information asymmetry between a seller and a buyer could undermine the market and lead to what is known as adverse selection. That is the phenomenon where, because of that information asymmetry, (i) fewer good products are sold at a higher price that a buyer would – were he aware that it was a good product – otherwise be prepared to pay, and instead (ii) sellers end up selling poorer products for lower prices that buyers are prepared to pay in circumstances where there is a risk that the product is indeed of lower quality. The parallel problem arises in insurance where insurers cannot identify good risks from bad risks and, because the latter have greater need for – and are thus more likely to buy – insurance, insurers end up insuring more bad risks than good, with the consequent risk of claims liabilities exceeding premium income.

This problem was identified first by George Akerlof in his paper 'The Market for Lemons',[21] which posited a market for used cars where really good used cars were referred to as 'peaches' while the duds were referred to as 'lemons'. Suppose that buyers in the used-car market valued a 'peach' at £1,000, and sellers at slightly less. Then suppose that a malfunctioning used car – a 'lemon' – is worth only £500 to buyers (and, again, slightly less to sellers). If buyers can tell lemons and peaches apart, trade in both would flourish. But in reality, buyers might struggle to tell the difference between a peach and a lemon: scratches can be touched up; engine problems may initially be undiscoverable; and previous serious crashes concealed. To allow for the risk that a car is a lemon, buyers reduce the price they are prepared to offer. They might be willing to pay, say, £750 for a car they perceive as having an even chance of being a lemon or a peach. But used-car sellers who in fact know that they have a peach will reject that offer insofar as it was made for a peach. It is for this reason that buyers face adverse selection: the only sellers who will be prepared to accept £750 will be those who know they are selling a lemon. That is, at the price offered in circumstances of asymmetric knowledge, only lemons get sold.

However, an intelligent buyer can foresee this problem. Knowing that they will only ever be sold a lemon at an offer of £750, they offer only £500, the price they would be prepared to pay for a lemon. Sellers of lemons end up with the same price as they would have done were there no uncertainty (i.e. where everyone knows the car in question is a lemon). But the peaches stay in the dealer's yard. This is regrettable precisely because there are buyers who would happily pay the £1,000 asking price for a peach, if only they could be sure of the car's quality. The information asymmetry between buyers and sellers leads to adverse selection and undermines the operation of the market.

[21] George Akerlof, 'The Market for "Lemons": Quality Uncertainty and the Market Mechanism', *The Quarterly Journal of Economics*, Vol 84, No 3 (August 1970), pp 488–500.

The problem is potentially more pronounced in the context of insurance. Before the age of big data analytics, the same information asymmetry existed between the insurer (as seller) and the insured (as prospective buyer). Except that (i) unlike with the sale of used cars, the insurer, as seller, was in the position of the buyer of the used car: it is the insurer who has much less information than the insured; and (ii) the sale of insurance involves an additional uncertainty since the true cost of the cover (and the extent of the insurer's liability to indemnify the insured) turns on the occurrence of a future contingency, namely, whether the insured risk materialises or not.[22] Insurance is a contract for the sale of protection against the occurrence of future loss, the cost of which will be transferred to and borne by the insurer. Absent information about the nature of the risk, the insurer may equally struggle to tell a good risk from a bad risk. But how does adverse selection arise in the insurance market? One thing that insurers have always appreciated is that those insureds most keen to buy insurance were probably the insureds who constituted the riskiest bets. After all, those who think that the equivalent risk that they presented was very unlikely to materialise would be more likely to decide that they did not need insurance at all – particularly if an insurer was setting higher average prices to cover his liabilities in respect of those losses that will materialise – thus leaving the pool of potential insureds as one comprising, to a relatively greater extent, individuals who are poorer risks who require insurance more.

The problem was addressed by Joseph Stiglitz and Michael Rothschild in a paper published in 1976.[23] They considered that the risk of adverse selection in the insurance market could be remedied by insurers who allowed their customers to 'signal' their riskiness by offering two different forms of cover, one that would be bought only by individuals who were better risks and one that would be bought only by those who were worse risks. Suppose, therefore, a car insurer is faced with high-risk and low-risk drivers. Suppose, too, that they cannot, without any further investigation, tell these groups apart; only the customer knows whether he is a safe driver. Stiglitz and Rothschild showed that, in a competitive market, insurers cannot profitably offer the same deal to both groups. If they did, the premiums of safe drivers would subsidise indemnities paid to bad, risk-taking drivers. A second insurer could offer a deal with slightly lower premiums, and slightly less cover, which would attract only safe drivers because risky ones prefer to stay fully insured. The first insurer, left only with bad risks, would make a loss.[24] The first insurer must instead offer two forms of cover: the first would be an expensive form of cover with no deductible while the second would be a cheaper, less extensive form of cover with a sizeable deductible. Risky drivers will balk

[22] An insurance contract is an example of an aleatory contract, being a contract where the parties' final rights and obligations are based on a future and uncertain contingency: see F Schultz, 'The Special Nature of Insurance Contract: A Few Suggestions for Further Study' (1950) 15 *Law and Contemporary Problems*, 376.

[23] Joseph Stiglitz and Michael Rothschild, 'Equilibrium in Competitive Insurance Markets: An Essay on the Economics of Imperfect Information', *The Quarterly Journal of Economics*, Vol 90, No 4 (November 1976), 629–49.

[24] Some worried that a related problem would afflict 'Obamacare', which forbids American health insurers from discriminating against customers who are already unwell: if the higher premiums that resulted from this prohibition were to deter healthy, young customers from signing up, firms might have to raise premiums further to ensure they covered the remaining, more risky customers, thereby driving more healthy customers away (the so-called 'death spiral'.)

at the deductible, knowing that there is a good chance they will end up having to pay it when they claim. They will therefore opt for the expensive form of cover. Safe drivers will be more content with cover subject to a high deductible and pay a lower price for the reduced cover they do get.[25]

Both Akerlof and Stiglitz and Rothschild's respective analyses are simplified and stylised to consider the points of principle. The information asymmetries are never so stark: as is widely acknowledged, Akerlof's paper did not provide an accurate description of the used-car market and the buyer could take certain steps to ascertain the likelihood that the car was a peach or a lemon; similarly insurers can ask a prospective insured questions on proposal forms to ascertain the extent of the prospective risk. But in a world of mass-market consumer insurance, insurers offered cover based on relatively few questions about each prospective risk and segregated individual risks into very wide pools in accordance with risk modelled, for example in the context of motor insurance, on age, gender, driving experience, and claims history. More specifically, actuaries would analyse the impact of those variables against past losses to generate an average rate for those falling within each of those small number of very large risk pools.[26] The assessment of an individual risk involved the application of the average risk of the overall group to the individual insured who shared those broad characteristics. Those limited risk factors enabled insurers to more accurately segregate insureds into a relatively small number of large risks pools and would offer more expensive policies with no or smaller deductibles to those identified as poorer risks and the less expensive policies with higher deductibles to the better risks.

B. Solidarity-Based and Mutuality-Based Insurance

Insurance may be provided in one of two broad ways: solidarity-based insurance or mutuality-based insurance. In broad terms, the former is provided by government or public authorities, without regard to the risk profile of any individual and with the goal of risk spreading to ensure more universal cover, whereas the latter is provided on the basis of individualised risk assessment by insurers in a private market. Onora O'Neill describes the distinction at a time prior to the arrival of big data, as follows:

> Solidarity-based insurance takes no cognisance of the different levels of risk that different individuals bring to the pool: premiums are set at a uniform level, or based on ability to pay; entitlement to claim if the event insured against occurs is uniform. The NHS and similar health insurance schemes in other countries are examples of solidarity-based insurance provision. Everyone contributes, indeed the better paid may contribute more, but those who are likely to use the health service a lot do not pay more than the robustly healthy. Unsurprisingly, solidarity-based insurance has to be publicly organised: it requires universal or at

[25] In a world characterised by stark information asymmetries, good drivers still have to bear high deductibles when they suffer an insured peril and make a claim on their policy.

[26] At its most basic, the way in which actuaries set the price of policies (also known as ratemaking) involves looking at the frequency and severity of insured perils and the expected average payout resulting from these perils. Thereafter an insurance company will collect historical loss data, bring the loss data to present value, and compare these prior losses to the premium collected in order to assess rate adequacy.

> least very wide participation, hence an element of compulsion (usually via the tax system), since those whose risk is least are required to contribute in solidarity with others. Without an element of compulsion, those with least risk would have reason to leave solidarity-based schemes and seek private insurance which could cover their low risks more cheaply, the average risk (and cost) of those left in the pool would rise and yet others would then have reason to leave. By contrast mutuality-based insurance differentiates premiums on the basis of the level of risk each person is held to bring to the pool. Typically commercial insurance is based on mutuality. In this case there may be no compulsion (eg home contents insurance), or no more than conditional compulsion to take out insurance if one undertakes some activity (eg motor insurance). In either case there may be no compulsion to join a particular scheme: better risks will purchase their insurance from those who offer them lower premiums; worse risks will purchase despite higher premiums because they can get no better terms … Of course the calculation of the risk represented by an individual is unavoidably an approximate matter: some people with adverse risk factors are good drivers. Still, there is little objection to the practice of adjusting premiums in proportion to the risk level each driver is held to represent. Driving is optional, and if high premiums keep those whose driving is a menace off the roads and provides an incentive for safe driving for all, this is a benefit to all.[27]

However, one feature that private (or mutuality-based) insurance has traditionally shared with social (or solidarity-based) insurance is the wide pooling of risk. Each form of insurance involves the pooling of funds from a very large number of insureds in order to enable the insurer who collects those funds to cover the losses that only some of those insureds will incur. The wider the pool, the larger the class of contributors, and thus the greater the fund that is available to those in the pool who suffer an insured peril. Moreover, and specifically in the context of mutuality-based insurance, wider pools allow insurers to benefit from the law of large numbers, according to which the outcome from a large number of transactions should be close to the expected overall outcome and will tend to get closer to that outcome as more transactions are undertaken. In mutuality-based insurance the larger the number of transactions, the closer insurers' predicted losses will be to their actual losses. In circumstances where insurance markets were characterised by information asymmetries, with the consequent risk of adverse selection to which this characteristic gave rise, that risk was mitigated by seeking to profile insureds more accurately by reference to actuarially based risk factors, and to offer an increasing variety of policies to allow insureds to corroborate their relative degree of risk by virtue of the cover they sought. But large risk pools remained in circumstances where insurers did not have the means of more precisely profiling individual risks than by reference to the limited number of actuarially based risk factors that allowed underwriters to price risk according to the presence or absence of those factors. The width of those pools meant that, even as constituted by reference to actuarially based risk factors, they contained a wide spectrum of individual risks, where lower-risk insureds effectively subsidised higher-risk insureds through the medium of each pool's aggregated premium.

[27] O O'Neill, 'Insurance and Genetics: The Current State of Play', in *Law and Human Genetics: Regulating a Revolution* (Oxford, Hart Publishing, 1998), 124–25.

That is changing. All insurers in principle have access to a much wider source of risk- (and non-risk-) related information about individual insureds. And insurers have a powerful commercial and competitive incentive to avail of algorithms that enable them to profile each individual insured to a much more granular degree. The ability to more precisely profile each individual risk is the logical next step for insurers: the whole purpose of mutuality-based insurance is to better understand each individual risk in order to avoid adverse selection. However, one consequence of more granular risk profiling would be the much greater segmentation of the risk pools into which insurers can place each individual insured. More particularly, the increased segmentation of risk pools means more accurate pricing of individual risks: those profiled to be a higher risk will pay higher premiums, while those found to be lower risks will payer lower premiums. Further, the increased number of risk pools will gradually become more homogenous, thus reducing the extent to which members of each pool are subsidising others in that pool. The promise of big data is that individual insureds will no longer pay the average premium applicable to those with whom he shares a few actuarially relevant characteristics: the younger male driver may be able to rely on other factors that show him to be a less risky driver. Likewise the very risky middle-aged female driver may no longer be able to benefit from the relatively better premium to which those two characteristics give her access. Staying with the example of motor insurance, real-time driving data enables insurers to assess the riskiness of an individual insured's driving behaviour without regard to the modelled behaviour of broadly comparable third party drivers. It has been said that '[t]his ability is fostering new and innovative products that more accurately price risk and attract profitable new customers, making the traditional segmentation of pricing auto-insurance – based on average characteristics or certain populations' gender or age – completely obsolete'.[28]

The flip side of the greater segmentation of the risk pool and the more accurate pricing of cover is the risk that some insureds will be denied access to cover where once they might not have been. Whereas our mutuality-based system of general insurance cover did price on the basis of individual risks, that model was constrained by the relatively little amount of data insurers had on individuals. The absence of individual data allowed for a much greater degree of risk-spreading even within the context of a mutuality-based system of insurance. As that changes, and profiling becomes increasingly individualised, the less that good drivers will end up cross-subsidising bad drivers. The more accurate pricing of risk, if done by reference to behaviours objectively relevant to the risk, must be a good thing not least since if better behaviours lead to lower premiums, then the use of big data has the potential to incentivise such behaviours. In contrast, when the premium is based on aggregate factors which a particular insured cannot change, his incentive to improve is removed. Regulation should encourage the operation of incentives that help to deliver positive behavioural outcomes in society.

The increasing segmentation of the risk pool has further consequences for the insurance market: insurers who have more quickly developed predictive analytics in order

[28] Cognizant, 'The Telematics Advantage: Growth, Retention and Transformational Improvement with Usage-Based Insurance', January 2012.

to better identify the risk posed by each individual insured will be able to cherry-pick the best risks, being those individuals who are less likely to suffer an insured peril or, therefore, file claims. Recall the point made by Baker, discussed in chapter one, that '[a]n insurer that discovers a new way to identify and exclude high risks improves its competitive position in two ways: it lowers its average risk and, assuming the people it rejects go elsewhere, it increases the average risk of its competitors'.[29] Those insurers who write risk on a traditional, aggregated basis by reference to a few actuarially sound risk factors are at risk of losing out to those insurers cherry-picking the best risks, leading again to the former suffering adverse selection because they are left with poorer risks. Those insurers will be at a competitive disadvantage giving rise to a risk of (i) insolvency; or – in a world where capital requirements are monitored on an ongoing basis (which in the EU occurs under Solvency II principles) – (ii) a risk that they simply exit the market. More generally, should risk profiling accelerate, the market will come to be dominated by those insurers who continue to profile and who are thus able to offer increasingly customised cover to those individuals to whom they are prepared to make offers of insurance. Were the cherry-picking of good risks to continue, those who are left uninsured will either have to bear losses or liabilities themselves (with consequential risks for third parties in relation to liability risks), or the industry or government will have to consider whether to intervene and (i) provide premium subsidies;[30] (ii) preclude reliance on such factors; (iii) impose direct rate regulation; or (iv) establish either a scheme of insurance of last resort, as with Flood Re (for insured homeowners living on uninsurable homes on flood plains) or (as an *ex post facto* solution) schemes of compensation for third-party victims of uninsured perils (such as the Motor Insurers' Bureau). Either way, the costs of non-insurance, subsidies, rate regulation or risk pools of last resort fall on either the market as a whole or society as a whole. Therefore, the more that insurers engage in individual risk-profiling, the greater the segmentation of individual risks into a larger number of smaller pools until, in theory, the number of pools equates to the total number of individuals seeking insurance (which prospect is made real when big data is applied to genetic information). At that point, insurance will no longer involve pricing risk or offering terms on the averaged and aggregated basis that characterises traditional underwriting. As the ABI noted in 2013, '[i]nsurer behaviour is also changing as they increasingly "segment" the markets available to them to pursue customers who offer the best risk profile for their business model, using technology such as predictive underwriting'.[31] All that said, as long as the

[29] Baker, 'Containing the Promise of Insurance: Adverse Selection and Risk Classification', 9 *Connecticut Insurance Law Journal* 371 (2003), http://ssrn.com/abstract=322581. See also Kenneth Abraham, *Distributing Risk: Insurance, Legal Theory and Public Policy* (New Haven, Yale University Press, 1986).

[30] It is often suggested that premium subsidies are preferable to restrictions on the use of certain risk factors or rate regulation because it does not distort the price mechanism (leading to inefficiencies, insufficient coverage or adverse selection of insureds and allows the positive effects of premium differentiation to be maintained: see C Kousky and H Kunreuther, 'Addressing affordability in the National Flood Insurance Program', 2014 *Journal of Extreme Events* 01 (01), 1450; see also the Geneva Association, 'Big Data and Insurance: Implications for Innovation Competition and Privacy', March 2018, 13.

[31] ABI, 'Identifying the Challenges of a Changing World', 2013: https://www.abi.org.uk/Insurance-and-savings/Topics-andissues/~/media/0D97E1A140F84636BFE2A938C194EFDA.ashx.

occurrence of individual risks retain some level of uncertainty, risk pooling has a role to play; for so long as insurers do not know which insureds exhibiting each individual risk factor will suffer insured loss, insurers will have to continue to model the risk level to which each risk factor, individually and in combination, gives rise. That modelling will still, therefore, have to be undertaken by reference to the aggregate incidence of insured loss.[32] The difference in a big data age is that aggregated assessment of the likelihood of risk can be modelled by reference to so many more risk factors and with the benefit of much greater amounts of data. And for that reason, the segmentation of the risk pool will continue to accelerate.

C. Regulatory Assessment of Risk Segmentation

Regulators are alive to the fact that big data is changing insurance by allowing insurers to move away from aggregated risk assessment to individualised risk assessment.[33] In 2015, the research that accompanied the CMA's Report on the Commercial Use of Consumer Data observed that micro-segmentation of the risk pool might reduce the degree of risk-sharing across individuals with a 'shift from being a "big underwriting pool of risk" to more targeted and strategically set prices'.[34] Micro-segmentation involves an extreme extension of the operation of mutuality-based insurance. Where risk classification is increasingly based on 'micro segments', this will – left unchecked – conflict with any general or solidarity-based conception of insurance as a means of spreading risks among a large pool of consumers, where lower-risk individuals do subsidise higher-risk individuals across larger risk pools. The FCA illustrates the process of risk – and micro – segmentation as follows:[35]

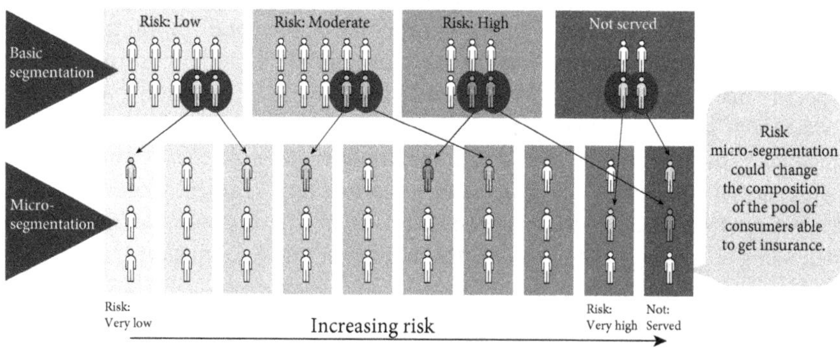

[32] That is true even at the genetic level where, absent those single gene disorders where the genotypic trait invariably leads to the phenotypic expression, risk modelling by reference to aggregated data in order to assess the likely incidence of loss will continue to be necessary.

[33] 'The Challenges for insurance and regulators in a Big Data world', speech by Andrew Bailey, Chief Executive of the FCA on 22 November 2016: https://www.fca.org.uk/news/speeches/challenges-insurance-regulators-big-data-world.

[34] 'Insurers to demand more data via telematics to fine-tune insurance prices, says AXA CIO', *Computing*, August 2014: http://www.computing.co.uk/ctg/news/2362319/insurers-to-demand-more-datavia-telematics-to-fine-tune-insurance-prices-says-axa-cio.

[35] Feedback Statement, figure 1, p 21.

However, in its Feedback Statement of 2016, the FCA observed that:

> In the parts of the GI sector we reviewed, our broker survey and PCW data analysis indicated that these concerns are not yet materialising. We recognise that our analysis does not look at particular providers, nor other parts of the GI sector that are not in the scope of our work. As the use of big data and sophisticated data analysis becomes more common across retail GI providers, we may see more consumers deemed higher risk who are unable to obtain or afford insurance through more accurate risk modelling, recognising that other consumers may benefit from greater accuracy.[36]

The FCA thus recognised the limited extent to which they could assess the incidence of risk segmentation across general consumer insurance and thus fairly acknowledged that its assessment of the risk of segmentation and price dispersion was constrained by that fact.[37] The Joint Committee of European Supervisory Authorities also considered the risk of segmentation of the risk pools and its implications in its Discussion Paper of December 2016 and observed that:

> More granular segmentations could however also lead to access issues for some consumers classified as undesirable. For example, in the insurance sector, the result of a more granular risk segmentation could lead either to higher premiums for certain customers or to certain customers (with high risks or unusual profiles) having difficulties accessing (certain types of) insurance cover. This could create difficulties for consumers seeking household insurance for real estate properties located in geographical areas exposed to high risks such as floods,[38] earthquakes or crime. The latter could eventually have broader social consequences and require action protecting the general good, since obtaining household insurance is a legal requirement in several Member States for renting or owning real estate properties.[39] The increasing individualisation of risk profiles could have, to a certain extent, implications for the principle of solidarity and risk pooling in the insurance sector.[40]

In her report on big data of September 2017, the Information Commissioner similarly observed that:

> In insurance, big data analytics can be used for micro-segmentation of risk groups; it may be possible to identify people within a high-risk (and therefore high-premium) group who actually represent a slightly lower risk compared to others in that group. Their premiums can be adjusted accordingly in their favour. In this case big data is being used to give a more accurate

[36] ibid, para 1.23.

[37] The FCA indicated that it would continue to monitor the market through their normal supervisory and intelligence activities for any notable increase in risk segmentation for different groups: p 26.

[38] The ABI notes that: 'In the past, the risk of your house flooding was calculated based on postcode – which grouped your home with on average 18 others or even a simple yes/no on proximity to a river, as insurers lacked the data to differentiate between individual houses … More accurate data allows insurers to differentiate between individual homes, so if your house is at a lower risk than all others in your postcode, that would be reflected by a lower insurance premium.' 'How Big Data makes insurance work better for you', September 2015, p 17.

[39] Giving the example of Flood Re in the UK.

[40] Joint Committee, Discussion Paper, December 2016, para 38. That fine-tuning risk classification could result in particularly high premiums for certain consumer types and even create consumer segments that are left without affordable cover, which has been acknowledged as a concern by Paul Evans, CEO of AXA UK and chairman of the Association of British Insurers (ABI). He noted that 'The industry will have to take great care to ensure we're not creating, because of big data, sectors of society that can't buy insurance.' Alistair Gray, 'Insurers warned to use "big data" responsibly, *Financial Times*, 1 February 2015, http://www.ft.com/cms/s/0/08f6049c-a7cd-11e4-8e78-00144feab7de.html.

> assessment of risk that benefits those individuals as well as the insurer. The corollary of this, given that insurance is about pooling risk, is that the remaining high-risk group members may find they have to pay higher premiums. Arguably this is a fair result overall, but inevitably there are winners and losers.[41]

The above analysis of course assumed that more individualised risk-profiling by reference to predictive analytics was indeed more accurate such as to offer early-moving insurers a competitive advantage and leaving those in their wake to suffer the consequences of adverse selection. The fact that predictive analytics operates on the basis, not of causation, but of correlation gives rise to the prospect that while insurers are profiling by reference to an increasing number of risk factors specific to each insured, it does not follow – without more concrete evidence – that any of the non-traditional factors are indicative of a greater likelihood of risk. Until insurers can isolate those risk factors and provide actuarially sound evidence that that factor does indicate a greater degree of risk – at least across the wider cohort of those insureds to whom that risk factor applies – then there is a risk that individual insureds will be incorrectly profiled and end up paying more (or less) than they would have paid had the algorithm been accurate. That in turn leads to a new 'tyranny of the group': predictive analytics was supposed to liberate individuals from the price offered by virtue of exhibiting a small number of actuarially relevant risk factors. But if individual insureds are being priced according to risk factors they share with third parties, which risk factors have been shown algorithmically – if not actuarially – to correlate with higher risk, then insureds may continue to be tied to the price of these new, big data-derived groups. However, the likely market response to the reliance on these non-causal proxies will be (i) to strive to improve the algorithm; and (ii) use the increased datasets to better analyse the incidence of insured loss on the part of those with the relevant risk factors. In that way, big data will be able to replicate actuarially based risk modelling but on a much bigger and more accurate scale.

III. Access to Insurance

Big data's ability to allow insurers to segment the risk pool to a much greater degree than before gives rise to the possibility that insureds will be discriminated against on two bases: (i) discrimination on the grounds of protected characteristics; (ii) discrimination that results from pricing practices that raises consumer and competition concerns. These are very different forms of discrimination and give rise to two distinct sets of legal issues.

A. Segmentation and Discrimination on the Grounds of Protected Characteristics

Insurers have in the past differentiated between men and women, young and old, and able-bodied and the disabled when assessing risk and calculating premium. Sex, age and

[41] ibid, para 37. The same concerns were expressed by the Joint Committee of European Supervisory Authorities in its final report on Big Data at para 36.

disability are each protected characteristics that are the subject of anti-discrimination and equality laws. But insurers have historically been able to point to the relevance of those characteristics to the assessment of risk by reference to actuarial data. Permitting insurers to take account of these characteristics where they can be shown to impact, in the aggregate, on the level of risk will enable risk to be assessed and priced more accurately. But taking account of those individual characteristics, particularly where they are inherent or immutable, strikes many as being inherently unfair. Equality law as it applies to insurance is thus required to make a normative judgement as between the benefits of accurate risk assessment and the potential for differential treatment on grounds of considerations deemed to be legally irrelevant.

i. Direct Discrimination

Were insurers to charge different prices on the basis of race, sexual orientation or religion, that would plainly amount to unlawful direct discrimination.[42] In the United Kingdom, direct discrimination is prohibited by the Equality Act 2010 (EA 2010), s 13. Section 13(1) provides that: 'A person (A) discriminates against another (B) if, because of a protected characteristic, A treats B less favourably than A treats or would treat others.'[43] The protected characteristics, for these purposes, are age, disability, gender assignment, marriage or civil partnership, race, religion or belief, sex and sexual orientation.[44] It would therefore be unlawful for insurers to profile individual insureds on these bases. A consequence is that if an insurer would be prohibited from asking questions about a protected characteristic (such as sexuality) on a proposal form and making an underwriting decision based on the answer, it follows that it should not be permitted to parse Facebook, Twitter, geolocation data or purchasing information for the same purpose.[45]

The Explanatory Notes to EA 2010 observe that the definition of direct discrimination is 'broad enough to cover cases where the less favourable treatment is because of the victim's association with someone [else] who has that [protected] characteristic (for example, is disabled), or because the victim is wrongly thought to have it (for example a particular religious belief)'.[46] These forms of direct discrimination are known as: (i) 'associative discrimination'; and (ii) 'perception discrimination', and may be highly relevant in relation to how insurers might seek to profile insureds by reference to certain new risk factors said to correlate with insured loss. If an insurer charged a person a higher premium because of that person's relationship with someone with a protected

[42] There is no general defence of objective justification available in direct discrimination save in relation to age.

[43] Although, as discussed in ch 8, modifications are made in relation to what amounts to direct discrimination on the basis of some of those characteristics.

[44] Equality Act 2010, ss 4–12.

[45] As the FTC noted in 'Big Data: A Tool for Inclusion or Exclusion', 'one study combined data on Facebook "Likes" and limited survey information to determine that researchers could accurately predict a male user's sexual orientation 88 percent of the time; a user's ethnic origin 95 percent of the time; and whether a user was Christian or Muslim (82 percent), a Democrat or Republican (85 percent), or used alcohol, drugs, or cigarettes (between 65 percent and 75 percent); FCA's Feedback Statement of 21 September 2016, 10.

[46] Explanatory Notes, para 59.

characteristic, that would be unlawful direct discrimination by association. Similarly, if through big data an insurer wrongly thought the prospective insured had a protective characteristic and charged him higher premiums when in fact he did not, that would be unlawful direct discrimination by reason of perception.[47] EA 2010, s 13 prohibits direct discrimination 'because of' a protected characteristic. That is wide enough to capture both associative discrimination and perception discrimination.[48]

As to what counts as less favourable, it has been held that merely depriving a person of a choice because of a protected characteristic will suffice.[49] It is not necessary to know of a disadvantage for it to cause actionable less favourable treatment.[50] Moreover, it is not necessary for the protected characteristic to be the sole basis for any treatment in order to establish direct discrimination: it is enough if the protected ground had a significant influence on the outcome.[51] Where the protected characteristic is race EA 2010, s 13(5) provides that 'less favourable treatment includes segregating' the victim from others. That creates the possibility that if algorithms were to segment prospective insureds along racial lines, that segmentation would violate EA 2010, s 13(5). It would appear that accidental or incidental segmentation is insufficient: a policy of segregation must exist.[52] Establishing discrimination based on a protected characteristic will require the court to assess the allegedly less favourable treatment as against the treatment afforded to a relevant comparator: EA 2010, s 13 does not require that comparator to be someone similarly situated but who does not share the same protected characteristic.[53] When establishing the relevant comparator it will be important not to attribute some of the characteristics leading to the differential treatment on the basis that they are a material or relevant differences, since to do so will make it harder to establish less favourable treatment. The question is complicated and a detailed discussion is beyond the scope of this work, but the decision of Baroness Hale in the *Roma Rights* case is instructive:[54]

> 73. The underlying concept in both race and sex discrimination laws is that individuals of each sex and all races are entitled to be treated equally. Thus it is just as discriminatory to

[47] See eg *English v Thomas Sanderson Blinds Ltd* [2008] EWCA Civ 1421; [2009] ICR 534, where the claimant was subject to homophobic abuse though it was known that he was not gay.

[48] The scope of the 'because of' formulation – used in the Framework Directive – was considered by the CJEU in Case C-303/06 *Coleman v Attridge Law* [2008] ECR I-5603; [2008] CMLR 7777. The Advocate General stated: 'One way of undermining the dignity and autonomy of the people who belong to a certain group is to target not them, but third persons who are closely associated with them and do not themselves belong to the group.' And see the judgment of Underhill P on remission to the Employment Appeal Tribunal in *EBR Attridge LLP (formerly Attridge Law) an Anor v Coleman (No 2)* [2010] 1 ICR 242; [2010] IRLR 10.

[49] *Gill v El Vino Co Ltd* [1983] QB 425; [1983] IRLR 206.

[50] *Garry v London Borough of Ealing* [2001] IRLR 681.

[51] See *Owen and Briggs v James* [1982] ICR 616 and *Nagarajan v London Regional Transport* [2000] 1 AC 501 at 513. Where a protected characteristic has had a material influence on a decision which would have happened in any event for other lawful reasons, a claim in direct discrimination may yet succeed, albeit with an impact on the relief given: *Chagger v Abbey National Plc & Anor* [2009] EWCA Civ 1202.

[52] See the discussion in *Furniture Timber and Allied Trades Union v Modgill; Pell Limited v Modgill* [1980] IRLR 142.

[53] Less favourable treatment could thus be established where a woman was assumed to be less reliable for reasons relating to childcare commitments than a woman who did not have children.

[54] *R (on the application of European Roma Rights Centre) v Immigration Officer at Prague Airport* [2005] 2 AC 1.

> treat men less favourably than women as it is to treat women less favourably than men; and it is just as discriminatory to treat whites less favourably than blacks as it is to treat blacks less favourably than whites.[55] The ingredients of unlawful discrimination are (i) a difference in treatment between one person and another person (real or hypothetical) from a different sex or racial group; (ii) that the treatment is less favourable to one; (iii) that their relevant circumstances are the same or not materially different; and (iv) that the difference in treatment is on racial grounds. However, because people rarely advertise their prejudices and may not even be aware of them, discrimination has normally to be proved by inference rather than direct evidence. Once treatment less favourable than that of a comparable person (ingredients (i), (ii) and (iii)) is shown, the court will look to the alleged discriminator for an explanation. The explanation must, of course, be unrelated to the race or sex of the complainant. If there is no, or no satisfactory explanation, it is legitimate to infer that the less favourable treatment was on racial grounds …
>
> 74. If direct discrimination of this sort is shown, that is that. Save for some very limited exceptions, there is no defence of objective justification. The whole point of the law is to require suppliers to treat each person as an individual, not as a member of a group. The individual should not be assumed to hold the characteristics which the supplier associates with the group, whether or not most members of the group do indeed have such characteristics, a process sometimes referred to as stereotyping. Even if, for example, most women are less strong than most men, it must not be assumed that the individual woman who has applied for the job does not have the strength to do it. Nor, for that matter, should it be assumed that an individual man does have that strength. If strength is a qualification, all applicants should be required to demonstrate that they qualify.

This point goes to one of the themes in this book: big data profiling promises to assess risk on the basis of the characteristics of the individual insured. But where such profiling involves the replacement – or, more likely, the supplementing – of existing, actuarially based risk factors with a set of new risk proxies that rely on correlation rather than actuarial assessment, big data risks profiling individuals by reference to the characteristics of new groups albeit where the incidence between those risk factors and the occurrence of insured loss has not been demonstrated across the group, never mind that it may not be an accurate indicator of risk in relation to the individual. In *R (on the application of Gillan & Anor) v Commissioner of Police for the Metropolis*,[56] the House of Lords considered that whereas a protected characteristic might be used to identify someone (in that case, for police questioning), their further treatment could not be based on the fact that they were members of that group absent a further and more fact-specific attempt to determine whether that particular individual raised the concern that led to their initial identification. That is the difference (albeit often easier to state than apply) between treating people differently on the basis of a group stereotype and treating people as individuals and without reference to the protected characteristic.[57] However, it is submitted that, unlike the case of police officers trying to identify terrorist suspects, algorithms cannot, at stage 1, be permitted to distinguish between prospective insureds on the basis

[55] The prohibition reflects a model of formal equality.

[56] [2006] UKHL 12; [2006] 2 AC 307.

[57] The issue in that case being the lawfulness of powers conferred that allowed police officers to stop and search persons in a specified area for articles which could be used in connection with terrorism.

of group-based stereotypes even where they sought to apply a series of criteria that in fact assess the risk profile of that individual as stage 2 of the profiling process.

As Baroness Hale observed, as 'people rarely advertise their prejudices and may not even be aware of them, discrimination has normally to be proved by inference'. Insurers may not design analytics tools that so expressly encode questions and consequences based on race or sex and so on. However, it is possible to differentiate on a ground that cannot but apply to a racial minority or a particular gender etc. Where a protected characteristic is 'inherent'[58] or 'indissociable'[59] from a particular criterion, then even where neutrally expressed it is likely to be directly, not indirectly discriminatory. The criteria of pensionable age, where men and women reach that age at different times, is a good example.[60] When the ground or reason for the less favourable treatment is clear from the act itself (eg applying a pensionable age criterion) there is no need for further enquiry into the putative discriminator's motives or the question of differential impact. However, where that person applies a criterion that does not refer to or is, on its face, indissociably linked with a protected criteria (eg when an applicant is told he will be considered on merit) then there will nevertheless be direct discrimination where it is demonstrated that the putative discriminator intended to or was motivated by the desire to treat that person less favourably because of that protected characteristic.[61] The further away a reason for less favourable treatment is from protected characteristics, the more likely it is that the less favourable treatment will only be capable of challenge on the basis that the reason or criterion applied has a differential impact amounting to unlawful indirect discrimination. The boundary between direct and indirect discrimination can be hard to identify.

ii. Indirect Discrimination

Algorithms may also use data to identify purported risk factors which do not differentiate because of a protected characteristic but which disproportionately disadvantage people with that characteristic. That may give rise to indirect discrimination, albeit that such differential treatment can be objectively justified. Indirect discrimination is prohibited in the United Kingdom by EA 2010, s 19. Section 19(1) provides that 'A person (A) discriminates against another (B) if A applies to B a provision, criterion or practice which is discriminatory in relation to a relevant protected characteristic of B's'.[62] If the criterion puts, or would put,[63] B at a disadvantage, it will be discriminatory

[58] *R(E) v Governing Body of JFS and Anor (United Synagogue and Ors Intervening)* [2009] UKSC 15; [2010] 2 AC 728.

[59] *Bressol v Gouvernement de la Communauté Française* (Case C-73/08) [2010] 3 CMLR 559, Opinion of Advocate General Sharpston, paras 52–57.

[60] *James v Eastleigh Borough Council* [1990] 2 AC 751.

[61] See, on this point, the discussion of the majority in *R (E) v Governing body of JFS and the Admissions Appeal Panel of JFS and others* [2009] UKSC 15; [2010] 2 AC 728, and Underhill P's judgment in *EBR Attridge LLP (formerly Attridge Law) an Anor v Coleman (No 2)* [2010] 1 ICR 242; [2010] IRLR 10.

[62] The Services Code of Practice para 5.7 observes that 'On the face of it, the provision, criterion or practice must be neutral. If it is not neutral in this way, but expressly applies to people with a specific protected characteristic, it is likely to amount to direct discrimination.'

[63] s 19(2)(a)–(d). The use of the word 'would' means that a person can bring a claim even if he has not been the subject of the offending criteria because they had chosen to avoid it or had no choice but to avoid it.

if A cannot show it to be a proportionate means of achieving a legitimate aim. Indirect discrimination is likely to be far more prevalent as a result of the use of predictive analytics. If a much wider range of factors are being correlated against insured loss, and thus constitute proxies for risk, then (i) it will be very easy to side-step forms of direct discrimination; and (ii) regulators will have to be vigilant about precisely what factors are the subject of these analyses.[64] Postcodes have of course been used by car insurers to identify levels of risk, but higher premiums in higher-risk areas may result in certain ethnic groups paying more for car insurance.

The question under s 19 would be whether the postcode criterion is a proportionate means of achieving a legitimate aim. The cases impose a three-stage test. First, is the objective sufficiently important to justify limiting a fundamental right; second, is the measure rationally connected to the objective; and third, are the means chosen no more than is necessary to accomplish the objective? In undertaking the proportionality exercise, it is necessary to 'weight the need against the seriousness of the detriment to the disadvantaged group'.[65] The reasons given by the putative discriminator will be considered, as will any business considerations relied upon to justify the criteria, but in the end it is for the court to decide what is reasonably necessary to accomplish the objective.[66] To return to the example, the desire to avoid adverse selection, objectively accurate pricing of high-risk insureds, and fairness to lower-risk insureds would all be legitimate aims were insurers to rely upon the insured's postcode. Other proxies include a person's credit history, loan information, or purchasing data on the basis of which the person might be refused services. Except, the real reason for the differential treatment may be that the consumer has a name that suggests they are a member of an ethnic minority group. Indeed, there were media reports in 2018 of claims that PCWs were quoting significantly higher car insurance premiums for people with such names.[67] And given existing structures of inequality, those in most need of protection from profiling that leads to refusals of services are disproportionately likely to be those who suffer the greatest level of discrimination in the first place.[68]

The role of a new range of risk proxies again raises the problem of opacity: if individuals are to challenge underwriting decisions, they need to understand which new factors are being correlated against risk, and how they have been applied to them. Swedloff has argued that 'if it is not clear who is charged more for insurance or why, there is little argument that insurers are reinforcing stereotypes or that policyholders are suffering dignitary harms'.[69] While that might be true if insurers are not obliged to

[64] There are three ways to demonstrate differential impact: proof of an inherently discriminatory criterion; statistical evidence; or by means of a forensically sound hypothesis.

[65] *Secretary of State for Defence v Elias* [2006] EWCA Civ 1293; [2006] 1 WLR 3213.

[66] The fact that the court considers what was 'reasonably' necessary does not create a margin of appreciation for the putative discriminator; the criteria will either be indirectly discriminatory or it will not. There is no scope for justification on the basis that the steps taken in pursuit of the objective might be thought to be one of a reasonable range of responses: *Hardys and Hansons plc v Lax* [2005] EWCA Civ 846; [2005] IRLR 726.

[67] https://www.bbc.co.uk/news/business-43011882.

[68] In the US, the potential for big data to result in exclusion and discrimination was discussed by the Federal Trade Commission in 'Big Data: A Tool for Inclusion or Exclusion?', January 2016, https://www.ftc.gov/system/files/documents/reports/big-data-tool-inclusion-or-exclusion-understanding-issues/160106big-data-rpt.pdf.

[69] R Swedloff, 'Rick Classification's (R)evolution', *Connecticut Insurance Law Journal*, Vol 21.1, 2014, 339 at 363.

stipulate the basis for the differential treatment, insurers do come under such an obligation in the United Kingdom.[70] Moreover, the fact that algorithms may be opaque and an insured may not know on what basis they have been differentially treated (or even know that their treatment was wrongly different at all) is no justification for discrimination, direct or indirect.

One way in which insureds may challenge the lawfulness of risk proxies that impose a criterion on a person with a protected characteristic that disadvantages him relevant to another person without that protected characteristic would be to show that they are not causal and cannot – either in their personal circumstances, or more widely – have any material bearing on the level of risk. If those proxies have no bearing on risk, then it would appear that insurers could not justify indirect discrimination as a result of their application. The broader question arising is whether insureds can challenge non-causal risk proxies even where they do not give rise to unjustified indirect discrimination to the insured. If a policy is priced more highly in part on the basis of that criterion, yet it has no bearing on risk, that suggests that the data relied upon is inaccurate. Whether insureds can object to higher pricing on the basis of non-causal risk proxies which, for that reason, are said to be inaccurate, is considered in chapters six and seven.

B. Should Insurers be Prohibited from Taking Certain Risk-related Information into Account?

A further question to which the segmentation of risk pools gives rise is to what extent are there risk factors – beyond an insured's protected characteristics – that insurers should not, as a matter of principle or public policy, be entitled to base underwriting decisions upon at all. In particular, if cherry-picking good risks through predictive analytics were to lead to the cost of higher risks being borne by society more generally, should regulators or the law forbid insurers from taking account of certain information that might render an individual uninsurable on the private market?[71] By what principle might we explain why certain risk factors, including protected characteristics, should not be the basis of underwriting decisions?

One approach is suggested by the principle of equality of opportunity which distinguishes between choices and circumstances. Individuals who have legal competence are responsible for their actions; legal competence – and the capacity for legal responsibility – arises because those actions were chosen. It is then for the law to determine whether

[70] See ch 6, section III.A.iv.e.

[71] Or, more fundamentally, should certain types of risk be provided only by way of solidarity-based insurance as opposed to mutuality-based insurance? O'Neill notes that if health insurance is organised on a mutuality basis there are likely to be many who can obtain no (or no affordable) private health insurance, who cannot therefore meet the costs of their healthcare. See O O'Neill, Insurance and Genetics: The Current State of Play', in *Law and Human Genetics: Regulating a Revolution*, Hart Publishing, 1998, 125. In most western countries, health insurance is organised in two tiers, with a solidarity-based scheme providing a baseline of care for everyone, with a private market operating for those seeking additional levels of health insurance. As this book is concerned with mutuality-based provision of insurance, the real issue is whether private insurers should be entitled to have access to or rely upon certain types of personal data in underwriting and claims handling.

harm caused by those actions renders the individual liable on a fault-based or strict-liability standard. By contrast, the law does not punish individuals for circumstances that they have not chosen. For example, the concept of a status crime (the punishment of someone merely because they are, for example, of a certain race or sexual orientation) is a fundamental violation of the rule of law.[72] The principle of equality of opportunity seeks to ensure that a person's fate is determined by their choices, rather than their circumstances. If a person pursues some endeavour in a society that adheres to this principle then his success or failure will be determined by his performance (choices), not his race or sexuality (which are circumstances). That leads to the conclusion that inequalities (such as the price of access to insurance) may be justified if they are the product of an individual's choices; but inequalities are not justified where based on unchosen social or genetic circumstances. As Kymlicka argues:

> No one deserves to be born [disabled] or with an IQ of 140 any more than they deserve to be born into a certain class or sex or race. If it is unjust for people's fate to be influenced by the latter factors, then it is unclear why the same injustice is not equally present when people's fate is determined by the former factors. The injustice in each case is the same – distributive shares should not be influenced by factors which are arbitrary from a moral point of view. Natural talents and social circumstances are both matters of brute luck and people's moral claims should not depend on brute luck.[73]

People should pay for the cost of their own choices. Paying for choices is the flip side of our intuition about not paying for unequal circumstances. It is unjust for me to demand that someone else pay for the costs of my choices. As Dworkin puts it, 'a distributive scheme should be endowment-insensitive and ambition-sensitive'.[74] That analysis prima facie suggests that insurers should be entitled to have access to and use data regarding the riskiness of the choices that we have made or are likely to make, but not to information about circumstances beyond our choice and control, such as our genetic inheritance. In that regard, the biggest US life insurer John Hancock has announced that all future insureds would be required to wear activity tracking devices:[75] why should those who jog every day continue to subsidise those who do not exercise at all? The differential in premium reflects choices of those respective insureds. Except that

[72] The rule of law is a virtue of law and legal systems. What the rule of law requires rather depends on the standards against which the principle of the rule of law measures individual legal systems. If the rule of law is a unique (and potentially the first) virtue of legal systems, it might be thought that it is concerned with the law's ability to operate as a distinct normative system. As a normative system, the law seeks to guide its subjects. J Raz, 'The Rule of Law and its Virtue' in J Raz, *The Authority of Law: Essays on Law and Morality* (Oxford, Clarendon Press, 1979); J Finnis, *Natural Law and Natural Rights* (Oxford, OUP, 1980), pp 266–80; and L Fuller, *The Morality of Law* (New Haven, Yale University Press, 1964), pp 33–91 all approach the rule of law as constituting a set of principles designed to assess the extent to which the law is capable of guiding its subjects. Status crimes are, on this analysis, a fundamental violation of the rule of law as such laws are incapable of guiding or altering conduct: one cannot change the colour of one's skin or sexuality. The law should not punish an individual for circumstances that are not chosen but should instead provide guidance by which we can choose how to act.

[73] W Kymlicka, *Contemporary Political Philosophy* (Oxford, Clarendon Press, 1990), 56.

[74] Ronald Dworkin, 'What is Equality? Part I: Equality of Welfare; Part II Equality of Resources, Philosophy and Public Affairs', 311.

[75] https://www.johnhancock.com/content/johnhancock/news/insurance/2018/09/john-hancock-leaves-traditional-life-insurance-model-behind-to-incentivize-longer--healthier-lives.html.

although wearable devices provide information about choices individuals are making, they also increasingly provide biometric data which are matters of circumstance not choice.

However, in the context of equality law, it has been pointed out that we do regard it as legitimate – and far from morally arbitrary – to judge people on the basis of certain immutable (unchosen) characteristics. A person's intelligence is a proper basis for selection for an academic job, just as physical strength is a qualification for employment as a nightclub bouncer. Every person has immutable features by which they are judged, yet the law only steps in to preclude judgment on the ground of certain immutable traits and in certain circumstances. As Janet Halley rightly suggests, an additional factor of moral (or legal) significance is always necessary to determine the boundary between cases where judgment by reference to an immutable factor is permissible, for example, a decision not to employ a person who is blind as a driving instructor, from those cases where it is impermissible, such as a decision only to employ white males. We need, Halley suggests, to find a 'principled way of distinguishing the many discriminations based on immutable characteristics that we do not find normatively or legally troubling'.[76]

It might be suggested that the reasons distinguishing between Halley's examples of permissible and impermissible differentiation relate to the fact that immutable characteristics of intelligence, eyesight and strength are all legitimately relevant to employers of academics, driving instructors and bouncers whereas being a white male simply is not. But relevance of those immutable characteristics to access a particular social good (here, insurance) might lead insurers to contend that a person's age, sex or genetic inheritance is entirely (and actuarially) relevant to the assessment of motor, life and health risks. If the test of whether insurers should have access to, for example, genetic information is whether that characteristic is relevant to the value of the social good (insurance) on offer, then relying on the fact that one's genetic inheritance is an immutable characteristic would not appear to prohibit insurers from taking account of this information: that a prospective insured is predisposed to a severe early onset disorder in principle has a clear impact on the pricing of that person's life insurance cover. Drawing a distinction between choice and circumstances may therefore not always provide a complete answer.

Individuals need access to insurance. Insurance is enabling in that it allows people to undertake activities knowing that should those activities lead to loss or result in liabilities, the insured will not have to fund those losses or liabilities himself. Were it otherwise, the risk of such large contingent losses or liabilities would disincentivise individuals from engaging in what are otherwise socially useful or personally empowering activities. In this regard, insurance is required in relation to activities where individuals have a prior choice over whether to engage in those activities. We are not compelled to drive, run a business or provide professional services. But if we choose to engage in these activities they come with contingent risks. In making a choice to

[76] Janet Halley, 'Sexual orientation and the politics of biology: A critique of the argument from immutability' (1994) 46 *Stanford Law Review* 503 at 519 as discussed in N Bamforth, *Sexuality Morals and Justice: A theory of lesbian and gay rights law* (London, Cassell, 1997); see also the discussion in P Kitcher, *The Lives to Come: The Genetic Revolution and Human Possibilities* (London, Penguin, 1996) 133.

engage in those activities, are our predispositions, behavioural and genetic, not each relevant to the cost of cover? Insurance also allows individuals to guard against future contingencies such as the risk of ill-health or permanent disablement. Such contingencies may be entirely unchosen, not having arisen out of some activity that we made a prior choice to engage in. Why should a person's ability to access insurance – and thus to the security that such access facilitates – be distributed on the basis of characteristics that are unchosen and beyond one's control? Given that health insurance is provided by way of a solidarity-based scheme in the UK, the real debate over whether the principle of equality of opportunity justifies restricting insurers from accessing this information will be played out in the context of life insurance, critical illness insurance and income protection insurance.[77] The fact that these forms of cover are, at least in the UK, provided through private, mutuality-based schemes, insurers might claim to have a greater entitlement to access some genetic information for the purpose of these more specific forms of cover. These policies are designed to provide financial assistance in the event of death (for the benefit of others, under a life policy), illness or loss of employment whereas health insurance, more fundamentally, provides access to healthcare and treatment. For that reason, insurers may have a much stronger case to access some genetic information when assessing premiums for these sorts of cover.[78] The answer as to why some immutable characteristics should not be available to insurers to take account lies in a combination of empowerment and dignitary concerns: denying access to insurance for reasons beyond the person's control and which otherwise restricts their ability to form and execute life plans in the same way as others may compound existing inequality, preclude personal advancement and give rise to significant dignitary harms. There can be no blanket rule and normative judgments will often have to be made on a more case-by-case basis such as would be the case if an insurer can take account of disability in assessing risk and offering terms but only where the link between the disability and the risk insured is clear and justified. Even then society might consider that the equality, empowerment and dignitary justifications might tell in favour of premium subsidies to be paid out of a fund that all insureds who would not be penalised on that basis might pay into.

The above is designed merely to sketch out the parameters of the debate as to how far the principle of equality of opportunity might constrain underwriting decisions. But the principles are not altered by the contingency of technology: it does not matter that new data sources might yield more information or that predictive analytics might yield greater insights into individual risks. Just because more information is accessible and

[77] Which, by virtue of the fact that they are not, unlike health insurance, provided by way of a solidarity-based scheme in the UK suggests that access to this form of protection is less important than access to healthcare.

[78] That access to life insurance does not have the same moral force as access to health insurance is made by Kitcher thus: 'the case for a system of guaranteed life insurance … is less clear-cut. Because the purpose of life insurance is almost always to enable to secure for their loved ones a range of opportunities which at least some members of society, often a significant number, do not enjoy, considerations of justice pull in different directions … [What such people] aim to preserve is a level of well-being greater than that enjoyed by members of other groups, many of whom are not responsible for their lack of opportunities.' P Kitcher, *The Lives to Come: The Genetic Revolution and Human Possibilities* (London, Penguin, 1996), 141.

capable of shaping insurance decisions, does not mean it ought to be accessed and relied upon by insurers.

These competing intuitions are especially problematic in the context of genetic information, particularly where big data provides the means of more accurately assessing the incidence of health and life risks than ever before.[79] The revolution in genetics and genetic testing continues to raise difficult questions as to what insurers are entitled to know and take account of in a mutuality-based system of consumer insurance. The FCA noted the increase in prospective life insureds undergoing DNA screening in its Feedback Statement of September 2016.[80] Specifically, consumers can submit to diagnostic or predictive genetic testing to rule out certain conditions. If someone's chances of suffering from a late-onset genetic condition can be accurately assessed, insurers will be able to price premiums more precisely and/or impose conditions permitting termination of cover and/or an increase of premium at certain times or on the occurrence of certain events. But just because an insured 'has the gene for' some disorder does not mean he is necessarily going to suffer from that disorder. There needs to be sound actuarial evidence as to the extent to which those who carry the gene acquire the disorder.[81]

Let's suppose that genetic identification – supported by robust statistical and actuarial evidence linking the gene to the incidence of disease – really does revolutionise the prediction of life expectancy and each person's probability of suffering from, for example, dementia. The implications for life and critical illness insurance are potentially profound. Individuals with the relevant genetic traits cannot simply react by changing their lifestyles, at least not as regards single-gene disorders (although changes in lifestyles can to some extent mitigate the risk of phenotypic expression in relation to many multifactorial diseases depending on the strength of the genetic component of that disease). Should this information be available to insurers? In the past, insurers argued that they should be able to obtain disclosure of any genetic test result that the insured obtained for other reasons (eg medical, reproductive or wider research purposes). Any other policy would, they argued, enable those who had discovered that they are at risk of serious disorders to withhold that information, and take out cover at an unfairly low

[79] Another risk that raises difficult questions as to the applicability of the division between choice and circumstance is flooding. There may be an obvious moral difference in the position of those who moved to a flood plain and those who did not. But what of those encouraged to move to a flood plain where planning permission for development was given to developers? Or where an area previously subject to one-in-100-years events now, through climate change, experience flood events on a one-in-20-years basis? The answer to this dilemma in the UK was the creation of Flood Re. Flood Re is a (not-for-profit and publicly accountable) reinsurance company, which enables insurance companies to insure themselves against losses because of flooding by purchasing subsidised reinsurance against flood risks which they are not prepared to underwrite themselves. The Flood Reinsurance (Scheme Funding and Administration) Regulations 2015 (SI 2015/1902) and the Flood Reinsurance (Scheme and Scheme Administrator Designation) Regulations 2015 (SI 2015/1875) (the Regulations) were made on 10 November 2015 and came into force on 11 November 2015. The *vires* for these Regulations were provided by the Water Act 2014.

[80] Albeit that health and life insurance were beyond the scope of the FCA's study into the use of big data in general insurance.

[81] As Philip Kitcher more generally puts it: 'If genetic information is to be used to classify people, and to treat the classes differently, then those applying the information are responsible for understanding how the variation in genotypes bears on phenotypic traits.' P Kitcher, *The Lives to Come*, above n 78, p 131.

premium. The problem of adverse selection would arise again: people at very high risk, for example, of late onset disorders, could buy extra cover but those with a very low genetic risk may not bother to insure themselves at all (thus leaving the higher risk, paying even higher premiums in a smaller pool comprised of higher-risk insureds). And without the ability to identify who represents what risk, claims will outstrip premiums resulting in wider loss. Contrary to the position of insurers, it was argued that this sort of information should be off-limits since otherwise it would create unacceptable divisions within society for reasons that relate not to our choices, but largely to circumstances wholly beyond our control. Losing the genetic lottery only to be refused cover for that reason would be a regrettable double whammy.[82]

A moratorium on the use of certain genetic test results originally came into effect in the United Kingdom in November 2001 while the first agreement with the insurance industry on the restricted use that could be made of such test results first came into effect in March 2005. In 2011 the Government of the United Kingdom renewed the 'Concordat and Moratorium on Genetics and Insurance' with the Association of British Insurers. That agreement was reviewed and revised in 2014.[83] The moratorium on insurers' use of predictive genetic test results was thereby extended to November 2019. The principles in the 2011 and 2014 agreements are materially identical and are referred to here collectively as the Concordat.[84]

The Concordat states that the Government accepts 'the commercial principle that, unless otherwise agreed, insurance companies should have access to all relevant information to enable them to assess and price risk fairly in the interest of all their customers'.[85] In other words, unless anything similar to the Concordat is entered into, there is no rule of law that prevents insurers gaining access to all 'relevant' information for underwriting purposes, including genetic information. In that regard, the Concordat provides that the framework for co-operation in relation to insurers' use of genetic information should be transparent, fair and subject to regular reviews.[86] Given the content of the Concordat, the Government has confirmed that it sees no reason to introduce legislation on the use of genetic test results or family history during the term of the agreement.[87]

Specifically, the Concordat is only concerned with genetic tests that could be used to predict future illness (predictive genetic tests). It does not apply to diagnostic genetic tests, nor does it apply to non-genetic medical tests – for example, blood or urine tests for cholesterol, liver function or diabetes. It was driven in part by the concern that but for a moratorium, insureds would be deterred from taking predictive tests which they

[82] The debate in the UK is softened because health insurance is provided on a solidarity basis via the NHS. The debate is much more pressing in the United States, where health insurance is mutuality-based.

[83] https://assets.publishing.service.gov.uk/government/uploads/system/uploads/attachment_data/file/390174/Genetics_and_Insurance_guidance_2014.pdf.

[84] References to paragraphs in the Concordat are references to the 2011 version.

[85] https://assets.publishing.service.gov.uk/government/uploads/system/uploads/attachment_data/file/216821/Concordat-and-Moratorium-on-Genetics-and-Insurance-20111.pdf.

[86] Adoption of the Concordat is a condition of membership of the ABI in which the ABI and its members commit to specific, agreed circumstances under which predictive genetic test information can be obtained and used. However, it is described as a 'statement of intent' and 'does not create legal obligations between the parties'.

[87] Concordat, 2011, para 3.

might otherwise wish to take. The Concordat does not apply to existing test results or conditions. And so it observes that if a customer for life insurance knows (from medical information, family history or tests) of a specific risk to his or her health, it should in all normal circumstances be disclosed (where, post CIDRA 2012, insureds will have to reveal if expressly asked about such tests by life insurers). If the risk is not disclosed, the insurance company may face ever more costly claims than it was able to assume in setting the price of its insurance policies.[88] That approach is sought to be justified in the Concordat on the basis that a rise in future pricing would affect the availability of insurance to all individuals. The key general principle agreed was that insurers should not treat customers who have an adverse predictive genetic test result less favourably than others without justification. However, it was further agreed that applications to approve the use of predictive genetic test results by insurers would only be for conditions that were (i) monogenic (single gene disorders that are inherited in a simple fashion);[89] (ii) late-onset (symptoms that are delayed until adult ages); and (iii) of high penetrance (ie where there was a high probability that those with the gene will develop the disorder). As regards disclosure, insurers agreed to the following:

i. customers would not be asked, nor would they be put under pressure, to take a predictive genetic test to obtain insurance cover;[90]
ii. customers would not be required to disclose any of the following:
    i. a predictive genetic test result from a test taken after the insurance cover has started, for as long as that cover is in force;
    ii. the predictive test result of another person, such as a blood relative; or
    iii. a predictive or diagnostic test result acquired as part of clinical research. To avoid doubt, customers could be asked to disclose details of any symptoms, diagnosis or treatment received outside of the clinical research programme, even if those related to a condition they found out about through the research programme;
iii. customers making relevant insurance applications would be required to disclose a predictive genetic test result only if all of the following applied:
    i. the customer was seeking insurance cover above the financial limits set out in the Moratorium;
    ii. the test had been assessed by a panel of experts and
    iii. approved by Government; and
    iv. the insurer asked the customer to disclose the information;
iv. that they would make available information to customers, before an application for insurance cover was completed, about what customers would and would not have to disclose about their genetic tests;

[88] ibid, para 6.

[89] As opposed to more complicated diseases that have a multi-genetic/factorial cause. The links between genetic test results for certain single gene disorders such as haemophilia or cystic fibrosis are well established. But these are early-onset diseases and not much use to insurers considering diseases that may arise in the future. Examples of late-onset single gene disorders include Huntington's chorea and certain hereditary forms of breast cancer. The point at which those diseases arise vary considerably.

[90] And indeed, one would have thought that those who didn't want to know their genetic fortune should not be forced to know as a result of disclosure requirements for insurance purposes.

v. that they were permitted to seek, with the person's consent, access to appropriate family medical history, diagnostic genetic test results, and to reports from GPs to accurately price the risk from any health information an applicant discloses;
vi. that they would maintain stringent procedures for seeking access to relevant medical information held by a GP or other clinician, agreed between the ABI and the British Medical Association;
vii. they would protect personal medical information in accordance with the ABI Confidentiality Policy; and
viii. they would destroy medical evidence when it was no longer relevant to them.

The classes of insurance to which predictive genetic test results are relevant is confined to life insurance, critical illness and income protection insurance. The moratorium on insurers' use of predictive tests thus made an exception to the principle of disclosure. It allows customers who have taken a predictive genetic test to obtain significant levels of cover without disclosing the results of that test.

> Insurers are only prepared to bear the risks and costs of this non-disclosure, which are spread across the broad pool of policyholders, whilst the number of policies affected by non-disclosure of predictive genetic tests appears to be low. On this basis, the Government and the ABI have agreed that the Moratorium should remain in place.[91]

The Concordat gives customers the right to ask an insurer to provide information on whether, and if so how, a predictive test result has contributed to an underwriting decision. They also have a right of appeal against an underwriting decision and a right to have a complaint dealt with fairly. Ultimately where a contract had been entered into, the insured is entitled to pursue a complaint to the Financial Ombudsman Service or to bring a legal claim.

The Concordat thus seeks to achieve a balance between insureds and insurers in a number of ways. First, whereas now predictive genetic test results are off-limits while uncertainty over incidence remains, pressure is likely to grow if big data is shown to remove some of that uncertainty. Second, until insurers can show that either the number of policies affected by the protected non-disclosure is increasing (something with which big data will assist) or that insurers can track onset of more complex diseases with much greater certainty, the constraints are likely to remain. Unless some system of subsidy, premium restriction or a two-tiered scheme of the sort that characterises the Flood Re arrangement in the UK is introduced, there will be a risk of more extreme segmentation of the risk pool as a result of predictive genetic testing. The need for such a scheme will proceed on the basis that without the identification of good and bad genetic risks to insurers, adverse selection will again lead to claims payments exceeding premium income, not least because – as noted above – those who obtain a clean genetic bill of health may not bother to insure at all. A form of premium subsidy or a two-tier system would thus allow insurers to avoid the losses arising from adverse selection, while mitigating the impact of allowing them to price risk by reference to unchosen genetic traits.

In October 2016, the Committee of Ministers of the Council of Europe issued a Recommendation on the processing of personal health-related data for insurance purposes,

[91] Concordat, 2011, para 24.

including data resulting from genetic tests.[92] The object of the Recommendation – which is not legally binding – is that Member States should take appropriate measures to ensure respect for the fundamental rights of persons, without discrimination, in the context of the insurance contracts covered by this recommendation.[93] The Recommendation sets out a number of principles. Principle 1 requires insurers to justify processing health-related personal data. Principle 4 states that insurers should not require genetic tests for insurance purposes and provides as follows:

> 15. In accordance with the principle laid down in Article 12 of the Convention on Human Rights and Biomedicine, predictive genetic tests must not be carried out for insurance purposes.
>
> 16. Existing predictive data resulting from genetic tests should not be processed for insurance purposes unless specifically authorised by law. If so, their processing should only be allowed after independent assessment of conformity with the criteria laid down in paragraph 5 by type of test used and with regard to a particular risk to be insured.
>
> 17. Existing data from genetic tests from family members of the insured person should not be processed for insurance purposes.

In addition, Member States should recognise the social importance of coverage for certain risks and should, where appropriate, take measures to facilitate affordable access to insurance coverage for persons presenting an increased health-related risk.[94] Although not legally binding, the Recommendation will likely inform the interpretation of the Convention on Human Rights and Biomedicine as well as the European Court of Human Rights' interpretation of Article 8 of the European Convention on Human Rights. The UK has neither signed nor ratified the Convention on Human Rights and Biomedicine.

C. Moral Hazard and the Problem of Data Creep

The limits on what information insurers can ask insureds to provide them with will be tested in another, practical way. The use of connected devices is giving rise to new forms of moral hazard. Take the case of the dog-walker who, each day on his dog-walking rounds, wore 10 separate activity tracking bands belonging to 10 separate clients for whom he provided a dog-walking service. The US health insurer providing health cover to those clients discovered this practice which came about because each insured could benefit from a complete reduction on the annual deductible so long as the insured hit three fitness metrics per day for the policy period, including walking 10,000 steps.[95] This highlights the fact that the adoption by insurers of connected devices to provide

[92] Recommendation CM/Rec(2016)8 https://search.coe.int/cm/Pages/result_details.aspx?ObjectId=09000016806b2c5f.

[93] ibid, para 1.

[94] ibid, para 20.

[95] The average number of steps taken per day by a US citizen is lower than that of the average European citizen: https://well.blogs.nytimes.com/2010/10/19/the-pedometer-test-americans-take-fewer-steps/.

real-time monitoring of risks enables unscrupulous insureds to 'game' the system. On this theme, the Financial Services User Group (FSUG)[96] states:

> there are many ways to 'game' the system and falsify data and information provided online. One can easily attach a pedometer to a dog, trick a fridge into thinking there is 'healthy' food in it, downloading 'healthy cooking apps', create 'fake' shopping lists for healthy foods, 'liking' healthy restaurants, manipulating your geolocation data with an app like Fake GPS to make algorithms believe you are in 'safe' places.[97]

FSUG thus argues that:

> [i]n short, in the 'best' case scenario, with accurate data, vulnerable users will be even more discriminated against, and in an alternative scenario, those who will have technical knowledge will be able to profiteer from the system, putting an extra burden on those who 'play fair'. Indeed, should many people 'cheat' and falsify their data, risk-hedging models will have to take that into account and increase the price of their products to hedge for that risk, making certain services even more expensive.[98]

The Joint Committee of European Supervisory Authorities also noted in its Final Report on Big Data that:

> Some respondents … highlighted the emergence of new moral hazard risks related to the use of Big Data. In particular, they saw a risk, against the backdrop of increased segmentation and price optimisation that some consumers may potentially seek to artificially improve their ratings either by paying online reputation management companies or by tampering with data generated about them, and tailor their profiles with data that is 'helpful' to them.[99]

In order to combat these new forms of moral hazard, it is likely that insurers will seek to impose additional verification requirements to ensure that it is indeed their insureds who are walking 10,000 steps a day and thus genuinely entitled to a reduction in their excess or the premium. In particular, it is likely that insurers will require greater proof in the form of more highly personal, biometric data: whereas one cannot ordinarily tell whether A or B is wearing a self-tracking device that monitors steps, additional verification is available in the form of: (i) assessing the meta-data on a phone to consider whether it was possible that the insured walked 10,000 steps on any given day (if the phone's metadata indicates that it was located at the insured's home all day, the inference is that the insured may not have done the steps); or, more compelling (ii) the use of new activity trackers that record the insured's heart rate variability, a metric that is very personal, or even his breathing rate (which can be correlated to heart rate for even greater personal verification). Insureds who say 'no' to such verification requirements will be excluded from available discounts and ultimately may be excluded from cover.

[96] The FSUG is an expert group set up by the European Commission to pursue the objective of securing high-quality expert input to the Commission's financial services initiatives from representatives of financial service users and from individual financial services experts.

[97] FSUG, p 5, https://ec.europa.eu/info/sites/info/files/file_import/1606-big-data-on-financial-services_en_0.pdf.

[98] ibid, p 5.

[99] Joint Committee of the European Supervisory Authorities, Final Report on Big Data, 15 March 2018 https://www.esma.europa.eu/sites/default/files/library/jc-2018-04_joint_committee_final_report_on_big_data.pdf, para 43.

As more and more individuals provide biometric information to avail of these offers, the giving of this information will become normalised. In that way, insurers will, over time and by default, obtain greater amounts of very personal data.

D. Segmentation and Price Discrimination

Risk segmentation leads to some insureds paying a higher price for the same cover than others. All risk classification within insurance burdens some individuals or groups more than others. Differential pricing is inherent to insurance. Price discrimination (or optimisation) is defined as the sale of different units of the same product at price differentials that do not correspond to any cost difference. The most common form is the sale of identical products to different customers at different prices. Charging customers different prices that reflect different costs is not discriminatory. If Insured A presents a much greater risk than Insured B, then if the insurer charges A £200 and B £100 for the same cover, there is no price discrimination: the different prices respond to different – albeit contingent – costs. Price discrimination can operate in three ways.

First-degree price discrimination occurs where the seller charges each buyer the maximum amount they are willing to pay. This is rare because it requires the seller to have perfect information about each customer. Although rare, big data is enabling sellers to have a much more accurate idea of what each of us is prepared to pay than once they did. Personalised pricing is becoming more common in online markets as a result.[100]

Second-degree price discrimination occurs when a company offers a selection of deals and allows each customer to choose the one that most suits them. This is common practice across a wide range of markets. Take the example of coffee: offering fair trade coffee for a premium price (albeit where the uplift largely ends up in the coffee seller's coffers) allows concerned citizens prepared to pay more to be identified as such.[101] As a further example of second-degree price discrimination, mobile phone users can choose from a variety of packages with different bundles and different prices. No one suggests that these practices – which allow coffee and mobile phone sellers to optimise prices – are problematic.

Third-degree price discrimination, like second-degree price discrimination, is practised because of the seller's lack of information about the price sensitivity of its customers. Sellers segment its market and price each segment differently. Student discounts and regional pricing variations are examples of third degree price discrimination. The seller charges different prices to consumers with different observable characteristics (such as age, gender or location).

Economic theory shows that in many circumstances, price discrimination enhances economic welfare and efficiency by increasing total market output compared with a situation of uniform pricing. It allows sales to customers that would not occur if the

[100] See OFT Paper, 'Personalised Pricing: Increasing Transparency to Improve Trust in the Market', May 2013.

[101] This example comes from T Harford, *The Undercover Economist* (London, Abacus, 2006) 38–40.

price charged to each was the same.[102] But generating more sales (output) usually occurs by charging less to the more price-sensitive customer who would not otherwise buy the product at the previously uniform price.

Insurers may charge different prices for the very same policy (being a product that has the same cover, exclusions and excess) supplied to two insureds whose risk profile is identical. Big data can identify people who are less price sensitive (as can be gleaned from online and offline purchasing data) and/or whose behaviour over time shows inertia in the sense that they do not switch between service providers. Insurers could use that information to offer different prices to two consumers who present the same level of risk and who are being offered precisely the same policy, but where one is revealed to be price sensitive and shops around whereas the other is less so and/or inert. Is it right that the latter may be charged more on the basis of this non-risk-related information? On this issue, the FCA's Andrew Bailey observes that:

> There is a choice for society – do we permit this sort of behaviour to go on, or not? … [O]ur view is that we should not. Why? If you take the argument apart, it is because we think that to do so would be to exploit a feature of individual behaviour which should not be exploited in this way. The reason is either because some of the public act on the basis of ignorance or naivety (and I am not using either of these two words in a critical or pejorative context) which should not be exploited, or because some of the consumers involved are more vulnerable (in whatever way) and cannot reasonably be expected to act in a way that prevents the exploitation of the information on their behaviours.[103]

The FCA's concern over pricing practices arises because insurers take into account information that is neither risk- nor cost-related in determining the price of cover. The FCA observed that 'the models used to determine prices will not clearly label which factors relate to risk, which have no relation to risk, and which have some relation but not to the extent factored into the pricing model'.[104]

Insurers can identify to some extent how price-sensitive an insured is by assessing the scope of the cover sought (comprehensive vs third party), the level of additional benefits (or add-ons) that the insured requires (eg no excess, wider scope of cover, preparedness to pay up front etc). But the first two of these features impact on the scope of the cover (and thus impact on the insurers' contingent costs). When considering whether price discrimination is problematic, the hypothesis above assumed that the two differently priced policies were otherwise identical, where the cover, exclusions and excesses were the same for two different insureds with the same risk profile. So although

[102] For a clear discussion of price discrimination in a competition law context see Niels, Jenkins and Kavanagh, *Economics for Competition Lawyers* 2nd edn (Oxford, OUP, 2016).

[103] 'The Challenges for insurance and regulators in a Big Data world', speech by Andrew Bailey, Chief Executive of the FCA on 22 November 2016: https://www.fca.org.uk/news/speeches/challenges-insurance-regulators-big-data-world. The National Association of Insurance Commissioners (NAIC) is a US regulator created and governed by insurance regulators from all 50 states. In its 2015 paper on the subject, the NAIC recommended that consideration of the following factors are inconsistent with the statutory requirements that rates shall not be unfairly discriminatory: price elasticity of demand, propensity to shop for insurance, retention adjustment at an individual level, and a policyholder's propensity to ask questions or file complaints: www.naic.org/documents/committees_c_catf_related_price_optimization_white_paper.pdf, p 16.

[104] para 1.19. And noted further that, for example, data concerning a consumer's income and credit rating may help to predict both risk and sensitivity to price.

the insured's ability to seek more extensive cover and add-ons is a means of enabling the customer to signal his price sensitivity, there cannot be price discrimination if the insurance products (and insurers' potential costs) are different. The question then is whether a first-party policy falls within the same product market as a third-party policy and whether the provision of additional cover, benefits and add-ons renders a policy a different product from one that does not have those additions. If these policies all fall within the same market, then an issue of price discrimination arises; if they don't, then it won't.

Economics offers insight on how to determine whether two products are comparable for, amongst other things, price discrimination purposes, by asking whether they fall within the same product market. Most products are to some extent substitutable. Market definition tries to separate close substitutes from more distant substitutes. To test whether two products compete against each other such that they might be said to be substitutes that fall within the same product market, one should hypothetically monopolise the supply of one of those products (eg first-party motor cover), imagine imposing a Small but Significant Non-Transitory Increase in Price,[105] and consider whether that increase would lead those customers to purchase, for example, third-party cover. If so, the types of policy will fall within the same market. That will, in each particular case, be a matter of expert economic evidence.

If two policies are in two different product markets, insurers charging different prices for them can avoid complaints of price discrimination. However, if they are not, regulators will seek to use their consumer protection powers to prevent insureds who otherwise present the same risk profile being charged different prices for the same cover because of inertia or vulnerability. Whether insurers are permitted to charge more for the same cover to those who are less price-sensitive but not because of evidence of vulnerability or non-switching behaviour will depend on whether the FCA's proposal applies to all insureds to avoid the potentially difficult task of differentiating vulnerable or inert insureds from those who might be thought to be better able to look after their own interests.

IV. Conclusions

All of the above developments – and the issues which accompany those developments – ultimately stem from the fact that big data enables insurers to know more about each individual risk than was ever previously possible. Real-time monitoring of individual risk through connected devices creates new opportunities for insurers to impose terms and conditions that enable them to tailor the scope of cover in response to the occurrence of real-time events. Can a motor insurer impose conditions excluding cover at certain speeds or if the car is driven or parked in certain locations? Can a household insurer suspend cover while a connected fire alarm indicates that its battery needs to be changed? Can a health insurer increase the premium if its insured's activity tracker

[105] The so-called SSNIP test.

indicates that they have not walked more than 3,000 steps a day for the past month? The extent to which such terms and conditions could be imposed compatibly with the law of insurance is the subject of chapter four.

On the assumption that algorithms continue to be used to profile individual risk and connected devices continue to be used to monitor those risks in real time, a further question arises as to what the consequences will be of the continued erosion, as between insured and insurer, of the information asymmetries in relation to risk. That of course depends on the relevance of information asymmetries as a justification for existing legal principle: if the traditional existence of information asymmetries as between the insured and insurer provided the justification for the imposition of duties of good faith and, more particularly, duties of disclosure, then the disappearance of such asymmetries would suggest that those duties may no longer be justified. Moreover, even if the information asymmetry between insured and insurer previously justified duties of disclosure on the insured, the question arises as to what the rationale is for insurers' duty of good faith disclosure: does it arise only where, unusually, insurers happen to know something about the risk that the insured does not? Does it relate to knowledge about the risk at all, as opposed, for example, to knowledge about the nature of the insurance product? If information asymmetries provide the justification for duties of good faith on insureds and insurers, and those duties relate to their respective knowledge of the proposed risk, then that would (i) explain the historic paucity of cases that consider the nature and scope of the duty as it falls upon insurers (since ordinarily they will not hold the information surplus) and (ii) might lead to a very significant expansion of that duty in a world in which big data enables insurers to potentially know more about the insured risk than the insured might be able to provide himself. These questions are explored in detail in chapter five below.

PART II

Big Data and the Principles of Insurance Law

4

Big Data and the Permissible Constraints on the Scope of Cover

It is one thing to identify the techniques by which insurers might in principle profile prospective insureds; it is another to consider to what extent insurers can use that information in relation to the scope of the cover they offer. Having considered how big data analytics enable insurers to more accurately evaluate individual risks, this chapter considers how that data might be used to more precisely delineate the scope of the cover offered. The scope of any insurance policy is determined by the scope of the insuring clause together with the imposition of specific endorsements or exclusions. The efficiency gains are again clear: not only can poorer risks be priced more accurately or excluded in their entirety; insurers can additionally protect themselves from claims by identifying the behaviours most likely to lead to insured loss and seek to impose terms that either encourage alternative behaviours or which remove liability for those behaviours from the scope of the cover. In that regard, insurers can not only more specifically tailor the terms of the policy before the risk incepts; but as big data permits insurers to monitor insured activities (such as motor and health risks) in real time, data about an insured's behaviours in principle permits insurers to vary the scope of the cover by way of real-time variations, including by way of terms that will operate contingently on the occurrence of real-time events. Take, for example, a telematics motor policy. An insurer might include terms to the effect that the policy will terminate if certain driving behaviours (eg excessive speeding) are recorded by the 'black box' as having taken place on three occasions. Or, upon renewal, and in light of the analysis conducted on the insured's driving in the previous policy period, insurers might seek to exclude cover for certain geographical locations, or impose warranties on how the insured will drive at certain times or places, compliance with which will again capable of being tracked in real time. The accumulated data over the policy period also allows insurers to adjust the scope of the insuring clause on renewal as well as adjusting the premium. Examples of telematics policies that insurers are currently using are discussed below.

This chapter begins by considering the terms and conditions that insurers might use in order to maximise the utility of real-time risk-related data. It then seeks to identify the types of terms that insurers might wish to impose, availing of the knowledge acquired both pre and post inception. It then considers the extent to which insurers are permitted to impose terms that contingently alter the scope of the cover within the policy period where real-time data provides a verifiable basis upon which insurers might come off risk in the course of the policy period. It does so by looking first at some general legal constraints which preclude insurers from imposing terms whose operation might overly restrict the cover provided. It then considers how terms that have been used in motor and home and contents risks have been constrained by the law applicable to those specific risks.

I. Terms of Insurance Contracts

The key terms of an insurance contract are either conditions (of various kinds) or warranties. A condition in insurance law can either impose an obligation on the insured to act in a particular way or stipulate a contingency upon which the validity of the policy or any subsequent claim may depend. A warranty in insurance law is a promise by the insured that a particular fact is or will remain true or that the insured will behave in a certain way.

A. Insurance Conditions

Conditions fall within one of three categories: conditions precedent[1] to the validity of the policy or the attachment of the risk; conditions precedent to liability under the policy; and other, ordinary conditions.

i. Conditions Precedent to the Validity of a Policy or Attachment of the Risk

A condition may be precedent to the commencement of the contract, absent the fulfilment of which there is no contract. A condition precedent to the attachment of the risk assumes a contract has been entered into, but absent fulfilment of which will mean the insurer never comes on risk. In each case, insurers cannot be liable for loss without the fulfilment of those conditions. Moreover, each type of condition can only be imposed prior to the contract having been entered into and cannot be imposed to remove the insured's accrued rights.

Three standard conditions relevant to the use of big data are conditions as to (i) the provision of further information by the insured; (ii) satisfactory presentation of the risk; and (iii) the receipt of a satisfactory proposal form. These conditions are likely to be

[1] Insurers can make clear that a condition is a condition precedent in a number of ways: (i) it can describe the condition as a condition precedent (see, eg, *Gan Insurance v Tai Ping Insurance (No 2)* [2002] Lloyd's Rep IR 612). This will be so unless on a proper construction of the condition, it appears that the condition cannot operate as a condition precedent, eg where the obligation in question is to be performed significantly later than the loss occurs); (ii) a general clause may render all, or certain stipulated policies conditions as precedent to, eg, liability (see, eg, *Pilkington United Kingdom Ltd v GCU Insurance Plc* [2004] Lloyd's Rep IR 891; (iii) the consequences of the breach of the condition may only be consistent with the condition being a condition precedent (see, eg, *AXA Insurance UK Plc v Thermonex Ltd* [2012] EWHC B10 (Mercantile)); or (iv) the wording or significance of the condition is otherwise such as to indicate that it could only have been intended to operate as a condition precedent (eg *Eagle Star v Cresswell* [2004] Lloyd's Rep IR 437).

much less relevant in future where insurers will have most if not all relevant details about the proposed insured and the proposed risk such that proposal forms will either be dispensed with or prepared by insurers and returned to the insured to confirm their accuracy.

ii. Conditions Precedent to the Insurer's Liability

Failure to fulfil these conditions means that the insured cannot make a claim to recover under the policy. Policies often contain conditions requiring the insured to take reasonable care, or to adopt certain measures to mitigate risk or protect the subject-matter of the insurance. Some of these conditions may be general in the sense that the insurer can have no liability at all until they are fulfilled. That would be true of a condition requiring the payment of premium whereby no claims can be made until payment is received.[2] Conditions precedent to liability may also operate such as to suspend the insurer's liability but only in respect of claims to which the breach related but not to other claims to which the breach did not relate.[3] At common law, no distinction was drawn between risk conditions and non-risk conditions.

iii. Ordinary Conditions

Policies often contain conditions not expressed to be conditions precedent but which cover similar issues to those which are so expressed. Such conditions are directed to the conduct of the insured during the policy period and deal with matters such as increases in risk and taking reasonable care. That these conditions are not expressed to be precedent to insurers' liability will have an impact on the available remedies for their breach. The policy may stipulate what the consequences of breach may be but if it fails to do so, this will be determined by ordinary common law principles depending on whether the breach is repudiatory (such as to entitle insurers to terminate) or not. That will depend on how fundamental the breach is, which will be determined either by reference to the nature of the condition itself, or the seriousness of the consequences of the breach if the term is innominate.[4] If an insurer (correctly) elects to treat the policy as repudiated, the insurer will have a full defence to any claim for losses occurring after the date of the insured's repudiatory breach. Alternatively, insurers can elect to affirm the policy and instead sue for damages for breach.

It will be important to know whether a condition is a fundamental or minor term. Insurers would be wise to draft terms to make it clear what conditions are regarded as fundamental. Absent an express stipulation, conditions will be classified as fundamental only exceptionally. One example of where a condition was held to be fundamental came in the case of *Svenska Handelsbanken v Sun Alliance & London Insurance Plc*.[5]

[2] *Aspen Insurance UK Ltd v Pectel Ltd* [2009] Lloyd's Rep IR 440.

[3] *Kazakstan Wool Processors (Europe) Ltd v Nederlandsche Credietverzekering Maatschappij NV* [2000] Lloyd's Rep IR 371.

[4] The intermediate term recognised in *Hongkong Fir Shipping Co Ltd v Kawasaki Kisen Kaisaha Ltd* [1962] 2 QB 26.

[5] [1996] 1 Lloyd's Rep 519.

In that case, the insured bank lent money in the course of a refinancing operation, where the funds loaned were secured by commercial mortgage indemnity policies,[6] some of which were underwritten by the defendant insurers. Insurers sought to avoid the policies in part because of the bank's failure to undertake a proper credit/risk analysis of the refinancing transactions. The court held that the obligation to investigate the credit risk posed by the transaction was fundamental, the breach of which released insurers from liability for the loss. That raises the question of whether, in a motor policy that operated by way of telematics, a condition not expressed to be precedent to liability, but which nevertheless required an insured to drive in a particular way, is sufficiently fundamental, the breach of which would be evidence that the insured no longer wished to be bound by the agreement.

It will be more common for standard conditions to be found to be innominate terms such that insurers' entitlement to treat the contract as having been repudiated will turn on the seriousness of the breach. The court will then consider the extent to which insurers are prejudiced by the breach or whether it could be remedied by an action in damages. Breach of claims clauses will rarely be held to entitle insurers to treat the policy as having been terminated.[7] Breach of clauses going to the risk itself may be more amenable to the contention that insurers are entitled to treat the contract as having been terminated, but even then much more often than not the courts are likely to find that the breach gives rise to no more than a claim in damages (where insurers will have to pay the insured's claim but seek to deduct from the value of the claim the extent of their own loss caused by the insured's breach of the condition). In any damages claim insurers will have to show what would have happened but for the breach and that that breach caused insurers' loss. These cases thus become loss of chance claims, where the courts will assess the likelihood of compliance making a difference to the risk materialising.[8]

B. Insurance Warranties

A warranty is defined by the Marine Insurance Act 1906 (MIA 1906), s 33(1) as 'a promissory warranty, that is to say, a warranty by which the assured undertakes that some particular thing shall or shall not be done or that some condition shall be fulfilled, or whereby he affirms or negatives the existence of a particular state of facts'. In other words, a warranty encompasses a promise by the insured to do or not do certain acts

[6] Which thus amounted to a form of commercial credit insurance.

[7] *Alfred McAlpine Ltd v BAI (Run-off) Ltd* [2000] Lloyd's Rep IR 352; *K/S Merc-Skandia XXXXII v Certain Lloyd's Underwriters* [2001] Lloyd's Rep IR 802.

[8] See, eg, *Hussain v Brown* (No 2) [1996] 1 Lloyd's Rep 627, where the insured breached an increase of risk notification clause by failing to notify insurers that the insured premises had become unoccupied. The premises were then damaged by fire. Insurers argued that had the notification been given, they would have inspected and insisted upon the installation of additional security such as to have prevented the loss. The Court concluded that there would have been a 50% chance of the fire being averted had the condition been complied with and reduced the insured's claim for indemnity accordingly.

and/or a promise that a certain state of affairs is true. Warranties may be sub-divided between present warranties and continuing warranties. Colinvaux gives the following as examples of each:[9]

> Present warranties – which operate at inception only – contain the following promises:
>
> (1) A promise that a state of affairs does or does not exist. In this regard insurers are free to specify conditions that must be warranted if a risk is to attach. For example, in relation to health cover the insured might be required to undergo a medical examination;
> (2) A promise that the insured has or has not acted in a certain way; e.g. in relation to motor cover the insured might be required to warrant that he has not been convicted of certain driving offences; and
> (3) A promise that the insured holds a particular belief.
>
> Non-compliance with a present warranty prevents the risk from attaching. They therefore must be complied with in full at inception.
>
> Continuing warranties contain obligations that apply post-contractually, i.e. only once the risk has incepted and include:
>
> (1) A promise that a state of affairs will continue to exist or will not come into being during the currency of the policy;
> (2) A promise that the insured will, or will not, act in a stated way during the currency of the policy;
> (3) A promise that the insured intends to act or to refrain from acting in a particular fashion during the currency of the policy.

As a continuing warranty applies to the insured's conduct after the risk has attached, breach of warranty may entitle insurers to refuse to pay any claim that relates to that breach.

At common law, the consequences of the insured giving a warranty were of enormous import: the insured was guaranteeing the truth of his statement and undertook to ensure exact compliance.[10] Prior to the reforms of insurance law in 2012 and 2015, breach of warranty automatically terminated the policy, even if the warranty was not material to the risk and even if its breach did not in any way contribute to the insured's loss. Their application was particularly inapposite and thus particularly harsh in the context of consumer insurance, to which these principles were extended.

The law relating to present warranties – and the effect of their breach – was fundamentally altered by CIDRA 2012, s 6 and IA 2015, s 9. In the context of consumer and business insurance respectively, the provisions prevent insurers from requiring insureds to warrant the correctness of statements made to insurers. IA 2015, s 9(2) thus provides that representations in connection with a proposed business insurance contract are

> not capable of being converted into a warranty by means of any provision of the non-consumer insurance contract (or of the terms of the variation), or of any other contract (and whether by declaring the representation to form the basis of the contract or otherwise).

This has the effect of abolishing the operation of 'basis' clauses by which insurers had previously required the insured to warrant the truth of all statements made as to

[9] *Colinvaux's Law of Insurance* 11th edn (London, Sweet and Maxwell, 2016), para 8-041 (precis).
[10] Marine Insurance Act 1906, s 33; and see, eg, *Trickett v Queensland Insurance* [1936] AC 159.

the risk[11] by way of a declaration made at the end of the proposal form.[12] Now, any statements made by the insured in connection with their proposed insurance will thus be treated as a representation rather than a warranty.[13] As regards future warranties, IA 2015, s 10 – which applies to consumer and business insurance – abolishes the rule that breach of such warranties brings the contract to an end automatically and replaces it instead with the principle that the risk is merely suspended during the period of breach. Its effect is that insurers are not liable for any loss occurring after the un-remedied breach of the warranty.[14]

IA 2015, s 11 – which not only applies to consumer and business insurance but applies to warranties as well as conditions – has the effect that an insurer cannot rely on a breach of any term unless it is related to the loss.[15] It provides:

> (1) This section applies to a term (express or implied) of a contract of insurance, other than a term defining the risk as a whole, if compliance with it would tend to reduce the risk of one or more of the following—
>
> (a) loss of a particular kind,
> (b) loss at a particular location,
> (c) loss at a particular time.
>
> (2) If a loss occurs, and the term has not been complied with, the insurer may not rely on the non-compliance to exclude, limit or discharge its liability under the contract for the loss if the insured satisfies subsection (3).
> (3) The insured satisfies this subsection if it shows that the non-compliance with the term could not have increased the risk of the loss which actually occurred in the circumstances in which it occurred.
> (4) This section may apply in addition to section 10.[16]

[11] At common law, breach of a warranty arising out of a basis of contract clause entitled the insurer to refuse to make a payment under the policy: *Genesis Housing Association Ltd v Liberty Syndicate Management Ltd* [2013] EWCA Civ 1173; [2013] Bus LR 1399.

[12] The words of s 6 of the 2012 Act and s 9 of the 2015 Act do not appear to merely prohibit basis clauses but any provision which seeks to convert a representation into a warranty. Therefore, on or after 6 April 2013 a statement in an application for an insurance policy cannot be a warranty breach of which entitles the insurer to avoid the policy: see *Ashfaq v International Insurance Co of Hanover Plc* [2017] EWCA Civ 357.

[13] s 6 of the 2012 Act and s 9 of the 2015 Act do not apply to warranties imposed by insurers as to present or future states of affairs or conduct (as opposed to the insured's representations as to those matters, which are caught by those provisions). Representations are therefore to be assessed by reference to the rules on presentation of the risk.

[14] This is made subject to IA 2015, s 10(4)(a), which provides that the insurers will be liable to the insured for a loss occurring during the period of the breach as long as it was attributable to some event that happened before the breach. By the same token, s 10(4)(b) provides that insurers will not be liable where the loss occurs after the warranty has been remedied but attributable to an event that occurred during the period of breach.

[15] These provisions were necessary to address three particular criticisms of the common law, and in particular the operation of warranties, given the fact that their breach led to automatic discharge of liability, the lack of any requirement of a connection between the breach and the insured's loss and the insured's inability to remedy the breach. IA 2015 s 11(4) states that s 11 may apply in addition to s 10. They will operate together in circumstances where the insured is in breach of warranty at the time when the insured loss occurs such that although the suspensory provision in s 10 is of no assistance to the insured, he is able to argue that the breach is irrelevant to the loss for the purposes of s 11; if such an argument can be maintained, insurers can refuse to pay the claim.

[16] s 11 does not apply to non-risk conditions which will continue to be enforceable in full subject only to the application of consumer protection legislation (either under the CRA 2015 or the obligations on insurers pursuant to the Insurance Conduct of Business (ICOBS) rules, issued under the Financial Services and Markets Act 2000 (FSMA 2000).

As the Explanatory Notes to the IA 2015 observe, the purpose of s 11 is to enable an objective assessment of the purpose of the policy provision, by considering what sorts of loss might be likely to occur as a consequence of the term not being complied with.[17] Section 11(1) effectively creates a distinction between terms that delimit the scope of the risk and terms that limit or exclude liability as discussed further below. Section 11(2) appears to draw a distinction between a failure to comply with a term excluding or limiting liability (that is, by way of an act or omission by the insured) but where the risk has otherwise attached, and an exclusion or limitation that arises as a result of a state of affairs, and where the failure entails that the risk has not attached or goes to the definition of the risk as a whole. In the latter case, the insured will not be able to rely on IA 2015, s 11. The purpose of s 11(3) is to prevent an insurer from relying on the failure of the insured to comply with a policy term where the loss that occurred is entirely unrelated to any non-compliance with that term.[18]

Although these reforms relate to remedies for breach of warranties, it is still necessary to understand what constitutes a present warranty and what constitutes a continuing warranty since (i) they operate at different times in relation to the policy, and (ii) insurers can still impose warranties as to present or future states of affairs or conduct. A policy may of course expressly stipulate what the warranty is and/or when it is required to be complied with. However, absent such clear indication, the nature of the warranty will be a matter of interpretation.[19] Factors that will impact on that interpretative question include whether requiring continuing compliance by the insured is feasible; whether a continuing warranty is appropriate to the particular risk; and whether the insurer requires continuing protection. And so a statement as to the address at which a motor vehicle would be garaged was found to be a continuing warranty.[20] However, a statement that premises were fitted with a security alarm – where the alarm subsequently stopped working – was held to be a present warranty only;[21] so too was a statement as to the future navigation route of a vessel.[22] Clearly cases as to whether the insured has warranted a fact will turn on the precise language and circumstances of the particular risk. In a world where risk can be monitored – and recalibrated – in real time, warranties as to facts such as whether a building is alarmed or where a vehicle would be driven may be more likely to amount to continuing warranties, particularly now that the harsh consequences of the common law have been removed by statute.

[17] Explanatory Notes, para 93.

[18] The Law Commission has explained that this is not a backward-looking test of causation, but rather a forward-looking assessment of whether non-compliance could have increased the risk of the loss that actually occurred whether or not it actually did so. The actual words of s 11(3), especially the concluding words – 'the loss which actually occurred in the circumstances in which it occurred – seems, however, to introduce a causal test.

[19] And use of the word 'warranty' may not itself be conclusive if the court considers that the provision in question is not capable of constituting a warranty: *Marina Offshore Pts Ltd v China Insurance Co (Singapore) Pte Ltd* [2007] 1 Lloyd's Rep 66; the word may also be disregarded if a court considers that it would be contrary to the parties' actual intention: *De Maurier (Jewels) Ltd v Bastion Insurance Co* [1967] 2 Lloyd's Rep 550.

[20] *Dawsons Ltd v Bonnin* [1922] AC 413.

[21] *Hussain v Brown* [1996] 1 Lloyd's Rep 627.

[22] *Grant v Aetna Insurance* (1862) 15 Moo PC 516.

Absent express wording, a term specifying that its breach will entail the automatic termination of the risk will indicate that the term is a warranty.[23] Further, Rix LJ in *HIH Casualty and General Insurance Ltd v New Hampshire Insurance Co*[24] listed three possible tests for a warranty: (i) did the term go to the root of the contract; (ii) was it descriptive of the risk or did it bear materially on the risk; and (iii) would damages be an inadequate or unsatisfactory remedy for breach. However, given the restrictive approach that the courts have taken to whether a particular warranty is a present or continuing warranty, insurers should, for the avoidance of doubt, stipulate whether something that the policy requires is a present or continuing warranty.[25]

II. General Constraints on Policy Terms

A. Increase in and Change of Risk: Limits in the Scope of the Initial Cover

In considering terms that might, in real time, regulate the scope of the cover in light of events that occur during the policy, it is worth recalling how the law of insurance differentiates between increases in the risk insured and changes to the nature of the risk during the policy period absent such terms. In particular, in circumstances where insurers can, with the benefit of data from connected devices, assess the way in which risk might be increasing or even changing over the course of the policy period, insurers may now seek to include terms defining the boundary between an increase in risk on the one hand and a change of risk on the other, and thus be able not only to stipulate when it will no longer be liable, but will be able to ascertain in real time when that moment occurs.

Insurance law distinguishes between an increase in the risk insured and a change to the risk insured. In non-marine insurance, increase in risk (and thus the prospect of loss) after the commencement of cover does not affect the insurer's obligation under the policy.[26] By contrast, a change in the risk involves an alteration to the very nature of the subject-matter of the risk insured, and will lead to the automatic discharge of the policy. If the increase in risk was envisaged by the terms of the initial cover, then the materialisation of that increased risk will fall to be covered.

i. Increase in Risk

Insurers can seek to avoid becoming liable for increased risks by requiring the insured to warrant that the risk will not increase and/or that he will not undertake certain forms of conduct. For example, in life insurance policies, insureds are often required

[23] Subject, now, to IA 2015, ss 10–11. An example of such a stipulation can be found in *Sceales v Scanlan* (1843) 6 LRIR 367.

[24] [2001] Lloyd's Rep 161.

[25] In that regard, non-marine warranties can only be express and cannot be implied: *Euro-Diam Ltd v Bathurst* [1988] 2 All ER 23.

[26] *Shaw v Robberds* (1837) 6 A & E 75.

to warrant that they will not take part in dangerous sports. The same result can be achieved by providing that the policy will terminate in those events, albeit that any such provision is now moderated by IA 2015, s 10, which merely suspends liability for the period of the unremedied breach.[27] Insurers may also impose an obligation on the insured to notify insurers of any increase to the risk, together with a reservation of rights as to the alteration of terms and/or an increase in the premium payable.

Increase in risk clauses will be interpreted to reflect the distinction between a mere increase and a fundamental change in risk: *Kausar v Eagle Star Insurance Co Ltd*.[28] It has been observed that the rationale underpinning that approach is that the insured should not be under onerous continuing duties[29] in the absence of clear wording.[30] This approach was adopted by David Steel J in *Scottish Coal Co Ltd v Royal and Sun Alliance Plc*,[31] where the increase of risk clause stated that in the event of 'material change in the original risk … the policy shall be avoided unless the continuance be agreed by endorsement signed by the company'. The judge applied the *Kausar* principle holding that there was only a material change in the risk if there was a fundamental change to its nature and not simply an increase in risk. Much will turn on the relationship of the increased risk and the wording of the clause by which it is governed. In *Ansari v New India Assurance Ltd*[32] the increase in risk clause provided:

> The insurance shall cease to be in force if there is any material alteration to the Premises or Business or any material change on the facts stated in the Proposal Form or other facts supplied to the Insurer unless the Insurer agrees in writing to continue the insurance.

The premises had been used for the sale of kitchens and were protected by an automatic sprinkler system. The premises were let and the tenant instead sold motorbikes, having disabled the sprinkler system. The Court of Appeal found that the insured had represented that the premises were protected by a properly functioning sprinkler system and not simply that one had been installed, and further found that the disabling of the system amounted to a 'material change', where materiality did not mean the threshold applicable in relation to duties of disclosure, but rather that the change had a significant bearing on the risk as compared to that which had been stated by the insured in the proposal form. The case highlights the distinction between a present warranty and future or continuing warranty. A present warranty in *Ansari v New India Assurance Ltd* would only have required the sprinkler system to be operative at the inception of the risk whereas a continuing warranty would have required the insured to maintain a properly functioning sprinkler system throughout the period of the insurance, a more demanding obligation. Clear words will be necessary where the insurer wishes to obtain a continuing, as opposed to a present warranty. The same will apply to increase of risk clauses, such as to require the insured to warrant that there will be no increase

[27] See the discussion of the IA 2015, s 10, below.
[28] [2000] Lloyd's Rep IR 154.
[29] Including by way of having to give insurers day-to-day notice of potential changes in use or risk.
[30] Colinvaux, above n 9, para 5-027.
[31] [2008] Lloyd's Rep IR 718.
[32] [2009] Lloyd's Rep IR 562.

in risk throughout the duration of the policy.[33] In light of s 10 of the IA 2015, any such clause will, if imposed, lead to the suspension of insurers' liability for the duration of the increase in risk.

ii. Change of Risk

A change of risk that meets the requisite threshold will be a risk different from that described and covered by the policy and will entitle insurers to be discharged. Much will depend on how the risk insured against is described in the policy. The subject-matter to be insured is the most important way in which the scope of the cover is delineated. If a motorist seeks cover to drive in a particular vehicle only, he will not be covered for loss arising out of his use of another vehicle. If a ship owner obtains cover for a particular voyage, by way of a particular route, he will not be covered for losses occurring on an alternative route or within excluded waters. If the risk run is different from that originally agreed, the risk will not attach and insurers will not be liable for losses arising. That was so, prior to the IA 2015, even if the alteration in the subject-matter did not necessarily increase the risk of loss and even where the alteration was beyond the insured's control. Changes of risk may occur at the outset of a policy where the risk in question never met the description of the risk in the policy, in which case the risk will never attach,[34] and those where the change in the nature of the risk incurs after the risk has attached.[35]

B. Clauses Providing for Variation of Cover

There is a difference between a clause which varies (or which is a prerequisite to the variation of) the scope of the cover but where that variation (if agreed) was not provided for at the outset of the contract of insurance, and one where the scope of the cover is varied during the policy albeit where that variation was, contingently, provided for. Examples of the former include simple variations where the scope of the cover is amended to reflect the change in risk during the policy period,[36] endorsements, or additional premium clauses.[37] Various notice clauses operate as potential precursors to a

[33] See, eg, *Beauchamp v National Mutual Indemnity Insurance Co* [1937] 3 All ER 19; and *Farnham v Royal Insurance* [1976] 2 Lloyd's Rep 437.

[34] See, eg, *Newcastle Fire Insurance Co v Macmorran & Co* (1815) 3 Dow 255.

[35] There are decisions that go both ways given the policy wording and the changes in question; an example of a change held to be meet the threshold was *Swiss Reinsurance Co v United India Insurance Co Ltd* [2005] Lloyd's Rep IR 341, where an all risks policy in relation to the construction of a power plant did not cover the risks left by unoccupancy of the plant when the contractors walked off site not having received payment.

[36] *Lishman v Northern Maritime Insurance Co* (1875) LR 10 CP 179; *Commercial Union Assurance Co Ltd v The Niger Co Ltd* (1922) 13 Ll L Rep 75. At common law, the extent of the alteration to the risk will impact commensurately on the extent of the duty of disclosure that must be given.

[37] The Insured may be contractually obliged to give information to insurers about prospective changes to the extent of the risk covered under the insurance. *Black King Shipping Corporation v Massie; The Litsion Pride* [1985] 1 Lloyd's Rep 437 concerned a war risks policy that contained clauses excluding certain geographical areas from cover, entry to which required the insured to give notice to the insurers whereupon additional premium would be payable.

variation. Insurance contracts may contain clauses obliging the insured to advise insurers of circumstances that increase the risk of the insured peril occurring, failing which (and prior to the IA 2015) the insured would not be covered or the insurer would be entitled to avoid.[38] Marine policies often contained 'held covered' clauses that enabled an insured to extend cover by giving notice to insurers. The additional cover would attract an additional premium and such clauses may also permit insurers to impose additional terms.[39]

With the advent of telematics and connected devices, each of which permit live tracking of insured activities, insurers may now seek to make increasing use of conditions precedent and warranties to tailor the scope of cover contingently on the occurrence of events that can be monitored in real time. There is no conceptual difference between the nature of conditions precedent or warranties pre and post big data. Rather, big data provides insurers the means of more accurately and efficiently tailoring and monitoring cover in real time without the need for either (i) notice of change of circumstance clauses or (ii) the parties having to reach an agreement to vary the cover. As noted above, conditions precedent and warranties each seek to circumscribe the extent of an insurer's risk: failure to adhere to a condition precedent will mean an insurer does not come on risk or will be discharged from liability; warranties protect insurers by requiring insureds to promise that a certain state of affairs will prevail or they will not engage in certain types of activity. Big data analytics provide a basis upon which insurers can accurately track events the subject of conditions precedent or warranties and thus to know in real time whether the insured is complying and therefore whether or not the insured is either on risk and/or potentially liable for insured loss. Insurers might now seek to delineate cover more precisely by reference to times covered and not covered; geographical locations covered or not covered; the condition of the subject-matter of the insurance and so on. However, these terms are now subject to the general constraint imposed by s 11 of the IA 2015.

Section 11(1) draws a distinction between terms 'defining the risk as a whole' and those which do not, and applies only to the latter. It was noted above that s 11(1) effectively creates a distinction between terms that delimit the scope of the risk and limitations or exclusions of liability.[40] The question thus arises as to what terms define the scope of the risk as a whole in contrast to those which merely carve out exclusions or exemptions from liability. It may, in that regard, be too simplistic to describe s 11(1) of the IA 2015 as positing a distinction between risk and non-risk clauses. The section clearly applies to terms that circumscribe the risk (and thus insurers' liability) insofar as it applies to terms, compliance with which 'would tend to reduce the risk' of insured loss of a particular kind, at a particular location or at a particular time. But the reference to terms that tend to reduce the risk is what leads to the conclusion that the section applies to terms that limit or exclude liability; that is, it encompasses terms that carve out the

[38] *Kausar v Eagle Star* [1997] CLC 129.

[39] *Overseas Commodities Ltd v Style* [1958] 1 Lloyd's Rep 456.

[40] Plainly clauses relating to the notification of loss or the fact that third party claims have been made are terms that do not define the risk as a whole. They do not define the risk at all. Rather, they are designed to enable insurers to investigate the loss as to which various consequential claims clauses will impose duties on the insured as regards not admitting liability, co-operating with insurers and so on. Plainly these clauses cannot increase or decrease the risk of insured loss.

insurers' risk but which presupposes a prior definition of the risk in relation to which the limitation or exclusion operates.

The delimitation of a term defining 'the whole of the risk' must be a substantive question. That is, the amenability of a term to the scrutiny of s 11 of the IA 2015 cannot turn, formally, on how the insuring clause is drafted. To give an example, an insuring clause in a motor policy might cover a particular driver, providing cover for third-party risks and only when the vehicle is being used for social or leisure purposes; that would appear, in its entirety, to be a term defining the risk as a whole, even though the condition as to the vehicle's use impliedly excludes business use from the scope of cover. By contrast, if an insuring clause covered a named insured for third-party risks, except for any travel on Christmas Day, the latter qualification would appear not to be something that defines the risk as a whole but which operates as an exclusion such as would be subject to s 11 of the 2015 Act. The more difficult cases will fall in between these two examples.

The Explanatory Notes to the IA 2015 simply state that 'section 11 does not apply to clauses which define the risk as a whole. This is expected to include, for example, a requirement that a property or vehicle is not to be used commercially.'[41] It appears that the extent of the application of s 11 will depend not on how the clause is described or where it is found in the policy but on the nature of the risk and the extent to which the clause in question qualifies. The issue of where the boundary lies as between the definition of 'the risk as a whole' and restricting cover by reference to specific clauses has been considered in more detail in case law in both Australia and New Zealand. The Australian Insurance Contracts Act 1984 s 54[42] (ICA 1984) does not draw an express distinction between risk definition on the one hand and limitation or exclusion of liability on the other. However, the courts have developed the concept of 'restrictions or limitations

[41] Explanatory Notes, para 94.

[42] s 54 is entitled 'Insurer may not refuse to pay claims in certain circumstances' and provides:

'(1) Subject to this section, where the effect of a contract of insurance would, but for this section, be that the insurer may refuse to pay a claim, either in whole or in part, by reason of some act of the insured or of some other person, being an act that occurred after the contract was entered into but not being an act in respect of which subsection (2) applies, the insurer may not refuse to pay the claim by reason only of that act but the insurer's liability in respect of the claim is reduced by the amount that fairly represents the extent to which the insurer's interests were prejudiced as a result of that act.

(2) Subject to the succeeding provisions of this section, where the act could reasonably be regarded as being capable of causing or contributing to a loss in respect of which insurance cover is provided by the contract, the insurer may refuse to pay the claim.

(3) Where the insured proves that no part of the loss that gave rise to the claim was caused by the act, the insurer may not refuse to pay the claim by reason only of the act.

(4) Where the insured proves that some part of the loss that gave rise to the claim was not caused by the act, the insurer may not refuse to pay the claim, so far as it concerns that part of the loss, by reason only of the act.

(5) Where:

(a) the act was necessary to protect the safety of a person or to preserve property; or

(b) it was not reasonably possible for the insured or other person not to do the act;

the insurer may not refuse to pay the claim by reason only of the act.

(6) A reference in this section to an act includes a reference to:

(a) an omission; and

(b) an act or omission that has the effect of altering the state or condition of the subject-matter of the contract or of allowing the state or condition of that subject-matter to alter.'

that are inherent in the claim'. *Prepaid Services Pty Ltd v Atradius Credit insurance NVi*[43] concerned a credit policy excluding cover for specified classes of debt; it was there emphasised that a restriction or limitation was 'inherent in the claim' if it did not define the event covered by the policy. This analysis was affirmed by the High Court in *Maxwell v Highway Hauliers Pty Ltd*,[44] in which a motor policy excluded liability for accidents occurring while vehicles were being driven by drivers who had obtained a minimum driver profile score in a personality test. The High Court held that the restriction was not one inherent in the claim where that concept was confined to 'a restriction or limitation which must necessarily be acknowledged in the making of a claim, having regard to the type of insurance contract under which the claim is made'. In *Stapleton v NTI Ltd*[45] cover under a motor policy was removed when any part of the assured's destination was more than 450 km from the assured's base of operations. The Queensland Supreme Court regarded this as an inherent restriction on the cover provided and the insured could not recover by showing that the loss was unrelated to the geographical limit. That is, the limitation was one that defined the risk as a whole. *Pantaenius Australia Pty Ltd v Watkins Syndicate 0457 at Lloyd's*[46] is a subtly different case from *Stapleton*. Here a yacht would not be insured if sailed outside Australian waters with the qualification that cover would only be restored once the yacht had cleared Australian customs. The yacht ran aground in Australian waters but before it had cleared Australian customs. The court's view was that the removal of cover while the vessel was outside Australian waters was a restriction inherent in the claim in that it defined the circumstances when the policy responded. However, the requirement to clear Australian customs did not define the risk but operated as an exclusion from cover and because the loss was unrelated to customs clearance the insured could rely upon s 54 of the ICA 1984 to secure cover. More recently in *Allianz Australia Insurance Co v Inglis*[47] the claimant, a 10-year-old girl, was injured by being run over by a ride-on lawn mower belonging to her family but being ridden by the defendant, a boy aged 11. Contribution proceedings were brought by the defendant against the claimant's father, and the question was whether the father's public liability policy – which excluded 'legal liability for … injury to any person who normally lives with you' – responded to the father's liability. The insurer argued that the limitation was one that was inherent in the claim against them, a suggestion rejected by McLure P: all that had to be acknowledged was that the claim arose under a liability policy, that bodily injury was covered and that the claim arose during the period and geographical scope of cover.

In New Zealand the equivalent distinction was articulated as follows by Hardie Boys J in *Barnaby v South British Insurance Co*:[48]

> [s 11 of the Insurance Law Reform Act 1977] is designed to deal with those kinds of exclusion clauses which provide for circumstances likely to increase the risk of a loss which the policy actually covers … the section is not designed to deal with exclusion clauses which specify the kind of loss or the quantum of loss to which cover does not apply at all.

[43] [2012] NSWCA 252.
[44] [2014] HCA 33.
[45] [2002] QDC 204.
[46] [2016] FCA 1.
[47] [2016] WASCA 25.
[48] (1980) 1 ANZ Insurance Cases 60-401.

That is, if the event giving rise to the claim could never have come within the scope of the cover in the first place, the restriction goes to the whole of the risk rather than being an event that, notwithstanding that it comes within the prima facie scope of the cover, is excluded.

It follows that a telematics motor policy that imposes a condition precedent or warranty to the effect that the car will not be driven X miles from the insured's home, or one that is not roadworthy, where the conditions for a vehicle's roadworthiness are defined, are restrictions that relate to the risk as a whole. However, a condition precedent precluding cover for driving above a certain speed[49] would not relate to the risk as a whole since loss arising from an accident where the vehicle was being driven above that speed limit was loss that would otherwise have fallen within the ordinary scope of the cover but for the limitation. Similarly, a property may be subject to a warranty requiring it to have an operative fire alarm and that the alarm should be tested by an engineer every six months. If a fire occurs and the property has no fire alarm, arguably s 11 does not apply as the property was never within the prima facie scope of the cover. However, if the property suffered a fire, did have an operative fire alarm, but one that had not been serviced in the last six months, the further qualification would appear to exclude liability for a loss that would otherwise have fallen within the scope of the cover.

C. Constraints on Terms Imposed by Financial Services Regulation

The extent to which Financial Services Regulation under the Financial Services and Markets Act 2000 (FSMA 2000) constrains the way in which insurers can collect and use an insured's data is discussed in chapter six. As explained in further detail there, the law relating to the conduct of insurance business is regularly updated by statutory instruments issued under FSMA 2000. Importantly, regulatory obligations are collected and consolidated in the PRA Rulebook and FCA Handbook. Rules (as opposed to guidance) within the Rulebook and Handbook have the force of law, breach of which can give rise to regulatory enforcement action by the PRA or FCA and which may give rise to a right of action in damages for breach of statutory duty under s 138D of FSMA 2000.

There are a number of rules and guidelines in the FCA Handbook that impact on the extent to which insurers can restrict or exclude liability. The Insurance Conduct of Business Sourcebook (ICOBS)[50] part 2 deals with general matters. ICOBS 2.5 deals with exclusion of liability. Rule 2.5.1 R provides:

> **Exclusion of liability and conditions**
>
> 2.5.1 R (1)
>
> (1) A firm must not seek to exclude or restrict, or rely on any exclusion or restriction of, any duty or liability it may have to a customer[51] or other policyholder unless it is reasonable for it to do so and the duty or liability arises other than under the regulatory system.

[49] Or that precludes driving in other particular manners.

[50] ICOBS is discussed further in ch 6 at section IB.

[51] A 'customer' is defined, in relation to ICOBS, as a 'person who is a policyholder, or a prospective policyholder (except in ICOBS 2 (general matters) and (in respect of that chapter) ICOBS 1 (application)) excluding

(2) A Solvency II firm must ensure that general and special policy conditions do not include any conditions intended to meet, in an individual case, the particular circumstances of the risk to be covered.[52]

As to (1), it appears that the rule will offer no better protection than that afforded by s 11 of the IA 2015; either a term relates to 'the risk as a whole' or is one, compliance with which would tend to reduce the risk of the types of losses set out. If a term relates to the risk as a whole and escapes scrutiny under s 11 of the IA 2015, then it is submitted that it follows that it will be reasonable for the purposes of rule 2.5.1 R (1). If the term tends to reduce the type of risk, the question under s 11 is whether non-compliance with that term increased the risk of the loss that occurred. If it did not, the insured will not be denied the benefit of the cover, and the reasonableness of the term under rule 2.5.1 R will be irrelevant. If non-compliance did increase the risk that in fact occurred, then in circumstances where the IA 2015 will permit insurers to rely on the term to deny liability, it can hardly be said that that statutorily mandated outcome is unreasonable.

As to (2), this rule appears to preclude an insurer seeking to impose exclusions which would foreseeably operate to exclude the very sort of losses and protections that the policy purports to put in place.[53] Therefore, if a policy's terms operated to exclude much of the cover that was prima facie provided by the policy, there will be grounds to argue that it is unreasonable.

Rule 2.5.2A R of ICOBS is entitled 'Conditions and warranties in policies' and states:

An insurer must ensure that any condition or warranty included in a policy with a consumer:

(1) has operative effect only in relation to the types of crystallised risk covered by the policy that are connected to that condition or warranty; and
(2) (for a warranty in a pure protection contract)[54] is material to the risks to which it relates and is drawn to the customer's attention before the conclusion of the contract.

The purpose of this rule is to prevent insurers from adopting conditions and warranties which appear to have no relationship with the risk underwritten. So a fire insurer can adopt conditions and warranties designed to both delimit and mitigate the risk of, for

a policyholder or prospective policyholder who does not make the arrangements preparatory to him concluding the contract of insurance'.

[52] Derived from Art 187 of the Solvency II Directive.

[53] 2.5.2 G states that 'The general law, including the Unfair Terms Regulations (for contracts entered into before 1 October 2015) and the CRA, also limits the scope for a firm to exclude or restrict any duty or liability to a consumer'.

[54] Defined as:

'(1) a long-term insurance contract in respect of which the following conditions are met:
   (a) the benefits under the contract are payable only on death or in respect of incapacity due to injury, sickness or infirmity;
   (b) [deleted]
   (c) the contract has no surrender value, or the consideration consists of a single premium and the surrender value does not exceed that premium; and
   (d) the contract makes no provision for its conversion or extension in a manner which would result in it ceasing to comply with (a) or (c); or
   (e) [deleted]
(2) a reinsurance contract covering all or part of a risk to which a person is exposed under a long-term insurance contract.'

example, fires but if they do not objectively do so, they cannot be relied upon. It appears, by extension, that the wider purpose of this rule is very similar to the purpose of s 11 of the IA 2015, namely that a condition or warranty whose breach is relied upon to deny liability can only be relied upon where they relate to the very sorts of risks of losses that are sought to be guarded against by those conditions or warranties. What the rule seeks to prevent is an insurer relying on a warranty requiring the insurer to have certain types of anti-theft locks on his property's doors but then seeks to rely upon a breach of that warranty in circumstances where the burglar got in the window, or, worse, where the property was destroyed by fire.

ICOBS 5.1.1 provides that an insurer is to take reasonable steps to ensure that the insured customer only buys a policy under which he is eligible to claim benefits. That appears to be aimed at the type of case (like the mis-selling of Payment Protection Insurance) where policyholders were sold policies that simply did not apply to their circumstances such as to prove worthless. That also reflects the purpose of Rule 2.5.1(2) as set out above.

D. The Consumer Rights Act 2015

To what extent does consumer legislation constrain the way in which insurers might tailor the scope of cover? The Unfair Contract Terms Act 1977 was not applicable to insurance contracts but they were caught by the Unfair Terms in Consumer Contracts Regulations 1999.[55] The latter were revoked by the Consumer Rights Act 2015 (CRA 2015) in relation to insurance contracts made after 1 October 2015. The CRA 2015[56] replaced three major pieces of consumer legislation: the Sale of Goods Act 1979; the Unfair Terms in Consumer Contracts Regulations 1999;[57] and the Supply of Goods and Services Act 1982. Chapter 4 of the Act (sections 48–57) applies specifically to contracts for services, including consumer insurance contracts.[58]

Section 49 of the CRA 2015 provides that every contract to supply a service – including a consumer insurance contract – is to be treated as including a term that the trader must perform the service with reasonable care and skill. Section 50 is entitled 'Information about the trader or service to be binding'. Section 50(1) provides that every service contract is to be treated as including as a term anything that is said or written to the consumer, by or on behalf of the trader, about the trader or the service if: (i) it is taken into account by the consumer when deciding to enter into the contract; or

[55] Which implemented Council Directive 93/13/EEC of 5 April 1993. The Directive was first implemented in the Unfair Terms in Consumer Contracts Regulations 1994, which were later replaced by the Unfair Terms in Consumer Contracts Regulations 1999.

[56] Which implements Directive 99/44/EC of the European Parliament and of the Council on certain aspects of the sale of consumer goods and associated guarantees, Directive 93/13/EEC of the Council on unfair terms in consumer contracts and some provisions of Directive 2011/83/EU of the European Parliament and of the Council on consumer rights.

[57] Which implemented EC Directive 93/13/EEC on unfair terms in consumer contracts.

[58] A consumer is, however, now defined as 'an individual acting for purposes that are wholly or mainly outside that individual's trade, business, craft or profession': s 2(3) and s 76(2).

(ii) it is taken into account by the consumer when making any decision about the service after entering into the contract. That implied term is subject to anything that qualified those statements and express variations of those statements, albeit where the consumer had in fact taken them into account. Section 51 relates to consumer contracts for which no price has been agreed or paid. It will apply where insurers have not stipulated a premium (or the means of calculating the premium). In such cases, the contract is to be treated as including a term that the consumer must pay a reasonable price for the service, and no more. The question of what is a reasonable price is a question of fact. Section 53 provides that nothing in Chapter 4 of the CRA 2015 affects any enactment or rule of law that imposes a stricter duty on the trader and further provides that the provisions of Chapter 4 are subject to any other enactment which defines or restricts the rights, duties or liabilities arising in connection with a service of any description. Section 54(2)–(4) provides that breach of any of the terms implied by ss 49–52 of the CRA 2015 will entitle consumers to repeat performance and/or a reduction in price. However, s 54(6) provides that s 54 does not operate to prevent 'the consumer seeking other remedies for a breach of a term to which any of subsections (3) to (5) applies, instead of or in addition to a remedy referred to there (but not so as to recover twice for the same loss)'. Section 54(7) sets out a list of available additional remedies, including a claim for damages or the exercise of a right to treat the contract as at an end.

These remedies are likely to be of limited relevance to consumer insureds who are more likely – for reasons of time and cost – to pursue complaints about breaches of ICOBS to the Financial Ombudsman Service (FOS). The implied terms, by definition, will only relate to matters arising post-contractually, so will not constrain the way insurers may acquire or profile personal data when considering whether to write the risk and if so on what terms. The duty, post-contractually, to exercise reasonable care and skill will be of most relevance in the context of claims handling. Were it the case under the law of insurance that insurers' post-contractual duty of good faith merely required insurers to handle claims honestly (and no more), the implied term requiring the exercise of reasonable care and skill may add to the insured's armoury were there to be any concerns over how reasonable it was for insurers to use big data to investigate or reach decisions in relation to claims.

Section 62(1) provides that an unfair term of a consumer contract is not binding on the consumer. Section 62(4) provides that a term will be unfair if, contrary to the requirement of good faith, it causes a significant imbalance in the parties' rights and obligations under the contract to the detriment of the consumer. Whether a term is unfair is determined by (a) taking into account the nature of the subject matter of the contract, and (b) by reference to all the circumstances existing when the term was agreed and to all of the other terms of the contract or of any other contract on which it depends. On its face, that may be of importance to the operation of terms which, as a result of real-time data monitoring, render the cover ambulatory: conditions may be imposed that can remove cover in real time as a result of exclusions being triggered by real-time events. Terms that might permit the 'hollowing-out' of cover at the very points when it is most needed may, to the extent that this is otherwise permitted by law, fall foul of s 62 of the CRA. In *Parker v National Farmers Union Mutual Insurance*

Society Ltd[59] the condition precedent required the insured to provide all written details and documents requested by insurers. The insured failed to comply. Teare J held that the condition survived the 1999 Regulations (which gave effect to Directive 93/113) because the condition was not unlimited, in that it was restricted by an implied obligation on the insurers to act reasonably; and compliance did not result in a significant imbalance in the rights of the parties, given that the assured alone possessed the information which might be required by insurers. The judge referred to rules of ICOBS under which insurers must not act unreasonably in rejecting a claim: given that insurers were subject to that constraint, it could not be said that the term could give rise to a significant imbalance in the rights of the parties. If this reasoning is correct, it means that the CRA 2015 will rarely have any part to play in determining the consequences of a breach of a condition precedent and the matter is to be resolved purely by application of ICOBS 8, enforceable either by complaint to the FOS or directly by means of an action for breach of statutory duty under FSMA 2000. Teare J concluded that reliance on the condition was not unreasonable under ICOBS 8 for much of the same reasons as he had ruled that it was not struck down by the 1999 Regulations.

Part 1 of Schedule 2 of the CRA 2015 contains an indicative and non-exhaustive list of terms of consumer contracts that may be regarded as unfair.[60] However, a term of a consumer contract will not be assessed for unfairness if it specifies the main subject-matter of the contract or if the assessment concerns the appropriateness of the price payable under the contract for the services provided,[61] so long as the term is transparent and brought to the consumer's attention.[62] In this regard, the identification of core terms which are excluded from a fairness assessment might appear to be similar to that under s 11 of the IA 2015. However, this section will be read in light of Recital (19) of Directive 93/13/EEC, which states:

> Whereas, for the purposes of this Directive, assessment of unfair character shall not be made of terms which describe the main subject matter of the contract nor the quality/price ratio of the goods or services supplied; whereas the main subject matter of the contract and the price/quality ratio may nevertheless be taken into account in assessing the fairness of other terms; whereas it follows, inter alia, that in insurance contracts, the terms which clearly define *or circumscribe* the insured risk and the insurer's liability shall not be subject to such assessment since these restrictions are taken into account in calculating the premium paid by the consumer.

Insofar as core terms will not only include terms that define the 'whole of the risk' but terms circumscribing the risk, then terms excluding or restricting the scope of the cover

[59] [2012] EWHC 2156 (Comm).

[60] Subject to Part 2 Schedule 2. Terms which may be regarded as unfair include those excluding the trader's liability in the event of death or personal injury to a trader (para 1); a term which has the object or effect of enabling the trader to alter the terms of the contract unilaterally without a valid reason which is specified in the contract (para 11). The Act contains certain restrictions in relation to terms that seek to exclude or restrict liability for negligence but these do not apply to insurance contracts: ss 65 and 66(1)(a).

[61] Case C-96/14 *Van Hove v CNP Assurances SA* [2015] 3 CMLR 31 at paras 34–35.

[62] CRA 2015, s 64. The decision of the House of Lords in *Director General of Fair Trading v First National Bank Plc* [2002] 1 AC 481 took a strict approach to the meaning of a core term which will continue in relation to the interpretation of s 64.

will also be regarded as core terms and will not be subject to a fairness assessment.[63] If a term is held to be unfair, it will not be binding on the consumer insured but the contract will continue to operate as far as is possible.[64] It would therefore appear that the requirement of fairness under s 62 of the CRA 2015 will not provide the consumer insured with any greater protection than s 11 of the IA 2015, certainly as regards terms that define the scope of the risk, whether those terms define the risk as a whole or limit or restrict the scope of the cover.

However, s 62 will apply to procedural clauses relating to timing, claims clauses and clauses relating to the provision of information and which require the notification of certain events. Terms making compliance with procedural requirements a condition precedent to indemnity are also likely to be regarded as unfair. Thus the CRA 2015 may operate to constrain use of early termination notices in consumer policies, particularly those written on the basis that cover can be withdrawn for no reason at all.[65] Paragraph 7 of Schedule 2 of the CRA 2015 contains, as an example of indicative unfairness, a term which has the object or effect of authorising the trader to dissolve the contract on a discretionary basis where the same facility is not granted to the consumer, or permitting the trader to retain the sums paid for services not yet supplied by the trader where it is the trader who dissolves the contract.

III. Constraints in Relation to Specific Classes of Risk

A. Profiling and Motor Insurance

As noted in chapter one, the way in which motor insurance is being underwritten is undergoing fundamental change as a result of telematics. Telemetry is an automated communications process by which data is collected by sensors and transmitted to receiving equipment for monitoring and analysis. As applied to motor cover, a device is plugged into the on-board diagnostics port of a vehicle which collects data about a range of driving behaviours including: time of day the vehicle is being driven; geolocation data on where the vehicle is being driven; the time that the driver is spending behind the wheel and the distances covered; and a range of metrics on how the vehicle is being driven in real time including speed, rates of acceleration and deceleration (that is, how hard a driver is braking) and cornering. That data is transmitted wirelessly (often via SIM cards in the device) to insurers enabling them to assess their risk profile from the riskiness of each individual journey. In the early days of telematics, it was largely used by companies operating fleets of vehicles. The data derived from telemetry enabled those companies to improve safety and efficiency.[66] It has since been adopted by insurers along much wider commercial lines and in consumer motor insurance.

[63] This will include suspensory conditions. It was thus held in *Bankers Insurance Co Ltd v South* [2004] Lloyd's Rep IR 1 that an exception to the cover was a core term. If conditions precedent or warranties therefore serve to define the parameters of the risk, they will be excluded from a fairness assessment as well.

[64] CRA 2015, s 67.

[65] See, eg, the clause in *Sun Fire Office v Hart* (1889) 14 App Cas 98.

[66] Including by way of targeted, pre-emptive maintenance.

Telematics has been the driver for the development of UBI or Pay-As-You-Drive cover. Such cover usually prices premium by reference to the type of vehicle, the time of use and/or distance covered, the location of the vehicle and, importantly, the driving behaviour of the insured. Motor insurers can not only more accurately discern the risk posed by an individual driver but, in offering discounts for certain types of driver behaviour, telematics policies encourage safer forms of driving, and thus have the potential to reduce the number and severity of accidents.[67] In addition to helping evaluate the riskiness of drivers, telematics offers further claims-related benefits to insurers including: (i) reducing fraud (information will be available to disprove certain claims about how accidents have occurred or whether there was an accident at all);[68] (ii) tracking vehicles such that stolen vehicles are more likely to be recovered, with insurers being able to avoid full replacement costs more frequently; and (iii) generating greater accuracy in post-accident investigations and the determination of liability.

Complementing the information generated by connected cars is that derived from the IoT about the environments in which cars are being driven. The tagging of roads with sensors (smart roads) will be able to provide information about their condition, while the tagging of sensors in various additional parts of vehicles provides analysis of the state of the engine, tyres and so on, all of which will be relevant to questions of roadworthiness, causation and liability in the context of claims.[69]

However, to fully inform insureds about their driving behaviour and the impact this has on the cost of their cover, insurers will have to consider what information they will provide to insureds about their driving practices and in what format.[70] This increasingly includes real-time feedback: such data is sent to insureds' dashboards and may also be sent by way of text or push notification to the insured indicating that, for example, their speed will take the insured outside the parameters of an available discount or the cover.

[67] And for which there is already evidence: see the review of data undertaken by the National Highway Transportation Safety Administration at www.NHTSA.gov. There are environmental benefits, too, as drivers are incentivised to reduce their mileage, reduce their speeds and the rate of acceleration and deceleration, all of which will consume less fuel and reduce CO_2 emissions.

[68] The CMA Research accompanying its 'Commercial Use of Consumer Data' report of 2015 noted that some motor insurance providers have already been able to detect fraud using information derived from social media: https://assets.publishing.service.gov.uk/government/uploads/system/uploads/attachment_data/file/435777/The_Commercial_Use_of_Consumer_Data_-_DotEcon_and_Analysys_Mason.pdf para 2.4.2.

[69] These developments were recognised by the FCA in its Feedback Statement where it stated: 'Telematics devices and mobile apps tend to record location, speed and information on driving style, e.g. braking and acceleration. Some providers collect more sophisticated data than others. We were informed that, with more analysis, insurers could build up a picture of precisely where and when accidents are more likely to occur, e.g. by analysing sharp braking trends of particular stretches of road at particular times. Insurance policies could then be adjusted to reflect the specific risk a driver represented, depending on when and where they drove.' FCA Feedback Statement, September 2016, para 3.5.

[70] For example, MyPolicy states: 'A feature of a Telematics Policy provided by MyPolicy is the ability to view information relating to your driving style through our website. It is safe, secure and simple. A dashboard view allows you to proactively manage your driving behaviour, shows you your mileage and ultimately allows you to control how your premium may be influenced. This feature is best illustrated using examples, for instance, in the event that you exceed the declared estimated mileage, you will be able to view up-to-date on-line information on the dashboard specifically relating to the number of miles used, enabling you to manage the future number of miles you might use rather than pay for extra mileage.'

i. Policy Terms and Constraints Imposed by Law

Imagine a motor policy that included conditions precedent or warranties designed to exclude cover for (1) loss that occurs in excess of a certain speed and/or (2) loss that might arise at particular locations or particular times; and/or (3) loss that arises where the roadworthiness of the car does not comply with certain metrics against which roadworthiness is measured. Even to the extent that those terms were characterised as risk-mitigating terms and amenable to scrutiny under s 11 of the IA 2015, a further question arises as to whether motor law permits the adoption of such terms at all.

Motor policies can cover first-party risks and/or third-party risks.[71] Provision for insurance against third-party liabilities is made in Part VI of the Road Traffic Act 1988 (RTA 1988). Section 143 of the RTA 1988 makes it compulsory to insure against liability for (i) death or bodily injury to third parties, and (ii) damage to a third party's property.[72] The requirements of a valid motor vehicle insurance policy are set out in s 145 of the RTA 1988. Motor policies often contain clauses restricting the liability of insurers in various ways, such as by reference to the qualifications or fitness of the driver of the vehicle, the purposes for which it is used and/or its condition or upkeep. Insurers are, of course, permitted to impose such restrictions, even in the context of compulsory third-party policies.[73] But whether a new range of telematics-facilitated restrictions may be deployed depends on s 148 of the RTA 1988. Section 148 is entitled 'Avoidance of certain exceptions to policies or securities' and assists third parties by avoiding certain conditions and terms in policies that could otherwise defeat claims. Section 148(1) of the RTA 1988 provides:

> (1) Where a policy or security is issued or given for the purposes of this Part of this Act, so much of the policy or security as purports to restrict—
>
> (a) the insurance of the persons insured by the policy, or
> (b) the operation of the security,
>
> (as the case may be) by reference to any of the matters mentioned in subsection (2) below shall, as respects such liabilities as are required to be covered by a policy under section 145 of this Act, be of no effect.

[71] Most motor policies cover the insured against a wider range of risks. In addition to providing cover against third-party risks (a form of (compulsory) liability insurance), often the costs of any associated litigation (a form of legal expenses insurance) will be covered. First-party policies will provide cover against personal injury or death to the insured (personal accident insurance) and some will additionally provide additional cover for, e.g., loss or damage to the contents of the car (a form of property insurance).

[72] It is the user of the vehicle and not the driver or owner that must be insured: *John T Ellis v Hinds* [1947] KB 475. The test of use is control of the vehicle. That will usually be the driver.

[73] In *John T Ellis Ltd v Hinds* [1947] KB 475 the appellants held a policy of insurance covering their liability to third parties, subject to an exception excluding liability whilst the insured vehicle was being driven with the general consent of the insured by any person who to the knowledge of the insured did not hold a licence to drive it. An accident was caused by a 17-year-old who was driving the insured vehicle. The 17-year-old neither held a driving licence nor was he qualified to hold a driving licence. On the facts, the insured appellants neither knew that he had driven the vehicle, nor that he did not hold a licence. The clause excluding cover thus did not operate. Had each condition been satisfied on the facts, the policy would not have been in force and insurers would not have had a liability in respect of the accident in question.

Three matters listed in s 148(2) are of particular relevance in the context of telematics motor policies:

1) the age or physical or mental condition of persons driving the vehicle (where real-time monitoring might show erratic driving suggesting that the person is driving under the influence of alcohol or drugs);[74]
2) the condition of the vehicle (where sensors in the car may, for example, reveal that there was a problem with the engine, the brake fluid was exhausted or the tyres were worn);[75] and
3) the time at which or the areas within which the vehicle is used[76] (which bears on the possibility of using conditions precedent or warranties to restrict liability by reference to time and place).[77]

It has been held that the list of excluded conditions in s 148 of the RTA 1988 is exhaustive. There is no question, therefore, that conditions relating to the use of a vehicle for 'social, domestic and pleasure' purposes only, restrictions on the mode of carrying passengers[78] or restrictions on particular forms of use[79] are valid and enforceable even in third-party policies.

Section 148(5) of the RTA 1988 is also important and provides:

> (5) A condition in a policy or security issued or given for the purposes of this Part of this Act providing—
>
> (a) that no liability shall arise under the policy or security, or
> (b) that any liability so arising shall cease,
>
> in the event of some specified thing being done or omitted to be done after the happening of the event giving rise to a claim under the policy or security, shall be of no effect in connection with such liabilities as are required to be covered by a policy under section 145 of this Act.

The effect of this clause is that once a third-party liability has accrued, no breach by the insured of any claims control clause will preclude the cover operating in order to discharge the insured's third-party liability.

Section 148 of the RTA 1988 does not apply to first-party claims and thus the conditions which it lists can be adopted in first-party policies. Its effect therefore is only to bar insurers' reliance on the conditions it lists for the purposes of meeting third party liabilities but remain valid exclusions as against the insured.[80] In those circumstances,

[74] RTA 1988, s 188(2)(a).
[75] RTA 1988, s 148(2)(b).
[76] *Palmer v Cornhill Insurance Co Ltd* (1935) 52 LI L Rep 78 for an example of such a clause.
[77] RTA 1988, s 148(2)(e).
[78] *Bright v Ashfold* [1932] 2 KB 153.
[79] *Gray v Blackmore* [1934] 1 KB 95; *Samuelson v National Insurance and Guarantee Corp* [1985] 2 Lloyds Rep 541.
[80] In *Cameron v Hussain, Liverpool Victoria Insurance Co* [2018] 1 WLR 657 it was observed that s 148 voids (for the purpose of meeting third-party liabilities, although not as against insureds) certain policy exceptions; thus s 148(1)–(2) nullifies certain policy restrictions relating to the features or circumstances of the driver, the vehicle or the loss event; section 148(5)-(6) nullifies any defence to liability arising because of contractual default subsequent to the loss event.

insurers can, where it has paid a third-party claim on one of the excluded bases under s 148(2), seek to recover from the insured under s 148(4) of the RTA 1988.[81] However, the s 148(2) exclusions cannot be relied upon for third-party claims or first-party claims where s 11 of the IA 2015 operates. That is, if the insured's non-compliance with the condition or warranty did not increase the risk, then insurers will be unable to pursue its right of recourse against insureds in third-party policies and they will be unable to exclude liability in first-party claims.

It is useful to consider how, prior to the introduction of s 11 of the IA 2015, the courts have analysed various restrictions imposed in motor policies, and then consider the impact that s 11 might now have on that analysis.

ii. User/Purpose

Restrictions on user are very common in consumer policies. If the car is used for purposes other than those specified in the clause, the policy ceased to cover the car,[82] although insurers were not entitled to avoid the insurance for breach of contract, or be discharged from all liability thereunder unless the insured had warranted that it would be used only for the specified purposes.[83] Section 10 of the IA 2015 now abolishes the remedy of avoidance for breach of warranty. It has been held that whether a restriction on use in a motor policy is operative has to be considered at the date of the event giving rise to the loss: *AXN v Worboys*.[84]

iii. Maintenance and Upkeep

Motor vehicle policies often provide that the insured shall take all reasonable steps to maintain the vehicle in an efficient condition. Where such clauses make roadworthiness a condition precedent to liability, insurers have previously been able to avoid liability if the vehicle had not in fact been maintained in an efficient condition, regardless of the question of whether such inefficiency caused or contributed to an accident: the term was, in effect, a warranty. Thus in *Conn v Westminster Motor Insurance Association Ltd*[85] the insured had allowed the tyres of a vehicle to become defective and, on proof of this, the court entered judgment for the insurance company without considering

[81] In *Charlton v Fisher* [2011] Lloyd's Rep IR 387 Rix LJ explained the effect of these provisions as follows (para 68): 'Where an insurer is required to discharge a liability only because of the interference of statute in arrangements between the insurer and insured, as in a case, among others, where s 148 bites or where the insurer's separate duty to the third party survives avoidance of the policy, the insurer is entitled to recover payment from his insured: see for instance ss 148(4) or 151(7) or (8). Normally of course an insurer cannot recover from his insured what it is required to pay out under the terms of his policy. Thus as between the third party and the insurer, the third party is protected as if the insured had been covered, but as between the insured and the insurer, the statute recognises that, in cases where the law compels a payment which would not otherwise be made under the terms of the policy, the insured is treated as if he was not insured.'

[82] *Farr v Motor Traders' Mutual Insurance Society* [1920] 3 KB 669.

[83] *Provincial Insurance Co v Morgan* [1933] AC 240.

[84] [2013] Lloyd's Rep IR 207.

[85] [1966] 1 Lloyd's Rep 407.

whether the defective tyres had contributed in any way to the accident out of which the claim arose. The latter analysis can no longer apply: a worn tyre clearly can increase the risk of insured loss but would not discharge insurers from liability if the accident had been caused by the insured losing concentration and hitting the third party for that reason. Section 11(3) of the IA 2015 entails that insurers cannot rely on the non-compliance if: '[t]he insured … shows that the non-compliance with the term could not have increased the risk of the loss which actually occurred in the circumstances in which it occurred'. The intention in the drafting of s 11 of the IA 2015 was not to impose a test of causation. However, in cases like this, deciding whether non-compliance diminished the risk of the loss which in fact occurred in the circumstances in which it occurred comes close to a causal inquiry. The lack of concentration may have led the insured to brake late, and if the tyres were worn, they would have been less effective. Could it be said in such circumstances that the non-compliance did not increase the risk?[86]

In *Barrett v London General Insurance Co*[87] Goddard J held, applying marine insurance decisions on unseaworthiness, that the insurer, in order to rely on the exclusion, must prove the vehicle was unroadworthy when it set out on its journey and not merely that it was unroadworthy at the time of the accident. He considered that, were this not so, insurers could avoid liability in a case where, for instance, the occurrence of a fault in the car caused an almost simultaneous accident. That reasoning was not accepted by the Privy Council in *Trickett v Queensland Insurance Co.*[88] There a vehicle was driven at night without lights for some time before an accident occurred. It was not shown whether the lights had been defective at the start of the journey, but the privy council held that liability was excluded by an exemption applying 'while any motor-vehicle … under this policy is (e) being driven in a damaged or unsafe condition'. That conclusion would survive s 11 of the IA 2015 on the basis that the term related to the risk as a whole. If, however, it was a risk-reducing term, then whether insurers could continue to rely will again depend on whether the non-compliance increased the risk of loss in the circumstances as they in fact occurred. In *Lefevre v White*[89] the insured's obligation to 'take every reasonable precaution' to maintain the vehicle in a safe condition was held not to require him to have the brakes tested on the vehicle which he had just purchased, but did oblige him to change the tyres which he knew to be in a worn condition. The test for breach of a roadworthiness clause is whether the insured has acted reasonably.[90] If such a clause was made a condition precedent

[86] As wear and tear is inevitable, its occurrence cannot be the subject of any indemnity. However, if a vehicle suffers from wear and tear and that results in sudden physical damage when a component gives way, that additional damage is not wear and tear: *Burts & Harvey Limited v Vulcan Boiler and General Insurance Co* [1966] 1 Lloyd's Rep 161. Insurers can, however, increasingly monitor wear and tear through sensors on connected vehicles. The risk of damage and accident can be mitigated by alerting insureds to the need for maintenance. Moreover, such information can assist, in a claims context, in establishing precisely what caused the loss.

[87] [1935] 1 KB 238.

[88] [1936] AC 159.

[89] [1990] 1 Lloyd's Rep 659.

[90] See *Amey Properties Ltd v Cornhill Insurance Plc* [1996] LRLR 259.

to liability, where the insured is found to act reasonably, insurers will not be able to disclaim liability. Where the insured acted unreasonably and the term is regarded as risk-reducing (rather than going to the whole of the risk), whether insurers will be able to rely on the non-compliance will yet again depend on an analysis of whether the unreasonable behaviour increased the risk of the loss which actually occurred.

iv. Conditions Relating to the Driver

Policies may contain clauses exempting liability for injury sustained by the insured while under the influence of alcohol or drugs. The question is whether they 'disturb the quiet, calm, intelligent exercise of the faculties': *Louden v British Merchants Insurance Co.*[91] Whether a condition precedent or a warranty, such terms will – if not otherwise relating to 'the whole of the risk' – plainly survive scrutiny under s 11 of the IA 2015 since, unless the insured can show that the loss would have occurred anyway because of the driving of a third party or some entirely external event, it will be a rare case where an insured will be able to contend that notwithstanding being drunk in charge of a vehicle, that non-compliance did not increase the risk of insured loss.

v. The Terms of Telematics Policies

Many telematics policies are arranged by specialist telematics insurance intermediaries who provide the telematics elements of the insurance (installation of the Smart Box and data monitoring and analysis) on behalf of insurers who provide the cover. An insured will thus enter into contracts with both the intermediary in relation to the provision of the telematics and the insurer who provides the cover. The contract with the intermediary will often provide more explicit information about how driving behaviours impact on premium and cover. The contract of insurance will often refer to the role of the intermediary in relation to the analysis of driving behaviours and their role in monitoring how those behaviours impact on cover.[92]

Many of these policies operate as mileage-based insurance where the insured's initial premium is typically calculated based on the annual mileage declared at the outset (a mileage allowance which operates as the basis for increased payments if exceeded or rebates if that allowance is not used in the policy period). However, if it appears that miles are consumed at a faster rate than envisaged by the total miles anticipated for the policy period, insurers will notify the insured and require a mileage top-up. Some telematics policies operate curfews. Virtually all will increase the premium the more

[91] [1961] 1 Lloyd's Rep 154.

[92] Highway's policy wording thus states: 'If your premium is based upon a telematics device being fitted to, or installed in, the vehicle, or for you registering and using any smartphone application provided to you, to monitor the driving behaviours of any authorised driver, failure to comply with your insurance adviser's terms or conditions relating to the telematics device may result in us, or our authorised agent, invoking our right to cancel under Cancelling Your Policy (Outside the Cooling-off Cancellation Right)': https://www.mypolicy.co.uk/media/1175/highway_policybook_pchwy8_07.pdf.

weekend and late-night driving that is undertaken. A typical example of the speeding restrictions and the consequences of their breach is as follows:[93]

Conditions	Action
+45mph is recorded in a 30mph zone *+60mph is recorded in a 40mph zone* *+75mph is recorded in a 50mph zone* *+90mph is recorded in a 60mph zone* *(Above are all examples of where the road speed limit has been exceeded by more than 50%)* *(this will result in your insurance policy to be cancelled)*	*Your telematics smart box will trigger a notification to us and we will notify you that a process of cancellation has started*
Speed in excess of 100mph is recorded *(this will result in your insurance policy to be cancelled)*	*Your telematics smart box will trigger a notification to us and we will notify you that a process of cancellation has started.*

Each individual journey is given a driving score based on the analysis of acceleration, braking, speed, location, cornering, time of use, mileage and types of roads used. As insurers gather more data, they will adjust their rating models on an ongoing basis. Some providers will charge a penalty if three high-risk driving scores are recorded in the policy period; if, after imposing a penalty, a further high-risk score is recorded, insurers may start a process of cancellation.

In addition to standard conditions in motor policies, many contain an additional section headed 'telematics conditions'. The Markerstudy wording[94] provides for the monitoring of the use of the insured vehicle and notes that information from the telematics device is used:

1. to monitor driving behaviour, in particular, compliance with speed limits;
2. to monitor the locations and times during which the insured vehicle is used, the way in which it is driven and where and when it is driven;
3. to provide further clarification as to the circumstance of a claim if you make a claim under the insurance policy; and
4. to calculate future premiums based on the information collected.

It goes on to state that the policy is

> intended for safe drivers and your premium at renewal will be affected by the way that the insured vehicle is driven and your mileage, as well as where and when you drive. Poor driving behaviour, and in particular extreme or consistent speeding, may result in the withdrawal of cover.

Its device is also able to detect accidents and states that 'in order to improve the speed with which road accidents and the resulting insurance claims are dealt with, your telematics device has been designed to automatically detect accidents'.

[93] This is taken from the My Policy Limited Terms and Conditions dated 25 May 2018: https://www.mypolicy.co.uk/media/1221/telematics_car_insurance_terms_and_conditions_v5_17may18.pdf.

[94] https://www.mypolicy.co.uk/media/1105/markerstudy_telematics_policy_booklet_v20_sept2017.pdf (accessed September 2018).

The Zurich policy refers to the insured's Driver Score as calculated by the driving data obtained.[95] It observes that the Driver Score is based on the following factors:

1. Smoothness – measures sharp acceleration, braking, deceleration and cornering over the course of each journey.
2. Speed – measures speed against the speed limit for the roads being driven.
3. Usage – measures time of day, journey volume, journey duration and types of road used.

The Zurich wording also contains an 'Unacceptable Driving Behaviour' clause, which provides:

> You and any driver of your vehicle must observe the law at all times. Poor driving behaviour (including your vehicle being driven at speeds which exceed the speed limit for the road on which it is being driven) will affect your Driver Score. In particular, if the telematics device detects that your vehicle is being driven at excessive speed the following conditions apply to this insurance:
>
> If during any one annual period of insurance you or any permitted driver of your vehicle:
>
> i) exceeds the speed limit for the road on which your vehicle is being driven by more than 100% in one journey; and/or
> ii) has three or more journeys which receives a Driver Score of between -6 and -10 which is a warning of high risk driving,
>
> your policy will be cancelled in accordance with Condition 6 of the policy.[96]

Finally, many telematics policies reserve the right to apply the acquired driver data for wider purposes. According to Direct Line's 2015 terms and conditions for its DrivePlus telematics policy, the third-party analytics provider may use the data for purposes that include analysis of road safety issues. The permitted purposes include:

1. Road and vehicle usage including for road safety issues, real time traffic flow, environmental impacts such as idle time at junctions, journey times, distances and speeds, and the analysis of junctions and the risk they represent;
2. Driving behaviour analysis and profiling including determining what constitutes safe and dangerous driving and the typical behaviours of various segments of the UK population;
3. Analysis of the causes of, and forces involved in, collisions and other road incidents; and,
4. Researching and refining techniques for analysing motor vehicle telematics data.[97]

According to Admiral's privacy and security statement in relation to its LittleBox telematics policy, the third-party technology company may use the data for policy-related purposes, but also for broader purposes, said to include: '[g]eneral research and analysis, mapping purposes, researching and refining techniques for analysing motor Telematics data and the supply of traffic information. In all such circumstances the information will be used anonymously and will not identify any individual, vehicle user, or the policyholder.'[98]

[95] https://www.mypolicy.co.uk/media/1101/zurich_policy_booklet.pdf (accessed September 2018).
[96] It is highly unlikely that such terms could be challenged for unfairness under the CRA 2015.
[97] http://faqs.directline.com/terms/disclaimers/black-box-terms-conditions.
[98] http://www.admiral.com/car-insurance/your-policy/your-privacy-andsecurity.php.

It is clear, therefore, that insurers are including terms and conditions that will operate to alter the scope of the cover on the occurrence of certain stipulated events which insurers can track in real time. There are constraints on the enforceability of terms as to the condition of the vehicle or the times and places where it may be driven in the context of compulsory third-party risks, but beyond those constraints, insurers will increasingly use terms that will tailor the scope of the cover in real time and in response to actual driving behaviours. Those terms will be constrained only by the fairness requirements under the CRA 2015 and s 11 of the IA 2015 in the event that they do not define or circumscribe the risk (for the purposes of the former Act) or constitute risk-reducing terms and where the breach has not increased the risk in question (for the purposes of the latter Act).

B. Profiling and Property Insurance

As the number of connected devices in properties multiplies, there are increasing opportunities for insurers to obtain data about the risk profile of their insureds in relation to home and contents cover. Automated household security systems collect and record data: doorlocks can be enabled and disabled by apps on smartphones. Insurers can thus tell when a property was secure and when it was not, information relevant to underwriting decisions and which will assist in the context of claims following break-in and theft. Other insurers have started to partner with Nest, a Google-owned company that makes smart smoke alarms. Pursuant to these partnering arrangements, insurers offer a discount if an insured installs a smart alarm. In 2015, the Chicago Tribune reported that one insurer stated: '[w]e believe customers seeking to monitor their homes with devices like Nest Protect demonstrate responsible behaviour [including helping to mitigate such incidents as fires]. As a result, we offer these customers discounts on their home insurance policy.'[99] These systems can not only detect smoke but additionally create a digital audit of the status of batteries, how long a detector has been chirping to let the homeowner know they need to be changed (with the length of time taken adding to a risk score), and can automatically alert emergency services when a fire breaks out. Insurers may increasingly require such smart security and fire detection systems to be installed as a condition of cover. Warranties may require insureds to undertake to keep them operative during the policy period.

i. *Property Policy Terms*

A term that is frequently found in property policies requires the insured to take all due and reasonable precautions to safeguard the property concerned: *Carlton v Park*.[100] Another form of wording requiring the insured to mitigate risk requires the insured to

[99] B Yerak, 'Home Insurers Gaining an Entry: Policyholders Offered Discounts for Installing Watchful devices, Privacy Concerns Arise', Chicago Tribune, 16 October 2015, http://www.chicagotribune.com/business/ct-insurers-home-monitoring-1016-biz-20151015-story.html.

[100] (1922) 10 Lloyd's Rep 818.

take 'such measures as may be reasonable for the purpose of averting or minimising a loss'. There will usually only be a breach of this clause if the insured had a reckless disregard for the safety of the property insured.[101]

ii. Terms as to Alarms

Many policies – particularly commercial property policies – require the insured to install an operative burglar alarm system.[102] The exact wording of the clause will be crucial but the courts have usually held that clauses requiring that a burglar alarm should be put into efficient working order will not usually be contravened if the insured was, through no fault of his own, unaware of a change or malfunction in the alarm.[103] In *Victor Melik & Co Ltd v Norwich Union Fire Insurance Society Ltd*[104] Woolf J held that a term which required a burglar alarm to be kept in efficient working order had not been broken where the alarm became defective; he held there would only be a breach where the insured had failed to repair it after the defects had come to his attention. In that case the telephone line that was necessary for the alarm to remain operative had been cut by a third party.[105]

The generous approach of Woolf J to this type of clause was followed in In *AC Ward v Caitlin (Five) Ltd (No 2)*,[106] where the policy contained a Protection Maintenance Warranty and a Burglar Alarm Maintenance Warranty. Those clauses provided:

> **Warranties applicable to Theft Insurance ... applicable only if specified in the Policy Schedule**
>
> **Protection Maintenance Warranty (PMW)**
>
> It is warranted that:-
>
> (a) the whole of the protections provided for the safety of the insured property shall be maintained in good order throughout the currency of this insurance and that they shall be in full and effective operation at all times when the Insured's premises are closed for business and at all other appropriate times, including when the said premises are left

[101] *Board of Trustees of the Tate Gallery v Duffy Construction Ltd (No 2)* [2008] Lloyd's Rep IR 159; *Shaw v Robberds* (1837) 6 A & E 75. In that latter case the fire was started by the gross negligence of the insured. However, if the proximate cause of the loss is a fire, it is immaterial in the absence of relevant warranties that the fire has been caused by the negligence of the insured or his servants.

[102] *Roberts v Eagle Star Insurance Co* [1960] 1 Lloyd's Rep 615.

[103] These clauses will to some extent be superseded by devices that can detect and provide analysis on their real-time status; the knowledge and diligence of the insured will only be engaged to the extent that the devices may need to be altered or repaired, something which insurers will be able to inform insureds of during the policy period.

[104] [1980] 1 Lloyd's Rep 523.

[105] See also *Hussain v Brown* [1996] 1 Lloyd's Rep 627 where the insured completed a proposal form which contained a question as to whether he had a security alarm fitted in the premises, to which he answered in the affirmative. Insurers submitted that this implied a continuing warranty that the alarm would be set when the insured left the premises and the insured's failure to do so breached the policy. The Court of Appeal dismissed the appeal holding that no principle existed in insurance law which implied continuing promises from answers given on proposal forms. To impose a continuing warranty, breach of which would lead to the automatic cancellation of cover, was a draconian measure and if underwriters required such protection then it should be stipulated in clear terms on the proposal forms.

[106] [2010] Lloyd's Rep IR 695.

> unattended, and that such protections shall not be withdrawn or varied to the detriment of the Insurers without their consent;
>
> (b) …
>
> All defects occurring in any protections must be promptly remedied.
>
> **Burglar Alarm Maintenance Warranty (BAMW)**
>
> It is warranted that:-
>
> (a) the premises containing the Insured property are fitted with the burglar alarm stated in the Schedule, which has been approved by Insurers and that no withdrawal, alteration or variation of the system or any structural alteration which might affect the system shall be made without the consent of the Insurers,
>
> (b) the burglar alarm system shall have been put into full and effective operation at all times when the Insured's premises are closed for business and at all other appropriate times, including when the said premises are left unattended,
>
> (c) the burglar alarm system shall have been maintained in good order throughout the currency of this insurance under a maintenance contract with a competent specialist alarm company who are approved by the Insurers,
>
> All defects occurring in any protections must be promptly remedied.

Flaux J held that neither warranty had been breached. He considered that the warranties had to be read as a whole. The judge held that the words 'the protections provided for the safety of the insured property' in the PMW referred to those protections in place when the risk incepted so that the PMW and the BAMW each applied to the burglar alarm in place on inception even though there was no alarm 'stated in the schedule'. He regarded the wording that required the prompt remedying of defects formed part of the warranties and would be deprived of their effect if the warranties were construed as imposing a strict obligation on the insured to ensure that the alarm system remained in effective operation at all times. He held that the words 'All defects occurring in any protections must be promptly remedied' meant that the warranties were confined to the defects of which the assured was aware but which had not been remedied. As the insured was not aware of the defects, there was no breach of either warranty. Flaux J held that the test arising from the wording in question was whether there had been a reckless failure to maintain.

By contrast, in *Milton Furniture Ltd v Brit Insurance Ltd*[107] the insured suffered a fire to a warehouse that had been deliberately started by unknown persons. The people on the adjoining premises were awoken by the fire alarm but the burglar alarm had not been set. The insurance policy contained a warranty (PW1) which stated:

> It is a condition precedent to the liability of the Underwriters in respect of loss or damage caused by Theft and/or attempted Theft, that the Burglar Alarm shall have been put into full and proper operation whenever the premises […] are left unattended.

General condition 7 (GC7) of the policy also stated:

> The whole of the protections including any Burglar Alarm provided for the safety of the premises shall be in use at all times out of business hours or when the Insured's premises are left

[107] [2014] Lloyds Rep IR 540.

> unattended and such protections shall not be withdrawn or varied to the detriment of the interests of Underwriters without their prior consent.

The judge found that GC7 was a condition precedent to insurers' liability, but that it was qualified by PW1, so that the insured was only required to set the burglar alarm if the premises were left unattended, which they had not been. However, he concluded that the insured had breached GC7 because the company responsible for monitoring the burglar alarm had stopped doing so as a result of the insured failing to pay its invoices. He held that the insured had been reckless as to the risk that the monitoring service would be cut off. Jay J held that the test as to whether the requirement that the 'alarm system shall have been maintained in good order', was more akin to ordinary negligence: 'In my judgment, an insured is in breach of the second limb of [the relevant condition] if it acts or fails to act in such a way that there is a real risk that the adverse consequence might flow.'[108] The Court of Appeal dismissed the appeal. It concluded that GC7 – which the Court of Appeal agreed was a condition precedent – required the whole of the protections provided by the burglar alarm to be in use in two alternative eventualities: at all times out of business hours or when the premises were left unattended. In light of that finding, it was not necessary to determine the issue about the burglar alarm monitoring service because the insured had been obliged to set the burglar alarm. However, the Court of Appeal considered that GC7 imposed a strict obligation on the insured in respect of the monitoring service. In addition, it held that if that conclusion was wrong, the test for determining whether the insured was in breach of GC7 was not a test of recklessness. It was whether the insured was aware of the facts which gave rise to the withdrawal of the monitoring service, or should have known of those facts.[109]

These decisions were made prior to the IA 2015. Section 11 will again require an analysis of whether risk-mitigating terms and in particular terms requiring the installation of alarm systems and other protections are risk-defining terms or risk-reducing terms. If the latter, insurers will again only be able to rely on their breach if that increased the risk of loss that in fact occurred.

Unlike with third-party motor policies, there are no additional risk-specific constraints on the terms that home and contents insurers can impose on insureds. As homes become increasingly connected, insurers may impose additional obligations on insureds by way of securing or maintaining properties by means of such devices as conditions of cover. The more connected devices in a home, the more evidence that will also be able to insurers not just in real time, but in any event upon the investigation of claims.

IV. Conclusions

Policies based on big data analytics whether prior to or during the policy period can adopt terms to provide increasingly tailored cover during the policy period. These are

[108] ibid, para 168.

[109] And applied the decision in *Melik & Co v Norwich Union Fire Insurance Society* [1980] 1 Lloyd's Rep 523 in so finding.

subject to some general and other risk-specific constraints. The general constraints will at most apply to risk-reducing clauses and the FCA Handbook and CRA 2015 will rarely offer any additional protection going beyond that offered by s 11 of the IA 2015. Risk-specific terms are also relatively limited. It follows that there is little restraint on the way in which insurers may avail of their increased knowledge of the risk, pre and post inception, to impose additional risk-specific limitations and incentives on individual policies. All of this additional information about the risk both pre and post inception not only impacts on the utility of certain terms that may respond to events occurring during the policy; it also raises the fundamental question as to the impact it will have on insureds' and insurers' duty of good faith disclosure, to the extent that those duties survive statutory modification. It is to that question that chapter five now turns.

5

Good Faith and Duties of Disclosure in Insurance Law

This chapter sets out how duties of disclosure arise in English contract law and in particular in English insurance contract law. It considers the rationale of duties of disclosure both in general law and in insurance law as the latter has evolved from the codes established under the law merchant to the recent overhaul of English insurance law pursuant to CIDRA 2012 and the IA 2015. A key purpose of this book is to consider the effect that big data has on the pre-existing information asymmetries that exist between insured and insurers. However, it will be seen that the impact of big data played no role at all in the Law Commission's review of existing law or in the formulation of its proposals for reforming the law. The chapter nevertheless considers whether the reforms that have been adopted in fact achieve an outcome that reflects the impact that big data has on insurance practice and in turn on insurance law. In particular, insofar as big data enables a very significant 'levelling-up' of the information asymmetry that previously characterised the relationship between insured and insurer, the effective abolition of the duty of good faith in consumer insurance reflects those changes, notwithstanding that this phenomenon was not relied upon in support of law reform. A duty of disclosure remains in non-consumer insurance but this may be appropriate given the differences between consumer and non-consumer risks and the fact that big data may (for the time being) play less of an overall role in assessing such risks: it would appear more difficult for predictive analytics to profile business interruption or professional risks than to assess motor or health risks. However, post-reform, the duty of good faith, albeit in modified form, continues to apply to insureds and insurers: while the duty of disclosure has either been abolished or modified for insureds, the recent legislative changes are silent on the extent of the duties owed by insurers. Yet if big data delivers on its promises in relation to risk assessment and claims handling, the duty as it applies to insurers might need to be extended to reflect how insurers use new sources of information and insight in understanding the nature of risk and in assessing the validity of claims. The chapter thus concludes that the duty of good faith as it applies to insurers ought to be maintained and may indeed require further development to accommodate the way in which insurers may use the information to which they increasingly have access.

I. Duties of Disclosure in English Contract Law

The structure of the general law of contract largely took shape in the nineteenth century with the explosion of the market economy. As Collins notes, '[a]s markets became the dominant instrument for the production and allocation of wealth, the nineteenth-century conception of contract law supplied the tool by which these market regulations could be understood and regulated.' As to the rationale for the structure of contract, he recalls that: '[t]he latent social idea of the nineteenth-century law of contract embodies a libertarian state, in which the law maximises the liberty of individual citizens, encourages self-reliance and adopts an avowedly neutral stance with regard to permissible patterns of social life. The law of contract secures these goals perhaps more effectively than any other category of the law by facilitating the creation of legal obligations on any terms which individuals freely choose.'[1] A core organising principle of the English law of contract is self-reliance, a principle born of classical contract's libertarian foundations. If parties are to remain free to choose whether or not to enter into a contract right up to the moment of accepting the offer, such flexibility militates against the existence of pre-contractual obligations. The absence of pre-contractual obligations during the negotiation phase gives parties room for manoeuvre and ultimately, the ability to walk away at any moment prior to a contract having come into existence. Pre-contractual obligations thus call for justification.

Parties to all contracts are under a duty not to make misrepresentations about the subject-matter of the proposed contract. Such an obligation exists to enable parties to be confident that they will be able to rely on what they have been expressly or impliedly told or promised. In the end, the duty not to make misrepresentations is a limited obligation: a seller need not, without more, say anything about the product he is selling; if he is asked a question, he is merely under a duty not to tell lies or answer in a way that is positively misleading. The courts have, on many occasions, recognised that parties owe pre-contractual duties in relation to the subject-matter of the proposed contract, duties which relate, amongst other things, to the information that ought to have been shared with the other party. And those duties have not arisen exclusively in relation to those limited categories of contract that may be described as contracts of utmost good faith. These duties have often been recognised where one party to a prospective contract is in a special position to know certain facts or to ascertain them, relative to the other party. In such circumstances, the former party has been obliged to take such reasonable care as would be expected of someone in that special position in communicating information to the other party.[2] Similarly, most pre-contractual statements as to the law may not be reasonably relied upon save where a statement as to the legal effects of a document are made by a person who ought to understand those effects. In such

[1] H Collins, *The Law of Contract* 3rd edn (London, Butterworths, 1997), 8.

[2] See, eg, *Howard Marine & Dredging Co Ltd v A Ogden & Sons (Excavations) Ltd* [1978] QB 574 where, during negotiations for the hire of some barges, the owner's agent stated their freight capacity on the strength of an inaccurate entry in the Lloyd's Register of ships, and omitted to check the owner's records of capacity. The agent was held liable for negligent misrepresentation because he was in a position to check the accuracy of the registers whereas other persons could have made the same statement without negligence, for normally the Lloyd's Register is a reliable document.

circumstances it has been held that the other party might reasonably rely on such statements: *Cornish v Midland Bank*.[3] Statements of opinion are also usually not capable of being relied upon save where they are given by those with sufficient expertise that those statements imply a basis in knowledge that is justified: *Esso Petroleum v Mardon*.[4] In that case Lord Denning said:

> If a man, who has or professes to have special knowledge or skill, makes a representation by virtue thereof to another – be it advice, information or opinion – with the intention of inducing him to enter into a contract with him, he is under a duty to use reasonable care to see that the representation is correct and that the advice, information or opinion is reliable.

In all of these cases, the party making the representation was in a special position of knowledge or expertise. The party in that position comes under a duty to make statements of fact with reasonable care in light of that special position or knowledge in circumstances where it was reasonable – in part because of the former's skill or position of knowledge – for the other party to rely on those statements. But in all of these examples, the duty on the party with special knowledge or in a special position is in reality a duty to take additional care in making positive representations about matters relevant to the proposed contract; they are not positive duties of disclosure as such.

However, the law will on occasion require parties to disclose information bearing on the terms of the proposed contract. Parties are entitled to be fully appraised of the terms of a proposed transaction in order to be able to make informed comparisons between alternative offerings. Drawing a party's attention to a particularly onerous term in what was otherwise a standard form contract provides one example.[5] That duty goes beyond merely requiring a party to take care in what is volunteered about matters pertaining to the contract. The cases where an obligation to disclose have been found to exist again arise as a result of one party's superior skill or knowledge and also where the relationship can be characterised as one of dependency. For example, disclosure of information may be required where, in the context of a relationship of dependence, a statement which, when made, was true, is rendered untrue prior to the formation of the contract. Thus, in *With v O'Flanagan*,[6] during negotiations for the sale of a business the seller stated the current value of the business but, prior to completion of the sale, fell considerably in value. The failure of the seller to disclose the change in value was treated as a misrepresentation and entitled the purchaser to rescind. The liability reflected the fact that the change of circumstances imposed a duty on the seller to disclose the changed circumstances.

Collins contends that the various instances of pre-contractual information obligations derive from a prior, general duty to negotiate with care, rather than a duty to bargain in good faith. He suggests that

> [w]hat English Law requires of parties is carefulness towards each other during the period of negotiation. The modern law rejects the strong protection of freedom of contract afforded

[3] [1985] 3 All ER 513.
[4] [1976] QB 801.
[5] *Interfoto Picture Library Ltd v Stiletto Visual Programmes Ltd* [1989] QB 433.
[6] [1936] Ch 575.

> by the absence of pre-contractual obligations, and instead recognises that some obligations of respect for the interests of others should be owed during negotiations.[7]

This is said to be justified for two reasons: (1) such rules are said to protect the operation of a competitive market where misleading claims about products (or, here, risks) can make it difficult to acquire the requisite information to make an informed choice about the various options (including, in the context of insurance, the decision whether or not to insure a risk). That reflects the concerns over adverse selection that pose an existential threat to the competitiveness of the insurance market: without knowing – or having some reliable guide – to which risks are good and which bad, insurers may end up with poorer risks leading to liabilities exceeding premium income; and (2) a duty of care during negotiations recognises that even in the absence of a concluded contract, the parties may enter into a relationship of dependence during the negotiations where the actions of one party may result in economic harm to the other.[8]

Similarly, Professor Beatson (as he then was) notes that the justification for the general rule whereby contracting parties are not required to provide pre-contractual disclosure is the need to give people an incentive to invest in the acquisition of skill and knowledge and consequently to allow 'good deals' to the more intelligent or hard-working. He states:

> This economic argument for the general rule does not obviously apply to information which has been acquired by pure chance or without any investment. Nor can it be dispositive where the information is acquired by a method regarded by the law as illegitimate – for example where it is 'inside' information. There may also be situations where it may be economically efficient to impose a duty of disclosure.

He further notes that the exceptions to the general rule are all based 'on inequality of information', noting (in 1997) that 'inequality of information is endemic'. He thus argued that

> [o]ne of two additional factors appears in the cases falling within the exceptions. It is either impossible for the other party to acquire the relevant information from any source other than the counterparty to the contract either at all or without incurring considerable expense. Alternatively, the relationship between the contracting parties is not a pure arm's length commercial relationship but one of trust and confidence or one of dependence.[9]

Clearly, he considered insurance to be a paradigmatic example of the former, and fiduciary or confidential relationships exemplars of the latter. But as we have seen already, it is no longer right to say that it is impossible or economically ruinous for insurers to obtain very substantial information about the insured and the proposed risk. That suggests the duty as it applies between insured and insurer will be justified only infrequently when it will be genuinely impossible for insurers to acquire the relevant information about the risk from other sources. That is particularly so where insurers

[7] Collins, above n 1, p 170.

[8] Collins contends that these cases support a duty to engage in pre-contractual negotiations with care, which is preferable to a duty to bargain in good faith. He contends that the 'latter formulation implies that the law merely requires honesty, which is plainly inaccurate in instances of negligence liability.' ibid, p 204.

[9] Jack Beatson, 'Has the Common Law a Future?', 1997 *CLJ* 291.

will habitually obtain information from other sources for the purposes of risk profiling. But what if insureds have, as a result of those practices, no idea as to the basis on which insurers are assessing the risk that they present? Insureds will not be able to know from any source other than the insurer what data the insurer has taken into account in offering the terms offered or in not making any offer at all. And the competitive markets rationale suggests that insureds ought to be put in a position to be able to compare offers of insurance and they will not be able to do that if they do not know what factors two different insurers took into account in assessing their risk.

II. The Good Faith Duty of Disclosure in Insurance Law

A. Evolution and Rationale of the Duty of Disclosure

This section considers in detail the development and precise rationale of the original duty of disclosure before considering the impact of the reforms of 2012 and 2015. This section charts the evolution and rationale of the duty, both as it applies to the insured and insurer, and as it applies pre- and post-inception.

i. Insured's Pre-contractual Duty

The origins of the duty of good faith disclosure are often traced to the judgments of Lord Mansfield and, in particular, his seminal decision in *Carter v Boehm*.[10] But the beginnings of the modern duty appeared certainly by the 1570s–1580s in the London Insurance Code of that time.[11] One article of that code provided:

> all persons whatsoever, that will cause any Assurance to be made, and meaneth to take any benefit by Assurance … shall not conceale any thing, that may tend to the hurt & hindrance of the Assurer, but with playne and true meaning shall give & continue his Assurance for as the Assurer putteth himself in place of the Assured… so ought the Assured to practice no sleight nor deceipt, to the hindrance of the Assurer, And if any deceipt be found & so judged by the Iudges, or Councellors appointed for the tyme being, such pollicy of Assurance shalbe voyd, and the Assurer shalbe free.[12]

In asking the insurer to step into his shoes, the insured was required to put the insurer into an equivalent position as regards his knowledge of the risk. If the insurer was not provided with knowledge of matters that bore on the risk, he could not in those circumstances be treated as having been put in the same position as the insured and could avoid the policy.

[10] (1766) 3 Burr 1905.

[11] Guido Rossi, *Insurance in Elizabethan England* (Cambridge, CUP, 2016), Ch 5.

[12] Art 35 (Harleian 5103, fol 165r) or Art 39 (Additional 48023, fol 256v–257r). And see Rossi, *Insurance in Elizabethan England*, above n 11, 244–45, 546–47, 676. The law merchant was fully subsumed within the common law by the 18th century. However, it was not until the late 19th century that the courts began to classify the duty as falling within the common law. See *Fletcher v Krell* (1873) 42 LJQB 55, where Blackburn J observed that the rule had its origins in mercantile custom.

a. *Carter v Boehm*

Carter v Boehm was decided over 200 years later and is regarded as the origin of the modern duty of good faith as it applies to insureds and insurers.[13] In that case the Governor of Fort Marlborough on the Island of Sumatra had foreseen the possibility of an attack on the fort and sought insurance cover in the event of such an attack.[14] The attack having duly materialised,[15] a claim was brought under the policy of insurance. The claim was disputed. The defendant contended that the claimant had concealed circumstances 'which ought to have been disclosed and particularly, the weakness of the fort[16] and the probability of its being attacked by the French'. Counsel for the defendant argued that 'the insurer has a right to know as much as the insured himself knows' and further contended that 'whatever really increases the [risk] ought to be disclosed'. In his judgment Lord Mansfield stated:

> The special facts, upon which the contingent chance is to be computed, lie most commonly in the knowledge of the insured only; the under-writer trusts to his representation, and proceeds upon confidence that he does not keep back any circumstance in his knowledge, to mislead the under-writer into a belief that the circumstance does not exist, and to induce him to estimate the risque, as if it did not exist.
>
> The keeping back such circumstance is a fraud, and therefore the policy is void. Although the suppression should happen through mistake, without any fraudulent intention; yet still the under-writer is deceived, and the policy is void; because the risque run is really different from the risque understood and intended to be run, at the time of the agreement.[17]

Lord Mansfield thus expressly considered that the information imbalance between insured and insurer in relation, specifically, to the risk to be insured, was the basis for the insured's duty. It appears that Lord Mansfield considered that there were two ways in which the duty could be breached: by concealment, as he defined it; and by a non-fraudulent mistake. As to the former, he stated:

> Good faith forbids either party by concealing what he privately knows, to draw the other into a bargain, from his ignorance of that fact, and his believing the contrary. But either party may be innocently silent, as to grounds open to both, to exercise their judgment upon. Aliud est celare; aliud, tacere; neque enim id est celare quicquid reticeas; sed cum quod tuscias,

[13] Probably the most detailed legal and historical analysis of the case is provided by Stephen Watterson in 'The History of a Landmark: Carter v Boehm', in Y Han and G Pynt (eds), *Carter v Boehm and Pre-Contractual Duties in Insurance Law: A Global Perspective after 250 Years* (Oxford, Hart Publishing, 2017).

[14] Carter insured against loss to trading stock in the event of an attack. The sum insured against was payable upon the occurrence of the attack. That gave it the prima facie appearance of a wagering policy, where a payment out would occur irrespective of the scope of the actual loss. However, Carter plainly had an insurable interest in the stock insured against and it appears that the sum agreed to be payable upon an attack rendered the policy not a wager but a valued policy whereby the parties agreed the measure of indemnity in advance.

[15] Albeit that the attack was made not, as had been expected, by the French, but by the Dutch.

[16] It was common ground between the parties that the fort, the powder and the guns were not in good and proper condition and that the Governor knew this. Moreover, it had previously been found as a fact that, as Lord Mansfield put it, 'the fort was a factory or settlement, but no military fort or fortress. That it was not established for a place of arms or defence against the attacks of an European enemy; but merely for the purpose of trade, and of defence against the natives.'

[17] At 1164.

> id ignorare emolumenti tui causa velis eos, quorum intersit id scire.[18] This definition of concealment, restrained to the efficient motives and precise subject of any contract, will generally hold to make it void, in favour of the party misled by his ignorance of the thing concealed.

The translation of the Latin passage is important to understanding what Lord Mansfield meant by 'concealment' and thus what constituted a breach of the duty of disclosure. In English, the passage translates:

> It is one thing to conceal, another to remain silent; for not everything you keep silent about is (a case of) concealment; but (rather) when, for the sake of your own profit, you want those, in whose interest it is to know, to remain ignorant of what you know.

The insured would thus be in breach of duty if he consciously failed to disclose a relevant matter because he believed that it will be to his advantage not to do so (for example, in order to obtain cover at all, or cover on better terms).

Concealment, in that conscious or fraudulent sense, was certainly sufficient to establish a breach, but it was not necessary as Lord Mansfield indicated that the withholding could lead to the policy being avoided where the suppression 'should happen through mistake, without any fraudulent intention'. That concealment is sufficient but not necessary appears clearly from the following further passages in his judgment:

> The reason of the rule which obliges parties to disclose, is to prevent fraud, and to encourage good faith. It is adapted to such facts as vary the nature of the contract; which one privately knows, and the other is ignorant of, and has no reason to suspect. The question therefore must always be 'whether there was, under all the circumstances at the time the policy was under-written, a fair representation; or a concealment; fraudulent, if designed; or, though not designed, varying materially the object of the policy, and changing the risque understood to be run.

Lord Mansfield then went on to explain where an insured may be 'innocently silent', that is, where he would not, by the non-disclosure in question, fail to fairly present the risk such as to breach the duty of good faith:

> There are many matters, as to which the insured may be innocently silent – he need not mention what the under-writer knows – Scientia utrinque par pares contrahentes facit. An under-writer can not insist that the policy is void, because the insured did not tell him what he actually knew; what way soever he came to the knowledge. The insured need not mention what the under-writer ought to know; what he takes upon himself the knowledge of; or what he waves being informed of.

Thus if the insurer discovers matters relevant to the risk, he cannot seek to avoid cover just because the insured did not himself make the insurer aware of those matters. Lord Mansfield went on at pages 1910–1911 of Burrough's report to list the circumstances when it could not be said that there was an information imbalance such as to require the insured to give disclosure. In summary, he considered that an insurer could not complain of non-disclosure of any matter he knew or ought to have known,

[18] There appears to be a typographical error in the law report: 'tuscias' is not a word; the report ought to read 'tu scias'.

nor of any matter of which he had waived disclosure or had assumed the burden of inquiry; insurers would be taken to know matters of general public notoriety and matters arising in the ordinary course of insuring risks of that nature. Importantly, Lord Mansfield expected the insurer to make his own assessment of the risk and he could not avoid a policy where the insured[19] failed to disclose matters that would serve to reduce the risk.

On the facts, Lord Mansfield found – in relation to the alleged concealment of the condition of the fort – that:

> The underwriter knew the insurance was for the governor. He knew the governor must be acquainted with the state of the place. He knew the governor could not disclose it, consistent with his duty. He knew the governor, by insuring, apprehended at least the possibility of an attack. With this knowledge, without asking a question, he underwrote. By so doing, *he took the knowledge of the state of the place upon himself.*[20] It was a matter as to which he might be informed in various ways: it was not a matter within the private knowledge of the governor only.

Evidently Lord Mansfield considered that if there was no significant information asymmetry, including where the insurer had other means of knowledge of the risk insured, then it was for the insurer to decide to what extent he would make enquiry of the risk from those other sources. It was thus only in relation to matters that (i) are within the private knowledge of the insured; (ii) which are not disclosed, whether through concealment or inadvertently through mistake; and (iii) which vary materially the nature of the risk to be underwritten, which give rise to a breach of the duty.

What is of most interest in Lord Mansfield's judgment is perhaps not points (ii) or (iii) above, but point (i). Lord Mansfield approached the question of what remained within the private knowledge of the insured in a way that substantially favoured the insured: insurers were obliged to further investigate matters that were publicly known or ascertainable. It followed that the insured's duty could be readily discharged by disclosing sufficient information to put insurers on notice of matters which, if considered material to the risk, insurers could investigate themselves. Only non-disclosure of matters material to the risk that remained within the private knowledge of the insured would violate the duty of good faith disclosure.

[19] On the facts insurers alleged non-disclosure of: (i) the condition of the fort; (ii) a letter from a third party as to the fact that the French had planned to attack the fort in the previous year; and (iii) the insured's own assessment of the likelihood of an attack. As to (i) Lord Mansfield considered that insurers knew that the fort was a trading post and not capable of defending an attack from a foreign military force; as to (ii) Lord Mansfield considered that insurers would be in a better position to know of the wider risk presented by French forces and considered that the previous year's attack not having materialised, it might now be less likely to occur; and as to (iii) an insured was not obliged to disclose his own speculations; it was for insurers to exercise their judgment on the facts of which they were or ought to have been aware. In each of these circumstances, insurers were not prejudiced by any information asymmetry and thus the duty did not arise in relation to any of the matters the subject of the allegations of non-disclosure. In all the circumstances, insurers had failed to take advantage of various means of knowledge available to them or make further inquiry even though insurers knew more than enough to have been put on inquiry.

[20] Emphasis added.

Hasson contends that Lord Mansfield's judgment in *Carter v Boehm*[21]

> has been cited in such a way as to make it appear that it is the insured's duty to supply information while the insurer's role in the process is an entirely passive one.[22] A reasonably careful reading of the opinion, however, makes it clear that Lord Mansfield placed the responsibility for obtaining the relevant information on the insurer.

He contends that it is only by properly emphasising the passage where his Lordship described the various aspects of the risk of which the insurer knew and in relation to which 'he took the knowledge of the place upon himself' will it be apparent that the insured's duty is relatively limited.[23]

Therefore, that of which the insurer was on notice and which was otherwise capable of being publicly ascertained would fall to the insurer to further investigate. Had big data been available to insurers at the time Lord Mansfield was developing the duty of good faith, he might have considered that, insofar as these technologies push back the boundary of what remains within the 'private knowledge' of the insured and radically alters the way in which information may be obtained, stored or retrieved, the duty was even more readily discharged by the insured.

b. Case Law Subsequent to *Carter v Boehm*[24]

In *Mayne v Walter*[25] a Portuguese ship was insured and warranted neutral. She carried an English supercargo, a fact which was not known to the underwriter, and which was contrary to a French Ordinance. On this ground she was captured, and condemned as a prize. The report records[26] that neither party knew of the Ordinance, which was said to be arbitrary, and contrary to the law of nations. The report noted: 'The parties are both innocent, and the underwriter who takes the risk ought to be the sufferer.' Lord Mansfield said: 'If both parties were ignorant of [the French Ordinance] the underwriter must run all risk: and if the defendant knew of such an edict it was his duty to enquire if such a super cargo were on board.' That the insured's duty of disclosure was a narrow one is again reflected in the fact that Lord Mansfield held that there must be a 'fraudulent concealment of circumstances that will vitiate a policy'. Although the

[21] And in particular the passage: 'The special facts, upon which the contingent chance is to be computed, lie most commonly in the knowledge of the insured only; the under-writer trusts to his representation, and proceeds upon confidence that he does not keep back any circumstance in his knowledge, to mislead the under-writer into a belief that the circumstance does not exist, and to induce him to estimate the risque, as if it did not exist.'

[22] RA Hasson, 'The Doctrine of Uberrima Fides in Insurance Law – a critical evaluation' (1969) 32 *MLR* 615.

[23] As Hasson notes, 'This passage would seem to indicate beyond any doubt that Lord Mansfield conceived of the insured's duty as being a very narrow one.' He further points out that it could not have been remotely straightforward for an insurer to ascertain information about the state of Fort Marlborough on the island of Sumatra in 1766. Yet, being on notice of what was sought to be insured, the insurer came under a duty to ascertain the state of its defences if they considered that material to the risk they insured.

[24] Lord Mansfield only referred to a duty of good faith. It was only in *Wolff v Horncastle* (1798) 1 B & P 316 that Buller J referred to the contract of insurance being a contract *uberrimae fidei*, that is, a contract of 'utmost' good faith.

[25] (1782) 3 Douglas 79.

[26] The report is in Park, 'The Law of Marine Insurances' (1787) at p 220.

existence of the supercargo was, in light of the terms of the French Ordinance, plainly material to the risk, the insured not knowing of the Ordinance was not obliged to disclose it.

Subsequently, in *Friere v Woodhouse*,[27] the insurer refused cover on the basis that the insured had not disclosed a detail that could have been ascertained by public means. Specifically, the claimants sought to insure a ship that was to sail from Brazil to Lisbon. It set sail with another ship called the Victorioso which duly arrived in port in Lisbon. The insurers contended that the claimant ought to have disclosed the fact that the Victorioso had arrived in Lisbon. However, that fact was capable of being ascertained from Lloyd's Lists. Burrough J held:

> the arrival of the other vessels at Lisbon from Maranham (however important this intelligence might be) must be presumed within the knowledge of the underwriters, from the circumstance of its being contained in Lloyd's printed Lists. What is exclusively known to the assured ought to be communicated; but what the underwriter, by fair inquiry and due diligence may learn from ordinary sources of information need not be disclosed.[28]

That again raised the question as to what a fair enquiry requires and what ordinary sources of information might consist in such that insurers could be expected or deemed to have investigated those sources.

However, in a series of later nineteenth-century cases, the courts recalibrated the requirements of the duty as it fell, respectively, on insureds and insurers. In particular, and contrary to Lord Mansfield's original views, these cases (i) required the insured to provide a much greater degree of disclosure such that (ii) the circumstances in which insurers came under a duty of enquiry were very significantly reduced. In *Lindenau v Desborough*,[29] a case about the failure of the doctors of a foreign life insured to disclose the existence of a tumour on the insured's brain, Bayley J found there was a wider obligation on the insured stating as follows:

> I think that in all cases of insurance, whether on ships, houses or lives, the underwriter should be informed of every material circumstance within the knowledge of the assured; and that the proper question is, whether any particular circumstance was in fact material and not whether any party believed it to be so. The contrary doctrine would lead to frequent suppression of information and it would often be extremely difficult to show that the party neglecting to give the information thought it material.

This passage expressly raises the prospect of exploitation of the insurer if the insured could effectively discharge his duty by providing minimal information and leaving it to insurers to make further enquiries. Littledale J similarly noted that

> there may also be circumstances affecting particular individuals which are not likely to be known … to the assurers and which had they been known would no doubt have been made the subject of specific enquiries. The general question appears to have been proposed in order to meet such cases, and I think the question on such a policy is not whether a certain individual thought a particular fact material, but whether it was in truth material.

[27] (1817) 1 Holt NP 572.

[28] The matter was left to a jury, a special jury of merchants, who considered that as this information was to be taken as in the hands of underwriters, there was no concealment.

[29] (1828) 8 B&C 586.

The broadening of the scope of the insured's duty of disclosure as regards the nature of the risk – and in particular the point at which insurers are regarded as having been put on notice or deemed to know or have the means of knowing the matters in question – clearly emerges in the case of *Bates v Hewitt*.[30] In that case a policy had been effected on a ship called the Georgia which had previously operated as a Confederate cruiser and whose history was well known to the British public. The defendant, a Lloyd's underwriter, had previously been aware of the ship's notoriety but at the time the risk was proposed, had forgotten these details. While the jury found the defendant to have been ignorant of the ship's history, they also found that at the time of insuring the cruiser, he had abundant means of identifying the ship and ascertaining material facts as to its history. Despite having the means of ascertaining those facts, a unanimous court held that that did not release the insured from the duty of disclosure. Lord Cockburn CJ stated:

> No proposition of insurance law can be better established than this viz that the party proposing the insurance is bound to communicate to the insurer all matters which will enable him to determine the extent of the risk against which he undertakes to guarantee the assured.

In contrast to the approach of Lord Mansfield in *Carter v Boehm*, Shee J, after conceding that the underwriter in the present case might 'if he had instituted enquiries' have discovered the material fact in question, nevertheless added: 'but that he is not obliged to do'. Again, and in contrast to Lord Mansfield's approach, it was no longer the case that only those matters material to the risk and within the private knowledge of the insured must be disclosed; even if insurers had the means of publicly ascertaining those matters, it was nevertheless for the insured to disclose all material facts in full.

But notwithstanding the shift away from Lord Mansfield's pro-insured approach, the rationale for the duty remained the same. In *Anderson v Pacific Fire and Marine Insurance Co*[31] Willes J thus said:

> The rule as to the good faith which is required to be observed on the effecting a policy of insurance is so strict that the assured is bound to make known to the underwriter all the information in his power which is not within the ordinary knowledge and experience of an underwriter.

In other words, the duty of disclosure principally fell on he who had the greater knowledge and information.

c. Codification in the Marine Insurance Act 1906

The common law principles were codified in the Marine Insurance Act 1906 (MIA 1906). The common law's acceptance that contracts of insurance were contracts of utmost good faith was recognised in s 17 of the MIA 1906, which codified the law of insurance in this respect, providing:[32] 'A contract of marine insurance is a contract

[30] (1867) LR 2 AB 595.

[31] (1872) LR 7 CP 65 at 68.

[32] That the principle of utmost good faith applies to all classes of insurance was confirmed prior to the 1906 Act: *London Assurance v Mansel* (1879) LR 11 QB 363, 367–69.

based upon the utmost good faith, and, if the utmost good faith be not observed by either party, the contract may be avoided by the other party.'[33] However, ss 18–20 of the MIA 1906 imposed further obligations of utmost good faith, but did so only in relation to the pre-contractual stage, and then only as against the insured or his agent: s 18(1) imposed a pre-contractual obligation on the insured to 'disclose to the insurer, before the contract is concluded, every material circumstance which is known to the assured which, in the ordinary course of business, ought to be known by him'. As the Law Commission later noted in 2014, the words of s 18 of the MIA 1906 suggest that an insurer 'may simply sit back and wait for the policyholder to disclose every material circumstance'.[34] Codification thus embodied the balance struck in the later nineteenth century cases, not that struck by Lord Mansfield.

In *London General Omnibus Co v Holloway*[35] Kennedy LJ held:

> no class of case occurs to my mind in which our law regards mere non-disclosure as a ground for invalidating the contract, except in the case of insurance. That is an exception which the law has wisely made in deference to the plain exigencies of this particular and most important class of transactions. The person seeking to insure may fairly be presumed to know all the circumstances which materially affect the risk, and, generally, is, as to some of them, the only person who has the knowledge; the underwriter, whom he asks to take the risk, cannot, as a rule, know, and but rarely has either the time or the opportunity to learn by inquiry, circumstances which are, or may be, most material to the formation of his judgment as to the acceptance or rejection of the risk, and as to the premium which he ought to require.

In *Greenhill v Federal Insurance Co*[36] Scrutton LJ said:

> insurance is a contract of the utmost good faith, and it is of the gravest importance to commerce that that position should be observed. The underwriter knows nothing of the particular circumstances of the voyage to be insured. The assured knows a great deal, and it is the duty of the assured to inform the underwriter of everything that he is not taken as knowing, so that the contract may be entered into on an equal footing.[37]

The same judge in *Newsholme Bros v Road Transport & General Insurance Co Ltd*[38] said: '[t]he contract of insurance requires the utmost good faith; the insurer knows nothing; the assured knows everything about the risk he wants to insure and he must disclose to the insurer every fact material to the risk.'

[33] Notwithstanding the fact that this provision was contained within a statute relating to marine insurance, the House of Lords has since held that the principle applies to all forms of insurance: *Manifest Shipping Co Ltd v Uni-Polaris Insurance Co Ltd (The Star Sea)* [2001] Lloyd's Rep IR 247.

[34] Law Commission, 'Insurance Contract Law: Business Disclosure; warranties; Insurers' Remedies for Fraudulent Claims; and Late Payment', No 353, July 2014, paras 6.6–6.8.

[35] [1912] 2 KB 72 at 86.

[36] [1927] 1 KB 65 at 76.

[37] The Judge relied further on Park's Marine Insurance and cited, inter alia, the passage at p 408 which stated: 'The second species of fraud, which affects insurances, is the concealment of circumstances, known only to one of the parties entering into the contract. Upon this head, the principles of law are perfectly clear, free from doubt or possibility of error. Concealment of circumstances vitiates all contracts, upon the principles of natural law. Insurance is a contract of speculation. The facts, upon which the risk is to be computed, lie, for the most part, within the knowledge of the insured only. The underwriter must therefore rely upon him for all necessary information; and must trust to him that he will conceal nothing, so as to make him form a wrong estimate.'

[38] [1929] 2 KB 356 at 362.

The rationale for the duty was repeated in cases throughout the twentieth century. In *Wales v Wadham*[39] Tudor Evans J thus observed that:

> [i]n contracts of insurance, the material facts upon which the insurer decides whether to assume the risk and, if so, upon what terms, lie exclusively within the knowledge of the insured. Contracts requiring *uberrimae fidei* are based upon the fact that from the very necessity of the case, only one party possesses knowledge of all the material facts. In the case of life assurance, for example, only the proposed assured can know the state of his health, past or present.

The imbalance in knowledge between insured and insurer was again emphasised in *Bank of Nova Scotia v Hellenic Mutual War Risks Association, The Good Luck*,[40] where Hobhouse J rejected the submission that an assignee of the benefit of an insurance policy owed or was owed a duty of good faith; it was a plain commercial agreement, not a contract of insurance. The Court of Appeal agreed and held that there was no necessary imbalance in the knowledge of the parties to warrant the classification of the undertaking as a contract of the utmost good faith. May LJ for the Court held: 'The common feature of … contracts [classified as of utmost good faith] is that

> 'by their very nature one party is likely to have the command of means of knowledge not available to the other': *per* Slade LJ, at p 769G–H.[41] The contract between the club and the bank does not seem to us to have been shown to be of that nature. It has not been demonstrated that the bank had at its command significantly less in the way of means of knowledge about the activities of the owners with reference to the risk insured than that which the club had. The bank had, of course, significantly less knowledge than the club as to what the club was saying or doing about any activities of the owners with reference to the risk insured. But any relevant action or inaction of the club would be a response to the activities of the owners and does not, in our view, so closely resemble the inequality of knowledge between the insured and the insurer at the stage of the making of a policy of insurance as to require the letter of undertaking to be treated as being itself a contract of utmost good faith.[42]

ii. Insurer's Pre-contractual Duty

In *Carter v Boehm*, Lord Mansfield also considered that a remedy would lie against the insurer for return of the premium if the insurer privately knew of facts which meant that he never came on risk. The example he gave was of the insurance of a ship's voyage where the insurer knew the ship had already arrived at her destination.[43] That would, he considered, amount to a breach of the insurer's good faith duty of disclosure. Again, the information asymmetry as between insurer and insured as regards the matters material to the risk was the basis for the duty. And having given examples

[39] [1977] 1 WLR 199 at 215.

[40] [1998] 1 Lloyd's Rep 514 (Hobhouse J); [1989] 2 Lloyd's Rep 238 (Court of Appeal).

[41] In *Banque Financière de la Cité SA v Westgate* [1990] 1 QB 665 (discussed further below).

[42] [1989] 2 Lloyd's Rep 238 at 264.

[43] In *Banque Financière de la Cité*, Lord Jauncey added the further example of an insurer agreeing to insure against fire a house that has already been demolished (960). Neither may be good examples as there would have been no insurable interest at the inception of cover such that the risk would never have attached.

of where remedies lay against insureds and insurers in light of their respective knowledge of the risk to be insured, it is apparent that Lord Mansfield considered the duty of good faith to apply both to insureds and insurers.

Very few authorities since *Carter v Boehm* have considered the mutuality of the duty. It was, however, confirmed a century later in *Britton v Royal Insurance Co.*[44] In that case Willes J merely stated that: 'The contract of insurance is one of perfect good faith on both sides, and it is most important that such good faith should be maintained.' There was no discussion of the rationale of the duty as it lay on insurers. Section 17 of the MIA 1906 did not confine the scope of the duty to a prospective insured; on its face, it is required to be observed by both parties to the contract, failure to do which will provide either party with the right to avoid. The nature of the duty as it fell on insurers was considered in a small number of cases at the end of the twentieth century. Steyn J made the first attempt to formulate the content of the insurer's duty in *Banque Financière de la Cité SA v Westgate Insurance Co*[45] and in doing so considered that the duty was not only mutual but based on the same rationale insofar as insurers would have to give disclosure of information bearing on the risk that was exclusively in their knowledge:

> The rationale of the rule imposing a duty of utmost good faith on the insured is that matters material to the risk are generally speaking peculiarly in his knowledge. In so far as matters are peculiarly in the insurer's knowledge, as in Lord Mansfield's example of the arrived ship, principle and fairness requires the imposition of a similar duty on the insurer.

In the Court of Appeal,[46] Slade LJ held, again relying on Lord Mansfield in *Carter v Boehm*, that: 'The common features of contracts which are classified by the law as contracts *uberrimae fidei* is that by their very nature one party is likely to have the command of means of knowledge not available to the other.'[47] His Lordship noted, as regards the application of the duty to insurers, that the MIA 1906 did not define the duties of disclosure falling on the insurer. He then said '[i]n our judgment, however, there is no doubt that the obligation to disclose material facts is a mutual one imposing reciprocal duties on insurer and insured. In the case of marine insurance contracts, section 17 in effect so provides.' However, he went on to state that:

> [t]he occasions where disclosure by the insurer is required may in practice be rare since the circumstances material to the insurance will ordinarily be known only to the proposed insured. Nevertheless, such occasions may arise. The mutuality of the duty under the common law was recognised by Lord Mansfield himself in *Carter v Boehm*.

The case confirms that where there is an information asymmetry between insurer and insured where insurers have exclusive knowledge of matters material to the risk (and information that might mean that the insured was overpaying or under-protected because of the impact that knowledge could have on the value of the cover), insurers would be obliged to disclose that information.

[44] (1886) 4 F & F 905, 909.
[45] [1987] 2 WLR 1300.
[46] [1990] 1 QB 665. At first instance the case was known as *Banque Keyser v Skandia*. The Court of Appeal's decision was later approved by the House of Lords in *Banque Financière de la Cité SA v Westgate Insurance Co Ltd* [1991] 2 AC 249.
[47] At 769.

iii. *Insured's Post-contractual Duty*

Lord Mansfield in *Carter v Boehm* said the duty of good faith is 'adapted to such facts as vary the nature of the contract'. He was referring to the fact that the duty of good faith is ambulatory and will revive when the nature of the risk presented to the insurer or undertaken by the insured changes or is proposed to be changed. That the duty revives and applies upon a proposed alteration of the risk, post-contractually, is reflected in a number of decisions. In *New Hampshire Insurance Co v MGN Ltd*[48] Potter J observed that:

> It is common ground as between the parties that, in accordance with general principles, there was a duty of disclosure upon the insureds (a) when the insurance was originally placed with the insurer in question; (b) when the insurance was renewed by the insurer in question and (c) on making and presenting a claim under the insurance, until such claim was accepted or rejected. To this should plainly be added, in my view, (d) when negotiating an endorsement or alteration in cover, in relation to facts concerning the subject matter of the endorsement or alteration.

He thus accepted that the obligation of good faith as between insurer and insured was one which continued throughout the policy, in particular in relation to the making of claims. However, he held that it did not apply 'so as to trigger positive obligations of disclosure of matters affecting the risk during the currency of the cover except in relation to some requirement, event or situation provided for in the policy to which the duty of good faith attaches'.[49] That the duty revives where the risk underwritten is proposed to be altered in the currency of the policy was again observed by Aikens J in *K/S Merc-Scandia XXXXII v Certain Lloyd's Underwriters (The Mercandian Continent)*,[50] who held:

> The rationale … must be that the right to cancel does not introduce a new risk nor does it involve the underwriter making a decision on a new situation in relation to the existing risk on which he has no knowledge and the assured has much. The right of cancellation gives him a right to terminate liability in respect of a risk that he has already accepted and in that there is no further element of speculation.

In the Court of Appeal in the same case, Longmore LJ listed the situations in which it had been suggested that good faith arose after the conclusion of a contract as including: (i) variations to the risk and 'held covered' clauses'; (ii) renewal; (iii) insurers asking for information during the policy;[51] and (v) the making of claims.[52] Longmore LJ held

[48] [1996] CLC 1692 at 1722.

[49] Reflecting the distinction, discussed in the previous chapter, between a material increase in the risk and a more fundamental change to the nature of the risk insured; that the risk of insured loss increases in the policy period not only does not avoid the policy; it does not trigger renewed duties of disclosure either. It followed that Potter J rejected the contention that a simple right of termination on notice constitutes such event or situation to which the duty of disclosure would re-attach. By extension, the mere decision to exercise any existing contractual right would not justify a duty of disclosure as the right had been created with the benefit of full disclosure when the contract was originally made (eg if a contingent condition subsequent occurs such as to trigger the insurer's entitlement eg to impose a further endorsement or raise premium, the exercise of that right flows from the original decision to offer cover subject to that term).

[50] [2000] 2 All ER (Comm) 731.

[51] Including, for example, by way of additional premium clauses.

[52] *K/S Merc-Scandia XXXXII v Certain Lloyd's Underwriters (The Mercandian Continent)* [2001] EWCA Civ 1275, [2001] 2 Lloyd's Rep 563. It is clear that the duty of good faith ceases once the parties enter into

that the duty of utmost good faith is a continuing duty and that it 'applies to all cases of fraudulent conduct', rejecting the submission that 'there are only some occasions when the requirement of good faith exists post-contract'. In that regard, he was not rejecting the ambulatory nature of the duty insofar as the requirement to give further disclosure arises where an underwriting decision that alters the scope of the cover is to be taken. Rather, he was observing that the duty operates at all times to prevent an insured acting fraudulently, most obviously by making a fraudulent claim.

The duty of good faith and the corresponding right to disclosure will apply in such degree as is appropriate for the circumstances in which it revives, whether that is renewal, the making of a claim or some other point where a decision has to be made about whether to continue cover and/or alter the scope of existing cover. Lord Clyde thus stated:

> The idea of good faith in the context of insurance contracts reflects the degrees of openness required of the parties in the various stages of their relationship. It is not an absolute. The substance of the obligation which is entailed can vary according to the context in which the matter comes to be judged.[53]

The proposed extension or alteration of a risk creates occasions on which the nature and extent of the risk falls to be reassessed. The duty is revived insofar (as is usually the case) the insured is required to provide information to the insurer to enable the latter to reassess the risk and thus the terms on which it is prepared to offer the revised cover. Insurers are entitled to know of material facts that alter the extent of the risk. In that regard, the duty mirrors that which is required of the parties pre-inception, albeit commensurately with the extent to which the risk has or is proposed to be altered.[54] If, upon renewal, there has been a very significant change to the nature of the risk, the insured will be obliged to provide detailed information of those changes.[55] If nothing has changed, the insured will not have to do more than confirm the same – he will not have to go through the motions of full disclosure all over again. As the Law Commission put it in its 2014 Report:

> Where the insured is being asked to make a further underwriting decision, the duty of good faith is justified in the same way as it is in respect of the precontractual duty of disclosure: the asymmetry of information between the parties. Where there is no underwriting decision to be made, it is less clear why the insurance relationship should be underpinned by a duty of good faith not imposed on other contractual relationships. This is reflected in the case law.[56]

litigation: *Manifest Shipping Co Ltd v Uni-Polaris Insurance Co Ltd (The Star Sea)* [2001] UKHL 1, [2003] 1 AC 469 at [77].

[53] *Manifest Shipping Co Ltd v Uni-Polaris Insurance Co Ltd (The Star Sea)* [2001] UKHL 1, [2003] 1 AC 469 at [7] and [48].

[54] And so upon a proposed variation to the cover (eg by the insured seeking to add additional interests by way of endorsement), the insured will be subject to a duty of fair presentation but only with respect to that aspect of the risk that is being increased or affected and not in relation to the contract as a whole: *Dalecroft Properties v Underwriters Subscribing to Certificate number 755/BA* [2017] EWHC 1263 (Comm).

[55] Subject to the fact that at the point at which the risk alters such as to render it entirely different from the risk insured, the policy will cease to cover that risk. If the insured wishes to reinstate the policy, a fresh duty of disclosure will arise.

[56] Law Commission 2014 Report, para 30.37.

The making of claims under the policy does not precisely mirror the pre-contractual duty in the way that the duty arising upon a variation of cover or renewal does. However, the courts have historically accepted that, just as with the seeking – or alteration – of cover, the insured will know much more about the circumstances of the peril that has occurred than insurers. There is again an information asymmetry which has justified the duty to disclose relevant information about the circumstances giving rise to the claim. That is reflected in *Rayner v Ritson*,[57] where Cockburn CJ held that:

> [t]he underwriter of a policy of marine insurance who is sued for a constructive total loss of the ship is so much at the mercy of the assured with respect to the circumstances under which the vessel has been abandoned, and there ought to be *uberrima fides* on the part of the latter, and he ought therefore to lay those circumstances before the underwriter. But that old practice goes far to shew us that … the assured must lay before the underwriter everything that throws light on a part of the transaction in which both parties are interested. It becomes very material to the assurer to see whether he ought to resist the demand of the assured if he should find material for so doing, or whether he ought not to give up defending the action and pay the amount of the insurance.[58]

Similarly in *Fargnoli v G A Bonus Plc*[59] Lord Penrose in the Court of Session said:

> I incline to the view that the duties associated with making a claim reflect the character of the contract and are duties of utmost good faith. Not only does the insured have control of the information required at the outset for the assessment of risk, if a casualty should occur he has at the date of making the claim exclusive control of the information on which the claim must be based. The insured is, typically, the dominant party in terms of having available relevant information. The risk of fabrication in such circumstances is real.[60]

Of course, if the insurer decides to investigate a claim before accepting it, good faith will require the insured to co-operate with that investigation. The insured will be required to allow insurers access to its files and databases to facilitate that investigation. As the investigation progresses, the imbalance between the insured and the insurer's knowledge declines and may approach equilibrium. The insured will have to answer questions arising from that investigation fairly and accurately. Such investigations will reduce the extent to which the insured is required to proactively disclose further information to the insurer.

In *Versloot Dredging BV v HDI Gerling Industrie Versicherung AG*[61] it was accepted that the duty not to present a fraudulent claim was part of the larger duty of utmost good faith but the court questioned whether the appropriate remedy was avoidance (a concern that is now mitigated by the operation of ss 12 and 14 of the IA 2015).

[57] (1865) 6 B & S 888, 891; 122 ER 1421.
[58] And see *Galloway v Guardian Royal Exchange (UK) Ltd* [1999] Lloyd's Rep IR 209 at 214.
[59] [1997] CLC 653 at 673.
[60] Similarly in *Orakpo v Barclays Insurance Services* [1995] LRLR 443 at 451 Hoffman LJ said: 'In principle insurance is a contract of good faith. I do not see why the duty of good faith on the part of the assured should expire when the contract has been made. The reasons for requiring good faith continue to exist. Just as the nature of the risk will usually be within the peculiar knowledge of the insured, so will the circumstances of the casualty; it will rarely be within the knowledge of the insurance company. I think that the insurance company should be able to trust the assured to put forward a claim in good faith.'
[61] [2016] UKSC 45; [2017] AC 1.

In any event, Lord Toulson referred to the information asymmetry as justifying the post-contractual duty:

> Insurance is about the assessment of risk and settlement of claims. Both processes depend on good faith and fair information and both are normally consensual ... The relationship of insured and insurer is a special one, in relation to which the good faith or *uberrimae fidei* has long been fundamental. As a special relationship it survived the failure of Lord Mansfield's attempt to introduce a general duty of good faith into English contract law. It did so rightly because of the general imbalance in information and control and the significance of moral hazard in insurance relationships. Insurance fraud is common place, often being regarded as a victimless crime in relation to which insurers are fair game. Of course insurers do not always pay claims as speedily as would be desired, but that is not an excuse for fraud and is something for which a separate remedy is under current legislative scrutiny.

However, just because the rationale of the duty derives from the information asymmetry that will exist and the desire to avoid fraud, it does not follow that the post-contractual duty will be breached if the insured fails to give the same degree of disclosure that would be required upon a proposed variation to the cover. In *Manifest Shipping Co Ltd v Uni-Polaris Shipping Co Ltd, The Star Sea*[62] the House of Lords agreed with the Court of Appeal's rejection of insurers' submission that the obligation to disclose facts after the contract is made is co-extensive with the obligation to disclose facts before the contract is made. However, it was clear that the reasoning was driven in part by the harshness of the potential remedy for breach, being avoidance, in circumstances where, although the presentation of the claim might have omitted certain material disclosure, it was nevertheless non-fraudulent.[63]

iv. Insurer's Post-contractual Duty

There are very few cases on the insurers' post-contractual duty of good faith. However, the duty is mutual and just as the insured owes duties of good faith post-inception, so too will the insurer in both considering or proposing variations and in handling claims. As to the former, if the insured sought to vary the contract during the policy period, not only is the insured obliged to disclose all facts material to the scope of the proposed variation, but were insurers to know of matters that bear on the nature of the risk, as varied, they would be obliged to disclose the same. Similarly, were a variation to be proposed by the insurer, a duty of disclosure will also arise. In *Lishman & Anor v Northern Maritime Insurance Co*[64] a proposal of marine insurance was made

[62] [2001] UKHL 1; [2001] 2 WLR 170.

[63] Lord Hobhouse thus observed (at [72]): 'It must be added that, on the facts found, had the defendants' defence succeeded it would have produced a wholly disproportionate result. The defence under section 39(5) failed after a full disclosure and investigation of all the material evidence. The claim was in fact a good one which the owners were, subject to quantum, entitled to recover under the policy. The defendants were liable to pay it. The policy was valid and enforceable. For the defendants successfully to invoke section 17 so as to avoid the policy ab initio and wholly defeat the claim would be totally out of proportion to the failure of which they were complaining. Fraud has a fundamental impact upon the parties' relationship and raises serious public policy considerations. Remediable mistakes do not have the same character.' There is thus no full duty of disclosure in respect of the making of a claim.

[64] (1875) LR 10 CP 179.

and accepted on 11 March. The ship was lost on 16 March. On 17 March, the insured with knowledge of the loss, but without communicating it to the insurers, demanded a stamped policy. On 17 March, insurers sought to impose an additional warranty that was additional to their acceptance of 11 March. Baron Bramwell held:[65]

> if the parties, after making the original agreement, were dissatisfied with the terms of it, and altered it in drawing up the final terms of the insurance, so as substantially to alter the nature of the bargain as affecting both sides. In that case it might well be that the obligation to communicate material facts would continue until the time of the execution of the policy, at any rate with respect to all matters material to the alteration of the terms.

As Aikens J observed, this is, in essence, precisely the same situation in which the parties find themselves when they negotiate the terms of the original contract.[66] And so where an insurer seeks to vary the contract for his own benefit, the insurer will, it is submitted, have to disclose all circumstances material to the proposed amendment.

B. Conclusion as to Rationale of the Duty of Disclosure

Insurers agree to indemnify insureds for loss that arises on the occurrence of the peril insured against. The cost of the cover is entirely contingent which makes it all the more important that insurers can accurately evaluate the risk of that contingency occurring and the magnitude of the loss should it do so. The courts have imposed the duty in response to the particular information asymmetry to which these features of insurance give rise. Historically, the insurers' principal source of information about the risk was the insured, whether directly or via his broker. It is unsurprising in those circumstances that the duty of disclosure was justified to require the insured to provide disclosure of facts material to the risk. The purpose of the duty was not merely to enable insurers to properly price the risk, but to avoid the insured exploiting the information imbalance, whether by obtaining cover at all (or on more favourable terms) or in obtaining payment upon the occurrence of the insured peril. That the duty of disclosure was designed to avoid fraud and exploitation has been clear throughout its evolution. It was expressly referred to by Lord Mansfield in *Carter v Boehm*. The anti-fraud rationale was relied upon by Lord Esher MR in *Blackburn Low & Co v Vigors*[67] as follows:

> It appears to me to be established by the cases to which I have referred, that in order to prevent fraud and wilful ignorance on the part of persons effecting insurances, no policy can be enforced by an assured who has been deliberately kept in ignorance of material facts by some one, whose moral if not legal duty it was to inform him of them, and who has been kept in such ignorance purposely in order that he might be able to effect the insurance without disclosing those facts. The person who allows the assured to effect a policy under such circumstances as I am now supposing, does not act fairly to the underwriters; and

[65] At 181; sic.

[66] *K/S Merc-Scandia XXXXII v Certain Lloyd's Underwriters (The Mercandian Continent)* [2000] 2 All ER (Comm) 731 at [43].

[67] (1886) 17 QBD 553 at 577–78.

> although such person may owe them no legal duty, the assured cannot in fairness hold the underwriters to the contract into which they have in fact entered under these circumstances.

In *Dalecroft Properties v Underwriters Subscribing to Certificate number 755/BA*[68] the Court again noted that '[t]he principles which [the MIA 1906 embodied] were developed at a time when the insured knew his business and while the insurer did not and were designed to protect the fledgling insurance industry against exploitation by the insured'.[69] The Law Commission in its Consultation Paper of July 2007 similarly recognised the role of the duty in preventing fraud: 'The law has long recognised that insurance is a special form of contract, which is particularly vulnerable to opportunistic behaviour by the insured.'[70] The aim of preventing fraud goes two ways. It is often easy for the beneficiary of the duty of good faith at any instance to abuse the good faith required of his counterpart by pressing for full compliance with the duty when such an end is truly not needed. In this way, the duty of good faith may actually result in the exercise of bad faith.[71] Although the concept of abuse of rights is not known to English law,[72] it is contrary to good faith if there is an abuse of rights, in this sense, by either party.[73]

But there is a second, separate rationale for the duty which might be called an efficiencies or market rationale. Insofar as there is an information imbalance and one that favours the insured, it would be more economically efficient to require the insured seeking cover to disclose facts material to the risk rather than insurers seeking to conduct an investigation for each new prospective insured. It would be inefficient for insurers to expend costs identifying information about risks that can be readily and cheaply provided by the insured. That is especially so when one thinks of the insured seeking cover from multiple insurers, each of whom will incur the cost of an investigation absent the duty falling on the insured. That will lead to each of those insurers who do not get the business wasting investigation costs which in turn reduces the total level of economic welfare. The market rationale explains the shift in the nineteenth-century cases away from Lord Mansfield's pro-insured stance of requiring disclosure of sufficient information to enable insurers to investigate the risk from publicly ascertainable sources, towards a much heavier duty on insureds to identify and disclose all matters material to the risk. The efficiency rationale has been expressly recognised in the cases.[74] It has also been recognised that the lack of such disclosure would result in

[68] [2017] EWHC 1263 (Comm).

[69] As MacGillvray notes, 'The national polity depended on the availability of affordable insurance against marine risks and war risks in those turbulent times and a rule of law which lightened the burdens of the emerging London market accorded with sound commercial policy'; 17-105.

[70] Law Commission Consultation Paper No 182, 'Insurance Contract Law: Misrepresentation, Non-Disclosure and Breach of Warranty by the Insured', para 1.59.

[71] The House of Lords warned against turning 'what is an indispensable shield for the underwriter into an engine of oppression against the assured' in *Commercial Union Assurance Co Ltd v The Niger Co Ltd* (1922) 13 LI L Rep 75 at 82.

[72] eg *Allen v Flood* [1898] 1 AC 1. In civil law jurisdictions, abuse of rights is the exercise of a legal right only to cause annoyance, harm, or injury to another. The abuse of rights principle is laid out in German law by the so-called *Schikaneverbot* ('ban on vexatiousness') BGB §226: 'The exercise of a right is unlawful if its purpose is only to cause harm to another.'

[73] *Pan Atlantic Insurance Co Ltd v Pine Top Insurance Co Ltd* [1994] 2 Lloyd's Rep 427 at 456; and see *Drake Insurance plc v Provident Insurance plc* [2003] EWCA Civ 1834 at [87]–[88] and [91]–[93] and [145].

[74] As expressly observed in *The Star Sea* [2001] 1 All ER (Comm) 193 at 208.

a 'waste of expedition'[75] and money in placing the insurance.[76] The need for a duty that levels up the parties' knowledge is the means by which a fair calculation can be made. In *Brotherton v Asegueadora Colseguros SA*[77] Moore-Bick LJ thus said:

> [t]he foundation of the insured's duty of disclosure lies in an insistence that the insurer must be given a fair opportunity to assess the risk and a recognition of the fact that he is unlikely to have that opportunity unless the insured discloses all material circumstances of which he is aware at the time the contract is made.

III. Legislative Reform

A. The Law Commission's Review and Reports 2006–2014

In 2006, the English and Scottish Law Commissions (the Law Commission) began the most recent review of the law of insurance,[78] including in particular, the duty of utmost good faith. In July 2007, the Law Commission published its Consultation Paper No 182 on 'Insurance Contract Law; Misrepresentation, Non-disclosure and Breach of Warranty by the Insured', in which it suggested a number of reforms depending on whether the insurance contract was a consumer contract or a business contract. The Consultation Paper was expressly prefaced on the basis that the MIA 1906 had not kept pace with the times and failed to meet expectations of the market.[79] On consumer insurance the Consultation Paper noted that the current law on disclosure can operate as a trap and allowed claims to be rejected even where policyholders have acted honestly and reasonably and proposed, inter alia, to replace the consumer's duty of disclosure with a requirement to answer questions carefully and honestly. The Law

[75] *Pan Atlantic Insurance Co Ltd v Pine Top Insurance Co Ltd* [1993] 1 Lloyd's Rep 496 506 *per* Steyn LJ.

[76] *Container Transport International Inc v Oceanus Mutual Underwriting Association (Bermuda) Ltd* [1984] 1 Lloyd's Rep 476, 496, Kerr LJ.

[77] [2003] EWHC 335 (Comm) at [26].

[78] In paper No 104 of 1980, the English Law Commission considered non-disclosure and breach of warranty and concluded that the law was 'undoubtedly in need of reform' and that such reform had been 'too long delayed'. Insurance Law, Non-Disclosure and Breach of Warranty (1980) Law Com No 104, para 1.21. The Law Commission again proposed statutory reform of the 1906 Act. However, in 1986, the Government thought that 'the case for legislation is outweighed by the advantages of self-regulation': Hansard (HC), vol 92, cols 356–57w.

[79] Noting that the ABI, the FSA (as it was) and the FOS respectively approached the practice and enforcement of insurance law contrary to the strict rights and entitlements provided for under the Marine Insurance Act 1906, and then largely only in respect of consumer insurance. The contrast between the law, market practice and enforcement practice was itself conducive to confusion. More particularly: (i) the ABI's Statement of Long-Term Insurance Practice and Statement of General Insurance Practice, which stated that the insurer would not repudiate liability if the assured reasonably failed to disclose a material fact or was guilty of misrepresentation which was neither fraudulent nor negligent; (ii) the FSA (and then the FCA)'s Rules prevented insurers from relying on the strict letter of the law dealing with non-disclosure, misrepresentation and breach of warranty. Since January 2005, the self-regulatory Statement of General Insurance Practice has been replaced by what is now ICOBS, which currently provides that insurers must handle claims promptly and fairly, provide reasonable guidance to policyholders and not unreasonably reject a claim; and (iii) the FOS where under section 228(2) of FSMA 2000, ombudsmen are directed to determine complaints 'by reference to what is, in the opinion of the ombudsman, fair and reasonable in all the circumstances of the case'. Ombudsmen may therefore depart from the law where they consider the law to be unjust.

Commission noted that sometimes the information that insurers required could only be obtained from a prospective insured,[80] and acknowledged that information asymmetries gave rise to the risk of adverse selection, stating:

> [t]he law of non-disclosure and misrepresentation guards against a particular problem with insurance, namely that the policyholder may know more about the risk than the insurer. Clearly, insurers need to receive this information in order to decide whether to accept risks and, if so, at what price and on what terms. Without this information exchange, the market may suffer from 'adverse selection'. In other words, those people who know their risk is high will be more likely to buy a policy than those who know their risk is low. If the insurer cannot differentiate the two, it will be forced to put up premiums. As the insurance becomes more expensive, the pool will become smaller, until the market is no longer viable.[81]

There was little further discussion of either the information asymmetry between insured and insurer or how that might be changing.[82] In fairness to the Law Commission, this Consultation Paper was issued at a time when big data and machine learning simply was not on the agenda, whether as a tool which insurers could deploy to better understand risk or at all. Perhaps more importantly, the Consultation Paper did not consider the duty of good faith as it applies to insurers.[83] The Law Commission thus did not consider the impact of the information revolution (which pre-dates the rise of big data) on how insurers should handle personal, but risk-related information. As to the need for the duty of disclosure in consumer insurance, the Consultation Paper stated:

> Our view is that we should bring the law into line with industry practice and ombudsman guidance by requiring insurers to ask clear questions about any matter that is material to them. We would abolish consumers' residual duty of disclosure. The insurer would thus have a remedy only if there had been a misrepresentation.[84]

In December 2009, the Law Commission published a report entitled 'Consumer Insurance Law: Pre-Contract Disclosure and Misrepresentation' along with a draft bill reflecting the recommendations in the report. The report made plain that the bill only related to pre-contract information, and then only to consumer insureds, not insurers. The Bill became CIDRA 2012, which is discussed below.

[80] Law Commission Consultation Paper No 182 on Insurance Contract Law; Misrepresentation, Non-disclosure and Breach of Warranty by the Insured, para 1.10.

[81] ibid, para 1.60.

[82] In its 2009 Report (discussed below), the Law Commission stated (para 2.15): 'Most insurers accept that in a mass, commoditised market, it is no longer practical for them to receive unstructured information from consumers.' What the first three chapters of this book show is that insurers are increasingly able to review and analyse vast amounts of unstructured data.

[83] Law Commission Consultation Paper No 182, above fn 80, para 2.10: 'The duty bears rather differently on the insurer than it does on the insured, and raises different issues of policy. We will not consider the insurer's duty of good faith in this consultation paper.'

[84] ibid, para 4.14. It further stated (para 4.20): 'Any unusual circumstance can be made the subject of a general "sweeper" question, which should bring home to the proposer the need to tell the insurer about the unusual fact just as well as a warning of a duty to disclose. We conclude that in consumer cases the duty to disclose is no longer needed. We think the law should now be brought into line with the FOS guidelines.'

In March 2010, the Law Commission published an issues paper entitled 'Damages for late payment and the insurers' duty of good faith'.[85] The paper considered the insurers' duty in the context of claims, that is, post-contractually, and had little to say about the nature or scope of insurers' duty of good faith as it applies pre-contractually and says nothing about how insurers can or should use personal data for underwriting purposes compatibly with their duty of good faith.[86] In a post-contractual (claims) context, the Law Commission proposed that insurers should investigate claims fairly; assess claims in an unbiased way; give reasons for refusing claims; and (where an insurer considers a claim to be valid) pay it within a reasonable time. The Law Commission proposed an amendment to section 17 of the MIA 1906 so as to provide insureds with a non-excludable right to damages where insurers acted in bad faith in the handling of claims.[87] The Law Commission considered that the duty of good faith would only become a truly mutual obligation if it were possible for policyholders to claim damages for losses which result from the insurer's bad faith.[88] The proposal did not discuss damages for insurers' breach of the duty of good faith in a pre-contractual context. In the event, the Law Commission did not pursue its suggestion of conferring a remedy in damages on the insured for post-contractual breach by insurers;[89] rather, it proposed merely to remove the remedy of avoidance for post-contractual breach of the duty of good faith, leaving the duty in place but apparently without any means of remedying its breach.

The Law Commission published updated proposals for commercial insurance in its June 2012 Consultation Paper.[90] In July 2014 the Law Commission published its report 'Business Disclosure; Warranties; Insurers' remedies for Fraudulent Claims; and Late Payment' (the 2014 Report). The 2014 Report made further proposals for reform of the duty of good faith insofar as it applied pre-contractually to commercial insureds (but not insurers, save as regards late payment of claims), and addressed further aspects of the duty as it applied to consumer and commercial insurance. The 2014 Report observed:

> 3.1 An insured often knows more than the insurer about the risk to be insured. It is therefore important to encourage a full and frank exchange of information before the insurance contract is made. Under the current law, the onus is on the prospective policyholder to disclose information to the insurer. This obligation to "present the risk" enables the UK insurance market to provide insurance for a wide variety of large and specialist risks, efficiently and cost-effectively.

[85] Issue Paper 6: https://s3-eu-west-2.amazonaws.com/lawcom-prod-storage-11jsxou24uy7q/uploads/2015/06/ICL6_Damages_for_Late_Payment1.pdf.

[86] And again, in fairness, not many people were talking about big data in the insurance context at this point in time.

[87] The Law Commission proposed that liability would be limited and controlled and that it would 'be a prerequisite to liability that the claim was valid. The policyholder would then need to prove actual loss and that this was foreseeable within the contract principles of *Hadley v Baxendale*': Law Commission Issues Paper, Damages for late payment and the insurers' duty of good faith, March 2010, s 36.

[88] ibid, 4.23.

[89] There was substantial opposition to the proposal from the insurance industry: see Insurance Contract Law: Post Contract Duties and other Issues (December 2011), Law Commission Consultation Paper No 201; Scottish Law Commission Discussion Paper No 152 paras 4.31–4.41.

[90] Insurance Contract Law: The Business Insured's Duty of Disclosure and the Law of Warranties (June 2012), Law Commission Consultation Paper No 204; Scottish Law Commission Discussion Paper No 155.

> 3.2 We think that this fundamental pre-contract duty is important to the successful operation of the UK insurance market. However, the law which governs the duty is more than 100 years old. It no longer works as well as it should. The law predates the information revolution, before which the volume of data that firms stored, analysed and accessed was much smaller. The law is unclear and difficult to comply with, and the consequences of breaching the duty are harsh.
>
> 3.3 Good disclosure requires co-operation between both parties: the policyholder knows how the business is run; the insurer knows which facts are relevant to assessing the risk. We think that the law should do more to encourage both sides to work together to exchange information.[91]

The Report went on to state:

> The 1906 Act codifies principles developed in the eighteenth and nineteenth centuries, when communications were slow and access to information was difficult. It was drafted on the principle that the proposer knows everything about the risk and the underwriter knows nothing. It therefore sought to protect insurers. Furthermore, businesses were smaller and their records were hand-written and hand copied; they simply held less information. Electronic communication and data storage have radically altered the scale of commercial enterprises and the way in which information can be transmitted, stored, accessed and processed. With so much information available, there is now a need both to define the limits of the duty and to prevent policyholders from 'dumping' huge quantities of undigested information on the insurer.[92]

The Law Commission thus engaged with the fact that (i) the duty of good faith was codified at a time when information and communications were such as to be unlikely to mitigate the informational imbalance between insured and insurer; and (ii) acknowledged the impact of the information revolution but did so in a way that emphasised the expansion in the volume of potentially relevant information – a point that prima facie supports the extension of the insured's duty of disclosure on the basis of the market rationale of not requiring insurers to investigate every new risk in a world where there may be much more information to sift through about each such risk. What the Law Commission did not consider was: (i) the impact of those technologies that enabled insurers to analyse that increased volume of data with much greater precision as compared with how they processed smaller datasets with traditional software; or (ii) the extent to which insurers are using that technology in either underwriting or claims decisions. The Law Commission describes 'dumping' as the process whereby prospective policyholders give large amounts of undigested information for the insurer to sort through and decide what is relevant. A lack of structuring and indexing combined with an overwhelming amount of information is known in extreme cases as a 'data dump'. Objections to data dumping[93] would appear to ring somewhat

[91] Similarly at paras 6.6–6.8 of the 2014 Report the Law Commission noted that 'good disclosure requires co-operation from both sides. The policyholder knows the facts; the insurer knows which facts are relevant. To provide an effective and efficient process … insurers should see their role as assessing what they are told and asking further questions as appropriate.' Law Commission report 'Business Disclosure; Warranties; Insurers' remedies for Fraudulent Claims; and Late Payment' (2014).

[92] ibid, paras 5.2–5.3.

[93] The Law Commission in any event recommended as follows: 'At present, a policyholder may be able to fulfil its duty of disclosure by sending large quantities of unsorted information on to the insurer, without

more hollow where insurers are, at the very same time, amassing large and unstructured datasets containing potentially relevant information about an individual risk (or where they are acquiring a pre-sifted and pre-profiled package from third party data brokers). Insureds are, of course, required to make a fair presentation of the risk. But if the amount of information they have obtained is in fact dwarfed by what insurers themselves are accessing and modelling, there is a very real question over whether the insurer should be taken to know of all the matters the subject of its own trawl (and thereby reducing the insured's duty commensurately)[94] or otherwise renders it more easy for an insured to contend that the insurer has waived the right to know more having raised no further issues further to its own aggregating and/or profiling exercises.

The Law Commission did acknowledge that as insurers became more skilled and had access to sophisticated risk models, there would be a need to reconsider what insurers should be taken to know, and how far they should use this knowledge to probe the insured's presentation.[95] But there is a difference between the sophistication of risk modelling (an actuarial exercise) and the sophistication of risk profiling (which benefits from risk modelling but relies on a wider range of sources of information and the use of predictive analytics to assess the risk of each individual insured).

The Law Commissions sought to adopt an evolutionary approach to reform and in its 2014 Report observed:

> Although we have identified problems with the duty of disclosure in its current form, we do not recommend removing the duty on policyholders to volunteer information, as we did for consumer insurance. The duty on policyholders to present the risk saves time and effort, and makes it easier to insure non-standard risks. In particular, it requires policyholders to tell insurers about surprising and unusual circumstances, which may not be covered by standard questions.[96]

Two further issues considered by the Law Commission of relevance here are: (i) what constitutes insurers' knowledge; and (ii) its discussion of the duty of good faith.

As to what insurers know or can be taken to know, the Law Commission recommended that any test should concentrate on information which is known or available to the underwriter. It recommended that (i) an insurer should only be regarded as knowing something if it is known to the people participating in the underwriting decision; (ii) an insurer ought to know something: (a) if it is known to the insurer's

a summary or signposting. We recommend that this should not constitute a fair presentation of the risk. Instead, policyholders should disclose information in a manner which would be reasonably clear and accessible to a prudent insurer': ibid, para 6.9.

[94] Where the insurer takes an active role in underwriting the risk and enquires into the specific features of the proposed risk, there is less need for a duty of disclosure. This may occur, for example, by the insurers instructing their own representatives to inspect the property to be insured or to analyse the financial records of the insured. In such cases, the necessity for a duty of disclosure reduces at least as regards those aspects of the risk that the insurer chose to investigate.

[95] Law Commission report 'Business Disclosure; Warranties; Insurers' remedies for Fraudulent Claims; and Late Payment' (2014), para 5.3.

[96] ibid, para 5.44.

employee or agent and ought reasonably to have been passed to the underwriter;[97] or (b) it is held by the insurer and was readily available to the underwriter;[98] and (iii) an insurer is presumed to know something if it is common knowledge, or it is something which an insurer offering that type of insurance ought to know in the ordinary course of business.[99] The Law Commission observed that one consultee had said:

> [t]he insurance (and reinsurance) market has evolved significantly since the 1906 Act and the cases that preceded it. Modern communication, particularly the internet, has led to a modern professional insurer being able actively to inform himself about a risk in a way that his predecessors, with access to far less information in times when communications were far slower, could not.[100]

Nonetheless, the Law Commission considered that the current law under s 18(3)(b) of the MIA 1906 was 'broadly right' but needed to be made clearer. On information available to the underwriter (including that held on its own files/databases) the Law Commission acknowledged that the decisions in *Mahli v Abbey Life Assurance Co Ltd* and *Strive Shipping Corp v Hellenic Mutual War Risks Association (Bermuda) Ltd (The Grecia Express)* may imply passivity among underwriters and 'fails to reflect adequately the availability of information in electronic systems'.[101] Insurers have been wary of accepting any positive obligation to search their records, particularly because claims information may not be available to the underwriting department. Further, the Law Commission noted that insurers may hold information on a variety

[97] Information will be known to the insurer if it was received by an agent of the insurer who is under an obligation to channel the information to the underwriter in question. In *Joel v Law Union & Crown Insurance Company* [1936] 1 KB 505 a doctor commissioned by an insurer to examine a prospective policyholder was considered to be the agent of the insurer for the purpose of channelling information. Information which the doctor acquired by his examination was attributed to the insurer. The Law Commission observed: 'We think it must be correct that the insurer is taken to know this type of information, particularly when it has been prepared specifically for the purpose of assisting the underwriter in the assessment of the risk.' If a risk profile has been prepared or purchased specifically for the purpose of evaluating the risk posed by an individual insured, then that will be attributed to the insurer as well.

[98] Raising the issue of whether the insurer has an obligation to search its records. In *Mahli v Abbey Life Assurance Co Ltd* [1996] LRLR 237 the insurer disclaimed liability on a 1984 life insurance policy on the ground of non-disclosure of the deceased policyholder's alcoholism and malaria. In 1986 the insurers were told about Mr Mahli's medical problems in the context of an application for a second policy, but they failed to relate them to his 1984 application. The underwriter checked the computer system, which noted that Mr Mahli had a previous policy, but failed to find the relevant documents. The court heard expert evidence that it was not the practice of underwriters to check earlier policies: 'the pressure of work in the offices is such that this would be quite impracticable.' On this basis the majority of the Court of Appeal upheld the trial judge's finding that the insurer did not have constructive knowledge of the nondisclosure when it continued to accept premiums. Lord Justice McCowan dissented on the grounds that the insurer had all the relevant information in its systems. In this regard McDonald-Eggers and Picken argue that majority were wrong: 'If the infrastructure of the insurer's organisation allows the various departments of the insurer to correlate the data they receive into a central database, the insurer should be presumed to know this data for the purposes of a risk, assuming that the connection between the risk and the information in the database can be made.' Respectfully, that must be right: P MacDonald-Eggers and S Picken, *Good Faith and Insurance Contracts* 4th edn (Abingdon, Informa Law, 2018), 8.37. A similarly surprising decision was reached in *Strive Shipping Corp v Hellenic Mutual War Risks Association (Bermuda) Ltd (The Grecia Express)* [2002] EWHC 203 (Comm), [2002] 2 Lloyd's Rep 88.

[99] Law Commission report 'Business Disclosure; Warranties; Insurers' remedies for Fraudulent Claims; and Late Payment' (2014), 6.17–6.18.

[100] ibid, 10.29.

[101] ibid, para 10.50.

of outdated 'legacy' systems which cannot be searched by all staff.[102] That was not an unreasonable point but, as previously noted, insurers have in fact been striving to synthesise those systems to use them for internal 'data mining' purposes. It will be a question of fact as to what legacy records have been integrated into insurers' electronic records or have otherwise been the subject of scan and search exercises. Indeed, the Law Commission acknowledged this, noting that IT systems' historical data about policyholders will

> become an increasingly important source of data. Indeed, an insurer may find it easier to assess information already processed and analysed by its own organisation than the same information presented by the insured as a 'material circumstance' in an unfamiliar format or from a different perspective.[103]

As to its discussion of good faith, the Law Commission proposed that the duty of good faith should continue as an interpretative principle but should not in itself give either party a cause of action.[104] The proposed removal of the right of avoidance from s 17 of the MIA 1906 would leave good faith as 'a general principle, with section 17 and the common law still providing that insurance contracts are based on the utmost good faith'.[105] The Law Commission explained the proposed use of the duty of good faith as an interpretive principle as one that would enable the courts to have continuing regard to it and that resort may continue to be had to the substantial and well-developed jurisprudence on the subject.[106] Specifically, three roles were envisaged for the principle:

> (1) To interpret the duty of fair presentation. Both parties are expected to act in good faith in exchanging information. For example, if a court were to find that an insured had intentionally disclosed only the bare minimum of information, hoping that the insurer would fail to make further enquiries to reveal the full picture, the insured would not have acted in good faith and would therefore be in breach of the duty of fair presentation.
>
> (2) To inform the need to imply contractual terms into the policy under the traditional "business efficacy" test. Good faith provides a background when considering whether it is necessary to imply a particular term.
>
> (3) To leave some room for judicial flexibility. It is possible that the principle of a mutual duty of good faith could provide a solution to an especially hard case <u>or emergent difficulty</u>. Although we think such cases would be extremely rare, it is possible that the courts could develop the concept to prevent an insurer from relying on a right to deny a claim where it would be manifestly unfair to do so.

While (1) may seem reasonable, (2) and (3) are not particularly convincing. as will be explained in chapter seven. However, the Law Commission's proposal that the duty of good faith was a component of business efficacy for the purpose of implying terms at the post-contractual stage (including as to how insurers could rely upon or exercise other contractual rights) provides no basis at all for how one might explain insurers'

[102] ibid, para 10.51.
[103] ibid, para 10.52.
[104] ibid, para 30.8.
[105] ibid, para 30.17.
[106] ibid, para 30.22.

pre-contractual duties which plainly cannot be based on implied terms absent any extant contract.

The 2014 Report made cursory mention of the insurers' pre-contractual duty of good faith. Referring to the example of the ship that had already arrived in port given by Lord Mansfield, the Law Commission said that although this is one of the few situations in which avoidance could be a suitable remedy for the insured, real examples of its use were rare. With respect, that entirely ignores the possibilities that insurers were already exploring as at 2014, namely the use of their own databases, public databases, third party data aggregators and more or less complex forms of profiling to evaluate individual risk. Insurers now have the ability to access new sources and obtain data about a prospective insured, or obtain a risk profile of that insured from the analysis of a wider variety of risk and non-risk related metrics, many of which may individually operate as non-causal proxies of risk. That form of analysis and profiling may affect the terms offered. And to the extent that this information relates to matters objectively material to the risk (and matters which insurers subjectively consider to be material to the risk), it would appear to be well within the scope of s 17 of the MIA 1906.

The only other example of insurers' breach of the pre-contractual duty suggested by the Law Commission was that of 'worthless policies' (for example, those sold for payment protection insurance that would never respond). Having raised that issue in its Scoping Paper, the Law Commission noted that respondents suggested that the issue would better be dealt with by the FCA or the FOS rather than through law reform, and indicated its agreement with that approach. It seems strange, however, that the Law Commission was manifestly not content to leave issues relating to the pre-contractual duty of good faith as it applies to insureds to the regulators, yet was prepared to adopt precisely that approach regarding equivalent problems arising in relation to breach of the insurers' pre-contractual duty, an approach that appears to undermine the mutuality of the duty. If the Law Commission took that view because it considered the issues arising pre-contractually as against insurers would be 'rare', then that view might already have to be reassessed in circumstances where insurers are beginning to use big data analytics to profile the risk of individual insureds.

In the event, having made no positive recommendations for law reform as regards insurers' duty, whether at the pre-contractual or post-contractual stage,[107] those issues will continue to be dealt with by reference to the principles that can be discerned at common law. They are discussed further below having considered the reforms as enacted in CIDRA 2012 and the IA 2015.

B. CIDRA 2012: Disclosure in Consumer Insurance

CIDRA 2012, s 1(1)(a) defines a consumer (for the purposes of a consumer insurance contract) to be 'an individual who enters into the contract wholly or mainly for purposes unrelated to the individual's trade, business or profession'. The key provisions

[107] At least beyond its proposals for delay in the payment of claims.

of the 2012 Act are ss 2–5. Section 2(2) requires the consumer 'to take reasonable care not to make a misrepresentation to the insurer'. The obligation bites pre-contract or on any variation of an existing contract. Section 2(4) provides that the duty imposed under s 2(2) replaces any duty relating to disclosure or representations by a consumer to an insurer which existed in the same circumstances before the 2012 Act applied. What 'reasonable care' requires is further defined in s 3. Section 3(4) provides that 'if the insurer was, or ought to have been, aware of any particular characteristics or circumstances of the actual consumer, those are to be taken into account' in ascertaining whether the insured took reasonable care. It is submitted that if the insurer profiles a prospective consumer insured before any contract is entered into, and is thereby aware of particular characteristics of that insured, what will be required of the insured to discharge his duty of reasonable care will be commensurately more limited. The 2012 Act then sets out a definition of 'qualifying misrepresentations' and provides differing remedies (set out in Schedule 1) depending on whether the qualifying representation was deliberate or reckless on the one hand or careless on the other: CIDRA 2012, s 5(1).

It follows that under CIDRA 2012, there is in effect no general duty of disclosure on the insured at the time of placing, at least as understood at common law; there is only instead a duty upon the assured to exercise reasonable care in making representations to the insurer. The 2012 Act thus abrogates the pre-contractual duty of disclosure on the insured and the previous common law on disclosure no longer applies to consumer insureds. There is now a duty to exercise reasonable care in making representations. That there can be no residual duty of good faith disclosure applicable to the insured in a consumer insurance contract is confirmed by CIDRA 2012, s 10, which makes it impermissible to contract out of the legislation where the proposed contractual terms put the insured in a worse position than he or she would be under the Act. The effect of this is that the law may have reached the position that it would have been compelled to reach as regards the duties of the insured as a result of insurers' use of big data and data profiling and the knowledge that insurers will have, actually or constructively, as a result.[108] As noted above, this was not considered by the Law Commission as a basis for removing the duty of disclosure on consumer insureds but reforms the law in such a way as to reflect the fact that big data and predictive analytics is in the process of eroding the information asymmetry that historically justified the duty of disclosure as between consumer insureds and insurers.

Notwithstanding that there is no longer a pre-contractual duty of good faith in consumer insurance contracts, there remains a post-contractual duty of utmost good faith applicable to such contracts. Part 4 of the IA 2015 deals with remedies for fraudulent claims and applies to both consumer and non-consumer insurance contracts. Nothing in the 2012 Act abrogates insurers' duty of good faith or, more specifically, their duty to give disclosure pre-contractually should the circumstances require it. In that regard there is now a lack of mutuality between what good faith requires of insured and insurer at the pre-contractual stage. However, that is the implication of the statutory modification of the insured's – but not the insurers' – duty.

[108] And which in turn will considerably widen the circumstances when an insurer will be taken to have waived his entitlement to further disclosure from the insured.

C. IA 2015: Disclosure in Non-consumer Insurance

The IA 2015 modifies the pre-contractual duty of disclosure on commercial insureds by replacing it with a duty of fair presentation. Section 2 of the Act provides that the duty applies to variations to the risk as well as to the original placing of the risk. Section 3(3) provides that a fair presentation of the risk is one (a) which makes the disclosure required by subsection (4);[109] (b) which makes that disclosure in a manner which would be reasonably clear and accessible to a prudent insurer; and (c) in which every material representation as to a matter of fact is substantially correct, and every material representation as to a matter of expectation or belief is made in good faith. The disclosure required under s 3(4) requires – subject to the operation of s 3(5) – (a) the disclosure of every material circumstance which the insured knows or ought to know, or (b) failing that, disclosure which gives the insurer sufficient information to put a prudent insurer on notice that it needs to make further enquiries for the purpose of revealing those material circumstances. That is designed to avoid the insured having to second-guess everything that the prudent insurer might have wanted to know. It means that so long as there is a fair presentation and no further questions are raised by insurers, the latter will be taken to have waived the need for any further disclosure.[110] Section 3(5) provides that in the absence of insurers making enquiry, subsection (4) does not require the insured to disclose a circumstance if (a) it diminishes the risk; (b) the insurer knows it;[111] (c) the insurer ought to know it; (d) the insurer is presumed to know it; or (e) is something to which the insurer waives information.[112] The exceptions exist because the non-disclosure of material facts in such cases is not seen as detracting from the purpose of the duty of disclosure, namely, to redress the imbalance of knowledge as between the insured and the insurer when they are negotiating terms.[113] As the opening clause of s 3(5) makes clear, these exceptions only arise in

[109] MIA 1906, ss 18–20 had specified the pre-contractual duty imposed on the assured. That is replicated now in modified form in ss 3–8 of the IA 2015 for non-consumer insurance.

[110] This re-balancing of the parties' respective duties has echoes of the approach of Lord Mansfield and reflects the view that insurers should not be wholly passive and should be required to play a more active role in making enquiries where appropriate.

[111] If a fact is known to an insurer, the insured is not required to confirm or disclose the same: *Kingscroft Insurance Co Ltd v Nissan Fire & Marine Insurance Co Ltd (No 2)* [1999] Lloyd's Rep IR 603 at 631 *per* Moore-Bick J. And nor does it matter from what source the insurer's knowledge is derived: *Carter v Boehm* (1766) 3 Burr 1905 at 1910; *Pimm v Lewis* (1862) 2 F&F 778; 175 ER 1281; *Bates v Hewitt* (1867) LR 2 QB.

[112] The use of a proposal form generally will not revoke the insured's duty of disclosure although it might enlarge it or restrict it. The fact that a proposal did not ask a particular question does not necessarily mean that the insurer intended to waive disclosure of such matters. In *Doheny v New India Assurance Co Ltd* [2004] EWCA Civ 1705 Longmore LJ proposed, as regards the construction of the proposal form, 'the test being would a reasonable man, reading the proposal form, be justified in thinking that the insurer had restricted his right to receive all material information, and consented to the omission of the particular information in issue'. In *Iron Trades Mutual Insurance Co Ltd v Companhia de Seguros Imperio* [1991] 1 Re LR 213, Hobhouse J commented that the waiver exception was unlikely to arise very often and would only do so where the insured made a fair presentation of the risk. If he did not, the insurer cannot be taken to have waived the duty by asking no further questions.

[113] As Lord Mustill said in *Pan Atlantic Insurance Co Ltd v Pine Top Insurance* '[t]he significance of these exceptions is that they were not written back by Lord Mansfield into his definition of materiality, but were aimed at the duty of disclosure and the consequences of failing to perform it. This is what one would expect. The materiality or otherwise of a circumstance should be a constant; and the subjective characteristics,

the absence of the insurers making enquiries; if they do make enquiries, for example, about something that would otherwise diminish the risk, clearly insurers want to know about it and the insured must answer those enquiries fairly.[114]

As noted above, the Law Commission felt that given the more specialised nature of commercial risks, it was appropriate that the duty of disclosure remained in modified form to enable insureds to draw unusual or specific material facts to insurers' attention. Although the proposed duty as it applied to commercial insureds was considered without any reference to the impact of big data or predictive analytics, there are differences between consumer and commercial insurance that would appear to justify the retention of a residual duty in respect of the latter risks. Many consumer policies have commercial analogues. A fleet policy is a commercial version of a consumer motor policy; an employer's corporate health insurance programme is a commercial version of a consumer health policy; commercial property cover is the commercial equivalent of a consumer home and contents policy. Big data analytics enables the monitoring of a fleet of vehicles, a block of flats and all employees as well as it enables the monitoring of a single vehicle, flat or employee. However, some commercial risks are less amenable to the sort of tracking and profiling that takes place in relation to individuals and their personal data. While big data might be able to better analyse the risk posed by certain forms of professional activity, there will be limits to what insurers can know about such risks. Some professional liability policies have contained exclusions or endorsements as regards the involvement of particular professionals: so architects or engineers who may have been involved in projects that previously led to claims might be more easily identified and potentially excluded from cover extending to construction projects. But big data is unlikely to know of individual circumstances that professional insureds are obliged to notify (and in any event disclose on renewal). Or a financial services firm may have been subject to a non-standard form of regulatory inspection which yielded the imposition of non-standard conditions that do not appear on a public register and which therefore cannot be parsed by big data. Those are the type of scenarios where specific facts material to a risk will be solely in the knowledge of the insured. It seems appropriate then for the duty to remain on insureds, albeit in modified form, even where insurers are increasingly modelling risk by reference to big data.

One indirect way in which big data will shape the insured's duty to make a fair presentation relates to the provisions on insured and insurer knowledge contained in ss 4–6 of the IA 2015. Section 4 deals with the question of whose knowledge counts – such as to be attributed to – the insured for the purpose of ascertaining whether a fair presentation was made in compliance with s 3(4). In addition s 4(6) provides that whether an individual or not, an insured ought to know what should reasonably have been revealed by a reasonable search of information available to

actions and knowledge of the individual underwriter should be relevant only to the fairness of holding him to the bargain if something objectively material is not disclosed.'

[114] See *Doheny v New India Assurance Co Ltd* [2004] EWCA Civ 1705; [2005] Lloyd's Rep IR 251 at [16] *per* Longmore LJ. Para 49 of the Explanatory Notes to the Insurance Act 2015 suggests the law concerning the meaning and effect of the words 'in the absence of enquiry' are the same under s 18(3) of the 1906 Act as they are under s 3(5) of the 2015 Act.

the insured (whether the search is conducted by making enquiries or by any other means),[115] where 'information' is defined in s 4(7) to include any information held within the insured's organisation or by any other person (such as the insured's agent or a person for whom cover is provided by the contract of insurance).

Perhaps more important is the definition of the insurers' knowledge in s 5 of the 2015 Act. It will be recalled that the Law Commission did not feel that the exceptions under s 18(3) and in particular the constituent elements of s 18(3)(b) of the MIA 1906 required a radical overhaul so much as clarification. IA 2015, s 5, to that end provides:

> (1) For the purposes of section 3(5)(b), an insurer knows something only if it is known to one or more of the individuals who participate on behalf of the insurer in the decision whether to take the risk, and if so on what terms (whether the individual does so as the insurer's employee or agent, as an employee of the insurer's agent or in any other capacity).
>
> (2) For the purposes of section 3(5)(c), an insurer ought to know something only if –
>
> (a) an employee or agent of the insurer knows it, and ought reasonably to have passed on the relevant information to an individual mentioned in subsection (1), or
>
> (b) the relevant information is held by the insurer and is readily available to an individual mentioned in subsection (1).
>
> (3) For the purposes of section 3(5)(d), an insurer is presumed to know–
>
> (a) things which are common knowledge, and
>
> (b) things which an insurer offering insurance of the class in question to insureds in the field of activity in question would reasonably be expected to know in the ordinary course of business.

Of most relevance to what insurers know or may be deemed to know in an age of big data is (i) what information is held or readily available to an insurer; and (ii) what an insurer offering that class of cover will be deemed to know.[116] There will, it is submitted, be no difficulty finding that an insurer knows that which has been the subject of internal or third-party risk profiling, the outcome of which has been provided to and held by the insurer.[117] What might objectively be readily available to an insurer will turn

[115] This replaces s 18(1) of the 1906 Act, where the insured was subject to the additional obligation of revealing all that ought to be known by him in the ordinary course of business. More specifically, the new obligation appears to expand the insured's deemed knowledge since what ought to have been known to the insured under s 18(1) of the 1906 Act was that which he would have known in the ordinary course of his business (which meant the insured's own business, not a reasonable business: *MacGillivray on Insurance Law* 13th edn (London, Sweet and Maxwell, 2015) paras 17-13–17-15) whereas information that would be available pursuant to a reasonable search would prevent the insured from merely looking in its own inadequate records to discharge its duty.

[116] Old examples where insurers were treated as having the relevant knowledge include *Friere v Woodhouse* (1817) Holt NP 572, where it was held that information contained on Lloyds List need not be disclosed to insurers if they could have ascertained that information by fair enquiry and due diligence; similarly in *Foley v Tabor* (1861) 2 F&F 663 it was held that where an insurer could have discovered the exact nature of the ship's proposed cargo by consulting a record kept at Lloyds and chose not to refer to it, such information is within the insurer's knowledge.

[117] para 64 of the Explanatory Notes to the Insurance Act 2015 states that this type of deemed knowledge is 'intended to require the relevant underwriter to make a reasonable effort to search such information as is available to them within the insurer's organisation such as the insurer's electronic records.' This is not dissimilar to the duty to search that rests on the insured pursuant to s 4(6) of the Insurance Act 2015, although no such duty is spelled out in s 5 of the Act.

on how the market continues to deploy big data analytics. If, for example, it became the norm for insurers writing that class of business to run certain types of analytics, but a particular insurer fails to follow that practice, there will certainly be an argument that in not following market practice it has failed to obtain information otherwise readily available to it. Market take-up of big data is also likely to shape what insurers are deemed to know. One area in which big data will have an important impact is on new sources of actuarial data. As discussed in chapter three, many existing risk proxies are, individually and collectively, non-causal proxies. As insurers refine their datasets and their modelling of risk, more information will become available, not just about correlations between certain factors and risks but the relationship between individual factors and the incidence of insured loss. The extent of the market's knowledge of the actuarially established relationship between new risk factors and the incidence of insured loss may depend on the extent to which actuarial data is shared in the market. But again, big data can only enhance the stock of insurers' knowledge. The relevance of this is that absent enquiry, where big data renders an insurer's knowledge, actual or constructive, much more extensive than would be the case previously, then (i) the duty on the commercial insured will be commensurately reduced; and (ii) absent further enquiry, insurers will more frequently be taken to have waived their entitlement to any further disclosure.

A recent decision on insurers' knowledge is that of *Sea Glory Maritime Co v Al Sagr National Insurance Co (The Nancy)*,[118] where Blair J considered the extent to which an insurer should be presumed or deemed to know information contained in electronic databases maintained outside the insurer's organisation. This case was decided prior to the IA 2015 but in circumstances where the Law Commission considered that the exceptions to the insured's duty of disclosure did not require an overhaul and for that reason is instructive. Blair J said:[119]

> I do not think that it is correct to say that electronic databases should be treated as equivalent to information in hard copy such as newspapers. The rationale for taking a restrictive view as to the latter is to be found in *Morrison v Universal Marine Insurance Co (1872–73) LR 8 Ex 40*. At page 54, Baron Bramwell said that to hold that the underwriter is bound to carry in his head all that is contained in Lloyd's List relating to a ship in which he has no interest, rather than to hold the owner of the ship bound to disclose it, would be to put a difficult and needless burden on the underwriter.
>
> That reflected the commercial realities of the day. However, an underwriter does not have to carry the information in an electronic database in his head. On-line information is available to be called up when required, and the evidence of the expert underwriters in the present case is that the usual practice in the market is to do so.
>
> A reasonable underwriter is presumed to know matters which he should have known from the facts in his possession or matters which he had means of learning from the sources available to him … However, I agree with the defendant that the fact that information is available to an underwriter on-line does not necessarily give rise to a presumption of knowledge. As the editors of Arnould put it in their discussion of this subject, the question ultimately reduces to whether there has been a fair presentation of the risk in all the

[118] [2014] 1 Lloyd's Rep 14 at paras 170–78.
[119] At paras 173–75.

> circumstances (ibid at 16–181). Whilst the circumstances may include the availability of on-line information, whether the insurer should be treated as having knowledge of it is something which has to be judged on the particular facts (ibid at 16–194).

In that case the insurer did not subscribe to the database that contained most detail of the relevant risk (although could have done). Those to which it did subscribe or have free access provided more limited, and in one respect inaccurate information about the risk. Blair J thus treated the fact that the relevant information was available on on-line sources as part of the background circumstances, but did not base his decision on it. In an age where insurers can immediately search databases that contain information about particular insureds and details of their claims history both in relation to the type of risk for which insurance is sought and for other risks, it is submitted that where the particular insurer holds or subscribes to a particular database, it is deemed to know details that could immediately be ascertained about a particular insured from that database. And while it is entirely reasonable to conclude that just because something exists on the internet, an insurer should not be taken to know it,[120] what of the position of a data trawl carried out by an insurer using algorithms that are designed to parse huge datasets (including information held on the internet) for information relevant to a particular risk or a particular insured? It is submitted that if the relevant detail was the subject of the insured's descriptive or predictive analysis, then it should be deemed to be within the insurers' knowledge. The question of insurers' knowledge – and the extent to which that knowledge would afford a commercial insured a defence to an allegation of unfair presentation – is likely to be one of the first questions to be determined under the IA 2015 arising out of the use of big data analytics. It is suggested that cases like *Bates v Hewitt*,[121] *Mahli v Abbey National* and *The Grecia Express* are unlikely to be decided in the same way today.

The requirements that (i) a matter that ought to be disclosed by way of a fair presentation of the risk be 'material'; and (ii) that any non-disclosure must have induced the insurer to write the risk on the terms offered, are retained in modified form under the 2012 and 2015 Acts. IA 2015 s 3(4)(a) thus requires disclosure 'of every material circumstance which the insured knows or ought to know'. The requirement of inducement appears in s 8(1) of the IA 2015, which provides that the insurer 'has a remedy against the insured for a breach of the duty of fair presentation only if the insurer shows that, but for the breach, the insurer (a) would not have entered into the contract of

[120] Which is different from the following, more specific example of common knowledge given by the Law Commission in its July 2014 Report: 'The issue of what constitutes common knowledge has become particularly current since the advent of social media, and we think it may be helpful to give an example of how we think the phrase would be interpreted. X, a well-known entertainer, is regularly rumoured in the mainstream media to have a drug problem and has not commenced libel proceedings against those making the allegations. When cancellation of event cover is sought for X's next tour, we think these rumours would be found to be matters of common knowledge that need not be disclosed to the underwriter:' ibid, paras 10.58–10.59. In this regard, Morrison J in *Brotherton v Aseguaradora Colseguros SA* [2003] EWHC 1741 (Comm) said: 'In a most general sense a London Underwriter ought to know the market in which he is writing business. With modern methods of communication, he can be expected to know more things than 50 or more years ago.' With the advent of big data, this point might be made with much greater force.

[121] The wider proposition in *Bates v Hewitt* might also be open to doubt insofar as it has been held to stand as authority for the proposition that past knowledge is relevant only if the insurer has an interest in the information at the time of its receipt: *London General Insurance Co v General Marine* [1921] 1 KB 104.

insurance at all, or (b) would have done so only on different terms. The concept of materiality is objective while the question of whether non-disclosure induced an insurer to offer cover on the terms in question is specific to the individual insurer. The question of inducement may be complicated where insurers use big data and predictive analytics. The algorithms are designed to identify that in which the individual insurer is interested. Where a particular insured is offered terms on an automated basis but the insurer seeks to rely on the fact that a certain risk factor was not disclosed, insureds may seek access to the operation of algorithms to identify what factors the algorithms themselves look for (i) to show either that insurers had constructive knowledge such that there was no unfair presentation of the risk; or (ii) to argue that because that factor was not something the algorithm was programmed to identify or analyse, then it was either not material and/or gives rise to a waiver of the right to disclosure absent any follow-up questions, or whose absence had no bearing on insurers' willingness to write the risk on those terms anyway.

As the IA 2015 considers the duties of the insured, and then only pre-contractually (or upon a variation), it does not, with some limited exceptions,[122] consider what good faith requires of insurers. It is clear from s 14 of the Act that the duty of good faith still applies to both parties, albeit that the effect of s 3 is to modify the disclosure requirements as they apply to insureds. Section 14 thus materially provides:

> (1) Any rule of law permitting a party to a contract of insurance to avoid the contract on the ground that the utmost good faith has not been observed by the other party is abolished.
>
> (2) Any rule of law to the effect that a contract of insurance is a contract based on the utmost good faith is modified to the extent required by the provisions of this Act and the Consumer Insurance (Disclosure and Representations) Act 2012.

And thus by s 14(3) of the IA 2015, s 17 of the MIA 1906 is modified to remove the right to avoid and which now provides that 'A contract of marine insurance is a contract based upon the utmost good faith'. The IA 2015 provides remedies for insurers in the event that the insured breaches the duty of fair presentation. However, no provision is made for any remedies in the event that insurers violate the duty of good faith and with the modification of s 17 of the MIA 1906 Act by s 14 of the IA 2015 there would be appear to be no existing remedies that an insured could avail of in the face of a breach by insurers. As the Law Commission observed in its 2014 Report – and as re-appears in the Explanatory Notes to the IA 2015 – the duty of good faith is regarded as an interpretative principle. Specifically, paragraph 116 of the Explanatory Notes to s 14 of the Act states: '[t]he intention of section 14 is that good faith will remain an interpretative principle, with section 17 of the 1906 Act and the common law

[122] Insurers' obligations in respect of the handling and payment of claims is now governed by s 13A of the IA 2015 as amended by s 28 of the Enterprise Act 2016, which applies to all insurance contracts concluded on or after 4 May 2017. Section 13A provides that it is an implied term in every insurance contract (including variations) that the insurer must pay an insurance claim within a reasonable time, allowing for investigation and assessment of the claim. Remedies for breach of the implied term include damages in addition to the payment of the claim and interest. In addition, consumer and commercial insurers are constrained to the extent to which they can opt out of these obligations: see s 16A and 17 of the IA 2015.

continuing to provide that insurance contracts are contracts of good faith.' What good faith means or requires, whether as an interpretative principle or as a substantive obligation, is considered further in chapter seven. However, absent any guidance in the IA 2015 as to how the duty applies to insurers, the common law principles will continue to apply.

D. Insurer's Duty of Good Faith after the IA 2015

Whilst the IA 2015 retains the duty of utmost good faith, it does not prescribe any remedies for a breach of the insurer's duty, having abolished the general remedy of avoidance for any breach by either party. Thus while a commercial insured's duty to disclose has been modified by way of the obligation to fairly present the risk, it would appear that the duty of an insurer to disclose facts that bear on the risk and which are only known to it, survives the passage of the Act. Yet, this is the area where big data is likely to have greatest impact on the insurance relationship, even allowing for the fact that it will not enable insurers to know everything about a particular commercial risk. If insurers have access to new troves of data about consumer and non-consumer insureds to which it can apply increasingly accurate predictive tools, this is the very scenario in which one would wish to ensure that insurers are required to use that data in accordance with the principles of good faith. And if such breaches were to occur, one might want the common law to afford insureds a remedy for such breaches. Before considering the extent to which the common law might develop the duty – and any associated remedies – one must consider (i) what precisely the duty of good faith requires of insurers, pre and post inception (which is considered below); (ii) whether there are other regulatory remedies that would apply to plug any gap left by section 14 of the IA 2015 (which is considered in chapter six); and (iii) how the common law might develop the duty and its remedies in light of the regulatory obligations that otherwise fall on insurers (considered in chapters seven and eight).

From the discussion above, it can be seen that the duty of good faith persists as against insurers notwithstanding the passage of CIDRA 2012 and the IA 2015.[123] It was also seen that insofar as the duty of good faith was characterised by mutuality, it applied to insurers as much as insureds, both pre-contractually and post-contractually. Where an information asymmetry arose over any aspect of the risk which required a further underwriting decision to be made, both pre and post inception, the duty required the party with the relevant knowledge to disclose that information. Whereas the post-contractual duty of good faith regarding claims merely required insureds to make non-fraudulent claims (as opposed to giving full disclosure), it is doubtful that that is all that is ever required of insurers when handling those claims.[124] IA 2015, s 13A implies terms requiring insurers to pay sums due in respect of claims in a reasonable time. Insofar as the duty of good faith in s 17 of the MIA 1906 survives and is to be used

[123] Indeed, parts of the Law Commission's July 2014 Report presupposes the continuation of the insurers' duty of good faith.

[124] If insurers avoid the policy knowingly and without cause, that may constitute bad faith: *Pan Atlantic Insurance Co v Pine Top Insurance Co Ltd* [1994] 2 Lloyd's Rep 427, 456. In *Fargnoli v G A Bonus Plc* [1997]

as an 'interpretative principle', it is submitted that good faith may require rather more from insurers in respect of claims handling.

The principal purpose of this section is to consider what the common law requires of insurers when considering whether to underwrite a risk or to vary that risk with consequences for the scope of the cover. Although it is clear that the insurer is obliged to disclose information to the insured before the contract is made and upon its variation thereafter, the extent of that disclosure obligation (which goes to the test of materiality) is not clear and the scope of the duty in other circumstances is the subject of scant authority. The most detailed discussion – and thus the necessary starting point – is the *Banque Financière* litigation. On the facts, a fraudster obtained credit facilities with the insured banks as part of an elaborate fraud. The banks obtained credit insurance with underwriters via their broker. The broker wrote cover notes on the basis that insurance was fully subscribed when it was not. Subsequently, before an amendment to the primary layer and the secondary layer becoming fully subscribed, the underwriter discovered the broker's wrongdoing. However, the underwriter wrote the final layer notwithstanding this knowledge, and failed to inform the insured banks of their own agent's wrongdoing. The question was whether the underwriter breached his duty of good faith in failing to inform the insured of their agent's wrongdoing.

As noted above, Steyn J at first instance proposed a reciprocal approach to the insurers' duty of good faith disclosure as that which applied to an insured. He said:

> The rationale of the rule imposing a duty of utmost good faith on the insured is that matters material to the risk are generally speaking peculiarly in his knowledge. In so far as matters are peculiarly in the insurer's knowledge, as in Lord Mansfield's example of the arrived ship, principle and fairness requires the imposition of a similar duty on the insurer.[125]

He went on to state:

> [The duty] must have some utility beyond the example given by Lord Mansfield. In my judgment the principle cannot be confined to a closed category of cases. I do not propose a definition. In considering the ambit of the duty of disclosure of the insurers, the starting point seems to me as follows: in a proper case it will cover matters peculiarly within the knowledge of the insurers which the insurers know that the insured is ignorant of and unable to discover but which are material in the sense of being calculated to influence the decision of the insured to conclude the contract of insurance. In considering whether the duty of disclosure is activated in a given case a court ought, in my judgment, to test any provisional conclusion by asking the simple question: Did good faith and fair dealing require a disclosure?[126]

It is not clear why the test should be constrained by requiring disclosure only of such material of which the insurer knows the insured is unaware. The insurer cannot know

CLC 653 Lord Penrose said that 'Of course it follows from the mutuality of the obligation of utmost good faith that it must be open to question whether an insurer would be in good faith in delaying an admission of liability or in advancing spurious defences to a claim or put the insured to proof of what the insurer knows is true or in delaying settlement of claims which he would, objectively, be obliged to admit before a court to be valid.' Moreover, insurers will be obliged by the duty to exercise claims co-operation clauses in such a way as to take into account the interest of both the insurer and insured: *Cox v Bankside* [1995] 2 Lloyd's Rep 437, 471–72.

[125] [1990] 1 QB 665 at 701.

[126] ibid at 703.

what the insured knows and does not know (although the underwriter in *Banque Financière* would have considered that the bank was unlikely to have been aware of its broker's wrongdoing). Otherwise the reciprocal test of materiality reflected the mutuality of the obligation. It would be for the insurer to assess what facts of which it was aware may be 'material in the sense of being calculated to influence the decision of the insured to conclude the contract of insurance', although the judge did not seek to apply a test of reasonableness by which that assessment might be judged. However, Steyn J's further test by which any assessment of materiality might be judged, namely 'does good faith and fair dealing require a disclosure', provides no guidance as it would be left to each court to make an individual assessment of what was required on the facts of each case. On the facts of the case before him, Steyn J concluded that disclosure ought to have been given.

The Court of Appeal considered this test to be too wide and uncertain: the test of materiality was considered to be too wide in that the insurer would be obliged to disclose his knowledge of cheaper quoted premium rates that would be offered by other insurers; equally, the Court of Appeal considered the sounding board of good faith and fair dealing against which any conclusion on disclosure could be assessed to be too uncertain to be a reliable guide as to when insurers would be required to give disclosure. The Court of Appeal proposed its own test of materiality as follows:

> the duty falling on the insurer must at least extend to disclosing all facts known to him which are material either to the nature of the risk sought to be covered or the recoverability of a claim under the policy which a prudent insured would take into account in deciding whether or not to place the risk for which he seeks cover with that insurer.[127]

The Court of Appeal considered that the fraud of the insured's broker, which was known to the insurer, but not the insured, was material in the above sense, given the existence of a fraud exclusion clause (such as to permit the rejection of a claim) or as the fraud might have affected the original placing with the insurer.

In the House of Lords, Lord Bridge indicated that he 'did not dissent from' the test of materiality proposed by Slade LJ,[128] but reached a different conclusion on materiality on the basis that the broker's fraud would not have come within the fraud exclusion clause. However, it has been pointed out that that considers the materiality only from the perspective of the impact on claims; the prior problem was that had the insured banks known of the broker's fraud, that would have been a disclosable fact; the banks were induced to enter into the contracts on the terms they did absent the knowledge of the broker's fraud and the jeopardy that created for the validity of the cover.[129] MacDonald-Eggers and Picken have suggested the following test of materiality in relation to insurers' duty of disclosure:

> If one were approaching the problem afresh and the Court of Appeal had not laid down a test of materiality, one would have wished for a definition along the following lines: a fact is material if it relates to the nature of the risk and would influence the judgment of a

[127] [1990] 1 QB 665 *per* Slade LJ at 772.
[128] [1991] 2 AC 249 at 268.
[129] P MacDonald Eggers and S Picken, *Good Faith and Insurance Contracts* 4th edn (Abingdon, Informa Law, 2018), 12.15.

> reasonable assured in deciding whether he will accept the terms of insurance offered by the insurer. There would of course be no duty of disclosure if the fact is known or ought, in the ordinary course of business, to be known to the assured or if the fact withheld would render the bargain more advantageous to the assured.[130]

It is not clear whether that is the test that Slade LJ had in mind, not least since his Lordship did not expressly refer to facts as being material only insofar as they tended to reduce the risk. The judgment of Lord Jauncey in the House of Lords proposed a test of materiality equivalent to that applicable to the insured. He held:

> [t]he duty of disclosure arises because the facts relevant to the estimation of the risk are most likely to be within the knowledge of the insured and the insurer therefore has to rely upon him to disclose matters material to that risk. The duty extends to the insurer as well as to the insured: *Carter v. Boehm* (1766) 3 Burr. 1905. The duty is, however, limited to facts which are material to the risk insured, that is to say, facts which would influence a prudent insurer in deciding whether to accept the risk and, if so, upon what terms and a prudent insured in entering into the contract on the terms proposed by the insurer. Thus any facts which would increase the risk should be disclosed by the insured and any facts known to the insurer but not to the insured, which would reduce the risk, should be disclosed by the insurer.[131]

A fact will be material to an insured where knowledge of that fact would influence a prudent insured in deciding whether to enter into the contract on the terms proposed by the insurer. MacDonald-Eggers and Picken refer to the following classes of facts that might be material for an insured to know in connection with his decision to contract with the insurer on the terms proposed:

1. The risk of loss under the policy or the status or safety of the subject-matter insured;[132]
2. The effect of the insurance and benefits available thereunder;[133]
3. The authorisation or constitution of the insurer permitting the insurer to issue the product that is to be taken by the insured and to pay claims;[134]
4. The existence of fraud in connection with the risk;[135]
5. Foreign illegality that might have an impact on the risk of the policy;
6. The financial impact of the policy as regards premium, provided it is material to the risk;[136]
7. Any defence that might be raised by the insurer under the proposed policy;[137]

These classes of fact are material because they relate to the risk and would, if revealed, show the insured either (i) that he doesn't need insurance; (ii) that he needs less

[130] ibid, 12.16.
[131] [1991] 2 AC 249 at 281.
[132] *Carter v Boehm* (1766) 3 Burr 1905; *Aldrich v Norwich Union* [1998] CLC 1621; *Duffell v Wilson* (1808) 1 Camp 401; 170 ER 999.
[133] *British Workman's & General Insurance Co v Cunliffe* (1902) 18 TLR 425, 502; *Tofts v Pearl Life Assurance Co Ltd* [1915] 1 KB 189; *Hughes v Liverpool Victoria Legal Friendly Society* [1916] 2 KB 482.
[134] See, eg, *Pontifex v Bignold* (1841) 3 Man & G 63; 133 ER 1058. If the insurer is not authorised under FSMA 2000, the insured by ss 26 and 28 of the Act, is entitled to compensation (including the premium paid by him) and may, subject to the discretion of the court, enforce the insurance contract.
[135] *Banque Financière de la Cité v Westgate Insurance Co* [1990] 1 QB 665.
[136] *Mutual Reserve Life Insurance Co v Foster* (1904) TLR 715.
[137] *Banque Financière de la Cité v Westgate Insurance Co* [1990] 1 QB 665.

insurance (either by reference to the time of cover or the extent of cover); (iii) that he could obtain insurance on better terms; (iv) the magnitude of the perceived risk is smaller than the insured may have appreciated; (v) the risk is less likely to arise than the insured might have appreciated; or (vi) that some action could be taken to avoid a loss that the insured would not be able to take or avoid if disclosure is not given.

In the big data age, algorithms are used to profile individual risks on the basis of many new risk factors, some of which demonstrate non-causal but correlative relationships with risk and of which the insured may be wholly unaware are being used as risk-proxies. The algorithm establishes a number of 'facts' that bear on the nature or extent of the risk and which establish the basis for the terms the insurer is prepared to offer. On Lord Jauncey's analysis, insurers are only required to disclose risk-reducing factors, not risk-increasing factors. Insurers might seek to 'price in' those risk-reducing factors to its offer of insurance. However, it is suggested that that would not discharge insurers' duty: those risk-reducing factors ought to be disclosed notwithstanding that insurers are prepared to reduce the price or widen the scope of the proposed cover. But a bigger question remains, namely, whether insurers are only required to disclose risk-reducing information or should also be required to disclose risk-increasing information they hold about the insured. It might be thought that if the information is sufficiently material such as to have an impact on insurers' pricing or terms, that they ought to be disclosed to the insured to allow him to make an informed decision about entering the contract on the basis of that offer.

On a traditional approach to underwriting, an insured who provides material facts to the insurer is not then entitled to ask to see how the insurer models those facts relative to the actuarial considerations which are the basis for the price. But that approach reflects a world in which both parties broadly know what material facts are in play. An insured can shop around because he at least knows that with risk factors A (eg age), B (eg sex), C (eg claims history) and D (eg driving history), the prices those factors produce allow him to compare the products. Where insurers begin to model risk by reference to predictive algorithms, and undisclosed risk factors – particularly those which may be not be actuarially established proxies for risk – prices and products are much harder to compare and insureds will not know what risk factors have been taken into account, never mind what positive (or negative) weighting such factors (or combination of factors) may have had on the price or the scope of the cover on offer. If they are material to the terms on which an insurer is prepared to underwrite the risk, they are also likely to influence a prudent insured insofar as that insured might consider that that combination of factors that have been taken into account by the insurer should have been priced differently whether because some of the risk factors did not apply to that insured or because the data was otherwise simply wrong. That fundamental lack of transparency not only leaves the question of materiality in the hands of insurers, but means that insureds may be offered terms on the basis of risk factors that may not be facts at all[138] and where the insured's own

[138] Because insurers have relied on a risk factor that correlates with the insured loss but which may not individually cause such loss at all.

knowledge of those 'facts' cannot be ascertained (or even assumed) by insurers.[139] Insurers will likely argue that these risk factors are ultimately all known to the insured, whether directly or indirectly, and as such engages Lord Jauncey's qualification that that which is required to be disclosed is only that which is not known (or which insurers assume is not known) to insureds.

More fundamentally, these difficulties arise because of the shift in the way in which risk-related information is being originated. Historically, the insured was the originator of information which he considered to be material to the risk. It was for the insured to assess the materiality of information to the risk sought to be insured. It would, as the cases recognise, be unusual for insurers to know of some fact that was material to the risk that was unknown to the insured and which would, if disclosed, potentially enable the insured to obtain cover on better terms. But in a big data age, insurers are increasingly the originators of risk-related information about the insured; in that regard they are, to a growing extent, stepping into the shoes of the insured in identifying and modelling risk factors which they consider apply to the insured. Insureds may not know what information is being relied upon or how it bears on the risk to be underwritten. It is arguable that confining the test of materiality applicable to insurers' duty of disclosure in such a way as to focus on (i) factors that reduce the insured's risk; and (ii) only those factors of which the insured is unaware, will not deliver transparency as to the information that is being relied upon in the pricing of risk. Insureds who are offered a lower price may be less likely to query the sources of information, the accuracy of that information or how it has been used; similarly, if the insurers' duty will only be breached in relation to material facts of which insureds are unaware, challenges to insurers' exercise of that duty will continue to be limited if insurers are permitted to contend that the information parsed about individual insureds is information that will at least be constructively known to insureds (particularly if there is no legal standards (whether of reasonableness or otherwise) against which insurers' assessment of an insured's knowledge might be tested).

The above comments related to disclosure of 'risk-reducing' information, the category of facts that fall within Lord Jauncey's test of materiality. However, it is suggested that a much greater concern arises in relation to the use of 'risk-increasing' information that leads to an increase in premium or more restricted forms of cover. If an insured does not know how insurers are sourcing information, or how they are relying on that information, he cannot challenge those uses. For as the European Data Protection Board (EDPB) in its guidelines on automated individual decision-making and profiling[140] state:

> the process of profiling is often invisible to the data subject. It works by creating derived or inferred data about individuals – 'new' personal data that has not been provided directly by the data subjects themselves. Individuals have differing levels of comprehension and may find it challenging to understand the complex techniques involved in profiling and automated decision-making processes.

[139] If insurers are using non-causal proxies (eg some information about shopping or purchasing habits), the insured may be entirely ignorant of either what the data says about them or how it is said to correlate with insured losses.

[140] http://ec.europa.eu/newsroom/article29/item-detail.cfm?item_id=612053, which was published on 6 February 2018.

IV. Conclusions

In those circumstances, it is submitted that it should not be assumed that insureds will know of all the risk factors relied upon or what inferences may have been drawn from their combined analysis; nor, it is submitted, should the question of whether a risk factor reduces the insured's risk be the sole trigger for insurers' duty of disclosure. Where insurers pre-emptively acquire information about insureds which is not visible to insureds, it is submitted that a better approach to materiality would be to reject the twin limitations that the insured disclosure is only required of risk-reducing factors and even then only where they are unknown to the insured. That approach is already available on one reading of Slade LJ's analysis in the Court of Appeal in *Banque Financière*. In the age of big data, it is submitted, with great respect, that such an approach is to be preferred to Lord Jauncey's obiter analysis in the House of Lords. Applying that test, insurers' modelling of risk through predictive algorithms should require them to disclose all those matters that bore on their evaluation of the risk. That would enable insureds to understand the basis upon which the proposed cover has been offered and would provide them with an opportunity to identify any errors in the data upon which insurers have sought to rely.

The next chapter considers what regulatory constraints operate in relation to insurers' use of personal data in underwriting risk. It is only by considering the extent of those constraints that we might identify (i) the sorts of regulatory requirements alongside which the common law might begin to develop in parallel; and (ii) whether there is, at least, a residual gap-filling role to be played by insurers' duty of good faith disclosure in the event that regulatory norms do not operate to provide all the sorts of protections that might be necessary where risk is increasingly being written using big data and predictive analytics.

PART III

The Impact of Regulatory Law on Insurance Law

6

Regulatory Constraints on the Collection and Use of Data

The previous chapter concluded that if insurers analyse information from most of the data sources to which they have access in principle, it would follow that (i) the justification for a duty of disclosure on insureds survives but only in respect of residual or exceptional matters of which insurers could not be aware, actually or constructively or as a result of waiver absent further enquiries; and (ii) given that the duty relates to information about the risk itself, the collection and use of that data engages insurers' duty of good faith and would require, at least, disclosure of all risk factors relied upon in insurers' evaluation and pricing of the risk, not least since that would give the insured the opportunity to correct inaccurate data. However, those conclusions can only be maintained if the application of regulatory law does not otherwise constrain insurers from collecting or using the new sources of data. This chapter thus considers the regulatory framework that applies to the collection and use of data by insurers. It is only once those constraints are considered that a final assessment can be made on the potential scope of insurers' duties of good faith at common law, a question that requires an assessment of the impact that the content of applicable regulatory duties may have on the scope of insurers' common law duty of good faith.

I. Financial Services Regulation

Prior to the regulation of insurers and insurance intermediaries by the EU, the regulation of insurance business was concerned, in broad terms, with insurers' ability to pay policyholders. Regulation proceeded incrementally across different classes of insurance, initially requiring insurers to make deposits[1] and then imposing solvency requirements.[2]

[1] The Assurance Companies Act 1909 expanded the scope of the deposit system to include fire, personal accident and employer's liability insurance.

[2] The Assurance Companies Act 1946 confined the right to carry on insurance business to insurance companies having a paid-up share capital of not less than £50,000. Moreover long-term (ie life) and general insurers had to maintain a margin of solvency whereby assets had to exceed liabilities by the greater of £50,000 or one-tenth of general premium income. These were inadequate and further amendments were made first by the Companies Act 1967 and then more substantially – as to the rules on authorisation, supervision and intervention – by the Insurance Companies Amendment Act 1973. The legislation was codified by way of the Companies Act 1974 which was itself repealed and replaced by the Insurance Companies Act 1982.

The law relating to authorisation, supervision and intervention was consolidated by the Insurance Companies Act 1982 but that was overhauled by the Financial Services Act 1986, which, although adopting a self-regulatory approach, marked the beginning of the modern form of insurance regulation. The 1986 Act was replaced by the Financial Services and Markets Act 2000 (FSMA 2000), which established the Financial Services Authority (FSA), which operated as a central regulator, replacing the self-regulatory model of the 1986 Act.[3] In light of the financial crisis of 2008, financial regulation was, further to the Financial Services Act 2012, divided between prudential regulation, which was the responsibility of the newly created Prudential Regulation Authority (PRA), and conduct regulation, which became the responsibility of the newly created Financial Conduct Authority (FCA). Between them, these two new bodies broadly have the same remit and powers that the FSA had before them.

Section 19 of the FSMA 2000 provides that, unless exempt, no one[4] may carry on a regulated activity by way of business in the UK without permission to do so.[5] A regulated activity is one which relates to investment or property, carried on by way of business and specified by secondary legislation made by the Treasury.[6] An investment includes rights under a 'contract of insurance'.[7] 'Effecting and carrying out contracts of insurance'[8] is a 'regulated activity' for the purposes of s 19 of the FSMA 2000.[9] A contract of insurance is defined by Article 3 of the Financial Services and Markets Act 2000 (Regulated Activities) Order 2001 (RAO) to mean 'any contract of insurance which is a contract of long-term insurance or a contract of general insurance'. Part I of Schedule 1 to the RAO sets out 18 classes of general insurance contracts which thereby fall within the definition of a contract of insurance in Article 3 of the RAO. Part II of Schedule 1 sets out nine classes of long-term insurance contracts. The law relating to the conduct of insurance business is regularly updated by statutory instruments issued under the FSMA 2000. Importantly, regulatory obligations are collected and consolidated in the PRA Rulebook and FCA Handbook. The sections of the FCA Handbook of particular relevance to the conduct of insurance business are: (i) PRIN (Principles for Business); (ii) COBS (Conduct of Business Sourcebook); and (iii) ICOBS (Insurance: Conduct of Business Sourcebook).[10] The provisions in each of those sourcebooks of potential relevance to insurers' collection and use of insureds' data are set out below.

[3] The FSA took responsibility for investment insurance in 2001, and for general insurance in 2005.

[4] Lloyd's became an authorised person in its own right pursuant to FSMA 2000. Following the Financial Services Act 2012, Lloyd's became an authorised person by virtue of the Financial Services Act 2012 (Transitional Provisions) (Permission and Approval) Order 2013. Lloyd's is regulated by both the PRA and the FCA but continues to supervise its members as required by the Lloyd's Act 1982.

[5] Permission is granted by the relevant regulator(s) under Part 4A of the FSMA 2000. Dual-regulated firms such as insurers who are supervised for prudential purposes by the PRA and for conduct purposes by the FCA must receive permission from both regulators in order to carry out regulated activities. The power of the Treasury to grant exemptions is conferred by s 38: see the Financial Services and Markets Act 2000 (Exemption) Order 2001 as amended.

[6] FSMA 2000, s 22.

[7] FSMA 2000, Schedule 2, para 20.

[8] Effecting insurance covers underwriting, while carrying out contracts of insurance includes administration and the payment of claims, and see *Re AA Mutual Insurance Co Ltd* [2005] 2 BCLC 8.

[9] And is a 'specified activity' pursuant to s 22 and Schedule 2 of the Financial Services and Markets Act 2000 and Art 10 of the Financial Services and Markets Act 2000 (Regulated Activities) Order 2001.

[10] COBS (Conduct of Business Sourcebook) applies to long-term insurance business in relation to life policies. See COBS 1.1.1.

A. PRIN

The Principles are a general statement of the fundamental obligations of regulated firms. Breaching a Principle makes a firm liable to disciplinary sanctions. However, the Principles do not give rise to actions for damages by a private person.[11] As the Principles are designed as a general statement of regulatory requirements applicable in new or unforeseen situations, the FCA's other rules and guidance do not exhaustively spell out the implications of the Principles themselves.[12] The Principles are set out in PRIN 2. The relevant Principles for these purposes include: (1) Integrity: a firm must conduct its business with integrity; (2) Skill, care and diligence: a firm must conduct its business with due skill, care and diligence; (5) Market Conduct: a firm must observe proper standards of market conduct; (6) Customers' interests: a firm must pay due regard to the interests of its customers and treat them fairly; (7) Communications with clients: a firm must pay due regard to the information needs of its clients, and communicate information to them in a way which is clear, fair and not misleading; (9) Customers: relationships of trust: a firm must take reasonable care to ensure the suitability of its advice and discretionary decisions for any customer who is entitled to rely upon its judgment; (10) Clients' assets: a firm must arrange adequate protection for clients' assets when it is responsible for them.[13]

Compliance with Principle 6 – Treating Customers Fairly (TCF) – requires insurers to demonstrate that they can meet six 'TCF Outcomes':[14]

- **Outcome 1:** consumers can be confident they are dealing with firms where the fair treatment of customers is central to the corporate culture.
- **Outcome 2:** products and services marketed and sold in the retail market are designed to meet the needs of identified consumer groups and are targeted accordingly.
- **Outcome 3:** consumers are provided with clear information and are kept appropriately informed before, during and after the point of sale.
- **Outcome 4:** where consumers receive advice, the advice is suitable and takes account of their circumstances.
- **Outcome 5:** consumers are provided with products that perform as firms have led them to expect, and the associated service is of an acceptable standard and as they have been led to expect.
- **Outcome 6:** consumers do not face unreasonable post-sale barriers imposed by firms to change product, switch provider, submit a claim or make a complaint.

The focus is again on the nature of the product, its suitability for the individual insured and that it operates in accordance with the insured's reasonable expectations.[15]

[11] See PRIN 3.4.4.R.
[12] PRIN 1.1.9.
[13] The territorial extent of the Principles are set out under PRIN 3.3.
[14] https://www.fca.org.uk/firms/fair-treatment-customers.
[15] The mis-selling of Payment Protection Insurance (PPI), whereby customers were sold policies under which they were ineligible to make a claim, was subject to enforcement action on the basis of a breach of Principle 6 and the TCF requirements.

The Principles thus do not expressly deal with personal data or the use of personal data. What amounts to a breach of the Principles will be guided by other, more specific norms, including financial services and data protection norms. Those norms will make clear what is required by way of skill and care, market conduct and how customers' interests must be met. Thus violations of more specific norms may also give rise to allegations of a breach of the Principles.

B. COBS and ICOBS

COBS applies to life and other long-term insurances while ICOBS applies, inter alia, to firms carrying out non-investment insurance (that is, general insurance) from an establishment maintained by it, or its appointed representative, in the United Kingdom with respect to, inter alia, their effecting and carrying out contracts of insurance.[16]

The Solvency II Directive[17] (Solvency II) makes some provision for insurer disclosure requirements.[18] Specifically, section 5 of Solvency II (Articles 183–187) provides for information to be made available to policyholders on matters such as the applicable law of the contract and complaints handling as well as more detailed information about benefits and other terms of life insurance policies. As the FCA put it in PS15/8 of March 2015: 'Articles 183–7 are primarily concerned with point-of-sale disclosure requirements and matters relating to the contract with policyholders.' The new Solvency II information requirements have been incorporated in changes made in the COBS.[19] The requirements relate to information that must be given in relation to the policy and the insurer. They do not relate to the information that the insurer may itself have acquired for the purposes of deciding whether to underwrite a risk or accept claims. In short, these information requirements relate to the insurance product, not the risk the subject of the proposed cover.

ICOBS 2.2 provides that an insurer must take reasonable steps to ensure that any communication of information is clear, fair and not misleading. This does not impose any positive obligation on insurers to set out what information it has itself obtained about the nature of the risk or the claim before determining whether to offer cover or pay a claim.

ICOBS 5.1.4 requires insurers to explain the duty of disclosure to the customer and provides:

> A *firm* should bear in mind the restriction on rejecting claims (ICOBS 8.1.1R (3)). Ways of ensuring a *customer* knows what he must disclose include:
>
> (1) explaining to a *commercial customer* the duty to disclose all circumstances material to a *policy*, what needs to be disclosed, and the consequences of any failure to make such a disclosure;

[16] This guidance applies in relation to a financial promotion that makes pricing claims, including financial promotions that indicate or imply that a firm can reduce the premium: ICOBS 2.2.4 G.

[17] Directive 2009/138.

[18] Recital (79) states: 'In an internal market for insurance, consumers have a wider and more varied choice of contracts. If they are to benefit fully from that diversity and from increased competition, consumers should be provided with whatever information is necessary before the conclusion of the contract and throughout the term of the contract to enable them to choose the contract best suited to their needs.'

[19] Specifically in COBS 1.1, COBS 1 Annex 1, COBS 13.1, 13.3, COBS 13 Annex 1 and 2, COBS 14.2, COBS 16.6, and COBS 20.4.7.

(2) ensuring that the *commercial customer* is asked clear questions about any matter material to the *insurance undertaking*;
(3) explaining to the *customer* the responsibility of *consumers* to take reasonable care not to make a misrepresentation and the possible consequences if a *consumer* is careless in answering the *insurer's* questions, or if a *consumer* recklessly or deliberately makes a misrepresentation; and
(4) asking the *customer* clear and specific questions about the information relevant to the *policy* being arranged or varied.

These obligations mirror the reforms made to the duty of disclosure in CIDRA 2012 and the IA 2015. No reference is made to what substantive information insurers might be required to provide to insureds in relation to their assessment of the proposed risk.

ICOBS 5.3.1 R applies to advised sales and provides that 'A firm must take reasonable care to ensure the suitability of its advice for any customer who is entitled to rely upon its judgment'. ICOBS 5.3.2 G provides suitability guidance for protection policies and provides:

(1) In taking reasonable care to ensure the suitability of advice on a *payment protection contract*[20] or a *pure protection contract*[21] a *firm* should:
(a) establish the *customer's* demands and needs. It should do this using information readily available and accessible to the *firm* and by obtaining further relevant information from the *customer*, including details of existing insurance cover; it need not consider alternatives to policies nor *customer* needs that are not relevant to the type of policy in which the *customer* is interested;
(b) take reasonable care to ensure that a *policy* is suitable for the *customer's* demands and needs, taking into account its level of cover and cost, and relevant exclusions, excesses, limitations and conditions; and
(c) inform the *customer* of any demands and needs that are not met.

(2) This guidance does not apply to payment protection contracts or pure protection contracts included in a packaged bank account.

The rule is thus concerned with information relevant to an assessment of the insured's insurance needs and demands rather than information for the purposes of insurers' underwriting or claims decisions.

ICOBS Chapter 6 sets out further general provisions, including what information must be provided to insureds about the policy being sold. ICOBS 6.1.5. R states that a

[20] Defined as: 'A *non-investment insurance contract* which has elements of a *general insurance contract* and the benefits of which are described as enabling a *policyholder* to protect his ability to continue to make payments due to third parties, or can reasonably be expected to be used in this way.'

[21] Defined as: '(1) a *long-term insurance contract* in respect of which the following conditions are met:
(a) the benefits under the contract are payable only on death or in respect of incapacity due to injury, sickness or infirmity;
(b) [deleted]
(c) the contract has no surrender value, or the consideration consists of a single premium and the surrender value does not exceed that premium; and
(d) the contract makes no provision for its conversion or extension in a manner which would result in it ceasing to comply with (a) or (c); or
(e) [deleted]
(2) a *reinsurance contract* covering all or part of a risk to which a *person* is exposed under a *long-term insurance contract*.'

firm must take reasonable steps to ensure a customer is given appropriate information about a policy in good time and in a comprehensible form so that the customer can make an informed decision about the arrangements proposed. ICOBS 6.1.6 G provides that the information rule includes matters relating to mid-term changes and renewals. It also applies to the price of the policy. Importantly, this obligation again relates to information that insurers must provide about their product, that is, the insurance policy and what it covers and what it does not; it will not extend to disclosing information as to the basis on which the proposed cover was offered. That the focus of the information rule is on the product, rather than the risk being underwritten, appears from ICOBS 6.1.7 G, which states that the level of information will vary according to matters including (i) the knowledge, experience and ability of a typical customer for the policy; (ii) the policy terms, including its main benefits, exclusions, limitations, conditions and its duration; (iii) the policy's overall complexity; and (iv) whether the policy is bought in connection with other goods and services.

ICOBS 6.1.12A R governs renewals and applies to general insurance contracts which have a duration of 10 months or more. It requires that insurers (or the intermediary dealing with the customer), in good time before renewal: (i) inform the insured of the proposed premium at which the insurer proposes to renew; and (ii) provide a statement indicating that the consumer should check that the level of cover offered by the renewal is appropriate to their needs. Again, insurers are not required to disclose what new information they gleaned from the existing policy period or through their monitoring of the risk in that period and which may have impacted on the renewal premium or terms.

Further information obligations arise under ICOBS Chapter 6 in relation to pure protection policies, and in compliance with the Solvency II Directive. But none of these information requirements relate to the information which insurers take into account when determining whether to offer cover or on what terms. Similarly in relation to mid-term changes, whereas an insurer is obliged to keep a customer informed throughout the term of a pure protection contract of any change concerning the policy conditions, both general and special,[22] it is not obliged to inform the insured of what information triggered the change. Broadly the same obligation covering all protection policies applies by virtue of ICOBS 6.4.11 R, which governs any term of the policy subject to a mid-term change. Insurers are also obliged to explain any implications of such a change. In this regard, ICOBS 6.4.12 R provides:

> (1) When explaining the implications of a change, a firm should explain any changes to the benefits and significant or unusual exclusions arising from the change.
> (2) Firms will need to consider whether mid-term changes are compatible with the original policy, in particular whether it reserves the right to vary premiums, charges or other terms. Firms also need to ensure that any terms which reserve the right to make variations are not themselves unfair under the Unfair Terms Regulations (for contracts entered into before 1 October 2015) or the [Consumer Rights Act].

Finally, Annex 2 of ICOBS 6 sets out what information must be contained within the summary of the policy to be provided to consumers. That must include the policy's

[22] ICOBS 6.3.3 R.

significant features and benefits, and any significant or unusual exclusions or limitations,[23] and cross-references to the relevant provisions in the policy document. There is no requirement to inform the insured of information the insurer had obtained pertaining to the nature of the risk or the basis upon which terms were offered.

Chapter 8 of ICOBS governs complaints handling. ICOBS 8.1.2 provides that the rejection of a consumer insured's claim is unreasonable where, in the absence of any evidence of fraud, the ground relied upon by the insurer is non-disclosure of a material fact that the policyholder could not reasonably be expected to disclose or non-negligent misrepresentation. ICOBS again imposes no obligation on insurers to provide information as to the basis on which a claim may have been rejected.

II. Regulation of Insurance – The Insurance Distribution Directive

The Insurance Distribution Directive (IDD) was promulgated on 20 January 2016, replacing the Insurance Mediation Directive (IMD). The IDD came into force on 1 October 2018. The IDD aims to enhance consumer protection when buying insurance – including general insurance, life insurance and insurance-based investment products (IBIPs). Like the IMD, the IDD covers the authorisation, passporting arrangements and regulatory requirements for insurance and reinsurance intermediaries. However, the application of the IDD is wider, imposing minimum harmonised standards across the EU in relation to organisational and conduct of business requirements for insurance and reinsurance undertakings. The IDD also introduces harmonised requirements in new areas, including product oversight and governance, and enhanced conduct rules for IBIPs.

The IDD introduces a requirement for non-life insurance distributors to provide customers with a standardised Insurance Product Information Document (IPID) prior to the conclusion of a contract. The IPID is created by the manufacturer of the insurance product but will be given to the customer by the distributor. The IPID must be provided before the conclusion of an insurance contract, when it will be most useful to customers. The FCA has clarified that commercial customers do not need to be given an IPID. However, the regulator made clear that distributors and manufacturers need to consider what type of information should be given to commercial customers and also when it should be provided to ensure that commercial customers are able to make an informed decision about purchasing the product.

The IDD also reinforces the pre-existing requirement that firms only offer customers insurance products that are consistent with the individual customer insurance demands and needs. It will be insufficient for firms to produce generic statements that the product meets a customer's demands and needs; rather they will have to explain more precisely why the products are consistent with their demands and needs.

[23] Examples of such terms include exclusion of certain conditions, diseases or pre-existing medical conditions, limits on the amounts of cover, limits on the period for which benefits will be paid or restrictions on eligibility to claim such as age, residence or employment status.

Article 2(2) of the IDD materially provides:

> For the purposes of points (1) and (2) of paragraph 1, the following shall not be considered to constitute insurance distribution or reinsurance distribution:
>
> (...)
>
> (b) the management of claims of an insurance undertaking or of a reinsurance undertaking on a professional basis, and loss adjusting and expert appraisal of claims;
>
> (c) the mere provision of data and information on potential policyholders to insurance intermediaries, reinsurance intermediaries, insurance undertakings or reinsurance undertakings where the provider does not take any additional steps to assist in the conclusion of an insurance or reinsurance contract.

Article 2(2)(c) makes clear that the IDD will not 'bite' on the information that an insurer obtains on a prospective insured from a data broker since the data broker (as provider of the data or information) would not take any additional steps to assist in the conclusion of an insurance contract.[24]

The information requirements imposed on insurance intermediaries and insureds by the IDD are set out in Articles 17–22 of the IDD. The general principle is set out under Article 17 materially as follows:

> 1. Member States shall ensure that, when carrying out insurance distribution, insurance distributors always act honestly, fairly and professionally in accordance with the best interests of their customers.
> 2. Without prejudice to Directive 2005/29/EC of the European Parliament and of the Council,[25] Member States shall ensure that all information related to the subject of this Directive, including marketing communications, addressed by the insurance distributor to customers or potential customers shall be fair, clear and not misleading. Marketing communications shall always be clearly identifiable as such.

Articles 18 and 19 impose obligations on intermediaries and insurers requiring them, prior to the entry into any contract, to provide information about themselves, whether they are providing advice on the products sold, their interest in an insurer (if an intermediary) or their interest in an intermediary (if an insurer) as well as information as to the remuneration that will be received for the conclusion of an insurance contract. Article 20(1) relates to the provision, or otherwise, of advice about an insurance product and provides that prior to the conclusion of an insurance contract, the insurance distributor shall specify, on the basis of information obtained from the customer, the demands and needs of that customer and shall provide the customer with objective information about the insurance product in a comprehensible form to allow that

[24] Reflecting Recital (13), which provides: 'This Directive should not apply to mere introducing activities consisting of the provision of data and information on potential policyholders to insurance or reinsurance intermediaries or undertakings or of information about insurance or reinsurance products or an insurance or reinsurance intermediary or undertaking to potential policyholders.'

[25] Directive 2005/29/EC of the European Parliament and of the Council of 11 May 2005 concerning unfair business-to-consumer commercial practices in the internal market and amending Council Directive 84/450/EEC, Directives 97/7/EC, 98/27/EC and 2002/ 65/EC of the European Parliament and of the Council and Regulation (EC) No 2006/2004 of the European Parliament and of the Council ('Unfair Commercial Practices Directive') (OJ L 149, 11.6.2005, p 22).

customer to make an informed decision. Any contract proposed must be consistent with the customer's insurance demands and needs. Where advice is provided prior to the conclusion of any specific contract, the insurance distributor must provide the customer with a personalised recommendation explaining why a particular product would best meet the customer's demands and needs. Article 20(4) then provides that, prior to the conclusion of a contract, whether or not advice is given, the insurance distributor is required to provide the customer with the relevant information about the insurance product in a comprehensible form to allow the customer to make an informed decision, while taking into account the complexity of the insurance product and the type of customer.[26] Article 20(8) sets out the information that must be provided in compliance with Article 20 on an IPID being:

(a) information about the type of insurance;
(b) a summary of the insurance cover, including the main risks insured, the insured sum and, where applicable, the geographical scope and a summary of the excluded risks;
(c) the means of payment of premiums and the duration of payments;
(d) main exclusions where claims cannot be made;
(e) obligations at the start of the contract;
(f) obligations during the term of the contract;
(g) obligations in the event that a claim is made;
(h) the term of the contract including the start and end dates of the contract;
(i) the means of terminating the contract.

Articles 29 and 30 of the IDD set out enhanced information and advisory requirements that intermediaries and insurers must comply with in relation to the distribution of insurance-based investment products, including as to continued suitability and (where relevant) proposed investment strategies.

Article 30(1) provides that

> without prejudice to Article 20(1), when providing advice on an insurance-based investment product, the insurance intermediary or insurance undertaking shall also obtain the necessary information regarding the customer's or potential customer's knowledge and experience in the investment field relevant to the specific type of product or service, that person's financial situation including that person's ability to bear losses, and that person's investment objectives, including that person's risk tolerance, so as to enable the insurance intermediary or the insurance undertaking to recommend to the customer or potential customer the insurance-based investment products that are suitable for that person and that, in particular, they are in accordance with that person's risk tolerance and ability to bear losses.[27]

There is no provision for how intermediaries or insurers may obtain information relating to the customer's knowledge, experience or risk tolerance, nor any provision as

[26] The obligation is without prejudice to those imposed by Arts 183 and 184 of Solvency II.

[27] Art 30(5) provides that when providing advice on an insurance-based investment product, the insurance intermediary or the insurance undertaking shall, prior to the conclusion of the contract, provide the customer with a suitability statement on a durable medium specifying the advice given and how that advice meets the preferences, objectives and other characteristics of the customer. The conditions set out in Art 23(1) to (4) shall apply.

regards how that information is held or used, other than obliging the intermediary or the insurer to assess the product's suitability and provide the relevant advice.[28]

The requirements in Article 37 of the IDD on data protection do not apply to insurers but rather to national competent authorities (the PRA and FCA) and EIOPA in relation to their processing of data further to the exercise of their functions under the IDD. In that regard, they are bound, not by the GDPR, but, respectively, by the Data Protection Directive (Directive 95/46) and Regulation 45/2001.

In the circumstances, nothing in the information or advisory obligations imposed by the new IDD oblige an insurer to disclose the prior information that it has obtained in determining whether to write a particular risk and if so, on what terms. Nothing in the IDD obliges the insurer to reveal what information it holds on the insured, or how it bore on its assessment of the individual risk or any subsequent claim made. The various information and advisory obligations relate not to the risk the subject of the insurance policy, but the nature of the policy itself. It therefore does not provide a basis upon which insurers might be constrained in their collection and use of risk-related data of their customers.

III. Data Protection Regulation

Europe is now at the forefront of data protection worldwide. The EU's data protection standards are based on EU legislation including, most importantly, the General Data Protection Regulation (GDPR), Council of Europe Convention 108,[29] as well as on the case law of each European legal order as determined, respectively, by the Court of Justice of the European Union (CJEU) and the European Court of Human Rights (ECtHR).[30] Reform and modernisation of Convention 108 in May 2018 (under the direction of the Council of Europe) and the promulgation of the GDPR (under the direction of the EU) was undertaken in parallel. Regulators in both legal orders have sought to ensure consistency and compatibility as between each framework. For the purposes of this Part, reference will predominantly be made to the EU framework. However, in view of the limitation that EU data protection law only confers rights in respect of personal data, being data relating to an identified or identifiable natural person, the question arises as to whether legal persons such as companies have any greater data protection under the ECHR. That question is considered further below.

A. EU Framework

The original treaties of the European Communities did not confer rights to personal data protection. Nor did they include any explicit competence on matters of fundamental

[28] Art 30 also imposes obligations as to the assessment of the suitability of a product in the context of execution-only sales.

[29] Convention for the Protection of Individuals with regard to Automatic Processing of Personal Data. The amending protocol (CETS No 223) to Convention 108 was adopted by the Committee of Ministers of the Council of Europe on 18 May 2018.

[30] All EU Member States, including the United Kingdom, are bound by each legal order. But non-EU states that are member states of the Council of Europe are bound by Convention 108 and the case law of the ECtHR.

rights. Prior to the changes made under the Lisbon Treaty, EU legislation on data protection – notably the Data Protection Directive 1998 and the Privacy and Electronic Communications Directive 2002 – were adopted on the internal market basis given the need to approximate national laws so that the free movement of data within the EU was not inhibited (currently Article 114 TFEU).

i. The Data Protection Directive 1995

The EU's first comprehensive data protection legislation was the Data Protection Directive of 1995.[31] The latter was implemented in the UK by the Data Protection Act 1998 (DPA 1998). The DPA 1998 has now been repealed by the Data Protection Act 2018 (DPA 2018), which gives effect to the GDPR, which has itself repealed the Data Protection Directive of 1995. As the GDPR and the DPA 2018 provide more extensive data protection, the Data Protection Directive and the DPA 1998 are not considered further.

ii. The Privacy and Electronic Communications (EC Directive) Regulations 2003

The Privacy and Electronic Communications (EC Directive) Regulations 2003 (PECR) implement, in part, the Directive on privacy and electronic communications (the e-Privacy Directive).[32] The e-Privacy Directive, unlike the Data Protection Directive (or, now, the GDPR) extends its protections to a limited extent to legal as well as natural persons. In particular, it protects the confidentiality of communications and the legitimate interests of legal persons concerning the increasing capacity for the automated storage and processing of data relating to subscribers and users.[33]

The e-Privacy Directive focuses on the confidentiality of users' electronic communications; it requires electronic communication services operators (including telecommunications providers) to ensure, among other things, that access to personal data is limited solely to authorised persons and take measures to prevent personal data from being destroyed, lost or accidentally damaged. The confidentiality of communications requires that the listening, tapping, storage or any type of surveillance or interception of communications and metadata is, in principle, prohibited. Importantly for present purposes, the Directive and the implementing regulations apply to the use

[31] Directive 95/46/EC on the protection of individuals with regard to the processing of personal data and on the free movement of such data.

[32] Directive 2002/58/EC of the European Parliament and of the Council of 12 July 2002 concerning the processing of personal data and the protection of privacy in the electronic communications sector. PECR was amended in 2004 and 2011. See ICO, *Privacy and Electronic Communications Regulations* https://ico.org.uk/about-the-ico/what-we-do/legislation-we-cover/privacy-and-electronic-communications-regulations/.

[33] Recital (7) thus states: 'In the case of public communications networks, specific legal, regulatory and technical provisions should be made in order to protect fundamental rights and freedoms of natural persons and legitimate interests of legal persons, in particular with regard to the increasing capacity for automated storage and processing of data relating to subscribers and users.' Article 1(2) provides: 'The provisions of this Directive particularise and complement Directive 95/46/EC for the purposes mentioned in paragraph 1. Moreover, they provide for protection of the legitimate interests of subscribers who are legal persons.'

of cookies which, as discussed in chapter one, are a key means by which an individual's internet use is tracked.[34] Under PECR, before a business can use cookies, it must: (i) provide clear and comprehensive information; and (ii) obtain freely given, specific and informed consent, unless it is 'strictly necessary' to provide the service. These requirements do not merely apply to cookies which store personal data but to the storage of all forms of data.[35]

In January 2017, the European Commission published a proposal for a regulation concerning the respect for private life and the protection of personal data in electronic communications, intended to replace the e-Privacy Directive. The reform aims to align the rules governing electronic communications with the new data protection regime established under the GDPR. The new regulation (the ePR) will be directly applicable throughout the EU. The ePR is broader in scope than the e-Privacy Directive and aims to ensure privacy in all electronic communications – including over-the-top service providers such as instant messaging apps (such as Facebook's Messenger and WhatsApp) and VoIP (Voice over Internet Protocol) platforms (such as Skype), and machine-to-machine communications such as the IoT. Importantly, the draft e-Privacy Regulation extends protection of communications and related legitimate interests to legal persons. Recital (3) in the draft regulation states:

> Electronic communications data may also reveal information concerning legal entities, such as business secrets or other sensitive information that has economic value. Therefore, the provisions of this Regulation should apply to both natural and legal persons. Furthermore, this Regulation should ensure that provisions of the [GDPR], also apply to end-users who are legal persons. This includes the definition of consent under [the GDPR]. When reference is made to consent by an end-user, including legal persons, this definition should apply. In addition, legal persons should have the same rights as end-users that are natural persons regarding the supervisory authorities; furthermore, supervisory authorities under this Regulation should also be responsible for monitoring the application of this Regulation regarding legal persons.

The intention is therefore to extend the provisions of the GDPR to legal persons insofar as the GDPR governs matters within the scope of the new ePR[36] and to afford equivalent levels of protection to natural and legal persons in relation to those matters (including the protection of electronic communications and the rights to control electronic

[34] The PECR of course apply equally to similar technologies such as locally stored objects (flash cookies) and device fingerprinting (see Data Protection Working Party, *Opinion 9/2014 on the application of Directive 2002/58/EC to device fingerprinting*).

[35] The requirements are discussed in ICO's 'Guide to the Privacy and Electronic Communications Regulations' of May 2018 at 29: https://ico.org.uk/media/for-organisations/guide-to-pecr-2-4.pdf. The ICO issued more specific guidance on the use of cookies in May 2012: https://ico.org.uk/media/for-organisations/documents/1545/cookies_guidance.pdf.

[36] As draft Recital (9) notes: 'This Regulation should apply to electronic communications data processed in connection with the provision and use of electronic communications services in the Union, regardless of whether or not the processing takes place in the Union.' The ePR raises interesting questions for the application of the GDPR to legal persons such as how can a legal person freely give consent (which will presumably involve some principle of attribution arising from the consent of certain officers with the requisite authority) and what are the legitimate interests of a legal person. See the discussion of these issues by the EDPB in its Opinion of April 2017: https://iapp.org/media/pdf/resource_center/wp247_ePrivacy-Reg_04-2017.pdf.

communications). For example, Draft Article 15(3) provides, in relation to publicly available directories, the right of legal persons to object to their data being included within the directory and the right to verify, correct and delete any such data. The new ePR was intended to come into force in May 2018 with the GDPR but that has been extended. At the time of writing, the new Regulation had still not come into force.

iii. The Charter of Fundamental Rights of the European Union

In addition to the EU legislature using the Treaties' harmonisation basis for the adoption of the above directives, the CJEU has developed rights in relation to data processing as part of its evolving fundamental rights jurisprudence. Some of these cases are discussed below. Following the Lisbon Treaty, Article 16 of the Treaty on the Functioning of the European Union provides: 'Everyone has the right to the protection of personal data concerning them.'[37] Article 16 thus creates a new and free-standing legal basis for the adoption of EU primary law affording personal data protection to EU citizens. Article 7 of the Charter of Fundamental Rights of the EU (the Charter)[38] confers the right to respect for private life.[39] Article 8 of the Charter also established the right to the protection of personal data requiring that it 'must be processed fairly for specified purposes and on the basis of the consent of the person concerned or some other legitimate basis laid down by law'. Additionally it provides that 'Everyone has the right of access to data which has been collected concerning him or her, and the right to have it rectified'. Compliance with the right is required to be subject to the control of an independent authority.[40] The right is not absolute 'but must be considered in relation to its function in society'.[41] Article 52(1) of the Charter recognises that limitations may be imposed on the exercise of rights such as that set out in Article 8 of the Charter, as long as those limitations are provided for by law, respect the essence of those rights[42] and freedoms

[37] Art 16(3) states that '[t]he rules adopted on the basis of this Article shall be without prejudice to the specific rules laid down in Article 39 of the Treaty on European Union'. Art 39 of the TEU provides: 'In accordance with Article 16 of the Treaty on the Functioning of the European Union and by way of derogation from paragraph 2 thereof, the Council shall adopt a decision laying down the rules relating to the protection of individuals with regard to the processing of personal data by the Member States when carrying out activities which fall within the scope of this Chapter, and the rules relating to the free movement of such data. Compliance with these rules shall be subject to the control of independent authorities.'

[38] The EU proclaimed the Charter in 2000. The Charter was not, at that stage, legally binding, the EU having no competence under the existing Treaty to promulgate it as such. However, it became binding as EU primary law pursuant to Art 6(1) of the Treaty on European Union (TEU) when the Lisbon Treaty came into force on 1 December 2009. The provisions of the Charter are addressed to EU institutions and bodies, obliging them to respect the rights listed therein while fulfilling their duties. The Charter's provisions also bind Member States when they implement EU law. As to the meaning of 'implementing EU law', see the decisions of the CJEU in Case C-617/10 *Åklagaren v Åkerberg Fransson* [2013] 2 CMLR 46 (paras 27–28) and Case C-206/13 *Siragusa v Regione Sicilia* [2014] 3 CMLR 13 (paras 24–32).

[39] The right is conferred on 'everyone', raising the issue whether it includes legal persons as well as natural persons.

[40] Which in the UK is the role of the Information Commissioner's Office.

[41] See, eg, CJEU, Joined Cases C-92/09 and C-93/09, *Volker und Markus Schecke GbR and Hartmut Eifert v Land Hessen* [2010] ECR I-11063, 9 November 2010, paras 48–50.

[42] See Case C-362/14, *Maximillian Schrems v Data Protection Commissioner* [2016] CMLR 2, 6 October 2015, relating to the Commission decision of 2000 allowing transfers of data held by companies such as,

and, subject to the principle of proportionality, are necessary and genuinely meet objectives of general interest recognised by the EU or the need to protect the rights and freedoms of others. As personal data protection is a distinct and stand-alone fundamental right in the EU legal order, protected under Article 8 of the Charter, any processing of personal data by itself constitutes an interference with this right. It is immaterial whether the personal data in question relate to an individual's private life, are sensitive, or whether the data subjects have been inconvenienced in any way. To be lawful, the interference has to comply with all the conditions listed in Article 52 (1) of the Charter.

iv. The GDPR

a. Application

The GDPR, promulgated under Article 16 of the TFEU, came into force on 25 May 2018.[43] Its principal aim is to protect EU citizens from privacy and data breaches in an increasingly data-driven society.[44] In particular, it introduces new provisions to address the risks arising from profiling and automated decision making.[45] The GDPR does not just focus on the decisions made as a result of automated processing or profiling. It applies to the collection of data for the creation of profiles, as well as the application of those profiles to individuals.

The GDPR forms part of the data protection regime in the UK, together with the new DPA 2018. It applies to 'controllers' and 'processors'. Someone is a 'controller' if they are the natural or legal person, public authority, agency or other body which, alone or jointly with others, determines the purposes and means by which personal data

in this case, Facebook, to US companies that self-certified that they would protect personal data transferred from the EU and would comply with the so-called 'Safe Harbour principles'. The CJEU regarded legislation permitting public authorities to access, on a general basis, the content of electronic communications as 'compromising the essence of the fundamental right to respect for private life, as guaranteed by Article 7 of the Charter'. Moreover, the CJEU observed that 'legislation not providing for any possibility for an individual to pursue legal remedies in order to have access to personal data relating to him, or to obtain the rectification or erasure of such data' is incompatible with the fundamental right to effective judicial protection (Art 47 of the Charter).

[43] In parallel, Directive 2016/680 on the protection of natural persons with regard to the processing of personal data by competent authorities for the purposes of the prevention, investigation, detection or prosecution of criminal offences or the execution of criminal penalties, and on the free movement of such data was promulgated to address, inter alia, the use of profiling techniques by law enforcement authorities. See, on profiling and discrimination, the prohibitions in Art 11 in particular. That Directive came into force on 6 May 2018.

[44] It had also become clear that the Data Protection Directive had been implemented in a diverging manner across the EU. That together with more fundamental technological changes – such as the growth of big data – created the need for a harmonising regulation. Even though the GDPR is directly applicable, Member States were expected to update their existing national data protection laws which the UK has done via the Data Protection Act 2018, discussed below.

[45] The European Data Protection Board (EDPB) notes the key concern is privacy but further states: 'Profiling can perpetuate existing stereotypes and social segregation. It can also lock a person into a specific category and restrict them to their suggested preferences. This can undermine their freedom to choose, for example, certain products or services such as books, music or newsfeeds. In some cases, profiling can lead to inaccurate predictions. In other cases it can lead to denial of services and goods and unjustified discrimination.' Guidelines on automated decision-making and profiling, February 2018, pp 5–6.

is processed.[46] Someone is a 'processor' of personal data if they are a natural or legal person, public authority, agency or other body which processes personal data on behalf of the controller.[47] Article 2(1) of the GDPR provides that it 'applies to the processing of personal data wholly or partly by automated means and to processing other than by automated means of personal data which form part of a filing system or are intended to form part of a filing system'. Article 4(1) defines 'personal data' to mean

> any information relating to an identified or identifiable natural person ('data subject'); an identifiable natural person is one who can be identified, directly or indirectly, in particular by reference to an identifier such as a name, an identification number, location data, an online identifier or to one or more factors specific to the physical, physiological, genetic, mental, economic, cultural or social identity of that natural person.[48]

Personal data thus includes only data relating to natural persons.[49] Use of the words 'relating to' means that the data in question must do more than simply identify the individual: it must concern the individual in some way, such as providing information on their activities, preferences, needs and so on. It further defines processing to mean

> any operation or set of operations which is performed on personal data or on sets of personal data, whether or not by automated means, such as collection, recording, organisation, structuring, storage, adaptation or alteration, retrieval, consultation, use, disclosure by transmission, dissemination or otherwise making available, alignment or combination, restriction, erasure or destruction.[50]

[46] Art 4(7).

[47] Art 4(8). The Information Commissioner observes that whereas it is often easy to distinguish the role of a controller and a processor, when personal data is processed in the context of big data, AI and machine learning, this can make it more difficult to distinguish: 'This is because, typically, big data analytics is about finding correlations, making predictions and aiding decision-making; all of which blur the lines between who is actually determining the purposes and manner of the processing when an organisation has chosen to outsource the analytics to another company – one that specialises in AI, for example.' ICO 2017, para 126.

[48] Online identifiers such as IP addresses or cookie identifiers are caught by this definition. If it is possible, directly or indirectly, to identify an individual from the information being processed (whether from a single identifier (such as a name) or a combination of identifiers), that will or at least may involve the processing of personal data. Information which has had identifiers removed or replaced in order to pseudonymise the data is still personal data for the purposes of GDPR.

[49] Information about companies is not personal data. Information about their employees (which includes all directors and officers) is, so long as it relates to them as individuals. In Joined Cases C-92/09 and C-93/09 *Volker und Markus Schecke and Hartmut Eifert v Land Hessen*, the CJEU, referring to the publication of personal data relating to beneficiaries of agricultural aid, held that 'legal persons can claim the protection of Articles 7 and 8 of the Charter in relation to such identification only in so far as the official title of the legal person identifies one or more natural persons. … [T]he right to respect for private life with regard to the processing of personal data, recognised by Articles 7 and 8 of the Charter, concerns any information relating to an identified or identifiable individual' (para 53). In the event the contested provisions were held invalid against the individual recipient named but not the partnership named even though the partnership contained the names of two individuals who thus could be readily identified. This contrasts with the opinion of Advocate General Sharpston, who considered the provision to be invalid against the partnership as well.

[50] If information that seems to relate to a particular insured is inaccurate (ie it is factually incorrect or is about a different individual), the information is still personal data, as it relates (albeit wrongly) to that individual. Moreover, even if insurers only hold certain identifying personal data on an individual insured, if it were possible for a third party to use that data, in combination with other data, to identify the individual, that will be sufficient to constitute the processing of personal data even if the insurer could not do so on the basis of the information it holds.

That would apply to insurers who, by themselves or via third party data aggregators, use algorithms to identify, collect and analyse information about an individual insured or insureds covered under a wider commercial policy. Data profiling is defined as

> any form of automated processing of personal data consisting of the use of personal data to evaluate certain personal aspects relating to a natural person, in particular to analyse or predict aspects concerning that natural person's performance at work, economic situation, health, personal preferences, interests, reliability, behaviour, location or movements.[51]

Data aggregators building individual profiles on insureds are both profiling personal data and may do so either as a controller for the purpose of selling those risk profiles to insurers or as a processor if this is done under the control of or on behalf of insurers. Insurers will be controllers and engaged in profiling where the data, whether gathered by third parties or by insurers themselves, is used to evaluate certain personal aspects of the individual insured. The category of purposes for which data might be profiled set out in Article 4(4) is not exhaustive and plainly applies to processing used to assess eligibility or the degree of risk presented by a prospective insured.

The GDPR identifies certain categories of personal data for special treatment. Article 9(1) provides that the

> processing of personal data revealing racial or ethnic origin, political opinions, religious or philosophical beliefs, or trade union membership, and the processing of genetic data,[52] biometric data[53] for the purpose of uniquely identifying a natural person, data concerning health[54] or data concerning a natural person's sex life or sexual orientation shall be prohibited.

That prohibition is subject to exceptions including where (a) the data subject has given explicit consent to the processing of those personal data for one or more specified purposes, except where Union or Member State law provides that the prohibition referred to in paragraph 1 may not be lifted by the data subject;[55] and (b) processing relates to personal data which are manifestly made public by the data subject.[56] The GDPR applies extraterritorially, as it applies to all companies processing the personal data of data subjects residing in the Union, regardless of the company's location.[57]

b. The GDPR Principles

The GDPR sets out seven key principles in Article 5. It is worth setting this provision out in full since it addresses a number of the problems raised in chapter three about how

[51] Art 4(4).

[52] Defined in Art 4 as 'personal data relating to the inherited or acquired genetic characteristics of a natural person which give unique information about the physiology or the health of that natural person and which result, in particular, from an analysis of a biological sample from the natural person in question.'

[53] Defined in Art 4 as 'personal data resulting from specific technical processing relating to the physical, physiological or behavioural characteristics of a natural person, which allow or confirm the unique identification of that natural person, such as facial images or dactyloscopic data.' If personal data can be truly anonymised then the anonymised data is not subject to the GDPR.

[54] Defined in Art 4 as 'personal data related to the physical or mental health of a natural person, including the provision of health care services, which reveal information about his or her health status.'

[55] Art 9(2)(a).

[56] Art 9(2)(e).

[57] GDPR, Art 3.

insurers collect data from a wider range of sources and the issues to which the use of that data might give rise:

5(1) Personal data shall be:

(a) processed lawfully, fairly and in a transparent manner in relation to the data subject ('lawfulness, fairness and transparency');
(b) collected for specified, explicit and legitimate purposes and not further processed in a manner that is incompatible with those purposes; further processing for archiving purposes in the public interest, scientific or historical research purposes or statistical purposes shall, in accordance with Article 89(1), not be considered to be incompatible with the initial purposes ('purpose limitation');
(c) adequate, relevant and limited to what is necessary in relation to the purposes for which they are processed ('data minimisation');[58]
(d) accurate and, where necessary, kept up to date; every reasonable step must be taken to ensure that personal data that are inaccurate, having regard to the purposes for which they are processed, are erased or rectified without delay ('accuracy');[59]
(e) kept in a form which permits identification of data subjects for no longer than is necessary for the purposes for which the personal data are processed; personal data may be stored for longer periods insofar as the personal data will be processed solely for archiving purposes in the public interest, scientific or historical research purposes or statistical purposes in accordance with Article 89(1) subject to implementation of the appropriate technical and organisational measures required by this Regulation in order to safeguard the rights and freedoms of the data subject ('storage limitation');
(f) processed in a manner that ensures appropriate security of the personal data, including protection against unauthorised or unlawful processing and against accidental loss, destruction or damage, using appropriate technical or organisational measures ('integrity and confidentiality').[60]

5(2) The controller shall be responsible for, and be able to demonstrate compliance with, paragraph 1 ('accountability').[61]

The transparency, accuracy, repurposing, data-minimisation and temporal limitation concerns addressed in chapter three are all therefore the subject of the GDPR's

[58] In Joined Cases C-293/12 and C-594/12, *Digital Rights Ireland Ltd v Minister for Communications, Marine and Natural Resources and Others* and *Kärntner Landesregierung and Others* [2014] ECR I-238 the CJEU considered the validity of the Data Retention Directive, which aimed to harmonise national provisions for retaining personal data generated or processed by publicly available electronic communications services or networks for their possible transmission to competent authorities to fight serious crime, such as organised crime and terrorism. Notwithstanding that this was considered a purpose that genuinely satisfies an objective of general interest, the generalised way in which the Directive covered 'all individuals and all means of electronic communication as well as all traffic data without any differentiation, limitation or exception being made in the light of the objective of fighting against serious crime', was considered problematic. See paras 44 and 57 of the judgment.

[59] See, eg, Case C-553/07, *College van burgemeester en wethouders van Rotterdam v M E E Rijkeboer* [2009] ECR I-03889, 7 May 2009.

[60] The GDPR thus expands and enhances the eight data protection principles set out in the DPA 1998. Principally, the GDPR removes individuals' rights from being a separate principle and are separately addressed in Chapter III of the GDPR.

[61] One of the accountability requirements is that records of processing activities must be maintained in circumstances (among others) where organisations have more than 250 employees or where they are processing personal data that could result in a risk to individuals' rights and freedoms. It is likely that insurers engaging big data analytics may fall within one, or both, of the above situations. One of the records that must be maintained is the purposes of the processing of personal data: GDPR Art 30(1)(b). Insurers engaged in profiling will also have to appoint a Data Protection Officer: GDPR Art 37(1).

processing principles. Compliance with the principles is central to compliance with the GDPR. Failure to comply with the principles may leave a data controller or processor liable to substantial fines. Article 83(5)(a) states that infringements of the basic principles for processing personal data are subject to the highest tier of administrative fines. This could mean a fine of up to €20 million, or 4% of an insurer's total worldwide annual turnover, whichever is higher.

c. Lawful Basis for Processing

Insurers as controllers of personal data must identify and have valid grounds under the GDPR for collecting and using personal data. Insurers must have a lawful basis for the processing (which will include profiling as an automated form of processing).[62] Article 6 provides that processing will only be lawful if one or more of the six listed bases apply. They are that:

(a) the data subject has given consent to the processing of his or her personal data for one or more specific purposes;
(b) processing is necessary for the performance of a contract to which the data subject is party or in order to take steps at the request of the data subject prior to entering into a contract;
(c) processing is necessary for compliance with a legal obligation to which the controller is subject;
(d) processing is necessary in order to protect the vital interests of the data subject or of another natural person;
(e) processing is necessary for the performance of a task carried out in the public interest or in the exercise of official authority vested in the controller;
(f) processing is necessary for the purposes of the legitimate interests pursued by the controller or by a third party, except where such interests are overridden by the interests or fundamental rights and freedoms of the data subject which require protection of personal data, in particular where the data subject is a child.

Bases (a) (consent), (b) (contract) and (f) (legitimate interests) will be of most relevance to insurers engaged in data profiling or using profiled data. The lawful basis for processing can also affect which rights are available to individuals.[63] Many of these bases depend on the processing being 'necessary'. The Information Commissioner explains that this does not mean the processing always has to be essential, merely that the lawful basis will not apply if the controller can reasonably achieve the purpose by some other less intrusive means.[64] She observes:

> It is not enough to argue that processing is necessary because you have chosen to operate your business in a particular way. The question is whether the processing is necessary for the stated purpose, not whether it is a necessary part of your chosen method of pursuing that purpose.

As noted in chapter three, it might be argued that data profiling is not necessary for evaluating individual risks because more traditional and less intrusive means of

[62] Arts 6–10 of the GDPR govern the lawful basis aspect of this principle.
[63] For example, whereas there is a right to 'port' one's personal data if it was processed pursuant to the data subject's consent or a contract, there is no such right if it was processed on the basis of legitimate interests.
[64] https://ico.org.uk/for-organisations/guide-to-the-general-data-protection-regulation-gdpr/lawful-basis-for-processing/.

profiling are available. Indeed, some insurers have made data profiling optional, by offering those who opt in the prospect of greater discounts (and no increases) on premium, offers that are not open to those who do not opt in. The Information Commissioner further elaborates on the broad choice between consent and legitimate interests as a lawful basis for processing as follows:

> You may prefer to consider legitimate interests as your lawful basis if you wish to keep control over the processing and take responsibility for demonstrating that it is in line with people's reasonable expectations and wouldn't have an unwarranted impact on them. On the other hand, if you prefer to give individuals full control over and responsibility for their data (including the ability to change their mind as to whether it can continue to be processed), you may want to consider relying on individuals' consent.

The lawful basis for the processing has a profound impact on whether data can be repurposed. If a controller's purposes change, they may not need a new lawful basis as long as the new purpose is compatible with the original purpose. However, the GDPR specifically says this does not apply to processing based on consent. Consent must always be specific and informed. A controller needs to either get a further consent which specifically covers the new purpose, or find a different basis for the new purpose. In other cases, in order to assess whether the new purpose is compatible with the original purpose the controller should take into account: (i) any link between the initial purpose and the new purpose; (ii) the context in which the data was collected – in particular, the controller's relationship with the individual and what they would reasonably expect; (iii) the nature of the personal data – eg is it special category data or criminal offence data; (iv) the possible consequences for individuals of the new processing; and (v) whether there are appropriate safeguards – eg encryption or pseudonymisation.

Consent

The conditions for obtaining a valid consent to the processing are set out in Article 7 of the GDPR. Requests for consent must be made clearly and separately from other information or authorisation that an insurer may seek from a prospective insured.[65] As noted above, Article 9(1) has the effect that an insurer can only process sensitive categories of data where, inter alia, the data subject has given explicit consent to the processing of those personal data for one or more specified purposes. Controllers can only process special category personal data if they can meet one of the conditions set out in Article 9(2), as well as a condition from Article 6. This includes special category data derived or inferred from profiling activity.[66] The EDPB observes that

> Controllers seeking to rely upon consent as a basis for profiling will need to show that data subjects understand exactly what they are consenting to, and remember that consent is not

[65] The GDPR makes it clearer that the consent must also be 'unambiguous' and that it must be a 'clear affirmative action' such as ticking a box on a website or choosing particular technical settings for 'information society services' (services delivered over the internet, eg a social-networking app): GDPR Art 4(11) and Recital (32).

[66] As referred to in ch 3, profiling can create special category data through the combination of non-special category data where shopping habits and location data may reveal health conditions or ethnicity. The study of Facebook likes allowing researchers to predict sexual orientation with 88% accuracy is well known: Michael Kosinski, David Stilwell and Thore Graepel, 'Private traits and attributes are predictable from digital records of human behavior', 9 April 2013, Proceedings of the National Academy of Sciences of the United States of America, http://www.pnas.org/content/110/15/5802.full.pdf.

> always an appropriate basis for the processing. In all cases, data subjects should have enough relevant information about the envisaged use and consequences of the processing to ensure that any consent they provide represents an informed choice.[67]

In addition, consent will be inappropriate where the data subject is pressurised to provide the data in exchange for a service or where there is a significant economic or other imbalance in the relationship between controller and data subject. Typical examples of such imbalances arise where (i) employers process personal data of employees or (ii) public authorities process the personal data of citizens pursuant to the exercise of public law powers. A supermarket offering discounts for those who sign up to loyalty cards would not, however, prevent a consumer giving a valid consent in signing up. There will be no imbalance where an insurer offers a discount to those who take a telematics policy. If the insurer was only prepared to offer insurance if the insured agreed to a telematics policy, the insured's ability to give a valid consent is likely to turn on whether he has a sufficient choice of policies on the motor insurance market. If so, consent will again be valid. If the situation arises where most insurers only offer telematics cover, insurers might argue that that is proportionate insofar as such policies are more effective in identifying and pricing risk and thus necessary for them to avoid adverse selection and the competitive harm that this would entail. It may thus be difficult to contend that the imposition of policies based on the use of big data analytics vitiates the insured's ability to validly consent to such policies.[68]

If an insurer buys a large dataset of personal data for analytics purposes, it then becomes a data controller regarding that data. The insurer then needs to be sure it has a lawful basis for the further use of that data. If it is relying on the original consent obtained by the data broker for that purpose, it should ensure that this covers the further processing it plans for the data. As the Information Commissioner notes by way of example,

> just because people have put data onto social media without restricting access does not necessarily legitimise all further use of it. The fact that data can be viewed by all does not mean anyone is entitled to use it for any purpose or that the person who posted it has implicitly consented to further use. This is particularly an issue if social-media analytics is used to profile individuals, rather than for general sentiment analysis (the study of people's opinions). If a company is using social-media data to profile individuals, eg for recruitment purposes or for assessing insurance or credit risk, it needs to ensure it has a data protection condition for processing the data. Individuals may have consented to this specifically when they joined the social-media service. If the company does not have consent, it needs to consider what other data protection conditions may be relevant.[69]

[67] And see Art 29 Data Protection Working Party, Guidelines on Consent under Regulation 2016/679 WP259, 28 November 2017, http://ec.europa.eu/newsroom/just/document.cfm?doc_id=48849.

[68] GDPR Art 7(4) provides that 'When assessing whether consent is freely given, utmost account shall be taken of whether, *inter alia*, the performance of a contract, including the provision of a service, is conditional on consent to the processing of personal data that is not necessary for the performance of that contract.'

[69] ICO report, 'Big data, artificial intelligence, machine learning and data protection', September 2017, https://ico.org.uk/media/for-organisations/documents/2013559/big-data-ai-ml-and-data-protection.pdf, para 64. The Information Commissioner states that a key factor in deciding whether a new purpose is

It follows that were information that an insured may have sought by way of a Google search or that they put on social media to be used to assess their risk profile for insurance purposes, then unless they are informed of this and asked to give their consent, then this repurposed use of the data is unlikely to be fair.[70]

Contract

This basis[71] will be relevant, for example, when someone makes a purchase online, and the website has to process their name, address and credit-card details to complete the purchase. Specific consent is not required for such processing. The problem in applying this in a big data context is that the processing must be 'necessary'. Processing will be necessary for online purchasing to verify identity and authorise the transaction (which will cover insurance purchased online). Big data analytics in the insurance context goes beyond what is required simply to sell a product. It may allow for more accurate profiling and thus more accurate pricing and greater efficiencies, but it might again be argued that it is not necessary in the strict sense, given that insurance has been written without the benefit of big data for most of its history. The difficulty is that as predictive analytics is used by more insurers, those who do not will find it increasingly necessary in a competitive sense to use profiling to avoid the problem of adverse selection.[72] But that is not the relevant test of necessity: the test is as to necessity to perform the contract, not necessity to compete in the market. Insurers will doubtless argue that policies written on the basis of big data analytics are different from traditional policies and that processing personal data is necessary for the operation of these particular types of policy. This is one of many questions that remains to be tested.[73]

Legitimate Interests

Profiling is allowed if it is 'necessary' for the purposes of the legitimate interests pursued by the controller or by a third party. However, Article 6(1)(f) does not automatically apply just because the controller or third party has a legitimate interest. The processing is not necessary if there is another way of meeting the legitimate interest that interferes less with people's privacy. The controller must carry out a balancing exercise to assess

incompatible with the original purpose is whether it is fair. In particular, this means considering how the new purpose affects the privacy of the individuals concerned and whether it is within their reasonable expectations that their data could be used in this way; ibid, para 81. Recital (5) of the GDPR says that in assessing compatibility it is necessary to take account of any link between the original and the new processing, the reasonable expectations of the data subjects, the nature of the data, the consequences of the further processing and the existence of safeguards.

[70] The Information Commissioner thus states: 'If the new purpose would be otherwise unexpected, and it involves making decisions about them as individuals, then in most cases the organisation concerned will need to seek specific consent, in addition to assessing whether the new purpose is incompatible with the original reason for processing the data'; ibid, para 82.

[71] Which covers pre-contractual relationships.

[72] Which of course assumes big data analytics will become more accurate than traditional, aggregated modelling.

[73] See the discussion by the Information Commissioner in her 2017 Report on Big Data at para 73.

whether their interests are overridden by the data subject's interests or fundamental rights and freedoms.[74] The following are particularly relevant:

1. the level of detail of the profile (a data subject profiled within a broadly described cohort such as 'people with an interest in English literature', or segmented and targeted on a granular level);
2. the comprehensiveness of the profile (whether the profile only describes a small aspect of the data subject, or paints a more comprehensive picture);
3. the impact of the profiling (the effects on the data subject); and
4. the safeguards aimed at ensuring fairness, non-discrimination and accuracy in the profiling process.

The Information Commissioner notes that although an alternative basis to seeking individual consent to processing, the legitimate interests condition is not a soft option for the organisation; it means it takes on more responsibility.[75] This means that if a data controller is relying on legitimate interests, it will have to explain what these are in its privacy notice.[76]

d. Fairness and Transparency

Fairness requires insurers to (i) consider how the processing may affect the individuals concerned; and (ii) be able to justify any adverse impact. They must consider how a profile may be unfair and might deny vulnerable people access to insurance or lead to their being targeted with more costly or more restricted cover. They must handle personal data in ways insureds would reasonably expect, or can explain why any unexpected processing is justified.[77] The use of Data Protection Impact Assessments (DPIAs) can provide a structured way of ensuring fairness in processing conducted by big data analytics. Transparency requires insurers to be clear about when and why data is collected and comply with the transparency obligations as to the insured's right to be informed.

[74] The opinion of the Art 29 Working Party on legitimate interests under the current Data Protection Directive sets out in detail how to assess these factors and do the balancing exercise. Art 29 Data Protection Working Party, Guidelines on Consent under Regulation 2016/679 WP259, 28 November 2017, http://ec.europa.eu/newsroom/just/document.cfm?doc_id=48849.

[75] ICO, 2017, para 70. Under the consent condition, while the organisation must ensure its processing is fair and satisfies data protection principles, the individual is responsible for agreeing (or not) to the processing, which may not proceed without their consent. By contrast, the legitimate interests condition places the responsibility on the organisation to carry out an assessment and proceed in a way that respects people's rights and interests.

[76] GDPR Art 13(1)(d) and 14(2)(b).

[77] As the Information Commissioner says in 'Big Data, Artificial Intelligence, Machine Learning and Data Protection', 2017, para 39: 'Fairness is also about expectations; would a particular use of personal data be within the reasonable expectations of the people concerned? An organisation collecting personal data will generally have to provide a privacy notice explaining the purposes for which they need the data, but this may not necessarily explain the detail of how the data will be used. It is still important that organisations consider whether people could reasonably expect their data to be used in the ways that big data analytics facilitates.'

e. Individual Data Rights[78]

In the digital age, data processing has become ubiquitous and increasingly difficult for individuals to understand. The GDPR's conferral of individual rights in relation to the processing of personal data is to mitigate the informational and power asymmetries between data subjects and controllers.

The Right to be Informed[79]

Articles 13–14 of the GDPR confer on individuals the right to be informed about the collection and use of their personal data.[80] Controllers must provide individuals with information including: their purposes for processing an individual's personal data, the lawful basis for the processing, the categories and sources of personal data obtained (if not obtained from the individual himself), retention periods for that personal data, who it will be shared with and the details of the existence of automated decision making, including profiling, if applicable.[81] Where an insurer obtains personal data from a source other than the individual it relates to, it needs to provide the individual with privacy information within a reasonable period of obtaining the personal data and no later than one month.[82] In addition, if insurers obtain personal data from publicly accessible sources, they still need to provide insureds with privacy information to that effect. Where an insurer applies artificial intelligence to personal data, then the fact that the processing is for the purposes of both (a) profiling and (b) making a decision based on the profile generated, must be made clear to the data subject.[83] Importantly, the Information Commissioner observes:

> If the purposes for processing are unclear at the outset, give people an indication of what you are going to do with their data. As your processing purposes become clearer, update your privacy information and actively communicate this to people … If you use AI to make solely automated decisions about people with legal or similarly significant effects, tell them what information you use, why it is relevant and what the likely impact is going to be.

[78] Art 23(1) of the GDPR lists a series of objectives of general interest considered legitimate for limiting the rights of individuals, provided that the limitation respects the essence of the right to personal data protection and is necessary and proportionate. National security and defence, crime prevention, the protection of important economic and financial interests of the EU or Member States, public health and social security are among the public interest aims mentioned therein.

[79] WP29, the predecessor to the European Data Protection Board, adopted guidelines on the transparency requirements of the GDPR and which are here: http://ec.europa.eu/newsroom/article29/item-detail.cfm?item_id=622227.

[80] Art 13 applies to information to be provided where the personal data is collected from the data subject. Art 14 applies where the data has not been obtained from the data subject.

[81] In Case C-201/14 *Smaranda Bara and Others v Casa Naţională de Asigurări de Sănătate and Others* ECLI:EU:C:2015:638, the CJEU considered that the requirement under EU law to inform the data subject about the processing of their personal data is 'all the more important since it affects the exercise by the data subjects of their right of access to, and the right to rectify, the data being processed … and their right to object to the processing of those data.'

[82] Art 14(3). Where insurers buy personal data from data brokers, if the data is to be used for a purpose different from the basis on which it was collected by the broker, the insurer must tell people about this, as well as what its lawful basis is for the processing.

[83] Arts 13(2)(f) and 14(2)(g).

The Right of Access[84]

Article 15 of the GDPR confers a right of access to personal data held on a data subject and provides that 'the data subject shall have the right to obtain from the controller confirmation as to whether or not personal data concerning him or her are being processed, and, where that is the case, access to the personal data and [certain] information'.[85] The information which the data subject can access includes the purposes of the processing, the categories of personal data concerned, where possible the period for which the data will be stored, the source of the data if it has not been collected from the data subject, and 'the existence of automated decision-making, including profiling, referred to in Article 22(1) and (4) and, at least in those cases, meaningful information about the logic involved, as well as the significance and the envisaged consequences of such processing for the data subject'.[86] As the EDPB notes, in addition to general information about the processing, pursuant to Article 15(3), the controller has a duty to make available the data used as inputs to create the profile as well as access to information on the profile and details of which segments of a wider cohort (such as a risk pool) the data subject has been placed into.[87] The Information Commissioner observes that the volume and variety of big data and the complexity of the analytics could make it more difficult for organisations to meet this obligation: that will arise where an organisation is using and/or buying in a range of data sources, including unstructured data, as it can be difficult to produce all the data on one individual. Moreover, the increasing use of observed, derived and inferred data means the data held may not all have been provided directly by the data subject.

> However, such reasons cannot be an excuse for disregarding legal obligations. The existence of the right of access compels organisations to practise good data management. They need adequate metadata, the ability to query their data to find all the information they have on an individual, and knowledge of whether the data they are processing has been truly anonymised or whether it can still be linked to an individual.[88]

A controller cannot restrict the data subject's rights by refusing to provide information beyond a date one year prior to the subject access request.[89]

[84] See generally Joined Cases C-141/12 and C-372/12, *YS v Minister voor Immigratie, Integratie en Asiel* and *Minister voor Immigratie, Integratie en Asiel v M and S*, 17 July 2014; CJEU, C-615/13 P, *ClientEarth, Pesticide Action Network Europe (PAN Europe) v European Food Safety Authority (EFSA), European Commission*, 16 July 2015 (nyr).

[85] This information largely corresponds with what must be published in a privacy notice.

[86] Art 15(1)(h). The EDPB observes that the controller should provide the data subject with general information (notably, on factors taken into account for the decision-making process, and on their respective 'weight' on an aggregate level) which is also useful for him or her to challenge the decision; EDPB, 'Guidelines on Automated individual decision-making and Profiling for the purposes of Regulation 2016/679', p 27; see http://ec.europa.eu/newsroom/article29/item-detail.cfm?item_id=612053.

[87] WP251, 17 http://ec.europa.eu/newsroom/article29/item-detail.cfm?item_id=612053.

[88] Information Commissioner's report 'Big data, artificial intelligence, machine learning and data protection', September 2017; https://ico.org.uk/media/for-organisations/documents/2013559/big-data-ai-ml-and-data-protection.pdf, paras 99–101.

[89] In Case C-553/07, *College van burgemeester en wethouders van Rotterdam v M E E Rijkeboer*, 7 May 2009, the CJEU was asked to determine whether an individual's right to access information about the recipients or categories of recipient of personal data, and to the content of the data, could be limited to one year before his or her request for access. The CJEU held that 'that right must of necessity relate to the past. If that were not

The Right to Rectification

Profiling can involve an element of prediction, which increases the risk of inaccuracy. The input data may be inaccurate or irrelevant, or taken out of context. There may be something wrong with the algorithm used to identify correlations, or the reliability of the correlations themselves. A risk factor identified in relation to a particular insured may not apply to that insured. Under Article 16 of the GDPR individuals have the right to have inaccurate personal data rectified. It provides:

> The data subject shall have the right to obtain from the controller without undue delay the rectification of inaccurate personal data concerning him or her. Taking into account the purposes of the processing, the data subject shall have the right to have incomplete personal data completed, including by means of providing a supplementary statement.

The right is a manifestation of the principle of accuracy set out under Article 5(1)(d). The right – which will be exercised further to the individual obtaining access to their data – may be exercised repeatedly to enable the individual to reconsider the accuracy of their data upon request. Data is inaccurate if it is incorrect or misleading as to any matter of fact.[90] Individuals may wish to challenge the accuracy of the data used and any grouping or category that has been applied to them. Under Article 18 of the GDPR an individual has the right to request restriction of the processing of their personal data where they contest its accuracy.

Insurers holding inaccurate data will be obliged to amend it. If insurers consider the data is accurate, notwithstanding the request to rectify, it should provide the insured with reasons for so concluding and inform them of their right to complain to the Information Commissioner and their legal rights.

The Right to Erasure

Under Article 17 of the GDPR individuals have the right to have personal data erased. This is the 'right to be forgotten' introduced in chapter three. The right is not absolute and only applies in certain circumstances. The right applies, inter alia, if: (i) the personal data is no longer necessary for the purpose which it was originally collected or processed (eg if the insured no longer needs insurance of that type or from that insurer); (ii) the insurer was relying on consent as its lawful basis for holding the data and the insured withdraws that consent; (iii) the insurer was relying on legitimate interest as the lawful basis for processing and the insured objects to the processing and the insurer cannot point to an overriding legitimate interest to continue processing; or (iv) the insurer has processed the personal data unlawfully.[91] One relevant exception to the right is where the controller requires the data for the establishment, exercise or defence of legal claims. Where the personal data the subject of the erasure request has been made public in an online environment, the controller who made that data public must

the case, the data subject would not be in a position effectively to exercise his right to have data presumed unlawful or incorrect rectified, erased or blocked or to bring legal proceedings and obtain compensation for the damage suffered.'

[90] DPA 2018, s 205(1).

[91] The right applies to data stored on back-up systems and the data must be put beyond use while the data is being overwritten.

take reasonable steps to inform other controllers who are processing the personal data to erase links to or copies of that data. The rights to rectification and erasure apply to both the 'input personal data' (the personal data used to create the profile)[92] and the 'output data' (the profile itself or 'score' assigned to the person).

In the *Google Spain*[93] case the CJEU considered whether Google was obliged to delete outdated information about the applicant's financial difficulties from its search list results. When a search was undertaken on the Google search engine using the applicant's name, the results of the search provided links to old newspaper articles mentioning his connection with bankruptcy proceedings. The applicant considered this an infringement on his rights to respect for private life and for the protection of personal data, as the proceedings had been concluded years ago, making such references irrelevant.

The CJEU noted that the Data Protection Directive sought to protect fundamental rights and, particularly, rights relating to privacy.[94] It considered that its provisions ought to be interpreted in the light of the fundamental rights to private life and the protection of personal data enshrined in Articles 7 and 8 of the Charter of Fundamental Rights of the EU (the Charter). The Court found that insofar as search engines such as Google could establish a detailed profile of an individual, those search engines were capable of affecting these rights significantly. Where society is becoming increasingly digitised, the requirement for personal data to be accurate (and for its publication to not go beyond what is necessary to provide information to the public) is fundamental to ensuring a high level of data protection to individuals. This means that the right to have one's personal data erased when the processing is no longer necessary or outdated also covers search engines, which were found to be controllers, not merely processors.

On examining whether Google was required to remove the links related to the applicant, the CJEU held that, under certain conditions, individuals have the right to obtain erasure of their personal data from an internet search engine's search results. This right may be invoked where information relating to an individual is inaccurate, inadequate, irrelevant or excessive for the purposes of the data processing. The CJEU acknowledged that this right is not absolute; it needs to be balanced with other rights, in particular the interest and right of the general public in having access to the information. Each request for erasure needs a case-by-case assessment to seek a balance between the fundamental rights to personal data protection and private life of the data subject on the one hand, and the legitimate interests of all internet users on the other. The Court laid down an important presumption in favour of the rights to privacy and the protection of personal data. This presumption could only be rebutted

> if it appeared, for particular reasons, such as the role played by the data subject in public life, that the interference with his fundamental rights is justified by the preponderant interest of

[92] Recommendation Rec(2002)9 of the Committee of Ministers noted that personal data should also be deleted 'where a decision is taken to refuse insurance coverage': para 13.1.

[93] Case C-131/12, *Google Spain SL, Google Inc v Agencia Española de Protección de Datos (AEPD), Mario Costeja González* [2014] EMLR 27, 13 May 2014.

[94] ibid, para 80.

the general public in having, on account of its inclusion in the list of results, access to the information in question.[95]

The CJEU provided guidance on the factors to take into consideration during the balancing exercise. The nature of the information in question is a particularly important factor. If information is sensitive to the private life of the individual, and where there is no public interest in the availability of the information, data protection and privacy would override the right of the general public to have access to the information. On the contrary, if it appears that the data subject is a public figure, or that the information is of such nature to justify granting the general public access to such information, then the interference with the fundamental rights to data protection and privacy is justified. The CJEU then examined whether the interference could be justified on the facts. The CJEU stated that 'it is clear that [the interference] cannot be justified merely by reliance on the economic interest which Google has in that processing', and that 'as a rule' the fundamental rights under Articles 7 and 8 of the Charter override such economic interest and the interest of the general public in finding that information upon a search relating to the data subject's name.[96]

By contrast, the *Manni* case[97] concerned the inclusion of an individual's personal data in a public commercial register. Mr Manni had requested the Lecce Chamber of Commerce to delete his personal data from that registry, having discovered that potential clients would resort to the registry and see that he had been the administrator of a company which was declared bankrupt more than a decade before. The CJEU was called upon to determine if EU law recognised a right to erasure in those circumstances. In reaching its conclusion, it balanced EU data protection rules and Mr Manni's commercial interest in removing the information about his former company's bankruptcy with the public interest in access to the information. It took due note of the fact that disclosure to the public registry of companies was provided for by law, and particularly by an EU Directive aiming to make company information more easily accessible to third parties. The CJEU rejected Mr Manni's entitlement to erase his personal data: the need to protect the interests of third parties in relation to joint-stock and limited liability companies, and to ensure legal certainty, fair trading and thus the proper functioning of the internal market took precedence over his rights under data protection legislation.

The Right to Restrict Processing

Article 18 of the GDPR gives individuals the right to restrict the processing of their personal data in certain circumstances. This means that an individual can limit the way that an organisation uses their data. This is an alternative to requesting the erasure of

[95] ibid, para 97.

[96] ibid, paras 81 and 97. The right to be forgotten was applied in *NT1 v Google LLC* [2018] EWHC 799 (QB). See also the forthcoming decision in Case C-507/17 *Google v CNIL*, where the CJEU will consider the balance to be struck between the right to be forgotten, the right of access to information and the right of free expression. The French Data Protection Commissioner argued that the right entailed the worldwide delisting of the data whereas Google argued that the data should only be delisted from Google France.

[97] Case C-398/15, *Camera di Commercio, Industria, Artigianato e Agricoltura di Lecce v Salvatore Manni*, [2017] ECLI:EU:C:2017:197.

their data. The right can be availed of, inter alia: (i) where the individual contests the accuracy of their personal data and the insurer is verifying the accuracy of the data; (ii) where the insurer may no longer need the data but where the insured requires the insurer to keep it in order to establish, exercise or defend a legal claim; and (iii) where an insured objects to the processing of data under Article 21 and the insurer is considering whether there are legitimate grounds to override the objection.

In *Manni*, the CJEU confirmed that it is up to the national courts to assess in each case, and having regard to all the relevant circumstances of the individual, the existence or absence of legitimate and overriding reasons which could exceptionally justify the restriction of third parties' access to personal data.

The Right to Data Portability

Article 20 of the GDPR confers a right to data portability which gives individuals the right to receive personal data they have provided to a controller in a structured, commonly used and machine readable format. It also gives them the right to request that a controller transmits this data directly to another controller. Article 20 provides, materially, as follows:

> 1. The data subject shall have the right to receive the personal data concerning him or her, which he or she has provided to a controller, in a structured, commonly used and machine-readable format and have the right to transmit those data to another controller without hindrance from the controller to which the personal data have been provided, where: (a) the processing is based on consent pursuant to point (a) of Article 6(1) or point (a) of Article 9(2) or on a contract pursuant to point (b) of Article 6(1); and (b) the processing is carried out by automated means.[98]
> 2. In exercising his or her right to data portability pursuant to paragraph 1, the data subject shall have the right to have the personal data transmitted directly from one controller to another, where technically feasible.

This is an important right and resolves concerns that had been raised by a number of regulators as to the use of big data in the provision of insurance services. For example, research undertaken for the CMA in June 2015 observed:

> A consequence of these various factors is that there is currently no portability of telematics data or driving scores for consumers who wish to obtain quotes from other providers based on evidence of their driving behaviour, collected by their current provider. (This contrasts, for example, with no claims discounts, which are typically transferable.) In theory, the lack of portability may lessen the incentives for consumers to switch, potentially dampening competition.[99]

In addition, if the insured was unable to port their past behavioural data from insurer A to insurer B and the latter did not otherwise have access to it, insurer B is

[98] That is, the right to data portability only applies when the insurer's lawful basis for processing this information is consent *or* for the performance of a contract; and the controller is carrying out the processing by automated means.

[99] CMA Research, 50. That research also noted that the complexity of this information, combined with a lack of standardisation and the providers' reluctance to share data that can offer competitive advantage, means that consumers typically cannot access the full data and analysis or 'port' it to other insurance providers (unlike no claims discounts, which are typically transferable).

prejudiced insofar as it is prevented from more accurately evaluating the risk posed by the insured, a fact that creates an uneven competitive playing field and may disincentivise switching between insurers.

A further, structural issue that made this problem real was the fact that different insurers had pursued the development of their risk-specific/behavioural data (and the analysis thereof) in different ways. There is no common approach or standard either with regard to the type of raw data collected or with regard to the algorithms used to produce driving scores. Insurers may be entitled to conceal their proprietary technology to preserve commercial advantage, but that does not entail retaining the raw data against which those analytics are applied. However, even if their algorithms benefit from IP protection, there had been a concern over who owned the data generated by, for example, telematics devices in the insured's vehicle. On this issue the FCA in its Feedback Statement of 2016 observed that

> a number of firms and other stakeholders commented that motor telematics data may not be easily transferrable. This is because different providers use different devices, which could potentially add cost and inconvenience if a consumer has to have one device uninstalled and another reinstalled each time they switch providers. Two firms told us that consumers own much of the driving data and could request it from their provider. However, there is not a common standard for recording driving data. Additionally, as one firm explained to us, another insurer may not be able to use the data because it is difficult to condense meaningfully (many insurers record driving data on a per second basis) and each insurer will interpret driving behaviour differently.[100]

Article 20 seeks to resolve these problems. The right applies therefore to traffic, location and raw driving data, and raw data processed by connected objects such as wearables.[101] But it does not include any additional data that the insurer may have created based on the underlying data provided. So inferred or derived data created for a user profile (eg a driver risk profile or score) would not be required to be ported to a new motor insurer, although to the extent that it contains personal data the insured could still obtain it by way of a subject access request.[102]

The Right to Object

Article 21 of the GDPR gives individuals the right to object to the processing (and profiling) of their personal data. An individual must give specific reasons why they are objecting to the processing of their data. These reasons should be based upon their

[100] FCA Feedback Statement, September 2016, para 3.6, https://www.fca.org.uk/publication/feedback/fs16-05.pdf.

[101] The idea of personal data stores has been floated – these are third-party services that hold people's personal data and make it available to organisations as and when individuals wish to do so. This facilitates data portability across an individual's data profile and across all range of sectors: see Ira S Rubinstein, 'Big data. The end of privacy or a new beginning?' *International Data Privacy Law*, 25 January 2013, http://idpl.oxfordjournals.org/content/early/2013/01/24/idpl.ips036.full.pdf+html. For a contrary perspective that sees the emergence of a new class of data managers or auditors managing data on our behalf, see J Obar, 'Big data and the phantom public. Walter Lippmann and the fallacy of data privacy self-management', *Big Data & Society*, July–December 2015 Vol 2 No 2, http://m.bds.sagepub.com/content/2/2/2053951715608876.

[102] Recital (68) encourages interoperability stating: 'Data controllers should be encouraged to develop interoperable formats that enable data portability.' Controllers generally are obliged to act reasonably and avoid creating barriers to transmission of data. In that regard the EDPB has published guidelines on data portability: 13 December 2016 as revised and adopted on 5 April 2017.

particular situation. If such a request is made, the controller 'shall no longer process the personal data unless the controller demonstrates compelling legitimate grounds for the processing which override the interests, rights and freedoms of the data subject or for the establishment, exercise or defence of legal claims'. The right is therefore not absolute, but the more compelling the reason on which the objection is made, the more difficult it will be to justify continued processing.

The Rights Related to Automated Decision Making Including Profiling

Importantly for present purposes are the rights in relation to (i) automated decision making and (ii) profiling. Automated individual decision making is a decision made by automated means without any human involvement. Profiling is a subset of automated decision making. Article 4(4) of the GDPR defines profiling as:

> Any form of automated processing of personal data consisting of the use of personal data to evaluate certain personal aspects relating to a natural person, in particular to analyse or predict aspects concerning that natural person's performance at work, economic situation, health, personal preferences, interests, reliability, behaviour, location or movements.

The GDPR restricts data controllers and processors from making solely automated decisions, including those based on profiling, that have a legal or similarly significant effect on individuals. However, that prima facie right is subject to exceptions. The key provision is Article 22 of the GDPR, which imposes obligations additional to those discussed above where decisions based on solely automated processing are taken. It is entitled 'Automated individual decision-making, including profiling' and provides:

> 1. The data subject shall have the right not to be subject to a decision based solely[103] on automated processing, including profiling, which produces legal effects concerning him or her or similarly significantly affects him or her.
> 2. Paragraph 1 shall not apply if the decision: (a) is necessary for entering into, or performance of, a contract between the data subject and a data controller; (b) is authorised by Union or Member State law to which the controller is subject and which also lays down suitable measures to safeguard the data subject's rights and freedoms and legitimate interests; or (c) is based on the data subject's explicit consent.
> 3. In the cases referred to in points (a) and (c) of paragraph 2, the data controller shall implement suitable measures to safeguard the data subject's rights and freedoms and legitimate interests, at least the right to obtain human intervention on the part of the controller, to express his or her point of view and to contest the decision.
> 4. Decisions referred to in paragraph 2 shall not be based on special categories of personal data referred to in Article 9(1), unless point (a) or (g) of Article 9(2) applies and suitable measures to safeguard the data subject's rights and freedoms and legitimate interests are in place.[104]

[103] Art 4(4) refers to 'any form of automated processing' whereas Art 22 refers to 'solely' automated processing. Profiling has to involve some form of automated processing – although human involvement does not necessarily take the activity out of the definition. Where a human decides whether to offer insurance cover based on a profile produced by purely automated means, that engages Art 4, but where an algorithm decides whether the loan is agreed and the decision is automatically delivered to the individual, without any prior and meaningful assessment by a human, that is solely automated decision making and engages Art 22.

[104] This is a significant development from the DPA 1998, under which individuals had a right to be informed about automated decisions that significantly affected them but generally this type of processing could be carried out unless an objection was raised.

For something to be solely automated there must be no human involvement in the decision-making process. The EDPB notes that the controller cannot avoid the Article 22 provisions by fabricating human involvement. For example, if an insurer routinely applies automatically generated risk profiles to individual insureds without any actual influence on the result, this would still be a decision based solely on automated processing. To qualify as human involvement, the controller must ensure that any oversight of the decision is meaningful, rather than just a token gesture. It should be carried out by someone who has the authority and competence to change the underwriting or claims decision. As part of the analysis, they should consider all the relevant data.[105]

The restriction only covers solely automated individual decision making that produces legal or similarly significant effects. These types of effect are not defined in the GDPR, but the decision must have a serious negative impact on an individual to be caught by this provision. It is submitted that being denied insurance or being charged higher premiums as a result of the application of an algorithm brings the profiling of insureds within Article 22 as, at the least, a decision having 'similarly significant effects'.[106] The effect of Article 22 is that an insurer could only deploy solely automated decision making if the decision is (i) necessary for entering into or the performance of a contract with an individual; (ii) expressly authorised by law; or (iii) based on an individual's explicit consent. Where profiling relates to special category personal data an insurer is only likely to justify this requirement with the insured's explicit consent.[107]

As noted above, Articles 13(2)(f) and 14(2)(g) of the GDPR provide that the controller shall inform the data subject as to the use of automated decision making, including profiling, referred to in Article 22(1) and (4) and, at least in those cases, meaningful information about the logic involved, as well as the significance and the envisaged consequences[108] of such processing for the data subject. What is required to explain the logic involved in a system of solely automated profiling? The EDPB observes that, given the complexity of profiling, the controller should find simple ways to tell the data subject about the rationale behind, or the criteria relied upon in reaching the decision. The GDPR requires the controller to provide meaningful information about the logic involved, not necessarily a complex explanation of the algorithms used or disclosure of the algorithm itself. The information provided should, however, be sufficiently comprehensive for the data subject to understand the reasons for the decision.[109] The Handbook on European data protection law suggests, by way of example, that a 'health

[105] Guidelines on Automated individual decision-making and Profiling for the purposes of Regulation 2016/679 http://ec.europa.eu/newsroom/article29/item-detail.cfm?item_id=612053 at 21.

[106] Cancellation of an insurance contract as a result of profiling would be a decision 'producing legal effects' but one denying cover in the first place where there is no cover is one having 'similarly significant effects'.

[107] Although, as will be seen below, the DPA 2018 authorises the processing of sensitive data for insurance purposes where certain additional conditions are met.

[108] The EDPB gives the example of a telematics insurer using an automated decision-making process to set motor insurance premiums providing the insured with an app that allows him to see how improved driving habits might impact favourably on his premium.

[109] http://ec.europa.eu/newsroom/article29/item-detail.cfm?item_id=612053 p 25.

insurance company using automated decision-making on applications should provide data subjects with general information on how the algorithm works and which factors the algorithm uses to calculate their insurance premiums.'[110]

The safeguarding measures that a controller must take in relation to solely automated decisions should include, as a minimum, a way for the data subject to obtain human intervention, express their point of view, and contest the decision.[111] The EDPB considers that human intervention is a key element. Any review must be carried out by someone who has the appropriate authority and capability to change the decision. The reviewer should undertake a thorough assessment of all the relevant data, including any additional information provided by the data subject.[112] Recital (71) in this regard highlights that 'in any case' suitable safeguards should also include 'specific information to the data subject and the right … to obtain an explanation of the decision reached after such assessment and to challenge the decision.' As explained in chapter three, an insured can only challenge a decision if he knows the basis upon which it was taken.

A DPIA must be undertaken for processing that is likely to result in a high risk to individuals. If solely automated decision making is being used, a DPIA must be carried out. A DPIA will enable the controller to assess the risks involved in automated decision making, including profiling. It is a way of showing that suitable measures have been put in place to address those risks and demonstrate compliance with the GDPR. Even if Article 22 doesn't apply (because the processing isn't solely automated), a controller is still required to carry out a DPIA if the processing constitutes '*a systematic and extensive evaluation* of personal aspects relating to natural persons which is *based on* automated processing, *including* profiling, and on which decisions are based that produce legal effects concerning the natural person or similarly significantly affect the natural person.'[113]

f. Domestic Implementation: The DPA 2018

Section 4 of the DPA 2018 provides that Chapter 2 of Part 2 of the Act applies to the types of processing of personal data to which the GDPR applies by virtue of Article 2 of the GDPR. Specifically, Article 2(2) provides that the GDPR only applies to the processing of data in the course of an activity which is subject to Union law. Section 4(2)(b) provides that Chapter 2 of Part 2 of the DPA 2018 supplements and must be read with the GDPR. The distribution of insurance products is an activity that is subject to EU law

[110] European Union Agency for Fundamental Rights, 'Handbook on European data protection law', 2018 edition, p 234. See also the Profiling Recommendation, which, albeit not legally binding, specifies the conditions for the collection and processing of personal data in the context of profiling: Council of Europe, Recommendation CM/Rec(2010)13 of the Committee of Ministers to member states on the protection of individuals with regard to automatic processing of personal data in the context of profiling, Art 5(5).

[111] The safeguards are provided for in s 14 of the DPA 2018; and see the Explanatory Notes to the Act, p 26.

[112] This is implemented in s 14(4) of the DPA 2018 giving the data subject one month after being notified that a decision was taken on a solely automated basis to ask for the decision to be reconsidered or that the controller takes a new decision that is not based solely on automated processing.

[113] Art 35(3)(a) of the GDPR, which refers to evaluations including profiling and decisions that are 'based' on automated processing, rather than 'solely' automated processing. This would appear to include decisions that are not wholly automated as well as those that are solely automated for the purposes of Art 22(1).

(see the discussion of the IDD in II.A above). Chapter 3 of Part 2 of the Act provides for a separate regime to apply GDPR standards to general processing in the UK which is outside the scope of the GDPR. Schedule 6 to the DPA 2018 specifies how GDPR standards will be applied to areas outside the scope of EU law.

Section 10 of the DPA 2018 makes provision for the lawful processing of special categories of personal data described in Article 9(1) of the GDPR. It will be recalled that Article 9(2) sets out exceptions to the prohibition of processing of the various special categories of personal data. Article 9(2)(g) of the GDPR listed one such exception where the processing of that data

> is necessary for reasons of substantial public interest, on the basis of Union or Member State law which shall be proportionate to the aim pursued, respect the essence of the right to data protection and provide for suitable and specific measures to safeguard the fundamental rights and the interests of the data subject.

Section 10(1) of the DPA 2018 provides:

> (1) Subsections (2) and (3) make provision about the processing of personal data described in Article 9(1) of the GDPR (prohibition on processing of special categories of personal data) in reliance on an exception in one of the following points of Article 9(2) –
>
> (…)
>
> (b) point (g) (substantial public interest);
>
> (…)
>
> (3) The processing meets the requirement in point (g) of Article 9(2) of the GDPR for a basis in the law of the United Kingdom or a part of the United Kingdom only if it meets a condition in Part 2 of Schedule 1.

Schedule 1 to the DPA 2018 relates to the special categories of personal data. Part 2 of Schedule 1 sets out the substantial public interest conditions which must be met if the processing of special category personal data is to be lawful. Paragraph 20 makes clear that processing sensitive personal information for insurance is processing that may be of substantial public interest so long as the conditions set out under that paragraph are met. Paragraph 20(1) provides that those conditions will be met if the processing is (i) necessary for an insurance purpose; (ii) is of personal data revealing racial or ethnic origin, religious or philosophical beliefs or trade union membership, genetic data or data concerning health, and (iii) is necessary for reasons of substantial public interest. In other words, the insurance industry does not need to obtain explicit consent from an insured before processing sensitive personal information for the purposes of insurance. The third condition is somewhat odd: prima facie, processing sensitive data for insurance purposes is processing for a 'substantial public interest' (hence its inclusion in in Part 2 of Schedule 1). But an additional test whereby that processing must be shown to be necessary for reasons of substantial public interest is imposed. What constitutes necessity where consent is not required remains to be seen. However, it is suggested that the profiling revealing the insured's sensitive data listed must, at the very least, be shown to be material to the risk. Of potentially greater concern is whether paragraph 20 of Schedule will operate as a Trojan horse in relation to genetic data or data concerning health: could this provision signal the beginning of the end of the Concordat and Moratorium on Genetics and Insurance?

B. ECHR Framework

i. The Relationship between the Rights to Private Life and Personal Data Protection

The right to respect for private life and the right to personal data protection, although related and overlapping, are distinct rights.[114] The former is protected by Article 8 of the ECHR which includes the right in certain circumstances not to have private information retained by the state or disclosed by the state to third parties. The right to personal data protection is not a distinct fundamental right under the ECHR. For Article 8 to be engaged, it first has to be determined whether a private interest, or a person's private life, has been compromised. Processing personal data may infringe a person's private life but it is not necessary to demonstrate such an infringement for the rights in relation to data protection to operate.[115] In *Vukota-Bojić v Switzerland*[116] Article 8 was engaged in relation to the acquisition of data by an insurance company. The case concerned secret surveillance of a social insurance claimant by private investigators commissioned by her insurance company. The ECtHR held that, while the surveillance measure at issue in the complaint had been ordered by a private insurance company, that company had been given the right by the state to provide benefits arising from compulsory medical insurance and to collect insurance premiums. A state could not absolve itself from responsibility under the convention by delegating its obligations to private bodies or individuals. Domestic law had to provide sufficient safeguards against abuse for interference with the rights under Article 8 of the ECHR to be 'in accordance with the law'. The ECtHR concluded that there had been a violation of Article 8 of the ECHR because domestic law had failed to indicate with sufficient clarity the scope and manner of exercise of the discretion conferred on insurance companies acting as public authorities in insurance disputes to conduct secret surveillance of an insured person. In particular, it did not include sufficient safeguards against abuse.

Where personal data protection has engaged Article 8, the rights that Article confers have been vindicated against the state as a contracting party. In *Vukota-Bojić v Switzerland* the insurer was, effectively, an agent of the state. The positive obligations

[114] In Joined Cases C-92/09 and C-93/02 *Volker and Markus Schecke GbR v Land Hessen*, Advocate General Sharpston described the two separate rights: the 'classic' right to the protection of privacy and a more 'modern' right to data protection.

[115] This includes the retention of private information by the police (*S and Marper v United Kingdom* (2008) 48 EHRR 1169), the unnecessary disclosure of confidential medical data in legal proceedings (*Z v Finland* (1998) 25 EHRR 371) and the unauthorised passing on of medical information from a hospital to authorities in the process of verifying a claim for social insurance and disability benefit (*MS v Sweden* (1999) 28 EHRR 313). Moreover, most forms of surveillance by the state will constitute an interference with the right to respect for private life and may also interfere with the right to respect for correspondence. In *Malone v United Kingdom* (1984) 7 EHRR 14 the ECtHR found a violation of Art 8 as a result of the interception of the applicant's phone calls. See also *Halford v United Kingdom* (1997) 24 EHRR 523 (which concerned the interception of telephone calls); *Khan v United Kingdom* (2001) 31 EHRR 45 (which concerned the placing of a listening device in the applicant's home); and *Copland v United Kingdom* (2007) 25 BHRC 216 (which concerned emails). See also *Peck v United Kingdom* (2003) 36 EHRR 41 and *Uzun v Germany* App No 35623/05, 2 December 2010.

[116] No 61838/10, 18 October 2016, para 77.

imposed by Article 8 did not extend to require contracting parties to adopt laws to provide protection in respect of the processing of personal data, whether by public authorities or private undertakings. By the mid-1970s the Committee of Ministers of the Council of Europe adopted various resolutions on personal data protection. In 1981 a Convention for the protection of individuals with regard to automatic processing of personal data (Convention 108) was opened for signature. Convention 108 applies to all data processing carried out by both the private and public sectors. It enshrines the individual's right to know that information is stored on him or her and, if necessary, to have it corrected. Importantly, the convention also establishes the right of the individual not to be subject to decisions solely based on automated processing without having their own views taken into consideration. Convention 108 is binding for states that have ratified it. It is not subject to the judicial supervision of the ECtHR, but has been taken into consideration in the case law of the ECtHR within the context of Article 8 of the ECHR.[117] Convention 108 remains the only legally binding international instrument in relation to data protection.

ii. The Rights of Legal Persons[118]

According to Convention 108, data protection deals, primarily, with the protection of natural persons; however, the Contracting Parties may extend data protection to legal persons such as businesses and associations in their domestic law. The Explanatory Report to the Modernised Convention states that national law may protect the legitimate interests of legal persons by extending the scope of the convention to such actors.[119] It is well established that companies may rely on the ECHR and have rights thereunder.[120] Indeed, the ECHR expressly confers rights on natural persons, most obviously by way of Article 1 Protocol 1. Insofar as companies have rights under the Convention, they are entitled to an effective remedy pursuant to Article 13 of the ECHR. Moreover, it is well established that where they do enjoy the protection of the convention, companies do not enjoy an identical level of protection to that enjoyed by individuals.[121] Article 8 has

[117] See, eg, *Z v Finland* (1998) 25 EHRR 371, No 220009/93, 25 February 1997.

[118] The US Supreme Court was the first to recognise that companies could enjoy constitutional rights under the US Bill of Rights: see, eg, *Santa Clara County v Southern Pacific Railroad Company* 118 US 394 (1886); *Gulf, Colorado & Santa Fe Railway Co v Ellis* 165 US 150 (1891) at 154 *per* Brewer J; *First National Bank of Boston v Bellotti* 435 US 765 (1978), *Citizens United v Federal Election Commission* 558 US 310 (2010).

[119] Explanatory Report of Modernised Convention 108, para 30, https://rm.coe.int/16808ac91a.

[120] Art 1 of the ECHR requires states to secure 'to everyone within their jurisdiction' the rights and freedoms under the Convention. Art 34 provides that the Court may 'receive applications from any person, non-governmental organisation or group of individuals claiming to be a victim of a violation' of a Convention right. The first case in which a company succeeded in an action before the ECtHR was *Sunday Times v UK* (1979) 2 EHRR 245, where the court found a breach of Art 10. Similarly, in *Comingersol v Portugal* (2001) 31 EHRR 31 the court awarded pecuniary and non-pecuniary damages for harm to reputation in a finding of a breach of Art 6 as a result of excessive delay in civil litigation. And in *Steel and Morris v UK* (2005) 41 EHRR 22 it was held that the right of a company to sue in defamation fell within the concept of 'the protection of the reputation and the rights of others' in Art 10(2) ECHR.

[121] See the cases on the availability of legal aid including *VP Diffusion Sarl v France* (App No 14565/04; decision of 26 August 2008) and *Granos Organicos Nacionales v Germany* (App No 19508/0722; March 2012). In *Spacek v Czech Republic* (2000) 30 EHRR 17 it was held that a legal entity, unlike an individual taxpayer,

been applied to companies, extending the concepts of 'home'[122] and 'correspondence'[123] to companies, albeit not always consistently and with the prospect that infringements of company rights might be more readily justified under Article 8(2).[124] Between these rights under the ECHR and the conferral of rights under the ePR, the rights of legal persons – which would include non-consumer or business insureds – are growing as a matter of Convention and EU law.

IV. Conclusions

The key question arising out of the above analysis is whether the developments in data protection through, in particular, the GDPR, can act as a catalyst for or a constraint upon the common law's development of the insurers' duty of good faith in circumstances where insurers profile personal data but also, by analogy, where they process personal and non-personal data of business insureds. That depends on a deeper analysis of the relationship between statutory and regulatory developments and the common law. That is considered in chapter seven.

can be expected to take legal advice and that 'the level of diligence expected from an entity engaged in a commercial activity may be higher than that required from a natural person' – *Elcomp v Poland* (App No 37492/05; decision of 19 April 2011).

[122] *Société Colas Est v France* (2004) 39 EHRR 17.

[123] *Association of European Integration and Human Rights v Bulgaria* (App No 625400/00; decision of 28 June 2007); *Bernh Larsen Holding AS and Others v Norway* (App No 24117/08, 14 March 2013).

[124] *Niemietz v Germany* (1992) 16 EHRR 97; *Uj v Hungary* (App No 23954/10; Judgment of 19 October 2011) at [22]; *Bernh Larsen Holding AS and Others v Norway* (App No 24117/08, 14 March 2013) at [159].

7

Impact of Regulatory Duties on the Content of the Duty of Good Faith

At this stage it is worth taking stock. We have considered the rationale and purpose of the duty of utmost good faith and how that justified the duty of disclosure. The duty of disclosure – as it applied to the insured – reflected the fact that there was a substantial information asymmetry between insured and insurer. The insurer depended on the insured to provide him with all facts material to the risk. In the United Kingdom, that duty has been abolished in relation to consumer insurance, although, as we saw, the impact of big data on the levelling-up of the information asymmetry played no part in the justification for reform. The duty on the insured remains in modified form in non-consumer insurance, on the basis that there would still be circumstances where only the insured would know of unusual aspects of the particular risk. However, unlike other regulators who had, as of 2014, begun to grapple with the use of big data analytics by commercial service providers, the Law Commission did not discuss its impact in its review of the duty of disclosure in non-consumer insurance. Nevertheless, it was suggested that the conclusion reached by the Law Commission – and as implemented in the IA 2015 – broadly correspond with how big data will increasingly impact on the duty of disclosure as it applies to the insured.

Where the failure to consider the impact of big data has potentially greater consequence is in relation to the duty of disclosure as it applies to insurers, in both the consumer and non-consumer context. As we saw, the duty of good faith as it has applied to insurers was a relatively minor aspect of the Law Commission's review between 2006 and 2014. And even then the focus of the analysis was on the problematic issue of late payment of claims. As neither the 2012 nor the 2015 Acts applied to the insurers' duty of good faith disclosure, the common law remains further to the passage of those Acts. In light of the previous analysis as to the use and potential application of big data analytics by insurers, it is likely that they will come, in many instances, to have at least as detailed an insight into the risk presented as will an individual consumer or business insured. Pockets of off-grid knowledge not amenable to any form of automated analysis will of course remain. But the use of big data to profile risk is only going to increase. The importance of the announcement of the biggest life insurer in the United States to the effect that all life insureds will be required to wear activity tracking devices cannot be understated: it will inevitably lead to its competitors following suit and normalising the practice in relation to life and health insurance. As it does, insurers' duty of good faith will increasingly fall under the spotlight. Is the duty in its current form sufficient to accommodate the use – while mitigating the potential abuse of – big data analytics?

That enquiry is assisted only so far by the common law's exposition of the duty as it applies to insurers. That is no particular criticism of the common law or the position it has reached, so much as a recognition of the fact that relatively few cases have come before the courts to test the rationale and requirements of the duty as it applies to insurers. The question that arises is whether the common law needs to develop the duty as it applies to insurers at all now that the GDPR has been passed and there is a separate, regulatory regime that specifically governs the processing of data by both public and private organisations. Does the GDPR fulfil all the roles that one would expect the duty of disclosure to perform in a world in which insurers often have more detailed knowledge and a much clearer and more holistic picture of the insured's risk profile than the insured? While the concerns of the GDPR and the common law duty of good faith as it applies to insurers overlap, they do not share precisely the same ends, their content is not identical and their scope of application differs in important respects. It is important to be clear about those differences in order to identify why the GDPR might not be a panacea for insureds seeking greater transparency from insurers. It is only where those divergences emerge that the further question arises as to how the common law might develop the duty of disclosure by reference to regulatory law to deal with the exigencies of big data. And a further question arises as to whether the common law duty need only develop to fill in the gaps left by regulatory law or whether it should evolve in a more wholesale manner and take on board many of the norms and requirements imposed by, in particular, the GDPR. The question of the development of the common law raises a broader question of how common law and statutory law inter-relate and whether it is permissible at all for common law to develop its own principles by reference to analogous principles that can be discerned from statute. The chapter thus seeks to: (i) identify in more detail the potential deficiencies of the duty of disclosure in relation to insurers' use of big data; (ii) consider the extent to which regulatory law including the GDPR addresses those deficiencies; (iii) examine the extent to which the common law might develop by analogy with regulatory law; and (iv) assess how the common law might evolve to deal with the impact of big data analytics.

I. Deficiencies in the Good Faith Duty of Disclosure

Section III.D of chapter five considered the test for the duty of disclosure as it applied to insurers adopted by the House of Lords in *Banque Financière*. Lord Bridge did not dissent from the approach taken by Slade LJ in the Court of Appeal but a more detailed (if, strictly, obiter) analysis was provided by Lord Jauncey who (to repeat) held:

> The duty of disclosure arises because the facts relevant to the estimation of the risk are most likely to be within the knowledge of the insured and the insurer therefore has to rely upon him to disclose matters material to that risk. The duty extends to the insurer as well as to the insured: Carter v Boehm (1766) 3 Burr 1905. The duty is, however, limited to facts

> which are material to the risk insured, that is to say, facts which would influence a prudent insurer in deciding whether to accept the risk and, if so, upon what terms and a prudent insured in entering into the contract on the terms proposed by the insurer. Thus any facts which would increase the risk should be disclosed by the insured and any facts known to the insurer but not to the insured, which would reduce the risk, should be disclosed by the insurer.[1]

As foreshadowed in chapter five, three specific problems arise from that test. First, the duty is confined to the disclosure of 'facts' material to the risk. What, for these purposes, is a fact? A fact material to the risk plainly includes any matter that objectively and verifiably increases or decreases the risk. That the insured driver has three points on his licence or that the insured property is situated 50 feet from a major watercourse or that the insured's resting heart rate is between 80 and 85 beats per minute are all facts material to each respective risk. Risk evaluation involves drawing inferences from, at least, a series of such primary facts: the insured smokes 20 a day, is 20 stone, takes no exercise and has high blood pressure. It is from those primary facts that a premium is set by reference to actuarial data. The risk calculation considers the impact of each additional primary risk factor. The impact of each such factor is based on an assessment of historical evidence as to the likelihood of risks arising where such factors were present. The duty of good faith does not require insurers to disclose the methodology by which they infer the nature of a particular risk from primary facts. But that is problematic in circumstances where insurers are increasingly using a range of new data sources that seek to identify new risk factors which are said to correlate, whether individually or in the aggregate, with the incidence of insured loss. But those correlations may not hold for any particular insured. But that has always been true of risk factors that are used to model risk: a particular young male driver may be an extremely safe driver but historically he was penalised in the price of cover because of his membership of the wider cohort of young males who, actuarially, constituted the most risky group of drivers. But the actuarial evidence did at least demonstrate that particular risk factors had, in the aggregate, a strong bearing on the likelihood of the insured risk occurring across that cohort. No one was under any illusion when risk was calculated by reference to fewer risk factors over much larger risk pools: individual members of that group paid, at least initially, the premium reflective of the risk character of the group exhibiting those same, limited risk factors. As risk profiling gets more granular and more individualised, it would be unsatisfactory for insureds to continue to be burdened by higher premiums because they exhibit new risk factors which are said merely to correlate with the incidence of insured loss across the wider cohort of insureds who exhibit those same risk factors. Where insurers seek to profile at an increasingly granular level, and in the absence of the sort of rigorous actuarial assessment of risk factors upon which risk modelling was traditionally founded, insurers will be drawing inferences about individual insureds that in some circumstances may not have been demonstrated actuarially across the group let alone the particular

[1] [1991] 2 AC 249 at 281.

insured. If Lord Jauncey's test of materiality is confined to the disclosure of facts which, at the very least, have been actuarially shown to be objectively relevant to the level of risk, then insurers who profile risk by reference to non-causal risk proxies (such as shopping habits, or social media posts) may not be required to disclose their reliance on such non-causal risk proxies. But it would be deeply unsatisfactory to permit insurers to avoid disclosure of the use of those risk proxies on the basis that they had not been actuarially established and therefore could not amount to facts that were objectively material to the risk. Therefore, if the duty of good faith as it applies to insurers is to properly accommodate risk profiling through big data analytics, the material 'facts' to which Lord Jauncey refers must be taken to include these new risk proxies; even if they are not objectively material, the particular insurer regarded them as relevant and took them into account in evaluating the risk.

The second problem is that on the current formulation of the test, it necessarily falls to the insurer to assess whether that which is known to it, is not known to the insured such that the duty to disclose might be engaged. As an insurer cannot know what the insured does or does not know – and the point of the test is that it operates without insurers having recourse to the insured to ask the question – the matter is left either entirely to the insurer without constraint or the insurer is subject to some standard of conduct in assessing whether the 'fact' of which it is aware is something that will not be known to the insured. It is submitted that as part of a test that seeks to articulate what is required in order to discharge the duty of good faith, insurers' assessment of whether the 'fact' is not one known to the insured should itself be made in good faith. Insofar as we are positing the operation of the duty at a pre-contractual stage, and as the question relates to disclosure, good faith should demand that the insurer always err on the side of disclosing. However, that may not itself be sufficient. That is because insurers might plausibly contend that all of the individual risk factors identified by the insurers' algorithms will be known to the insured, whether actually or constructively. Were insurers to take account of wider risk factors like credit scores, shopping and purchasing information and web-browsing behaviour, they might claim that all of these facts will be known to the insured such that there will be no need to disclose. Accepting that contention would stifle the development of the duty: although an insured might well acknowledge their shopping or web-browsing habits, if they are otherwise unaware that such factors are being used to profile their level of risk, it is suggested that that lack of knowledge should trigger insurers' duty to disclose the use of that information for risk-profiling purposes.

The third problem, touched upon in chapter five, is that a test confined only to requiring insurers to disclose matters that reduce the risk rather misses the point. Where information is being gathered by insurers rather than being provided by the insured, there is a growing lack of transparency as to what factors are being relied upon or how. Insureds are at a disadvantage in not having this information: were they to know on what basis risk was being modelled, they could question insurers' reliance upon that information; more particularly, revealing the information on which the cover is proposed to be offered will enable the insured to pre-emptively identify concerns that might arise from the application of those risk factors to that person. If an insured knows that insurers are proposing to rely on certain factors which they can show to be wrong or do not materially increase the risk in relation to them, they should be put in a position to be able to make those points. That, after all, is part of the promise of more granular and individualised risk assessment through the use of big data. In not knowing what factors are being relied upon, insureds cannot begin to negotiate the price or the terms with the insurer. Moreover, the insured is put in a position of trust and dependency: they are being asked to trust that insurers are relying on only accurate and relevant information and they are dependent on the accurate application of algorithms that model the risk. That lack of knowledge, the superior position of the insurer and the insured's dependency on the insurer are all factors that, outside the law of insurance, have given rise to a limited duty of pre-contractual disclosure.[2] In circumstances where these features characterise the position of the insured relative to the insurer, it should follow more strongly that a duty of disclosure should be extended such as to require the insurer to disclose all the factors that it considers to be material to the risk, rather than merely those that tend to reduce it, which may remain confined to a relatively narrow and unlikely set of facts (being facts that demonstrate that the insured may not need insurance at all or may only need a much reduced level of cover; or second, by revealing facts that would cause the insured to take steps to avoid circumstances arising which would render the cover worthless).

In the circumstances, it is again contended that the test of materiality set out by Slade LJ in the Court of Appeal in *Banque Financière* should be preferred to that of Lord Jauncey insofar as it can more readily be read (or consciously developed) to require insurers to disclose the wider array of risk proxies upon which cover is proposed to be written and will apply irrespective of whether they are factors that are regarded by insurers as risk-reducing or risk-increasing.

II. Does the GDPR's Application to Insurers Address the Common Law's Deficiencies?

The question then is whether the GDPR operates in such a way as to require insurers to disclose the facts and matters that insurers consider to be and/or have treated as material to the risk? The GDPR requires proactive disclosure from insurers at two stages. First, pursuant to the privacy notices required under Articles 13–14. And second, where insurers are taking decisions on a solely automated basis. These principles are aspects of the principle of transparency under the GDPR. To assess the extent to which these transparency obligations would address the potential limitations of the common law duty of disclosure, it is important to consider, more specifically, how each of these sets of obligations may be discharged by an insurer.[3]

[2] As discussed in ch 5, section I.

[3] See the Article 29 Working Part Guidelines on Transparency of 11 April 2018, as adopted by the EDPB: http://ec.europa.eu/newsroom/article29/item-detail.cfm?item_id=622227.

A. Articles 13–14 GDPR and the Right to be Informed[4]

The basic right to be informed was discussed in chapter six. As to this right, the Information Commissioner observes:

> Using personal data in ways that are invisible to people can create risks. It can leave people unaware of uses of their personal data that may lead to discrimination or disadvantage, and prevents them from exercising their rights. Being transparent helps to mitigate against these risks. Actively telling people about [the] use of their personal data will help them retain control over it and anticipate the potential consequences of its use.[5]

The information required to be provided[6] to an insured when insurers collect data that have not been obtained from the insured are set out in Article 14.[7] The most important categories of information as regards insurers' evaluation of risk are: (i) the purposes of the processing for which the personal data are intended as well as the legal basis for the processing;[8] (ii) the categories of personal data concerned;[9] (iii) from which source the personal data originate, and if applicable, whether it came from publicly accessible sources;[10] and (iv) the existence of automated decision making, including profiling, referred to in Article 22(1) and (4) and, at least in those cases, meaningful information about the logic involved, as well as the significance and the envisaged consequences of such processing for the data subject.[11] It is submitted that none of these required disclosures would satisfactorily meet the deficiencies in Lord Jauncey's test:

1. Telling an insured that the purpose of the processing is to undertake risk evaluation does not tell him what factors have been considered or how they impacted on the terms offered, if offered. Nor will a description of the legal basis upon which processing is undertaken.[12]

[4] The transparency requirements apply across the lifecycle of the processing. Art 12 provides that it applies before or at the start of the data processing cycle, ie when the personal data is being collected either from the data subject or otherwise obtained for the purposes of making an underwriting decision; in the context of insurance it will apply again if new personal data is collected for the purposes of handling claims.

[5] https://ico.org.uk/for-organisations/guide-to-the-general-data-protection-regulation-gdpr/the-right-to-be-informed/what-is-the-right-to-be-informed-and-why-is-it-important/.

[6] In fact, the requirement to provide the information can be discharged by the insurer either furnishing the information to the insured or actively directing her to the location of that information, eg by way of direct link or use of a QR code etc. The point is that the insured must not have to actively search for information covered by these articles amongst other information, such as terms and conditions of use of a website or app. This can be done by a layered approach or push notifications where the notice is provided digitally. 'Just-in time' notices may also be used. These provide specific 'privacy information' in an ad hoc manner, as and when it is most relevant for the data subject to read. This method is useful for providing information at various points throughout the process of data collection. The various modalities are explained in Article 29 Working Party's Guidelines on Transparency at paras 33–40.

[7] The information must be provided in a privacy or data protection notice, albeit there is no specific form that such notices must take.

[8] Art 14(1)(c).

[9] Art 14(1)(d).

[10] Art 14(2)(f).

[11] Art 14(2)(g).

[12] The Article 29 Working Party Guidelines on Transparency stated (at para 10) that: 'In particular, for complex, technical or unexpected data processing, WP29's position is that, as well as providing the prescribed information under Articles 13 and 14 (dealt with later in these guidelines), controllers should also separately

2. Telling insureds what type of information is collected will be satisfied by reference to categories of information; so an insurer will comply with the obligation if it indicates that it relies upon browsing habits, shopping or purchasing information, credit score information or social media information. That does not tell insureds what precise information was regarded to be a risk factor or how it bore on a particular underwriting decision.
3. Telling the insured the source of personal data will again be capable of being satisfied if the insured is told that the information came from online retail information, social media or other sources by category. Again, this does not require the insurer to disclose the precise 'facts' relied upon in an underwriting decision.
4. Where decisions are taken on a solely automated basis, insurers can satisfy this requirement by indicating that automated decision making is used. Giving insureds 'meaningful information about the logic involved in the process and explaining the significance and envisaged consequences' can also be satisfied by stating that data acquired from various sources is used to assess risk through automated profiling tools, like algorithms. Again, that does not require an insurer to inform an insured about the specific factors taken into account in a particular underwriting decision. There appears, in this regard, to be some tension between the wording of Articles 13(2)(f) and 14(2)(g) and the EDPB's guidelines in relation to what, in particular, the obligation to provide 'meaningful information about the logic involves, as well as the significance and the envisaged consequences of such processing of the data subject', requires. The wording of the GDPR does not apply this requirement to individual decisions taken on the basis of personal data that insurers may have obtained from third-party sources. The obligation arises in relation to the collection of the data, not its subsequent processing. That is reflected in Articles 13(2)(f) and 14(2)(g) by reference to the need to disclose – generically – 'the existence of automated decision making' (that is, the fact that it is used at all) and the additional reference to the 'envisaged consequences' of the automated decision making, which appears to be a reference to the future consequences of subsequent processing. In addition, these obligations set out what goes into a privacy notice which is again to be provided upon the collection of the data. However, the EDPB observes that the controller should find simple ways to tell the data subject about the rationale behind, or the criteria relied upon in reaching *the decision*,[13] suggesting that it arises each time data is processed for the purpose of actual automated decisions. The EDPB guidance goes on to state: '[t]he information provided should, however, be sufficiently comprehensive for the data subject to understand the reasons for the decision'. This appears to be an unwarranted gloss on the wording of the GDPR, confusing data to be provided to help individuals understand that automated processing will be used and the

spell out in unambiguous language what the most important *consequences* of the processing will be: in other words, what kind of effect will the specific processing described in a privacy statement/ notice actually have on a data subject?' Again, that will be satisfied if insurers inform the insured that the type of information will be used in connection with underwriting or claims handling decisions.

[13] EDPB, 'Guidelines on Automated Decision-Making and Profiling for the Purposes of Regulation 2016/679', 25.

way in which decisions will in future be taken by such methods on the one hand, and a requirement to disclose reasons for every individual automated decision in fact taken on the other. No such right is conferred under Article 22 of the GDPR either, the very place where one might expect such a right in relation to automated decision making to be found. As stated above, notwithstanding the view of the EDPB, nothing constituting the right to be informed (or the right to disclosure) under the GDPR requires an insurer to inform the insured about the specific risk factors taken into account on a particular underwriting decision or the bearing particular factors had on that decision.

There are also exceptions to the duty to disclose. Article 14(5)(c) of the GDPR exempts disclosure where it is otherwise required by law. Insurers may contend that the scope of the obligation to disclose is already provided for in the common law duty of disclosure as it applies to insurers. However, the EDPB states that this exemption

> is conditional upon the law in question providing 'appropriate measures to protect the data subject's legitimate interests'. Such a law must directly address the data controller and the obtaining or disclosure in question should be mandatory upon the data controller. Accordingly, the data controller must be able to demonstrate how the law in question applies to them and requires them to either obtain or disclose the personal data in question.[14]

Reliance on this exemption by insurers would likely be in support of the more limited reading of Lord Jauncey's test; if that were a permissible response, the right to be informed under the GDPR would lead to the same three problems set out above. That narrow reading of insurers' duty of disclosure would be insufficient to 'protect the data subject's legitimate interests'.

B. Article 22 GDPR and the Right to Disclosure

In relation to automated decision making the Information Commissioner advises controllers:

> If you use AI to make decisions about people or to profile them, you need to be upfront about it and explain your purposes for doing so. If the decisions are solely automated and have legal or similarly significant effects, you must provide people with extra detail on the logic involved, the significance of the processing and the envisaged consequences of it. In practice, this means telling people what information you use, why it is relevant and what the likely impact is going to be. The way you provide this information to people must be clear and meaningful, you should not confuse people with overly complex explanations of the analytics.[15]

[14] EDPB, 'Guidelines on Transparency under Regulation 2016/679, para 66. That passage continues: 'This is in line with Recital 41 of the GDPR, which states that a legal basis or legislative measure should be clear and precise, and its application should be foreseeable to persons subject to it, in accordance with the case law of the Court of Justice of the EU and the European Court of Human Rights. However, Article 14.5(c) will not apply where the data controller is under an obligation to obtain data *directly from a data subject*, in which case Article 13 will apply. In that case, the only exemption under the GDPR exempting the controller from providing the data subject with information on the processing will be that under Article 13.4 (i.e. where and insofar as the data subject already has the information).'

[15] https://ico.org.uk/for-organisations/guide-to-the-general-data-protection-regulation-gdpr/the-right-to-be-informed/the-right-to-be-informed-in-practice/.

The requirements of Article 22 disclosure were fully summarised in chapter six.[16] As explained, it imposed additional obligations on data controllers to (i) identify one of a more limited number of lawful bases for automated decisions; (ii) adopt measures to safeguard the data, including the conferral of rights to obtain human intervention and contest the decision; and (iii) to obtain explicit consent for the processing of special category personal data and demonstrate that processing that data is necessary for reasons of substantial public interest.[17] As noted above, Article 22 imposes no additional duties of disclosure on insurers taking automated underwriting decisions.

In the circumstances, absent knowing what actual risk factors are causing premium to increase and/or the scope of cover to become more limited, insureds will be less able and less likely to exercise their other GDPR rights, including their right to access and correct information and their right to object to its processing. Moreover, the duties of disclosure under the GDPR do not on their own appear to remedy the problems identified with the scope of the duty of good faith disclosure as it applies to insurers. The gaps in protection that emerge, notwithstanding the implementation of the GDPR are, broadly, as follows: (i) as regards consumer insurance, the consumer insured will not be entitled to disclosure of the specific risk factors that insurers took into account (or the relative bearing they had on the price or the scope of cover) in a specific underwriting decision that was based on profiling, whether that decision was taken with human involvement or not. The insured can of course find out how a particular underwriting decision was taken but that involves the individual insured proactively exercising his other GDPR rights to access and correct the data relied upon and his further rights to require human intervention and to contest the decision; (ii) as regards non-consumer insurance, the GDPR will often not apply since the beneficiaries of the GDPR are natural persons; companies do not have rights under the GDPR as data held about a company itself is not personal data. Individual officers or employees of a company can find out what data is held on them personally but an insured company cannot require the insurer to provide it with all data that bore on the insured risk or how all those factors impacted on the proposed cover. It may be able to obtain information as to how data about its individual employees was processed for those purposes, but (a) that will require the company to have each individual's authority to itself obtain that information and (b) understanding how the personal data on the company was used in underwriting decisions will not provide the full picture.

But the value of the GDPR lies not just in the scope of its duties of disclosure under Articles 13–14: focussing narrowly on whether those rights would, if applied analogically, address the narrowness of the common law's duty of disclosure would be to miss the point. Rather, the GDPR must be considered as a whole in order to ascertain the values which it embodies and which the common law might seek to apply in developing the scope of the good faith duty of disclosure. That duty, as discussed in chapter five, seeks to remedy information imbalances and to avoid those subject to an information deficit being exploited. In the past, exploitation was understood to mean either fraud, or the fact that material non-disclosure can result in better terms,

[16] At section III.A.iv.e.

[17] Which the provision of insurance will prima facie satisfy: see para 20 of Schedule 1 to the DPA 2018, discussed in ch 6, section III.A.iv.f.

terms that would not have been offered had the disclosure been given. As we have seen, exploitation by insurers could arise through their underwriting a risk knowing something that, had it been known to the insured, would have led the latter to either not insure at all or to take steps to avoid the policy being rendered worthless before it incepted. But the GDPR's purpose extends beyond the removal of information asymmetries to avoid the risk of exploitation of data subjects (although that of course is part of its wider purpose). In a digital age, the GDPR seeks to protect privacy by promoting transparency and fairness, where those principles are given more specific expression through the conferral of rights and the imposition of duties relating to how personal data can, consistently with those principles, be collected and used. In this way, data subjects are enabled to make more informed choices about who collects their data and how it is used. Those goals are much more ambitious than merely avoiding exploitation of data subjects because of, inter alia, informational deficits. Transposed to the insurance context, it is submitted that these principles provide a foundation for the coherent and consistent development of insurers' good faith duty of disclosure where insurers underwrite risk or make claims decisions on the basis of big data analytics. Moreover, these principles should not just apply to automated processing of personal data in a consumer context but should additionally apply to automated processing in the non-consumer context. Business insureds should also be provided with all risk-related information which insurers have derived from their use of big data analytics in order to take underwriting or claims decisions.

III. Can the Good Faith Duty of Disclosure Evolve by Analogy with the GDPR?

Statutory and common law norms are separate sources of law. However, the question arises as to the impact that the enactment of statutory law has on the development of common law in the same or an overlapping field of activity. Does statutory law constitute a comprehensive code, such as to replace common law in respect of the matters subject to regulation? Or does the enactment of statutory law encourage the common law to develop a parallel framework consistently with statutory law? Statutes may expressly state whether they operate such as to exclude or replace existing common law. A statute might state that it is setting down a code; additionally it may state that the code is comprehensive or exhaustive; or it might state that it does not affect the operation of the general law save as expressly provided. But rarely will such indications resolve all questions arising as to the impact on common law norms. The question arising in this section is whether, notwithstanding the fact that the GDPR does not remedy the deficiencies in the duty of disclosure as it applies to insurers, the common law can look to the rights and principles embodied in the GDPR, and draw support from those rights and principles in developing the duty of disclosure on insurers such as to fully protect insureds' disclosure interests where underwriting and claims handling operate by way of big data analytics? And, by extension, can those rights and principles be called upon in order to fashion new or expanded remedies at common law?

In considering whether common law development can take place by analogy with statute, it is useful to distinguish a number of different situations where statute law and common law might interact, where those differences impact upon the extent to which analogical development might be possible:

1. Statute replaces the common law in a particular field of activity. This is often the most difficult area in which to consider the relationship because the statute is enacted within a wider legal framework and often assumes the continuation of certain common law concepts and principles.[18] Moreover, the extent to which the common law is expressly or impliedly excluded will be a matter of interpretation.[19] That is not the situation we are dealing with: nothing in the GDPR seeks expressly to replace the duty of good faith as it applies to insurers within the law of insurance. On the contrary, it imposes additional obligations that will apply to insurers in the course of processing personal data. Nothing in the passing of the GDPR in any way cuts down the common law rules applicable to what insurers must disclose to insureds in the course of underwriting or claims.
2. The enactment of a statute precludes the further development of the common law in the same field of activity. This is often expressed through the argument that because the statute addressed issues A and B but not C, Parliament must be taken to have intended not to regulate C and thus it would be inappropriate for the judges to impose obligations in the context of C. However, as Professor Burrows states in his analysis of cases arising in relation to this scenario, 'the starting point is that the common law should be developed as the courts think appropriate. It should only be if a statute clearly makes a common law development inappropriate – because it would be inconsistent with the statute – that one should interpret it as holding back the development.'[20] In this case, there is no reason why the development of the common law duty of disclosure to reflect the principles embodied in the GDPR would cut across[21] or be inconsistent with those principles. On the contrary, it is plain to see how the common law and regulatory law would pursue the same ends in an entirely consistent manner.
3. The enactment of statute may be used by analogy in the development of the common law. The common law evolves and refines legal principles. Often, courts and commentators have regarded statutes not as embodying principle,

[18] As Bennion notes (code 25.6, p 656), where a new Act is passed it may be expected to fit into the wider legal framework. The courts will usually adopt a construction which is most consistent with the area of law to which the Act relates. This contributes to upholding the principle of legal policy discussed in Code 26.10 that law should be coherent and self-consistent. *Bennion on Statutory Interpretation* 7th edn (London, LexisNexis, 2017).

[19] It is plain that Parliament can, if it chooses, displace any principle or rule of law. But it is equally plain that, unless Parliament does so, the principle or rule, if relevant, continues to operate in relation to an enactment. So in *R v Morris* (1867) LR 1 CCR 90, Byles J said 'it is a sound rule to construe a statute in conformity with the common law, except where or in so far as the statute is plainly intended to alter the course of the common law'. Pausing there, the GDPR is clearly not intended to alter the course of the common law as regards insurers' duty of good faith. It is not concerned with the insurers' duty of good faith at all. It must therefore be construed as not altering the existing scope of that duty.

[20] Andrew Burrows, 'The Relationship Between Common Law and Statute' (2012) *LQR* 128, p 232.

[21] Which was the reason why the claims in cases such as *X v Bedfordshire CC* [1995] 2 AC 739 and *Marcic v Thames Water Utilities Ltd* [2003] UKHL 66 failed.

> but rather policy, and often the policy that arises from political compromise.[22] On that view, the courts have historically developed the common law separately to statute and have viewed with circumspection the idea that statute can be a source of principle in the development of the common law at all.

Roscoe Pound considered that there were four broad ways in which the common law might respond to statute in his classic 1908 *Harvard Law Review* piece as follows:[23]

> Four ways may be conceived in which courts … might deal with a legislative innovation. (1) They might receive it fully into the body of the law as affording not only a rule to be applied but a principle from which to reason, and hold it, as a later and more direct expression of the general will, of superior authority to judge made rules of the same general subject; and so reason from it by analogy in preference to them.[24] (2) They might receive it fully into the body of the law to be reasoned from by analogy the same way as any other rule of law regarding it, however, as of equal or co-ordinate authority in this respect with judge-made rules upon the same general subject. (3) They might refuse to receive it fully into the body of the law and give effect to it directly only; refusing to reason from it by analogy but giving it, nevertheless, a liberal interpretation to cover the whole field it was intended to cover. (4) They might not only refuse to reason from it by analogy and apply it directly only, but also give to it a strict and narrow interpretation, holding it down rigidly to those cases which it covers expressly.[25]

Pound observed that the fourth approach characterised the orthodox common law attitude to legislative innovations at the time at which he was writing. In the UK, there

[22] 'Statutes are said to be rooted in policy not principle so that it is not possible to reason by analogy from statutory provision of common law or even, in some cases, from one statutory provision to another.' Jack Beatson, 'The Role of Statute in the Development of Common Law Doctrine' (2001) 117 *LQR* 247.

[23] Roscoe Pound, 'Common Law and Legislation' (1908) *Harvard Law Review* 383 at 385.

[24] A good example of the first of Pound's suggested approaches is the decision of the US Supreme Court in *Moragne v State Marine Lines Inc* 398 US 375 (1970) which, in refusing to follow previous case law to the contrary, recognised a right of recovery for wrongful death in maritime law. Harlan J held, referring to the fact that every State had enacted a wrongful death statute, 'These numerous and broadly applicable statutes, taken as a whole, make it clear that there is no present public policy against allowing recovery for wrongful death. The statutes evidence a wide rejection by the legislatures of whatever justifications may once have existed for a general refusal to allow such recovery. This legislative establishment of policy carries significance beyond the particular scope of each of the statutes involved. The policy thus established has become itself a part of our law to be given its appropriate weight not only in matters of statutory construction but also in those of decisional law … This appreciation of the broader role played by legislation in the development of the law reflects the practices of common-law courts from the most ancient times. As Professor Landis has said, "much of what is ordinarily regarded as 'common law' finds its source in legislative enactment." … It has always been the duty of the common law court to perceive the impact of major legislative innovations and to interweave the new legislative policies with the inherited body of common law principles – many of them deriving from earlier legislative exertions.'

[25] Professor Atiyah raised the issue, albeit with some residual circumspection, in the following way: 'is it possible for the courts to take account of statute law, in the very development of the common law itself? Can the courts, for instance, use statutes as analogies for the purpose of developing the common law? Can they justify jettisoning obsolete cases, not because they have actually been reversed by some statutory provision, but because a statute suggests that they are based on outdated values? Could the courts legitimately draw some general principle from a limited statutory provision and apply that principle as a matter of common law? It must be clear that using statutes in this way is fundamentally different from any process of construction, however benevolent or liberal that might be. Construction, as a matter of theory at least, requires the court to give effect to what it thinks the legislation actually enacts. Using statutes by way of analogy quite clearly involves using them to produce results which the legislation does not enact.' Patrick Atiyah, 'Common Law and Statute Law" (1985) 48 *MLR* 1.

is now considerable evidence that the courts are prepared to develop the common law by analogy with statute along (at the very least) Pound's second conceptual approach, leading Sir Rupert Cross to suggest that 'in England, a legislative innovation is received fully into the body of the law to be reasoned from by analogy in the same way as any other rule of law'.[26] The following examples reflect this approach.[27]

In *Parry v Cleaver*[28] the House of Lords held that a disability pension should not be taken into account in assessing damages for loss of earnings in a claim for personal injury. In reaching that decision, two of their Lordships derived some support from s 2(1) of the Fatal Accidents Act 1959, that a pension should not be taken into account in assessing damages for a fatal accident. Lord Reid said:

> If public policy, as now interpreted by Parliament, requires all pensions to be disregarded in actions under the Fatal Accidents Act, I find it impossible to see how it can be proper to bring pensions into account in common law actions … In my judgment, a decision that pensions should not be brought into account in assessing damages at common law is consistent with general principles, with the preponderating weight of authority and with public policy as enacted by Parliament and I would therefore so decide.

In *Warnink v Townend & Sons (Hull)*, the House of Lords adopted what has been described as an 'attenuated' version of the doctrine. In that case, the House of Lords held that the cause of action for passing off should not be confined to cases where the name indicated the product's origin; rather, it should be extended to cases where the name denoted the particular characteristics of the product by reason of its ingredients. In the course of doing so, Lord Diplock stated:

> Parliament … beginning in the 19th century has progressively intervened in the interests of consumers to impose on traders a higher standard of commercial candour than the legal maxim caveat emptor calls for, by prohibiting under penal sanctions misleading descriptions of the character or quality of the goods; but since the class of persons for whose protection the … statutes are designed, are not competing traders but those consumers who are likely to be deceived, the Acts themselves do not give rise to any civil action for breach of statutory duty on the part of a competing trader even though he sustains actual damage as a result … Nevertheless the increasing recognition by parliament of the need for more rigorous standards of commercial honesty is a factor which should not be overlooked by a judge confronted by the choice whether or not to extend by analogy to circumstances in which it has not been applied a principle which has been applied in previous cases where the circumstances although different had some features in common with those of the case which he has set aside. Where over a period of years there can be discerned a steady trend in legislation that reflects the view of successive parliaments as to what the public interest demands in a particular field of law, development of the common law in that part of the same field which has been left to it ought to proceed upon a parallel rather than a divergent course.[29]

[26] R Cross and JW Harris, *Precedent in English Law* 4th edn (Oxford, Clarendon Press, 1991), 174–75.

[27] For full discussion of the cases relied upon in support of the analogical approach, see the articles by Atiyah (1985), Beatson (1997), Beatson (2001) and Burrows (2012), all cited herein.

[28] [1970] AC 1.

[29] *Warnink v Townend & Sons (Hull)* [1979] AC 731. More recently in Australia, some jurisdictions passed legislation altering the common law of legal professional privilege, so that the test for whether a particular document attracted privilege was a test of dominant purpose rather than sole purpose. In light of the legislation, the High Court of Australia developed the common law, particularly as it applied in the remaining

The judge would only have a 'choice' as to how to develop the common law, were the statutory provisions silent on whether the framework imposed was to be treated as comprehensive or otherwise made clear how the common law was to respond. In those circumstances, the courts would have to be satisfied that the regulatory tide made clear what the policy of the law was such that the courts may be confident in developing the common law along the same lines. In relation to the processing and use of data, the legislation has gone in one direction and overtime has provided increasing protection of personal data. European data protection law establishes a harmonised minimum level of protection across the EU. Data protection law does not, however, apply specifically and solely to the insurance industry. It is generally applicable. There is no reason in principle why the common law of insurance should not take its cue from these laws to enhance the protection of personal data in the insurance field in parallel with, rather than diverging from, data protection legislation.

The relevance of statute in the determination of principle is also illustrated by *Malik v Bank of Credit & Commerce International SA*,[30] which qualified the ruling in *Addis v Gramophone Co Ltd*[31] that damages could not be recovered in a contractual action for injury to reputation per se. There the employees of a bank had sued for damage to reputation as a result of the corrupt way in which the bank had run its business. The House of Lords considered that there was no basis for excluding financial loss arising from damage to reputation from the ordinary principles of contract law and that such damages did not cease to be so recoverable because they were also recoverable in an action for defamation. But Lord Steyn stated that he was also reinforced in his view by the consideration that such losses are in principle recoverable in respect of unfair dismissal under what became s 123 of the Employment Rights Act 1996. He stated that 'in the search for the correct common law principle one is not compelled to ignore the analogical force of the statutory dispensation.'

Professor Beatson, pertinently for these purposes, has considered the way in which common law and statute law interact in relation to duties of disclosure. He observed that

> [t]he fact that the legislative schemes [in the consumer credit and financial services sectors] are so detailed means that it is not unreasonable to see them as self-contained codes. However, that part of the regimes which relate to disclosure might arguably be of wider significance. In both contexts the relationship is one of inequality; in financial services (and probably in consumer credit) there is also imbalance of information in the sense that the professional has information that the client cannot acquire from any other source – or cannot do so without incurring considerable expense. The imbalance can also be seen at the root of … the duty of disclosure in contracts *uberrimae fidei* and the other exceptions. It is accordingly arguable that the fact that the legislature has imposed a duty of disclosure in the specified cases can be seen, alongside the cases in which a duty exists at common law, as an indication of the underlying rationale and principle of such a duty. If so, such legislative

jurisdictions of Australia, so that it also applied a dominant purpose test: *Esso Australia Resources v Commissioner of Taxation* (1999) 2010 Commonwealth Law Reports 49.

[30] [1998] AC 20.

[31] [1909] AC 488.

> duties could therefore assist a court which is considering the scope of the exceptions [to the general rule] or the extension of the duty [of disclosure] to a new fact situation.[32]

In other words, the desire to level up information asymmetries in financial services – including insurance transactions – is a principle that underpins common law and statute and can be relied upon to develop the common law where new situations of information inequality arise.

It is submitted that the rise of big data analytics – a means by which information inequalities in financial services are at risk of being compounded – is precisely the type of new fact situation in which that underlying principle ought to be developed analogically in pursuit of the information equality which the principle is designed to achieve.[33] As explained above, it can also be seen that the GDPR's promotion of transparency through rights to be informed and rights of access as to how personal data is collected and used, creates a more level playing field between consumers and financial services providers, such as insurers. To that extent, common law duties of good faith disclosure, informational duties in financial services and the various transparency obligations under the GDPR are each pursuing, in parallel, the same broader set of goals. Insofar as the rights and duties set out in the GDPR constitute a principled approach to how data controllers ought to be transparent about precisely how they propose to collect and use data in the context of making important decisions affecting consumers, there is every reason why the common law might evolve the good faith duty of disclosure on insurers in a way that restores equality of information and secures greater transparency in underwriting and claims decisions.[34] Pre-GDPR, Professor Burrows observed[35] – by reference to the narrowness of the approach taken to the scope of the duty of disclosure by the House of Lords in *Banque Financière de la Cité v Westgate Insurance Co Ltd*[36] – that were

> the Supreme Court to be asked to decide whether to extend the pre-contractual duty of disclosure from its present relatively narrow limits at common law, it would surely be appropriate for the Courts to take into account statutory and pre-contractual duties of disclosure such as those to be found in the Consumer Credit Act 1974, the Financial Services Act 1986 and rr 7–8 of the Package Travel, Package Holiday and Package Tours Regulations 1992.

To this we can add, it is submitted with some force, the GDPR.

[32] Jack Beatson, 'Has the Common Law a Future?' [1997] *Cambridge Law Journal* 291.

[33] Beatson further suggests that the answer to the question of how to integrate the principle lies in embracing the purposive construction of statutes in order to identify their purpose and which may be applied analogically. He says where a principle can be discerned in a statute, 'such as, I would suggest, there is in the duties of disclosure in the Consumer Credit and Financial Services Acts, any statute is capable of being applied analogically'.

[34] 'Provided the courts are sensitive to the scope of the statute and do not extend it into an area in which the legislature has decided it should not go, the statutory context may be of vital assistance in determining the ambit of policy and its continued relevance.' Jack Beatson, 'The Role Statute in the Development of Common Law Doctrine' (2001) 117 *LQR* 247.

[35] Building on the points made by Beatson as to the common principles underpinning statutory and common law disclosure/informational duties in 'Has the Common Law a Future?' [1997] *Cambridge Law Journal* 291 at 306–07.

[36] [1991] 2 AC 249.

IV. The Evolution of the Common Law Duty of Disclosure on Insurers

Given that there can be little objection to the judges developing the insurers' duty of good faith by reference to the clear and coherent principles embodied in the GDPR, how and to what ends should they do so? The first question to arise is whether, as the Law Commission has suggested, the duty of good faith is to be deployed merely as an 'interpretative principle' or whether the duty should itself be expanded to reflect GDPR principles. That alternative raises the additional question as to the nature of the duty of good faith, since its further development could have wider remedial consequences. A yet further possibility is that, whether through the deployment of good faith as an interpretative principle, or through the analogical development of the duty of disclosure, the common law might expand the common law duty of care, breach of which would also have potentially important remedial consequences.

A. Good Faith as an Interpretative Principle

As was seen in chapter five, as a result of the modification of s 17 of the MIA 1906 by s 14 of the IA 2015, (i) contracts of insurance remain contracts of utmost good faith, but (ii) there would appear to be no existing remedies that an insured could avail of in the face of a breach by insurers.[37] As the Law Commission observed in its 2014 Report – and as re-appears in the Explanatory Notes to the IA 2015 – the duty of good faith is regarded as an interpretative principle. In Chapter 30 of the former, the Law Commission expressly envisaged that the judges would continue to develop the duty noting that there should be 'room for judicial flexibility' and stating that '[s]pecifically, paragraph 116 of the Explanatory Notes to s 14 of the IA 2015 state that "[i]t is possible that the principle of a mutual duty of good faith could provide a solution to an especially hard case or emergent difficulty"'[38] although it considered that such recourse would be rare. It is suggested that the use of big data analytics by insurers is such an emergent difficulty. The Explanatory Notes continue: 'The intention of section 14 is that good faith will remain an interpretative principle, with section 17 of the 1906 Act and the common law continuing to provide that insurance contracts are contracts of good faith.' That approach suggests that the interpretative principle will apply to interpreting terms in insurance contracts and might additionally operate as a principle of statutory interpretation. However, notwithstanding the remarks that appear in the Explanatory Notes, there is nothing in the IA 2015 itself which provides an express foundation for such a principle.

But before one can assess the scope of the principle's application, one must again start by asking what good faith means such that contractual terms and statutory

[37] The Insurance Act 2015 abolished the remedy of avoidance although that was never particularly helpful to insureds complaining of breaches of the duty by insurers.
[38] Law Commission, 2014 Report, para 30.24(3).

obligations might be applied in accordance with its requirements. Following the analysis set out above, it is suggested that good faith should not only draw on existing common law requirements, but should encompass the purposes pursued by other legislative measures that seek to promote transparency and informational equality in the provision of financial services. Any interpretative principle should thus draw on the various rights and obligations in the GDPR as reflecting a broader aim to ensure transparency in the use of data by financial service providers. The principle ought to apply to consumer and non-consumer insurance but it does not follow that the principle's content would be uniform where one size would be required to fit all: what an expanded duty of good faith would require would depend on the circumstances of a particular case. The principle would thus potentially apply with greater force in the consumer context, and in circumstances where it could not be assumed that the insured had relevant knowledge about factors bearing on the risk (or knowledge that certain factors had been taken into account in assessing the risk). However, the principle would appear to be constrained in one respect: the common law duty of good faith disclosure operates, pre-contractually,[39] by reference to knowledge of material facts that relate to the risk itself. The interpretive principle ought also to apply post-contractually in the context of claims. It is suggested that when considering when and where the principle operates, it ought to be anchored to the concern over the relative risk-related knowledge of the parties to an insurance contract. There are of course two forms of information asymmetry prevalent in the context of insurance: one which relates to the facts bearing on the risk itself and another which relates to knowledge of the insurance product. The common law duty of good faith only applies to the former. It is suggested that informational duties[40] including as to non-risk, and particularly price-related, information might be better left to regulatory and consumer law subject to any competition issues to which differential pricing might give rise.[41] What, then, are the more precise ends to which the interpretative principle might be put, pre- and post-contractually?

i. *The Contractual Application of the Interpretative Principle*

As to its contractual application, the principle would operate in relation to the interpretation of express terms. But two more substantial applications of the principle in a contractual setting suggest themselves: (i) the implication of terms to give effect to the principle; and (ii) the operation of the principle to restrict the exercise of express terms or which otherwise govern the performance of the contract.

As to its role in implying further terms, this was expressly envisaged by the Law Commission in its July 2014 Report where the purpose was stated to be: 'to inform the need to imply contractual terms into the policy under the traditional "business efficacy" test, Good faith provides a background when considering whether it is necessary to

[39] And post-contractually upon a variation to the scope of the cover that was not pre-ordained.

[40] The two information asymmetries therefore map a distinction between disclosure duties at common law (which require disclosure of risk-related facts) and information duties imposed by regulators (which require the provision of product-related information).

[41] Discussed in ch 8, section IV.

imply a particular term.'[42] There is an oddity in this suggestion. If the preponderant view – as the Law Commission itself accepted – is that the source of the duty is not an implied term, it is unclear why the duty should be used to imply further terms in the name of good faith. More likely, as has been pointed out, is that the Law Commission envisaged the use of the idea of 'utmost good faith' as a matter of construction or interpretation of existing insurance contracts, albeit even then, the fact that the contract to be interpreted is one of utmost good faith will be part of the relevant circumstances taken into account when applying ordinary principles of contractual interpretation.[43] It would appear to follow that if there is no separate role for a principle of good faith contractual interpretation, any constraints on the exercise of contractual rights must derive from the operation of the duty itself. This possibility is thus discussed below.

ii. The Legislative Application of the Interpretative Principle

However, the problems with the suggestion that there is a free-standing interpretative principle of good faith in relation to contracts does not preclude the reformed s 17 of the MIA 1906 from supporting a wider interpretative principle applicable to statutes. If the common law can reason analogically from, inter alia, the principles espoused by the GDPR, the courts can further develop what Burrows calls the statute-based common law when interpreting the requirements of wider regulatory duties.[44] If good faith operates as an interpretative principle that is – in an evolved or expanding form – concerned with the fair and transparent conduct of insurance business, then there would appear to be no reason preventing its application to existing regulatory frameworks which apply to the conduct of insurance business. For example, we saw in chapter six how PRIN and ICOBS set down a range of conduct principles and standards which insurers are required to adhere to as a matter of law. For example, PRIN 6 requires that an insurer must pay due regard to the interests of its customers and treat them fairly;[45] PRIN 7 applies to communications with clients and requires that an insurer must pay due regard to the information needs of its clients and communicate information to them in a way which is clear, fair and not misleading. While these principles only apply to consumer insurance, those standards could be interpreted – by the FCA, the FOS and the Courts – to ensure transparency in the use of big data analytics at the underwriting and claims-handling stages. The same approach could be applied to the more specific (and civilly enforceable) obligations imposed by ICOBS, such as the communication obligations at ICOBS 2.2 and ICOBS 6.1.5 R which relate to the steps an insurer must take to ensure a customer is given appropriate information in order to make an informed decision about the arrangements proposed. That may include the provision of details about what risk factors insurers took into account and to what effect in relation to the offer of insurance made to the insured.

[42] Law Commission, 2014 Report, para 30.24(2).

[43] A Tettenborn and B Soyer, 'Mapping (Utmost) Good Faith in Insurance Law' (2016) *LQR* 618 at 621–22.

[44] Burrows, above n 20. Statute-based common law is the body of judge-made law that develops in the context of interpreting statute.

[45] Where Outcomes 1 and 3 appear particularly ripe for development according to the interpretative principle.

The interpretative principle might also be brought to bear when applying other consumer legislation that applies to consumer insurance contracts. Again we saw in chapter six that s 62(4) of the CRA 2015 provides that a term will be unfair if, contrary to the requirement of good faith, it causes a significant imbalance in the parties' rights and obligations under the contract to the detriment of the consumer. The difficulty, however, is that the unfairness assessment applies to existing terms: it does not impose obligations on insurers to draw risk factors derived from the use of big data analytics to the consumer's attention. In addition, as we saw, s 64 of the CRA 2015 provides that terms specifying the main subject matter of the contract and the price payable are not amenable to the fairness assessment under s 62 if they have been brought to the attention of the consumer. On these bases, it is difficult to see what role a wider good faith interpretative principle could have in the context of the CRA 2015.

The principle might also be applied to the informational obligation under Article 20 of the IDD. However, there might be an argument against this proposed application of the principle because Article 20 is a regulatory obligation that relates to an insured's knowledge and understanding of the insurance product, rather than the risk, and interpreting the obligation to include a duty on insurers to provide information as to the risk factors that were taken into account might be regarded as overly stretching the language and purpose of the provision.

In addition, any proposed application of the principle to the above schemes of legislation would apply largely to consumer insurances and would not catch a large proportion of non-consumer insurances notwithstanding the non-consumer insured's cover might also be offered, at least in part, as a result of profiling conducted by big data analytics and where the risk factors determining the terms of the offer have not been disclosed to the insured.

B. Good Faith and the Development of the Duty of Disclosure

The Law Commission's observations in its July 2014 Report suggest that the requirement of good faith – re-imagined as an interpretative principle – may cease to operate as a matter of substantive insurance law. However, the Law Commission's preference that the reformed s 17 of the MIA 1906 merely gives rise to an interpretative obligation sits ill with the fact that Parliament did not, in the IA 2015, abolish or in any way amend insurers' good faith duty of disclosure. It merely abolished the only remedy to which its breach had previously given rise. It was silent as to the duty of good faith disclosure.[46] As Bennion points out, '[w]here an Act is silent on an issue the existing law is taken to apply unless excluded expressly or by implication.'[47] Insurers' common law duty of disclosure not having been amended, the position must remain that

[46] And MIA 1906, s 91(2) preserves the common law insofar as it is not inconsistent with the express provisions of the Act itself. Nothing in the Insurance Act impacts on the settlement reached under the 1906 Act.

[47] Bennion, above n 18, code 25.6. The existing law is therefore available to supplement the legislative scheme so long as it does not cut across the legislative scheme: *Re B (A Child) (Habitual Residence: Inherent jurisdiction)* [2016] 1 *FLR* 561 (Lord Sumption at [85]).

insurers are subject to such duties: just because the remedy of avoidance has been abolished does not have the effect of setting the duty at nought. In those circumstances, it is strongly arguable that Parliament's intent in abolishing a remedy that was unacceptable for many reasons but retaining the duty was to leave it to the courts to develop the scope of those duties.

Before considering how the duty might be developed, it is important to briefly consider the juridical basis for that duty. It has variously been argued that the duty of utmost good faith is an implied term of the contract, alternatively constitutes a tortious duty, or alternatively is a sui generis common law duty that does not have a contractual or tortious basis. As to the contractual analysis, while that explanation might be available once the contract has been entered into,[48] plainly there can be no implied terms at the pre-contractual stage and the suggestion that compliance with the duty is an implied condition precedent either to the formation or performance of, or liability arising under, the contract is inconsistent with the remedies that arise for its breach (as compared to those that would be available were the duty an implied condition precedent in one or other of those senses).[49]

In *Banque Financière de la Cité v Westgate*, Steyn J examined the nature of the duty and rejected the suggestion that the duty existed by virtue of an implied term in the contract or because of any collateral contract. He said:

> it is often said that a term is implied in a contract when in truth a positive rule of contract law is applied because of the category in which a particular contract falls ... [T]he body of rules, which are described as the *uberimmae fides* principle, are rules of law developed by the judges.

The Court Appeal in *Bank of Nova Scotia (the Good Luck)* approved its own reasoning in *Banque Financière* and expressly rejected the suggestion that the pre- or post-contractual duty arose out of an implied term. It considered that there was no reason for distinguishing the character of the duty depending on the time at which it was owed. It held that the duty arose out of the principle of *uberimmae fides*, but was amorphous, taking shape only to meet the circumstances in which the parties found themselves. Both *Banque Financière* and *Bank of Nova Scotia* were appealed but in neither case did the House of Lords consider the juristic basis of the obligation to observe good faith in insurance contracts.[50] Lord Hobhouse in *The Star Sea*

[48] Particularly in the duty's most limited incarnation, namely, the prohibition of fraudulent behaviour, since the parties to the contract would readily agree the fraudulent performance or breach of the contract would be contrary to what the contract required. Hobhouse J in *Bank of Nova Scotia (the Good Luck)* [1998] 1 Lloyd's Rep 514 considered that once the contractual relationship existed, the source of the obligation ceased to be relevant. He considered that the post-contractual duty of disclosure (he said nothing about the pre-contractual duty) was distinctly contractual (ie an implied term).

[49] See the discussion in P MacDonald-Eggers and S Picken, *Good Faith and Insurance Contracts* 4th edn (Abingdon, Informa Law, 2018) para 4.32 ff.

[50] The Court of Appeal's conclusion that the duty was a common law duty has been followed in a number of cases; see, however, the observations of Lord Hobhouse in *Manifest Shipping Co Ltd v Uni-Polaris Shipping Co (The Star Sea)* [2001] UKHL 1 at [76]. Lord Mustill in *Pan Atlantic Insurance Co Ltd v Pine Top Insurance Co Ltd* [1994] Lloyd's Rep 427 at 449 suggested the question as to the juridical basis of the duty was academic. However, that ignores, amongst other things, the fact that the basis of the duty directly determines the remedial consequences of its breach. In light of the abolition of the remedy of avoidance by the Insurance Act 2015, it again becomes important to understand the nature of the duty if it, and its remedial consequences, are to be developed anew by the courts.

noted that both counsel had accepted that *Banque Financière* (and the conclusion as to the basis of the duty of good faith) was good law, such that there was no remedy in damages for want of good faith. He commented: 'It follows from this that the principle relied on by the defendants is not an implied term but is a principle of law which is sufficient to support a right to avoid the contract of insurance retrospectively.'[51] This remark related to the pre-contractual duty. However, he went on to suggest that where a breach of the duty of good faith occurs post-inception, avoidance would be anomalous and disproportionate, noting that 'the result is effectively penal'. He went on to say this of s 17 of the MIA 1906:

> A coherent scheme can be achieved by distinguishing a lack of good faith which is material to the making of the contract itself (or some variation of it) and a lack of good faith during the performance of the contract which may prejudice the other party or cause him loss or destroy the continuing contractual relationship. The former derives from requirements of the law which pre-exist the contract and are not created by it although they only become material because a contract has been entered into … The latter can derive from express or implied terms of the contract; it would be a contractual obligation arising from the contract and the remedies are the contractual remedies provided by the law of contract.[52]

The Law Commission in its 2010 Issues Paper considered the discussion as to the basis for the duty of good faith in the cases and stated:

> it is not easy to characterise the duty of good faith. We do not think it is an implied term or that it should give rise to an action in tort or delict. It is best seen as a separate, non-excludable duty, giving rise to specific remedies.[53]

As to the development of the duty itself, it has been suggested that the duty can constrain the exercise of rights conferred in insurance contracts, and in a way that would go beyond merely precluding such exercises that would constitute an abuse of rights.[54] Tettenborn and Soyer give the example of an insurer taking conduct of the defence of a claim against the insured under a liability policy being required to do so consistently with the reputational and financial interests of the insured.[55] They also refer to the duty embodying a duty to correct mistakes, albeit in a context where one party knows that the other has made a clear but unrecognised mistake (eg in the calculation of premium). It is submitted that this example already falls within the duty since it relates to something that is material to and either increases or decreases the risk for the insurer or insured, respectively.[56] More pertinent is their observation that the

[51] *Manifest Shipping v Uni-Polaris Insurance Co (The Star Sea)* [2001] UKHL 1; [2003] 1 AC 469, 518.

[52] It is likely that the analysis of the basis of the duty was driven in significant part with an eye to the lack of an appropriate remedy for the breach of the duty by insurers. That concern militates in favour of finding that at least the post-contractual duty has a basis in contract since breach opens the door to a claim for damages for breach of contract.

[53] Law Commission Issues Paper 6: 'Insurance Contract Law, Damages for Late Payment and the Insurer's Duty of Good faith', S.22; the Law Commission repeated that view in its issues paper of March 2010 at para 4.45.

[54] As discussed in ch 6, III.B.

[55] A Tettenborn and B Soyer, 'Mapping (Utmost) Good Faith in Insurance Law' (2016) *LQR* 618 at 625, citing *Groom v Crocker* [1939] 1 KB 194.

[56] Other obvious mistakes of which advantage might be taken may be avoided on ordinary principles of construction or rectification; however, good faith will constrain exploitative exercises of strict contractual rights.

duty of good faith may now require a more muscular approach to the provision of information akin to the ongoing duties between partners or parties to a joint venture where the duty has been interpreted expansively as one 'to observe reasonable commercial standards of fair dealing in accordance with their actions that related to the agreement'.[57] This approach is on all fours with the duty of disclosure expanded by reference to the principles of fairness and transparency set out under the GDPR. That would require, for example, an insurer who acquires new risk-related information (whether through predictive analytics or real-time data monitoring) to disclose that information in circumstances where it would rely upon that information in seeking to exercise a cancellation clause, the imposition of an endorsement, a clause permitting insurers to reduce the scope of cover or where it would impact negatively on their approach to renewal. Unilaterally exercising rights on the basis of information only known to insurers[58] would, it is suggested, violate this expanded duty.[59]

V. Conclusions

It is not proposed to set out a complete definition or justification for an expanded duty of good faith. The ambition of this book is more limited, merely being to suggest that where insurers make decisions on the basis of information derived or inferred from the application of big data analytics, the expanded duty of good faith ought, by analogy with the fairness and transparency principles in the GDPR, require, at a minimum, the disclosure of all risk factors that contribute to (i) an initial underwriting decision; (ii) any decision during the contract to exercise a contractual clause relating to the scope or price of the cover or the rights of the parties; and (iii) any decision on renewal similarly so based. This accords neatly with the aims of the GDPR and there is no reason why the common law should not take this approach, more comfortable as it now is with purposive interpretation and reasoning by analogy with statutory or regulatory principles and with what fair dealing consistently requires in consumer and commercial contexts.[60] The duty of good faith has not been rendered redundant by statutory reforms; on the contrary, as a result of those reforms and the opportunities that technology has opened up to insurers, it is suggested that the courts should embrace the principles embodied in the GDPR as giving new content to the insurers' duty of disclosure.

[57] *Berkeley Community Villages Ltd v Pullen* [2007] 3 *Estates Gazette Law Reports* 101 at [97].

[58] See the Australian case of *Beverley v Tyndall Life Insurance Co Ltd* (1999) 21 *Western Australian Reports* 327 at 329-33.

[59] Tettenborn and Soyer point out that this approach has been adopted in Germany, where the biggest difference appears to relate to what the duty requires of insurers. There good faith precludes insurers from relying on unusual limitations on cover likely to escape the insured's notice unless warned and further requires insurers to be fair and open in decision making where a discretion of the insurer is in issue, as well as preventing abusive reliance on technical exclusions: Tettenborn and Soyer, above n 55, p 634.

[60] As to the latter the judgment of Leggatt J in *Yam Seng Pte Ltd v International Trade Corp Ltd* [2013] EWHC 111 (QB) provides a detailed survey of the cases from which it might be said that English law has already implicitly developed principles of good faith and fair dealing even in a commercial setting.

The way in which underwriting and claims handling is evolving, and the fact that as part of that evolution, insurers may often know and take account of many risk factors that they have identified through their own enquiries and use of predictive analytics rather than from the insured, raises afresh the question of whether the duty of good faith imports – or should import – a duty to take reasonable care in the discharge of the duty of disclosure. In particular, if the duty of disclosure is expanded to require insurers to disclose to insureds all risk-related information that they have separately sourced and on which they propose to rely in offering terms or paying claims, should it not follow that insurers should be required to take reasonable care in relation to the information they provide to insureds so that the latter can know and understand what is proposed to be relied upon and how? The question of whether the duty of disclosure does – or ought – to require insurers to discharge that duty with reasonable care and skill is intimately connected with the remedial consequences of the breach of any such duty. As fundamentally a remedial question, it is addressed in the following chapter.

PART IV

Remedies

8

Remedies for Insurers' Misuse of Data

This chapter considers the remedies available to insureds whose data has been misused by insurers in the context, principally, of underwriting or claims handling. The discussion of the relationship in the previous chapter between common law and regulatory obligations, was, in this regard, necessary groundwork. Having concluded that it is generally permissible for the courts at common law not only to seek to identify principles from statute but also to develop the common law by analogy with those principles, the only further question was whether there was any reason why, more particularly, developing the common law duty of disclosure by reference to the rights and duties in the GDPR would be impermissible. It was suggested that there is no inconsistency between an expanded common law duty of disclosure on insurers and the GDPR itself. Nor does such a duty cut across the aims of other regulatory provisions that impact on the distribution of insurance. But analysis of that relationship is necessary for the further reason that the scope of any remedies that one might develop to enforce that expanded duty of disclosure depends not only on the juridical basis of the duty, but also depends on whether any proposed expansion of the remedies for breach of that duty would be inconsistent with the remedies regime operating within those overlapping regulatory frameworks. In this chapter, the regulatory remedies available under the FSMA 2000, the CRA 2015 and the GDPR are considered. The chapter additionally considers two separate sets of remedies, namely: (i) those available under domestic and European human rights and equality law; and (ii) those available for breach of competition law. It is only upon considering the nature and extent of the various available remedies for data misuse that an informed assessment as to the remedies that might be developed for breach of insurers' expanded duty of good faith might be made.

I. Financial Services Remedies

If an insurer breaches rules in the FCA Handbook, that may have two sets of consequences. First, the FCA may take disciplinary action against the insurer and may, for example, impose a fine.[1] However, this may be of little comfort to an insured seeking compensation for loss arising as a result of such a breach. Second, in principle,

[1] Financial Services and Markets Act 2000, s 66.

consumer insureds may bring a claim for damages against a regulated firm for breach of statutory duty under s 138D of the FSMA 2000.[2] And third, an insured may pursue the breach with the Financial Ombudsman Service. I shall take the latter two alternatives in turn.

A. Damages Actions

Section 138D of the FSMA 2000 is entitled 'action for damages' and materially provides:

> (1) …
> (2) A contravention by an authorised person of a rule made by the FCA is actionable at the suit of a private person who suffers loss as a result of the contravention, subject to the defences and other incidents applying to actions for breach of statutory duty.
> (3) If rules made by the FCA so provide, subsection (2) does not apply to a contravention of a specified provision of the rules.
> (4) In prescribed cases, a contravention of a rule which by virtue of subsection (1) or (2) would be actionable at the suit of a private person is actionable at the suit of a person who is not a private person, subject to the defences and other incidents applying to actions for breach of statutory duty.

The statutory right of action is not available for breaches of every obligation imposed by the FCA Handbook. In this regard, PRIN 3.4.4 R A states that a contravention of the rules in PRIN does not give rise to a right of action by a private person under s 138D of the Act (and each of those rules is specified under s 138D(3) of the Act as a provision giving rise to no such right of action).[3] However, ICOBS is binding upon insurers and a consumer insured will be able to bring a claim under s 138D for breach of ICOBS that causes it loss.[4]

The damages regime under s 138D of FSMA 2000 is exhaustive. That is, one cannot bring a common law claim for breach of statutory duty or a common law claim for damages in relation to a breach of ICOBS separately from or in addition to a claim under s 138D itself. The following principles are applicable when considering whether a free-standing action for breach of statutory duty is available in respect of a breach of statutory duty:[5]

1. Where a statute is silent (which FSMA 2000 is not), 'The initial, working presumption appears to be that there is no civil remedy for breach of the statute';
2. 'Where the statute does provide an alternative remedy to enforce the relevant duty that will normally indicate that the statutory right was designed to be enforceable by those means and not by private right of action';

[2] The successor to FSMA 2000, s 150.

[3] There was previously a right of action for damages for breach of the Principles but this was removed by PRIN 3.4.4.R as confirmed by PRIN Sch 5, 'Rights of action for damages'.

[4] See *Parker v National Farmers Union Mutual Insurance Society Limited* [2012] EWHC 2156 (Comm), where it was held that the obligations under ICOBS were not implied terms of the insurance contract.

[5] For a discussion of the source of the following principles see *Brown & Ors v InnovatorOne & Ors* [2012] EWHC 1321 (Comm) at paras 1271–76.

3. 'A common law action for breach of statutory duty arises only when the Claimant can establish that Parliament intended that breach of the relevant statutory duty should be actionable by an individual harmed by that breach.' Because FSMA is a regulatory statute for the benefit of everyone, no such intention arises.

There is clear authority that no claim for breach of statutory duty is available for breaches of FSMA 2000 which are not specifically defined in the Act as giving rise to a claim for breach of statutory duty: see *Hall v Cable and Wireless plc*.[6] In that case, Teare J held that:

> [Those provisions in FSMA which expressly provide for a claim for breach of statutory duty] indicate clearly that Parliament expressly considered which of the duties or obligations imposed by FSMA would give rise to a cause of action at the suit of a private person. Parliament did not provide expressly that a breach of the Listing Rules would give rise to a cause of action at the suit of a private person. Other remedies and penalties were provided by ss 382, 384 and 91. That is a clear indication that Parliament did not intend a breach of the Listing Rules would give rise to a cause of action at the suit of a private person. To hold that Parliament did so intend would interfere with the scheme and modes of enforcement provided by FSMA 2000.[7]

In *Brown & Ors v InnovatorOne & Ors*[8] the claimants brought claims in professional negligence against solicitors in relation to, inter alia, alleged breaches of ss 19 and 21 of FSMA 2000 in relation to the sale of tax efficient technology investment schemes. The claimants acknowledged that they were barred by authority from bringing a claim for breach of statutory duty in relation to any breach of the rules imposed under FSMA 2000; however, the claimants asserted that the defendant solicitors were under a common law duty of care to comply with the regulatory regime imposed by FSMA. That was also rejected since it would undermine the scheme of civil liability carefully created by the Act and would be contrary to the above-mentioned principles which preclude a claim for a 'free-standing' breach of statutory duty from arising in circumstances where it is plain from the relevant Act that the drafters had considered and expressly defined those provisions within the Act that could give rise to such a claim.[9]

B. Complaints to the FOS

The Law Commission in its July 2007 Consultation Paper stated that:

> the [FCA] Rules are not an adequate cure for defects in the law. First, it is not the task of the [FCA] to monitor individual cases. Relatively few consumers will complain to the [FCA] about individual matters of misrepresentation or nondisclosure, and serious disciplinary action is unlikely in what appear to be one-off cases. In principle a breach of the [FCA] Rules may lead to the insurer being liable for breach of statutory duty, but we doubt

[6] [2011] BCC 543 at 548–49.
[7] ibid at [16].
[8] [2012] EWHC 1321 (Comm).
[9] ibid, paras 1271–74. The judge further held that the very same reasons barring a claim for breach of statutory duty also applied to bar a claim in negligence.

> the practical efficacy of this remedy save when a very large sum is at stake. Those who can pursue the matter through the FOS are best advised to do so; those who cannot may well drop the matter.[10]

Similarly, in its July 2014 Report, the Law Commission stated that[11] a claim for damages under s 138D of FSMA 2000 may be useful, but noted that its predecessor (s 150) was very rarely used in practice. The Law Commission considered that the principal reason for that fact was that the damages remedy was confined to 'private persons', who it noted fell into two classes: (i) an individual (which included both a consumer who is not acting in the course of business, and a sole trader who is acting in the course of business); and (ii) a legal person, such as a company or corporate body (including partnerships) which is not acting in the course of business. The Law Commission thus observed:

> It is not surprising that the right has been so little used. Most consumers and small businesses will find it easier to complain to the FOS than bring a complex, novel action before the courts for breach of statutory duty. Most other potential claimants are excluded because they are companies and suffer losses in the course of business. Many of the cases we are concerned with involve small companies which have lost profits following catastrophic events, such as fires. These policyholders are not entitled to rely on the provision.[12]

The statutory scheme establishing three jurisdictions under which the FOS may resolve disputes is provided for in Part VXI of the FSMA 2000.[13] The three jurisdictions under which the FOS might act are: (i) the compulsory jurisdiction;[14] (ii) the consumer credit jurisdiction;[15] and (iii) the voluntary jurisdiction.[16] Section 228 of the FSMA 2000 relates to the compulsory jurisdiction (which for these purposes is the most relevant jurisdiction).[17] Section 228(2) provides that a 'complaint is to be determined by reference to what is, in the opinion of the ombudsman, fair and reasonable in all the circumstances of the case'. This means that the FOS is not bound by strict law. It has effectively developed its own jurisprudence on the issue, which in practical terms is more important than the legal rules. The FOS seeks wherever possible to settle complaints by mediation. Should this prove impracticable, the case will be investigated and a view reached by an adjudicator. If either party remains dissatisfied, an appeal may be made to an ombudsman. An ombudsman has the power to

[10] Law Commission, Insurance Contract Law Misrepresentation, Non-Disclosure and Breach of Warranty by the Insured, July 2007, para 3.19.

[11] para 26.68.

[12] ibid, para 26.69.

[13] FSMA 2000, s 225 and see further Schedule 17, making further provision for the ombudsman scheme.

[14] FSMA 2000, s 226.

[15] FSMA 2000, s 227.

[16] FSMA 2000, s 227.

[17] FSMA 2000, s 226(1) provides that a 'complaint which relates to an act or omission of a person ("the respondent") in carrying on an activity to which compulsory jurisdiction rules apply is to be dealt with under the ombudsman scheme if the conditions mentioned in subsection (2) are satisfied.' s 226(3) provides that '"Compulsory jurisdiction rules" means rules (a) made by the [FCA] for the purposes of this section; and (b) specifying the activities to which they apply.'

make an award against an insurer of up to £150,000, which becomes binding on the insurer if accepted by the complainant.

II. Consumer Law Remedies

Chapter six considered the relevant provisions of the CRA 2015.[18] As noted in chapter four, s 54(2)–(4) provides that breach of any of the terms implied by ss 49–52 will entitle consumers to repeat performance and/or a reduction in price. However, s 54(6) provides that s 54 does not operate to prevent 'the consumer seeking other remedies for a breach of a term to which any of subsections (3) to (5) applies, instead of or in addition to a remedy referred to there (but not so as to recover twice for the same loss)'. Section 54(7) sets out a list of available additional remedies, including a claim for damages or the exercise of a right to treat the contract as at an end. In the circumstances, there is no statutory right of action for damages conferred by the CRA 2015. However, if the consumer's right to repeat performance or a price reduction is unsatisfactory, he may be able to bring a claim under s 138D of the FSMA 2000.

III. Equality and Anti-Discrimination Remedies

The way in which discrimination can occur where big data is used to profile groups of individuals is illustrated in the following example given to the United States Senate Committee on Commerce, Science and Transportation:

> A data broker sells consumer profiles to financial companies … The profiles define consumers by categories (carrying titles such as 'Rural and Barely Making It', 'Ethnic Second-City Strugglers', 'Tough Start: Young Single Parents') or 'score' them, focusing on consumers' financial vulnerability. The financial companies offer these consumers payday loans and other 'non-traditional' financial services (high-cost loans and other financially risky products).[19]

Some of the new risk categories created by big data analytics may be directly discriminatory; others may operate as proxies which have a disproportionate impact on those

[18] The Unfair Terms in Consumer Contract Regulations 1999 (SI 1999/2083) govern the terms of contracts made before 1 October 2015 between a 'seller or supplier' and a 'consumer'. Subject to saving and transitional provisions, the 1999 Regulations were repealed and replaced with effect from 1 October 2015 by the Consumer Rights Act 2015, Sch 4 para 34 and the Consumer Rights Act 2015 (Commencement No 3, Transitional Provisions, Savings and Consequential Amendments) Order 2015 (SI 2015/1630).

[19] This example is taken from United States Senate, Committee on Commerce, Science, and Transportation. A Review of the Data Broker Industry: Collection, Use, and Sale of Consumer Data for Marketing Purposes, Staff Report for Chairman Rockefeller, 18 December 2013, https://www.commerce.senate.gov/public/_cache/files/0d2b3642-6221-4888-a631-08f2f255b577/AE5D72CBE7F44F5BFC846BECE22C875B.12.18.13-senate-commerce-committee-report-on-data-broker-industry.pdf. See p ii of the Executive Summary and p 12 of the main body of the document in particular.

with a certain protected characteristic and thus constitutes indirect discrimination, each of which is prohibited in the UK and the EU.

A. UK Equality Law

The Equality Act 2010 (EA 2010) seeks, as one of its main purposes, to harmonise discrimination law in the UK having revoked – in order to revise and consolidate – almost the entirety of UK anti-discrimination law.[20]

As noted in chapter three, direct discrimination is prohibited by s 13 of the EA 2010. Section 13(1) provides that: 'A person (A) discriminates against another (B) if, because of a protected characteristic, A treats B less favourably than A treats or would treat others.'[21] The protected characteristics, for these purposes, are age, disability, gender assignment, marriage or civil partnership, race, religion or belief, sex and sexual orientation.[22] Indirect discrimination is prohibited in the United Kingdom by s 19 of the Equality Act 2010. Section 19(1) provides that: 'A person (A) discriminates against another (B) if A applies to B a provision, criterion or practice which is discriminatory in relation to a relevant protected characteristic of B's.' If the criterion puts B at a disadvantage, it will be discriminatory if A cannot show it to be a proportionate means of achieving a legitimate aim. The case law on what constitutes each is discussed briefly below.

Section 29 of the EA 2010 prohibits, inter alia,[23] discrimination in relation to the provision of services and materially provides – as far as private providers are concerned – as follows:

> (1) A person (a "service-provider") concerned with the provision of a service to the public or a section of the public (for payment or not) must not discriminate against a person requiring the service by not providing the person with the service.
> (2) A service-provider (A) must not, in providing the service, discriminate against a person (B) –
>
> (a) as to the terms on which A provides the service to B;
> (b) by terminating the provision of the service to B;
> (c) by subjecting B to any other detriment.

Section 29(2)(a) of the EA 2010 will be of most relevance to the provision of insurance. Section 29 applies to discrimination on the basis of all protected characteristics albeit subject to certain limitations and exclusions on which insurers are permitted to rely.

[20] Specifically, the EA 2010 repeals and revokes almost the entirety of: the Equal Pay Act 1970, the Sex Discrimination Act 1975, the Race Relations Act 1976, and the Disability Discrimination Act 1995, the Employment Equality (Religion or Belief) Regulations 2003, the Employment Equality (Sexual Orientation) Regulations 2003, the Employment Equality (Age) Regulations 2006, Part 2 of the Equality Act 2006 and the Equality Act (Sexual Orientation) Regulations 2007.

[21] Although, as discussed in ch 6, modifications are made in relation to what amounts to direct discrimination on the basis of some of those characteristics.

[22] Equality Act 2010, ss 4–12.

[23] It also prohibits harassment and victimisations on similar bases.

A 'person requiring a service' includes a reference to a person who is seeking to obtain or use the service.[24] The Explanatory Notes to the EA 2010 further explain that 'a person is protected both when requesting a service and during the course of being provided with a service'.[25] As to the meaning of providing a 'service to the public or a section of the public', s 31(7) of the EA 2010 provides that:

> (7) A reference to a service-provider not providing a person with a service includes a reference to –
>
> (a) the service-provider not providing the person with a service of the quality that the service-provider usually provides to the public (or the section of it which includes the person), or
>
> (b) the service-provider not providing the person with the service in the manner in which, or on the terms on which, the service-provider usually provides the service to the public (or the section of it which includes the person).

One person can therefore constitute a section of the public,[26] a relevant fact in circumstances where insurers begin to create risk profiles for each individual insured.

However, the EA 2010 contains a number of exemptions that limit the scope of the protections available in the context of the provision of services. A number of these exceptions are controversial because they exclude from the scope of protection groups who may be especially vulnerable because of their particular protected characteristic. The exemptions are set out in Schedule 3 and pursuant to s 31(10) of the EA 2010. Part 5 of Schedule 3 sets out the operative exemptions in the context of the provision of insurance. Paragraph 20 of Schedule 3 provides that s 29 of the EA 2010 does not apply to, amongst other financial services, insurance services arranged by an employer. Insurance provision arranged by an employer and which is said to be discriminatory will fall to be considered as against the employer rather than the insurer under Part 5 of the Act.[27] The exemptions which are applicable to the direct provision of insurance relate to age and disability and additionally create a limited exception in relation to existing insurance policies. Specifically:

- para 20A relates to age; para 20A(2) provides that 'where A [an insurer] conducts an assessment of risk for the purposes of providing the financial service to another person (B), A may rely on sub-paragraph (1) [which exempts age discrimination] only if the assessment of risk, so far as it involves a consideration of B's age, is carried out by reference to information which is relevant to the assessment of risk and from a source on which it is reasonable to rely';[28]

[24] EA 2010, s 31(6).

[25] Explanatory Notes, para 107.

[26] A bank may provide a service by way of a reasonable adjustment to a single disabled person: *Royal Bank of Scotland v Allen* [2008] EWCA Civ 1213.

[27] The Explanatory Notes to the Act give the following example: 'An employer enters into a contract with an insurer for the provision of health insurance to employees. As the health insurance is part of the package of benefits provided by the employer to the employee, the employer must ensure that the provision complies with Part 5. So, if benefits under the health insurance policy differ between men and women, the employer may have to justify the difference by reference to paragraph 20 of schedule 9 (Insurance contracts etc).' Above n 25, para 713.

[28] para 20A was inserted by Article 3 of the Equality Act (Age Exceptions) Order 2012, which was made under s 197 of the 2010 Act.

- para 21 of Schedule 3 relates to disability and provides there will be no contravention of s 29 of the Act so far as relating to disability discrimination, to do anything in connection with insurance business if: (a) that thing is done by reference to information that is both relevant to the assessment of the risk to be insured and from a source on which it is reasonable to rely, and (b) it is reasonable to do that thing. A test of reasonableness will be easier for an insurer to satisfy than a test of objective justification;
- para 23 sets out the exemptions in relation to existing insurance policies and provides that s 29 of the Act will not be contravened in relation to discrimination based on age, disability, gender reassignment, pregnancy and maternity, race, religion or belief, sex or sexual orientation, 'to do anything in connection with insurance business in relation to an existing insurance policy'. An existing insurance policy is one entered into before the date on which para 23 came into force.[29] It will thus be of greater continuing relevance to long-term policies entered into before October 2010 but will have diminishing relevance to most forms of consumer insurance. Moreover, if an existing policy has been renewed or reviewed after para 23 came into force, the dispensation will not apply.[30]

Paragraph 22 of Schedule 3 to the EA 2010 had provided for exemptions in relation to sex, gender reassignment, pregnancy and maternity. It provided that it would not be a contravention of s 29 in relation to those forms of discrimination to do anything in relation to an annuity, life insurance policy, accident insurance policy or similar matter involving the assessment of risk if: (a) that thing is done by reference to actuarial or other data from a source on which it is reasonable to rely, and (b) it is reasonable to do that thing. In that respect, the permitted discrimination had at least to be supported by actuarial evidence demonstrating the relationship between the risk factor and the incidence of loss. However, para 22 of Schedule 3 was repealed in light of the litigation brought in relation to the insurance derogation contained with the Gender Goods and Services Directive.[31] That Directive requires Member States to prohibit sex discrimination in the calculation of premiums and benefits for the purposes of insurance and related financial services for all contracts of insurance entered into after 21 December 2007. Notwithstanding that prohibition, Article 5(2) provided:

> Member States may decide before 21 December 2007 to permit proportionate differences in individuals' premiums and benefits where the use of sex is a determining factor in the assessment of risk based on relevant and accurate actuarial and statistical data … These Member States shall review their decision five years after 21 December 2007 … and shall forward the results of this review to the Commission.

[29] However, an existing policy will be unenforceable against a person if at the time it was made it was otherwise unlawful: see, eg, Sex Discrimination Act 1975, s 77; Race Relations Act 1976, s 72.

[30] The Joint Committee raised serious concerns over the width and acceptability of this exemption: see its 'Legislative Scrutiny: Equality Bill, 26th Report of Session 2008–09, para 159.

[31] Directive 2004/113/EC.

The UK and Belgium each availed of the derogation. On a challenge to the Belgian legislation, the CJEU ruled in *Association Belge des Consommateurs Test-Achats ASBL v Conseil des Ministres (Test-Achats)*[32] that

> [t]he use of actuarial factors related to sex was widespread in the provision of insurance at the time when the Directive was adopted. Consequently it was permissible for the EU legislature to implement the principle of equality for men and women – more specifically, the application of the rule of unisex premiums and benefits – gradually, with appropriate transitional periods.[33]

That was the basis for the prohibition in Article 5(1) and the (apparently permitted) derogation in Article 5(2). However, as the court noted, the Directive was silent as to the length of time during which those differences may continue to be applied as a result of which Member States had made use of the option and permitted insurers to apply the unequal treatment without temporal limitation.[34] The court found that position to be contrary to Articles 21 and 23 of the Charter such that it was considered to be invalid on the expiry of the five-year transitional period. The CJEU concluded that 'Article 5(2) is invalid with effect from 21 December 2012'.[35] Thus, as at that date, insurers were not permitted to take gender into account when setting premiums based on risk. The Equality Act 2010 (Amendment) Regulations 2012[36] came into force on 21 December 2012 to reflect the judgment in *Test Achats*. Paragraph 22 in Part 5 of Schedule 3 was thereby repealed.

As for the remaining age and disability exemptions, where they apply insurers will be able to refuse to provide cover or charge higher premiums expressly on the basis that those characteristics increase the prospective insured's risk profile. Regarding age, the Explanatory Notes to the EA 2010 gives the following example: 'An insurer can lawfully quote higher motor insurance premiums for young men if this is based on actuarial and statistical up-to-date data that is published so that customers can see the information that justifies proportionate differences in male and female premiums and benefits.'[37] That is an important statement both for policies which might differentiate between insureds on the basis of one of the exempted characteristics, and beyond insofar as it makes clear that insurers cannot simply use algorithms that happen to have found a correlation between age and risk or certain disability and risk;[38] rather, the insurer must be able to show that, at least in the aggregate, the evidence clearly supports the proposition that insureds with these characteristics present higher risks for certain types of insured loss.[39] Findings made by algorithms must thus be actuarially supported

[32] Case C-236/09; [2011] Lloyd's Rep IR 296.
[33] ibid, paras 22–23.
[34] ibid, para 26.
[35] ibid, paras 32–34.
[36] SI 2012/2992.
[37] EA 2010, Explanatory Notes, para 720.
[38] Regarding disability, differential treatment must be based on reasonable and reliable information: Explanatory Notes, para 714.
[39] Regarding disability, as the Services Code of Practice observes at paras 13.77–13.78: 'Information which might be relevant to the assessment of the risk to be insured includes actuarial or statistical data or a medical report. An insurer cannot rely on untested assumptions or stereotypes or generalisations in respect of a disabled person.' It goes on to give the following example: 'A disabled man with HIV+ applies to a motor

and publicly available if they are to permit differential provision of insurance cover to people based on age or disability: insurers ought to be obliged to show that the correlation relied upon is not mere coincidence but has a basis in evidence. Moreover, an expanded duty of good faith on insurers based on the transparency values set out in the GDPR is further supported by the requirement that differentiation between insureds must be supported by publicly available actuarial data. This is another statutory basis to which the courts can refer in the analogical development of the common law duty of good faith.

Even then, if insurers are permitted to rely on actuarially based differentiation in the aggregate, that still permits risk profiling based on the level of risk presented by the group, and not the individual. However, the very promise of big data is to provide insurers with the means of assessing the risk of each individual insured. If a motor insurer has black box telematics data that shows an individual insured is a much lower risk than that of the group considered in the aggregate, it is submitted that the insurer cannot avail of the exemption. But where actual data about the risk profile of an individual is not available from a connected device, an individual insured may have greater difficulty in rebutting the presumption that his risk profile is equivalent to the group's risk profile. The Explanatory Notes to para 21 of schedule 3 to the EA 2010 give the following two contrasting scenarios regarding a disabled applicant:

> A disabled person with cancer applies for a life insurance policy. The insurance company refuses to provide life insurance cover based on a medical report from the person's doctor which provides a prognosis on the person's condition.
>
> An insurer charges higher premiums for travel insurance for a person with a particular disability because actuarial evidence suggests that people with this disability are at increased risk of having a heart attack.

There can be no objection to the former example. The refusal is based on the prognosis in the report, not the prospective insured's disability. The latter is more problematic. For although it is supported by actuarial data, if that individual is not at an increased risk, his cover will be increased by reference to the group assessment. This differential treatment is permitted by the exemption in para 21 of Schedule 3. But that again provides a further example of why identification of individual risk factors used by an insurer should be disclosed to an insured so that the insured has a chance to challenge the application of the group's risk profile to him.

B. Equality Act Remedies

The remedies available under the EA 2010 are administered by the County Court and the Employment Tribunal, in the first instance. Were an insured to complain that

insurer for comprehensive insurance on his motor car. In completing the application form he states that he has HIV+. The insurer is willing to provide him with insurance cover but only at a higher premium than would be charged to other motorists. The decision to charge a higher premium is not based on any sound data about HIV+ or on the man's actual medical condition. It is likely to be unlawful.' Services Code of Practice, para 13.79. On HIV status, in April 2018 it was revealed that the mobile app Grindr was sharing user data, including HIV status, with third-party companies: https://www.theguardian.com/commentisfree/2018/apr/04/grindr-gay-men-hiv-status-leak-app.

profiling by an insurer gave rise to unlawful discrimination, he would seek a remedy from the County Court.[40] This section therefore focusses on the remedies available in that court. Remedies in the County Court are governed by s 19 of the EA 2010. Section 19(2) provides that the County Court has power to grant any remedy which could be granted by the High Court (a) in proceedings in tort; and (b) on a claim for judicial review. Section 19(4) provides that an award of damages may include compensation for injured feelings, whether or not that award includes compensation on any other basis. Stigma damages[41] and aggravated damages[42] will also be available. Breach of s 13 or s 19 of the EA 2010 is a breach of a statutory duty and damages are assessed in broadly the same way as compared with other claims for breach of statutory duty.[43] Exemplary damages may be awarded in an appropriate case,[44] in particular where there has been oppressive, arbitrary, or unconstitutional action by servants of the Government, or where the defendant's conduct has been calculated to make a profit notwithstanding his likely liability for the wrong.[45] The only exception to the unconditional power to award damages or compensation in the County Court relates to claims of indirect discrimination in that where, following a finding of unlawful indirect discrimination, the Court is satisfied that the provision, criterion, or practice was not applied with the intention of discriminating against the claimant, the court should not make an award of damages unless it has first considered whether to make any other disposal.[46] In addition to damages awards, the new power to issue remedies under Part 54 of the Civil Procedure Rules enables the County Court to issue quashing orders, prohibiting orders and mandatory orders as well as granting declarations or issuing injunctions.[47]

IV. Competition Law Remedies

Three consumer-related competition issues arising from the use of big data in insurance are (i) portability of data; (ii) lowering of privacy standards; and (iii) comparability of products. The ability to port one's insurance-related data has now been addressed by the GDPR, as discussed in chapter six.[48] Lowering of privacy standards was an

[40] The major difference in the scope of the remedies regime between the County Court and the Employment Tribunal is that only the latter have the power to make an 'appropriate recommendation': EA 2010, s 124(2)(c). On a finding of unlawful discrimination, the Tribunal will be able to make recommendations for the purpose of 'obviating or reducing the adverse effect of any matter to which the proceedings relate' on the complainant or any other person. This may enable the Tribunal to make recommendations designed to address institutional issues giving rise to discrimination.

[41] *Chagger v Abbey National Plc and Anor* [2009] EWCA Civ 1202; [2010] ICR 397.

[42] *Alexander v The Home Office* [1988] ICR 685; [1988] 1 WLR 268.

[43] For example, damages will be assessed by reference to whether the discrimination caused the loss and not whether it was foreseeable: *Essa v Laing Ltd* [2004] ICR 746; *Hurley v Mustoe (No 2)* [1983] ICR 422.

[44] The other conditions for the award of exemplary damages must be satisfied in the ordinary way: *Virgo Fidelis Senior School v Boyle* [2003] IRLR 268.

[45] *Kuddus (AP) v Chief Constable of Leicestershire Constabulary* [2001] 1 UKHL 29; [2002] 2 AC 122.

[46] EA 2010, s 119(5)–(6)

[47] EA 2010, s 119(2)(b).

[48] Some EU Member States have gone beyond the requirements of the GDPR. Germany requires insurers jointly to maintain a set of statistics, including on car accidents, which smaller firms would not be able to compile on their own: *The Economist*, 'Fuel of the Future', 6 May 2017.

eventual feature of the merger between Facebook and WhatsApp (and their respective datasets). The GDPR now imposes standards to protect privacy but the amount of personal data one is required to give away as a condition of access to such social networks or messaging services itself raises a competition issue: privacy standards are a non-price, quality-related aspect of competition: this will relate more to insurers' sources of information (where higher privacy standards on social media platforms and web browsers might mean certain personal data may not be available to data brokers or insurers) than to insurers' use of that information (insurers are more likely to keep such information as they further refine an individual insured's risk profile).[49] The issue of comparability is rather more intractable. The increasingly personalised nature of insurance products makes it harder for consumers to compare one offer of insurance as against another. The Joint Committee of Supervisory Authorities' Final Report on Big Data noted that 'the increasing individualisation of products and services would reduce the capacity to compare between products/services'. It observed that some respondents

> also considered that risks will be heightened with the further development of AI/machine learning and the opacity of algorithms (making it more and more difficult for firms to explain the logic of decisions/services or products offered to clients). The capacity to compare products/services could be further diminished also in cases of firms applying different big data tools to similar offers, thereby increasing information asymmetry to the detriment of consumers.[50]

This lack of comparability is plainly a regulatory issue and will require mechanisms for data/comparison tools to be introduced should the problem not be resolved by the market. However, the lack of comparability does not itself give rise to any cause of action.

Competition law causes of action will be available where an insured can point to: (i) a breach of the Chapter I Prohibition under the Competition Act 1998 (CA 1998) or Article 101 of the TFEU (broadly, collusive behaviour between insurers); or (ii) a breach of the Chapter II Prohibition under the CA 1998 or Article 102 of the TFEU (broadly, abuses of dominance). The particular competition law issue depends on the particular use being made of big data analytics. Nazzini points out that

> Big data competition concerns typically relate to the possibility that data possessed by incumbents may give them a competitive advantage against new entrants. In contrast, competition concerns arising through the use of algorithms typically relate to whether such use may enhance the potential for coordination on pricing or, in exceptional circumstances, whether a dominant firm may use algorithms to engage in abusive conduct, for example to exclude

[49] The German Competition authority began an investigation into Facebook's privacy notice in March 2016. The Bundeskartellamt argued that Facebook may have exploited its dominant position in 'the market for social networks' by adopting terms of service on the use of user data 'in violation of data protection provisions'. Users, in the Bundeskartellamt's reasoning, would not accept Facebook's terms of service, should the company enjoy a lesser degree of market power. It may be the first major attempt to bring data protection and pure privacy issues into the realms of competition law: https://www.bundeskartellamt.de/SharedDocs/Meldung/EN/Pressemitteilungen/2016/02_03_2016_Facebook.html.

[50] Joint Committee of Supervisory Authorities' Final Report on Big Data, 15 March 2018 https://www.esma.europa.eu/sites/default/files/library/jc-2018-04_joint_committee_final_report_on_big_data.pdf, paras 39–40.

rivals or price discriminate so that downstream undertakings are placed at a competitive disadvantage.[51]

Many of these competition battles will therefore not take place between an insured and insurers, albeit that individual insureds will be harmed if anti-competitive conduct precludes new entry, fewer products and higher prices.[52] Rather, it will fall to other insurers to bring competition claims to contend why these access and behavioural issues causes anti-competitive harm.

A. Access to Data as an Essential Input[53]

The case law relating to whether an undertaking required to give access to some essential input that it has developed or created is careful not to intervene in such a way as to disincentivise those actors from creating or generating those inputs in the first place.[54] Data is an input and may be an essential input for insurers as risk profiling increasingly uses predictive analytics. This is particularly the case where data is 'rivalrous' and 'excludable'. Data is non-rivalrous where 'the use of the data by one person does not diminish the stock [or the value] of the good'.[55] Data is non-excludable if one person cannot prevent another person accessing that data. Predictive analytics cannot operate absent large datasets providing information on insureds. If the biggest insurers (or technology companies who might venture into insurance markets) amass large datasets, that creates market power and may give rise to significant barriers to new entry. Again that is particularly so if the data is (i) rivalrous (which risk-related information will, to an extent, be: the more insurers can access that data, the less of a competitive advantage will be available as between those insurers through its use); and/or (ii) excludable (where insurers can obtain a competitive advantage if only they have

[51] Renato Nazzini, 'The Italian Big Data Inquiry: A question of Method', Competition Policy International, 2017: https://www.competitionpolicyinternational.com/wp-content/uploads/2017/09/CPI-Nazzini.pdf.

[52] It might be queried whether, if a particular insurer acquires a dataset unique to the individual insured and then refuses cover, that individual dataset might constitute a unique product market on which that insurer, being the only insurer who has that dataset, is dominant. Such an argument is almost certain to fail: different insurers with very similar and overlapping datasets (albeit each slightly differently constituted) will not each be in a position of dominance since those datasets are substitutes, as are the insurance products based on those datasets. With competition between insurers based on different but overlapping datasets, no insurer is likely to be found to be dominant.

[53] This question can arise under Article 101 (in exclusive vertical supply agreements), Article 102 or in the context of mergers but will most often arise in relation to abuse of dominance cases.

[54] See Case C-6/73 *Commercial Solvents v Commission* [1974] ECR 223; Joined Cases C-241/91 and C-242/91P *RTE & ITP v Commission* [1995] ECR I-743 ('*Magill*'); Case C-7/97 *Oscar Bronner GmbH Co KG v Mediaprint* [1988] ECR I-7791; Case C-418/01 *IMS Health GmbH & Co OHG v NDC Health GmbH & Co KG* [2000] ECR I-5039; and Case T-201/04 *Microsoft v Commission* [2007] ECR II-3601. The test that the courts will apply as to whether a dominant undertaking's refusal to grant access to an essential input is difficult to meet. The refusal must: (i) concern a product which was (technically or economically) indispensable for carrying on the business in question (ie there is no actual or potential substitute for the facility); (ii) prevent the appearance of a new product or hamper innovation; (iii) exclude all effective competition in the relevant market; and (iv) not be justified by objective considerations.

[55] OECD, 'Exploring the Economics of Personal Data: A Survey of Methodologies for Measuring Monetary Value', OECD Digital Economy Papers No 220, 2013, 25.

access to certain data). The question of access to datasets was considered by the European Commission in *UK/Everything Everywhere/JV* (the M-commerce Decision).[56] In that case the Commission considered whether the collection of personal data through mobile wallet services offered by the three leading wireless operators in the UK would raise competition concerns. Specifically, the Commission assessed whether the joint venture vehicle established for the purposes (JV Co) would foreclose competing providers of data analytics or advertising services by combining personal information, location data, response data, social behaviour data and browsing data such as to create a unique database that would become an essential input for targeted mobile advertising that no competing provider of mobile data analytics services or advertising customer would be able to replicate. The Commission rejected this theory of harm, concluding that:

> JV Co would indeed be able to collect a broad range of consumer information, which will be very valuable for its (mobile) data analytics services and advertising services. However, many other strong and established players are also able to offer comparable solutions to the JV Co. Therefore, other providers of advertising services competing with the JV Co would not be foreclosed from an essential input and the creation of the JV Co would not have a negative effect on competition on the market for (mobile) data analytics, as well as for market research services or marketing information services.

By contrast, the Commission accepted commitments to divest copies of the combined database to third parties so that credible competition would remain in the marketplace following the merger of Thomson and Reuters.[57] A key question will be whether the necessary datasets can be replicated. If so, there will be no denial of access to an essential input. Commissioner Vestager recently confirmed that the Commission's interventions should be limited to exceptional circumstances, stating that: 'the problem for competition isn't just that one company holds a lot of data. The problem comes if that data really is unique, and can't be duplicated by anyone else. But really unique data might not be that common.'[58] In the context of the insurance industry, the fact that insurers can acquire technologies to develop datasets and the availability of data on a non-exclusive basis from data brokers is likely to mean that a challenge by smaller insurers to obtain access to the datasets of larger insurers is unlikely to succeed. There may also be disputes between insurers operating on downstream insurance markets seeking data from data aggregators (such as Google or Facebook or large data brokers) on upstream data markets. Whereas arguments based on data being an essential input

[56] Commission Decision of 7 March 2013 in Case COMP.6314.

[57] Commission Decision of 19 February 2008 in Case COMP/4726. Both Thomson and Reuters sourced, aggregated and disseminated real-time and historical market data and other types of financial content to respond to the needs of financial professionals, such as traders and sell-side people in the on-trading floor space, of investors on the buy-side and of analysts in the off-trading floor space within banks, investment funds and corporations. See also Commission Decision of 6 December 2016 in Case COMP/M.8124 *Microsoft/LinkedIn*, where the Commission considered the possible negative impact on competition resulting from the concentration of datasets. In particular, the Commission assessed whether a possible denial of access to LinkedIn's database by Microsoft could harm competition.

[58] Speech by Commissioner Vestager at the Data Ethics event on Data as Power, Copenhagen, 9 September 2016: https://ec.europa.eu/commission/2014-2019/vestager/announcements/making-data-work-us_en.

may equally fail, insurers may be able to obtain a remedy where upstream data providers are in a dominant position on the relevant data markets and abuse that dominance through price discrimination[59] by favouring certain downstream suppliers to the detriment of downstream rivals.[60]

B. Competition Issues as a Result of the Use of Algorithms

Algorithms give rise to conduct concerns since they are designed to make decisions in light of the data they analyse. They can thus engage in conduct that is collusive (where there is a growing issue of algorithms communicating with each other leading to information sharing and price fixing).[61] As discussed in chapter three, a key concern over the use of algorithms was to enable insurers to discriminate as to the price of cover. As we saw, price discrimination would occur where two identical risks were being offered at different prices for the same level of cover,[62] something big data is facilitating to a greater degree. There can be no objection if the differing cost of cover reflects the fact that one insured is a greater risk than another: here there is no price discrimination in the strict sense since the greater risk gives rise to a greater potential cost. However, it is potentially more problematic to charge someone who presents an identical risk to another on the basis that insurers have non-risk-related information suggesting that the former will pay more. Price discrimination is usually discussed in the context of abuse of dominance; the problem facing individual insureds is that the general insurance markets in the UK are highly competitive: no single motor, life or property insurer is dominant in the market for those individual risks. Insureds who suffer price discrimination because insurers' deeper profile suggests that they are less price conscious will thus not be able to bring a claim. More realistic is a contention that such practices violate the Principles in the PRIN Handbook or the rules in ICOBS such as to entitle individual insureds to bring a claim under FSMA or, more realistically, a complaint to the FOS. Moreover, the FCA has indicated that where the impact of price discrimination as between savvy and non-savvy (or vulnerable) purchasers of goods or services has sufficient distributional effects, it will exercise its consumer protection powers to intervene in such practices.[63]

[59] Art 102(2)(c) gives as an example of abuse 'applying dissimilar conditions to equivalent transactions with other trading parties, thereby placing them at a competitive disadvantage'. Discriminatory refusals to supply and preferential terms and conditions are further examples of abusive discriminatory treatment. Price discrimination is not, in and of itself, a prohibited exclusionary abuse: Case C-209/10 *Post Danmark* EU:C:2012:172, para 30. But where it is used as an exclusionary tool by a dominant firm, such conduct may be abusive.

[60] The idea of tech companies entering insurance markets is not a theoretical concern: see the Joint Committee of the European Supervisory Agencies Final Report on Big Data in March 2018, paras 27–30 and see also the discussion of the implications of tech companies entering the market by the Geneva Association, 'Big Data and Insurance: Implications for Innovation, Competition and Privacy', March 2018, 21–23.

[61] E Ezrachi and M Stucke, *Virtual Competition* (Cambridge, MA, Harvard University Press, 2016).

[62] And see the discussion by the FCA in Occasional Paper No 22, 'Price Discrimination and Cross-subsidy in Financial Services', September 2016 and further the discussion by the OFT in 'Personalised Pricing: Increasing Transparency to Improve Trust', May 2013.

[63] FCA, Occasional Paper No 22, 4. An example of the FCA exercising such powers was to cap pay-day loans where the loss of access to such loans by some was outweighed by the prevention of consumer harm

C. Market Investigations

Section 134 of the Enterprise Act 2002 gives the CMA the power to undertake market investigations where any feature, or combination of features, of each relevant market prevents, restricts or distorts competition in connection with the supply or acquisition of any goods or services in the United Kingdom or a part of the United Kingdom.[64] If upon finding any market features having adverse effects on competition in the relevant market, the CMA has power to impose structural remedies. Were data markets to become concentrated and lead to the restriction of access to data (whether by insurers or others), the CMA could in principle undertake a market investigation to identify features of the market having adverse effects on competition.

V. Data Law Remedies

A. GDPR, Article 82[65]

Article 82 of the GDPR is entitled 'Right to compensation and liability' and provides:

1. Any person who has suffered material or non-material damage as a result of an infringement of this Regulation shall have the right to receive compensation from the controller or processor for the damage suffered.[66]
2. Any controller involved in processing shall be liable for the damage caused by processing which infringes this Regulation. A processor shall be liable for the damage caused by processing only where it has not complied with obligations of this Regulation specifically directed to processors or where it has acted outside or contrary to lawful instructions of the controller.
3. A controller or processor shall be exempt from liability under paragraph 2 if it proves that it is not in any way responsible for the event giving rise to the damage.
4. Where more than one controller or processor, or both a controller and a processor, are involved in the same processing and where they are, under paragraphs 2 and 3, responsible for any damage caused by processing, each controller or processor shall be held liable for the entire damage in order to ensure effective compensation of the data subject.[67]
5. Where a controller or processor has, in accordance with paragraph 4, paid full compensation for the damage suffered, that controller or processor shall be entitled to claim back from the other controllers or processors involved in the same processing that part of the compensation corresponding to their part of responsibility for the damage, in accordance with the conditions set out in paragraph 2.

thereby forgone. That was an exceptional case. Big data can be used to achieve the same effects but may be less discernible.

[64] The CMA's 'Guidelines for market investigations: Their role, procedures, assessment and remedies (CC3)' explains how it will go about determining whether any feature of the market has an adverse effect on competition: https://assets.publishing.service.gov.uk/government/uploads/system/uploads/attachment_data/file/284390/cc3_revised.pdf.

[65] And see Recital (146).

[66] DPA 2018, s 168 provides that for the purposes of Art 82, 'non-material damage' includes distress.

[67] That is, liability will be joint and several.

6. Court proceedings for exercising the right to receive compensation shall be brought before the courts competent under the law of the Member State referred to in Article 79(2).

Article 82 relates to breaches of the GDPR. Judging from the case law under s 13 of the DPA 1998, Article 82 (unlike FSMA, s 138D) will not preclude individuals bringing claims under Article 82 from also relying on the same facts to establish causes of action for other pre-existing common law duties. Therefore if an insured could show that an act that might also amount to a breach of the GDPR equally constituted a breach of a common law duty, there would appear to be no reason why the individual could not vindicate that overlapping common law claim. Indeed, the courts have recognised that data breaches also constitute the tort of misuse of private information. That being so, there is no reason in principle why the same facts might not also give rise to a common law claim in damages for breach of the insurers' duty of good faith (if such a remedy were otherwise available, a question discussed in section VI below).

B. Case Law under s 13 of the DPA 1998

The case law under s 13 of the DPA 1998 will provide a guide as to the way in which damages claims will be resolved under Article 82. Section 13 had provided:

(1) An individual who suffers damage by reason of any contravention by a data controller of any of the requirements of this Act is entitled to compensation from the data controller for that damage.

(2) An individual who suffers distress by reason of any contravention by a data controller of any of the requirements of this Act is entitled to compensation from the data controller for that distress if –

    (a) the individual also suffers damage by reason of the contravention, or
    (b) the contravention relates to the processing of personal data for the special purposes.

(3) In proceedings brought against a person by virtue of this section it is a defence to prove that he had taken such care as in all the circumstances was reasonably required to comply with the requirement concerned.

Vidal-Hall v Google Inc[68] considered claims for misuse of private information[69] and breach of the DPA 1998. The claims arose out of the fact that Google had secretly tracked private information about the users' internet usage via the use of cookies without their knowledge or consent and given that information to third parties. That was contrary to its publicly stated position that such activity would not be performed without users' consent. The users sought damages under s 13 of the DPA 1998 for distress; they had suffered no pecuniary loss. That gave rise to a question as to the meaning of

[68] [2015] EWCA Civ 311.

[69] There is no law of privacy as such in the UK (*Wainright v Home Office* [2003] 3 WLR 1137). However, a right to privacy has long been recognised and protected under English law in different guises, most recently as a result of the requirement to give effect to Art 8 of the European Convention on Human Rights. The central cause of action, which has been developed out of the law of confidence (most notably in the leading case of *Campbell v Mirror Group Newspapers Ltd* [2004] 2 AC 457), is known as 'misuse of private information'.

'damage' for the purposes of s 13 and whether there could be a claim for compensation without pecuniary loss. It was common ground that on a literal interpretation, the users were not entitled to recover damages under s 13 because their claims did not fall within either s 13(2)(a) or s 13(2)(b) of the DPA 1998. The Court of Appeal noted that insofar as 'damage' was referred to in the Data Directive[70] that raised the question of whether it included the EU concept of 'moral damages', an unfamiliar concept in the UK which encapsulated a right to compensation for breach of an individual's non-pecuniary rights. Although there was no presumption in EU law that 'damages' included 'moral damages', and although there was nothing to suggest that the Data Directive required compensation for such damages to be paid, the natural and wide meaning of 'damage' in Article 23 of that Directive included 'moral', non-pecuniary damage, such as distress.[71] It was important that data subjects had an effective remedy for a distressing invasion of privacy falling short of pecuniary damage, especially as Articles 7 and 8 of the Charter made specific provision for the protection of personal data. The Court observed:

> Since what the Directive purports to protect is privacy rather than economic rights, it would be strange if the Directive could not compensate those individuals whose data privacy had been invaded by a data controller so as to cause them emotional distress (but not pecuniary damage). It is the distressing invasion of privacy which must be taken to be the primary form of damage (commonly referred to in the European context as "moral damage") and the data subject should have an effective remedy in respect of that damage. Furthermore, it is irrational to treat EU data protection law as permitting a more restrictive approach to the recovery of damages than is available under article 8 of the Convention. It is irrational because … the enforcement of privacy rights under article 8 of the Convention has always permitted recovery of non-pecuniary loss.
>
> Additionally, article 8 of … the Charter … makes specific provision for the protection of the fundamental right to the protection of personal data: "everyone has the right to the protection of personal data concerning him or her". It would be strange if that fundamental right could be breached with relative impunity by a data controller, save in those rare cases where the data subject had suffered pecuniary loss as a result of the breach. It is most unlikely that the Member States intended such a result.[72]

Following the decision in *Vidal-Hall*, Mitting J subsequently considered the issue of damages under s 13 of the DPA in *TLT v Secretary of State for the Home Department*.[73] In this case, the Home Office had published quarterly statistics about its family returns process by which those with children who had no right to remain were returned to their country of origin. In addition to anonymised statistics uploaded onto the government website, the Home Office mistakenly uploaded the spreadsheet of raw data on which those statistics were based. The spreadsheet included the personal

[70] Directive 95/46/EC on the protection of individuals with regard to the processing of personal data and on the free movement of such data.

[71] The court came to this conclusion in reliance on the opinion of the Advocate General and the CJEU in Case C-168/00 *Leitner v TUI Deutschland GmbH & Co KG* [2002] ECR I-2631. See [70]–[82].

[72] ibid, [77]–[78].

[73] [2016] EWHC 2217 (QB).

data of approximately 1,600 lead applicants[74] for asylum or leave to remain, including their names, ages, nationality, the fact of an asylum claim, immigration removal status and the regional office which dealt with their case, from which the general area in which they lived could be inferred. The defendants accepted that posting of the details amounted to a misuse of private and confidential information and was a breach of the DPA 1998. It was not disputed that, subject to proof, damages were recoverable for 'distress' at common law and under s 13 of the Act. The judge held that damages claims could be brought under both the common law and statutory causes of action notwithstanding the fact that the claimants were not named. The Court of Appeal dismissed the Home Office's subsequent appeal.[75]

Article 82 of the GDPR and s 168 of the DPA 2018 now explicitly state that it is possible to recover for 'non-material' damage. Following the above line of cases, it appeared that claimants would be able to bring compensation claims even if they have not suffered a financial loss arising from an infringement of the GDPR and potentially even if the damage suffered is very minor. This could include claims for, inter alia, distress, anxiety and reputational damage. However, some doubt has been cast on that proposition by the court in *Lloyd v Google LLC*.[76] In that case, the claimant sought to bring an action as a representative of a class of other residents in England and Wales who alleged that Google breached s 4(4) of the DPA 1998 by secretly tracking the internet activity of Apple iPhone users, collating and using the information it obtained by doing so, and then selling the accumulated data. The method by which Google was able to do this is generally referred to as 'the Safari Workaround'. On damages, the Court distinguished cases like *Vidal-Hall*, acknowledging there could be instances where a loss of control over personal data may have significantly harmful consequences such as to give rise to non-material damage. In *Lloyd* the claimant argued that the result of the collection, collation, aggregation and sale of the data obtained via the Safari Workaround was that individuals in the class (as well as others) received advertising that was targeted by reference to their interests and preferences, as inferred from the personal data that was processed in those ways, when they would otherwise have received advertising that was not so targeted. But the court held that the Particulars of Claim did not contain any complaint that this amounted to damage. The claimant's pleaded case on damage relied on (a) the lack of consent or knowledge of the representative claimant and each member of the claimant class to the defendant's collection and use of their personal data; (b) the fact that such collection and use was contrary to the defendant's public statements; (c) the fact that such collection and use was greatly to the commercial benefit of the defendant; and (d) the fact that defendant knew or ought to have known of the operation of the Safari Workaround from a very early stage during the relevant period. Plainly this was not a claim for pecuniary loss but for non-material damage. The court, however, held that it had 'not been shown any European authority to support the view that any of those three categories contains a description of something that, of itself, counts as

[74] They were 'lead' applicants in the sense that they were the named applicant who applied on behalf of themselves and other family members.

[75] [2018] 4 WLR 101.

[76] [2018] EWHC 2599 (QB).

"damage" for this purpose'. It was held that the concept of 'damage' had been extended in various contexts to cover 'non-material damage' but only on the proviso that 'genuine quantifiable damage has occurred'.[77] The court held that there was no rule or principle that substantial damages are invariably recoverable and must always be awarded for misuse of private information, just because the tort has been committed, and regardless of the nature of the wrong and its impact on the individual claimant.[78] '[T]he Court cannot make an award of "vindicatory" damages, merely to mark the commission of the wrong', saying this was 'wrong in principle'.[79] In the circumstances, it appears that the fact of a data breach alone will be insufficient to constitute the tort of misuse of information or give rise to damages under that tort or Article 82 of the GDPR.

While Article 82 makes no significant changes as regards the damages regime that operates under the GDPR, and while there have been no cases decided under the GDPR at the time of writing, the case law in this area is developing quickly. What is clear is that a claimant could not seek to pursue a damages claim for breach of the GDPR under the tort of negligence where remedies are available pursuant to the tort of misuse and under the GDPR itself. And if *Lloyd v Google* is followed, damages for the privacy invasion alone may not constitute damage for which any compensation may be payable.

VI. Insurance Law Remedies at Common Law

Two questions arise. First, does the breach of the common law duty of disclosure give rise to a claim in damages? And second, does the common law duty of disclosure import a duty to take reasonable care in relation to the discharge of that duty? Both questions are directed to the duties as they apply to insurers. Insofar as the 2012 and 2015 Acts set out in detail insurers' remedies for breach of the consumer and non-consumer insured's pre-contractual duties, there can be no question of insurers being able to bring common law claims for breach of those statutory duties in addition.

A. Damages and the Duty of Disclosure

The duty of disclosure as it applies to insurers is a common law duty. Insofar as insurers are subject to a duty, the person to whom that duty is owed, the insured, has a right to the discharge of that duty. If it is to be meaningful, the insured must have the ability to vindicate that right; he will only be able to do so if the common law provides him with a remedy.[80] But the only remedy that was previously available in respect of the breach of the duty, namely avoidance, was abolished by section 14 of the IA

[77] ibid, para 61, citing *Leitner* and *Vidal-Hall*.
[78] ibid, para 66.
[79] ibid, para 68.
[80] As Holt CJ said in a judgment approved by the House of Lords in *Ashby v White* (1703) 2 Ld Raym 938, 953, 'if the plaintiff has a right he must of necessity have the means to vindicate it and a remedy if he is injured in the enjoyment or exercise of it'.

2015.[81] Does it follow that insureds have no remedy, including as to damages, in respect of insurers' breach of duty?

The courts have determined that a breach of the duty of good faith does not of itself give rise to a right to damages. However, in *Banque Financière de la Cité,* Steyn J at first instance concluded that such a right existed:

> Once it is accepted that the principle of the utmost good faith imposes meaningful reciprocal duties, owed to the insurers and vice versa, it seems anomalous that there should be no claim for damages for breach of those duties in a case where that is the only remedy.

He made this ruling on the basis of 'justice and policy considerations': where there is a right, there should be a remedy.[82] He observed that 'occasionally judges have to apply an existing remedy to a new situation when a right already recognised by the law is not adequately protected'.[83]

However, Steyn J's conclusion on damages was rejected when the case came before the Court of Appeal. Slade LJ said damages for breach of the duty of good faith would only be available if there had been a tort. The court, however, held that the failure to observe good faith was not tortious, stating it could find 'no authority whatever to support the existence of such a tort'.[84] Furthermore, the court offered four reasons why such a tort should not be created:

(1) First, relief for non-disclosure shares an origin in the courts of equity with duress and undue influence. These do not give rise to a claim for damages. The difficulty with this is that the duty of disclosure arises at common law, rather than equity.[85]

(2) Second, when an underwriter (or possibly an insured) is seeking to avoid a policy for non-disclosure, the effect of the non-disclosure on the underwriter in question is not considered – merely the effect on a notional prudent underwriter.[86] This approach would not translate easily to a scenario where damages were sought. The difficulty with that argument is that it is superseded by the decision in *Pan Atlantic Insurance Co Ltd v Pine Top Insurance Co*, which created or confirmed

[81] The Law Commission noted in the December 2009 Issues Paper at para 3.19: 'The problem with the duty of good faith in insurance contracts is that only one remedy is available for breach: avoidance. This means that the contract is declared void from the start. The insurer may refuse all claims and simply return the premium. It is a one-sided remedy, of far more use to the insurer than to the insured.'

[82] *Banque Financière de la Cité SA v Westgate Insurance Co Ltd* [1990] 1 QB 665 at 706.

[83] *Banque Financière de la Cité SA v Westgate Insurance Co Ltd* [1991] 2 AC 249 (HL).

[84] Slade LJ, p 780.

[85] As MacDonald-Eggers and Picken point out, although it is true that the courts, including the House of Lords, have treated the remedy of avoiding insurance as originating in equity 'to prevent imposition', the availability of the remedy in equity would mean that it must be discretionary. And while of course the remedy of avoidance puts the innocent party to his election, and one which he will not be able to exercise in circumstances of delay or acquiescence (each conditions or bars imposed by equity in relation to the analogous remedy of rescission), '[t]his is at odds with the hundreds of cases heard by the courts where avoidance has existed as a remedy at the election of the innocent party without reference or reliance on an overriding jurisdiction of the court to deny or impose conditions on the relief. Certainly, the existence of the remedy in the Marine Insurance Act 1906 supports the absence of an overriding discretion to deny such relief'. P MacDonald-Eggers and S Picken, *Good Faith and Insurance Contracts* 4th edn (Abingdon, Informa Law, 2018), para 4.58.

[86] Where the requirement of materiality is an objective question for the court.

the requirement of inducement which is considered in relation to the particular underwriter in question.[87]

(3) Third, section 17 of the MIA 1906 does not refer to damages being available for a breach of the duty of good faith, merely avoidance. In this regard, Slade LJ said: 'We think the clear inference from the Act of 1906 is that Parliament did not contemplate that a breach of the obligation would give rise to a claim for damages in the case of such contracts. Otherwise it would surely have said so. It is not suggested that a remedy is available in the case of non-marine policies which would not be available in the case of marine policies.'[88] The court reasoned that in order to decide whether the remedy of damages is available, one has to start by analysing the nature of the right: 'If the banks' right to full disclosure of material facts is founded neither on tort nor on contract nor on the existence of a fiduciary duty nor on statute, we find it difficult to see how as a matter of legal analysis it can be said to found a claim for damages.'[89] The difficulty with this argument is that the absence of any reference to damages in section 17 should not be decisive as the 1906 Act was a codification of the then common law and is thus open to the further development of the common law. In other circumstances the courts have been content to read words into the Act.[90]

(4) Fourth, the obligation to disclose is an absolute one, not being dependent on any fault. Given its reciprocal nature, the availability of a damages remedy could cause hardship – for example if an insurer sought damages from an insured for an innocent non-disclosure. The difficulty here is that the fact that fault is not required for a breach should not be decisive in determining that its breach cannot give rise to damages: a party can be liable for damages for breach of warranty without any fault; some tortious duties give rise to damages on a strict-liability basis.[91] Moreover, insurers cannot, as noted above, claim damages from insureds where their own specific remedies for breach have been set out comprehensively in CIDRA 2012 and IA 2105.

Banque Financière was appealed to the House of Lords, but decided on a different point. However, the House of Lords approved the Court of Appeal's reasoning on this issue. Despite some contrary suggestions,[92] it seems to be accepted as settled

[87] The subjective test of inducement operates – whether this was the purpose behind its development or not – to soften the harshness of the remedy of avoidance.

[88] *Banque Financière de la Cité SA v Westgate Insurance Co Ltd* [1990] 1 QB 665 781, *per* Slade LJ. This despite admitting that, where the breach occurs after the insured event, avoidance and return of the premiums 'may be quite inadequate', at 775.

[89] ibid, at 776.

[90] And again see *Pan Atlantic Insurance Co Ltd v Pine Top Insurance Co* [1995] 1 AC 501, where the House of Lords held that inducement was an implied requirement in ss 18 and 20.

[91] These criticisms of the Court of Appeal's reasoning in *Banque Financière* are based on and set out in more detail in J Birds, *Birds' Modern Insurance Law* 7th edn (London, Sweet & Maxwell, 2007), at p 142.

[92] *HIH Casualty & General Insurance Ltd v Chase Manhattan Bank* [2001] EWCA Civ 1250; [2001] 2 Lloyd's Rep 483 at [48], [164] and [168]; see also *Conlon v Simms* [2006] EWHC 401 (Ch); [2006] 2 All ER 1024 (partnership).

law in England and Wales that even deliberate non-disclosure does not give rise to liability in damages, as deceit requires a positive misrepresentation.[93]

It would appear that there are perhaps two overarching reasons why breach of the duty of good faith has never been held to give rise to an action for damages: (i) the potential harshness on insureds; and (ii) the existence of avoidance as the stipulated remedy for the duty's breach. The two are of course related, since the harshness of an action in damages against an insured arises precisely because it would add to insurers' remedial armoury in circumstances where (a) avoidance was already a one-sided remedy that operates as a nuclear option for insurers but which provided no real assistance to the insured;[94] and (b) given that breaches of the duty of good faith would, it was posited,[95] be committed far more frequently by the insured than insurers, damages would be a remedy ordinarily being sought by insurers.

The concern over the impact of damages on the insured is reflected in the following passage of the Law Commission's March 2010 Issues Paper where it considered there to be two policy arguments for not creating a general tortious liability for bad faith in insurance contracts. The first was that such a liability could operate harshly against the insured:

> Where a policyholder has failed to disclose a relevant matter, or made a misrepresentation, we think the insurer's remedies should be limited to avoiding the policy or refusing all or some of the claim, and we have set out recommendations to this effect. We do not wish to see insurers also suing policyholders for damages.[96]

Nevertheless, the Law Commission asked for views on whether the law should be reformed to provide insureds with a claim for damages against an insurer who acted in bad faith through late payment of claims or taking spurious defences to resist claims. It considered that such reforms would only apply where the insurer acted dishonestly, or so unreasonably that no reputable insurer could act in that way. Insurers' strongly objected to the proposals on damages, and these views persuaded the Law Commission to shelve plans for any general, if limited, damages liability for the breach of the duty of good faith.[97]

[93] *HIH Casualty & General Insurance Ltd v Chase Manhattan Bank* [2003] UKHL 6; [2003] 1 All ER (Comm) 349 at [75] ('nondisclosure (whether dishonest or otherwise) does not as such give rise to a claim in damages'); *Manifest Shipping Co v Uni-Polaris Insurance Co, The Star Sea* [2001] UKHL 1; [2003] 1 AC 469 at [46].

[94] In that in circumstances where the insurer is in breach of duty, they will usually be circumstances where the insured most needs the policy to subsist and respond, rather than be unwound *ab initio*.

[95] That, however, views the relative knowledge of the parties from a pre-big data perspective.

[96] Law Commission Issues Paper 6, 'Insurance Contract Law, Damages for Late Payment and the Insurer's Duty of Good faith', 2010, para 4.46. If damages were generally available, it would be open to insureds to sue insurers; the Law Commission had concerns with this as well. The second policy objection was that tortious damages were 'more generous than those for breach of contract. For example, while contract damages are restricted to losses within the contemplation of the parties at the time of the contract, under tort law, the victim is entitled to any loss foreseeable at the time of the tort (that is when the insurer acts in bad faith). At this point, the insurer is likely to have much greater knowledge of the insured's specific circumstances. In the USA, the courts of several states have been prepared to provide high levels of tort damages against insurers. Although British courts would be unlikely to award damages on such a scale, we can understand concern about potentially unrestricted increases in an insurer's liability.' Issues Paper 6, 2010, para 4.47.

[97] Law Commission Issues Paper 6, 2010, para 26.62. Remedies for insurers' late payment of claims is dealt with in the Insurance Act 2015, s 13A on a stand-alone basis by way of an implied term specifically concerning payment of claims.

The constraining effect of the existence of the remedy of avoidance on the development of a remedy in damages is reflected in the decision of the Court of Appeal in *HIH v Chase Manhattan*,[98] which adopted similar reasoning to the Court of Appeal in *Banque Financière* as to why breach of good faith was not a tort. There, Lord Justice Rix held that it was not fair, just and reasonable to impose on insurers and insureds a duty of care to each other when a proposal is put. In giving his reasons (with which other members of the court agreed) he said that the theme running through the *Banque Financière* case:

> is that the duty of good faith which the law has developed especially for contracts of insurance provides a remedy only in avoidance and not in damages. It seems to me to follow that *if the established remedy in this context grants no remedy in damages* … then it ought to require very special factors to make it just and reasonable to superimpose an additional remedy for the narrower case of a negligent misrepresentation [emphasis added].[99]

That observation was made in relation to the question, addressed below, of whether the duty of good faith disclosure also imports a duty of care.[100] Lord Justice Rix's analysis of that further question was predicated on the existence of avoidance as the only remedy for breach of the duty of disclosure. His point was simply that if the common law had consciously set itself against damages as a remedy for breach of the duty of disclosure, then that approach would effectively be side-stepped by imposing a concomitant duty of care in relation to the discharge of the duty of disclosure. However, if avoidance is no longer available as a remedy for a breach of the duty of disclosure, leaving no other effective remedy for any breach of that duty by insurers, what are the remedial consequences of such a breach?

It is submitted that there is no good reason in policy or principle as to why insurers' breach of the good faith duty of disclosure should go unremedied. With respect to the Law Commission, the concerns raised by insurers that a general damages remedy would lead to the development of US-style damages claims with substantial punitive damages are unconvincing. As the Law Commission recognised, damages could be controlled by ordinary rules.[101] That point is *a fortiori* if the basis for the duty is neither contract nor tort but a stand-alone duty whose scope and extent can be controlled by the common law. The point has been made that as the law allows for the recovery of damages for many breaches of the duty of good faith on differing juristic bases, such as deceit, negligent misrepresentation and breach of an implied term, it should allow damages to be recovered for any breach of the common law duty of good faith.[102]

[98] *HIH Casualty and General Insurance Ltd and others v Chase Manhattan Bank and others* [2001] EWCA Civ 1250; [2001] 2 Lloyd's Rep 483.

[99] At [68].

[100] Albeit a duty of care not to make negligent misrepresentations, rather than a duty of care in relation to the exercise of a duty of disclosure: but the point of principle as to what damages would issue is the same.

[101] para 26.62 referred to control by 'normal contract rules'. That would be right if the basis for damages for breach of the duty of good faith disclosure was an implied term. But as noted above, that will never explain pre-contractual breaches. In fairness to the Law Commission, this discussion was in the context of post-contractual breaches where insurers unreasonably delayed the payment of claims and where an implied term analysis might be available.

[102] MacDonald-Eggers and Picken, *Good Faith and Insurance Contracts*, above n 85, para 16.162.

Moreover, not only is the absence of any extant remedy a compelling reason to permit the development of a damages remedy; so too is the fact that as insurers are increasingly required by regulatory obligations – at least in a consumer context – to provide certain pre-contractual disclosure (both proactively pursuant to the right to be informed and reactively pursuant to the right of access), they will have regulatory liabilities for breach of those obligations. The common law can again reason by analogy in developing a damages remedy for breach of the duty of disclosure. Specifically, if the duty of disclosure ought to be expanded to reflect the transparency principles embodied in data and consumer law, then it is a short further step to develop a damages remedy for breach of that expanded duty of good faith. It is no argument to contend that because damages are available in a regulatory setting, they should not be available for breach of an expanded duty of disclosure. That is because, while overlapping, the aims of the FSMA 2000, the GDPR and consumer law are not identical to those of the duty of good faith in insurance law. Further, Parliament cannot, in providing certain damages remedies in the regulatory and data context, for that reason be taken to have intended that there should be no similar development in the common law of insurance. An insured may not be able to fully recover his losses as a result of a breach of the expanded duty of disclosure under those statutory forms of redress.[103] Most obviously in that regard is the fact that those remedies are simply not open to non-consumer insureds. Nor should an insured be forced to shoehorn a claim for damages into a cause of action for misuse of private information (although absent a remedy in damages for breach of the insurers' duty of good faith, some insureds may be able to rely on that cause of action). A remedy in damages for breach of the duty of disclosure could be shaped to respond to loss specifically occasioned as a result of a breach of that duty. Developing the common law in this manner by analogy with statutory developments would lead to a more consistent and coherent set of duties and remedies than currently exists.

B. Damages and a Duty to Take Care

If, contrary to the above, damages for breach of the duty of disclosure continues to be resisted, what scope is there for the common law to develop a duty of care in relation to the discharge of the duty of disclosure? In that regard, it is not being suggested that a duty of care is a necessary incident of the duty of disclosure. As was argued by the insured banks in *Banque Financière*, a duty of utmost good faith and a duty of care are overlapping but not coincident duties; a breach of the duty of utmost good faith may not be negligent, and the relationship of insurer and insured would not in all circumstances entail that a duty of care was owed by the former to the latter. It will be necessary to separately ascertain whether the criteria for the establishment of a duty of care are met on the facts of the particular relationship between insurer and

[103] And to the extent that an insured were to bring a claim and additionally plead damages for regulatory breach, plainly the common law, applying the compensatory principle, would not permit double recovery and would discount a common law damages award where recovery was permitted in relation to loss caused by regulatory breaches.

insured. In order to establish liability in negligence, a duty of care must be owed by one person (here, the insurer) to another (the insured), a failure to comply with that duty and the occurrence of foreseeable damage resulting from the breach. Insofar as this question has arisen in the context of the scope of the duty of good faith disclosure, the first question as to whether a duty is owed has been determinative. Again, the key authority is *Banque Financière*. At first instance Steyn J found a duty of care to exist. He held that it was 'reasonably foreseeable by the insurers that there was a manifest and obvious risk that a failure to disclose would lead to financial loss' by the insured. As discussed in chapter five, the insured bank contended that the failure of the defendant insurers to advise them of the fraudulent activities of the insured's agent, and of which insurers were aware, was a breach of a duty of care that insurers owed to the insured. Steyn J found that there was sufficient proximity between the insurer and insured insofar as they had an established business relationship and as a result of the fact that they owed the insured a duty of good faith. The Judge held that 'the existence of a duty of care is consistent with the requirement of good faith and fair dealing, which ought to govern the relations between insured and insurer'.[104] The judge considered it would be fair, just and reasonable to find that such a duty existed because it was consistent with the understanding of the market and, as the non-disclosure in the case was one of fraud, such a duty would 'help to expose and eradicate fraud in the London insurance market'.[105]

The Court of Appeal overturned this decision, holding that the mere existence of a commercial relationship by itself could not give rise to a duty of care in tort, although it was held that economic loss was reasonably foreseeable on the facts. Further, the Court of Appeal rejected the suggestion that 'the nature of the contract as one of utmost good faith can be used as a platform to establish a common law duty of care' on the simple basis that the MIA 1906 did not provide any remedy for a breach of the duty other than avoidance and, in some circumstances, the return of premium. The court held that

> we are not satisfied that justice and reasonableness imperatively require the finding of a duty of care owed by [insurers] to [the insured]. This is not a case in which the denial to the banks of a cause of action in negligence will mean that the banks are left without any remedy at all.[106]

Thus the availability of the remedy of avoidance had a clear bearing on the finding that no duty of care arose.[107] The court further held that the insurers had not voluntarily assumed responsibility for any failure to disclose, although the court acknowledged in principle that liability could attach to a failure to disclose where a duty of care could be established.[108] Such voluntary assumption of responsibility was held to be marked by

[104] *Banque Financière de la Cité SA v Westgate Insurance Co* [1990] 1 QB 665 at 715.
[105] ibid, 715.
[106] ibid, 801E.
[107] As did the fact that the broking firm would have been vicariously liable for the insured's agent's deceit. The alternative remedy also told against a duty of care against insurers.
[108] The Court of Appeal suggested that had insurers positively represented to the banks that its agent was honest, then there might have been a claim in negligent misstatement, applying the principles in *Hedley Byrne v Heller and Partners* [1964] AC 465 (at 739D).

conduct 'signifying that he assumes responsibility for taking due care in respect of the statement or action'.[109] The Court of Appeal was influenced by the fact that as the parties could define their mutual obligations by contract, it was not for the law of tort to fill any gaps left in the contractual arrangements. The law in this regard has moved on and the existence of a contractual relationship is no bar to the finding that parties negotiating a contract might owe each other duties of care. That was already clear as a result of the decision in *Hedley Byrne & Co v Heller & Partners*[110] but extended by the House of Lords in *Henderson v Merrett Syndicates Ltd*.[111]

The House of Lords concluded that even if insurers owed a duty of care to disclose to the insured the fraud of its agent, the breach of that duty in the circumstances did not cause the loss which the banks suffered.[112] Specifically, much of the analysis was driven by the factual conclusion that the failure to inform the insured was not causative insofar as the loss was due to the insured's own fraudulent customer, rather than its fraudulent agent. In those circumstances, holding insurers liable for loss caused by an assumed breach which was not causative would have generated some bizarre results.[113] Lord Templeman addressed the question of the duty of care by observing that the underwriter

> did not do or say anything. [The underwriter] did not by his silence assume any responsibility for the trustworthiness in the future of [the insured's fraudulent agent] and the banks did not rely on his silence as a representation that [the underwriter] believed [the agent] to be honest.[114]

Lord Jauncey considered the issues through the question of whether insurers' knowledge of the fraud of the insured's agent was material to the risk insured such that it would be covered by the duty of disclosure. As discussed in chapter seven, Lord Jauncey considered that insurers were only obliged to disclose facts that would tend to reduce the risk to the insured (such matters being 'material'). He distinguished Lord Mansfield's example of a ship that had already arrived in port as follows:

> In the present case the risk to the insured was the inability, otherwise than by reason of fraud, of [the bank's customer] and his companies to repay the loan to the banks. [The insured's agent's] dishonesty neither increased nor decreased that risk. Indeed it was irrelevant thereto. It follows that the obligation of disclosure incumbent upon [the underwriter], as the insurer,

[109] ibid, 795.

[110] [1964] AC 465.

[111] [1994] 3 WLR 187.

[112] The insured bank had argued that a duty of care is owed by a person engaged in commercial dealings with another to disclose a fraud relating to those dealings of which the other is a victim, if he acquires actual knowledge of and appreciates that the victim is ignorant. The insured cited, for that proposition, cases such as *McKenzie v British Linen Co* (1881) 6 App Cas 82 and *Ogilvie v West Australian Mortgage and Agency Corporation Ltd* [1896] AC 257. The question arising more generally for present purposes is whether a duty of care is owed more generally upon discharging the duty of disclosure and not just in those instances where insurers might become aware of a fraud of which the insured was a victim.

[113] *Henderson v Merrett Syndicates Ltd* [1994] 3 WLR 187, 277F–H.

[114] ibid, 273E–F. His Lordship continued: 'It would be strange if in these circumstances one party to a contract owed a duty in negligence to the other party, to warn the other party of his suspicions of former misconduct by the agent of that other party; it would be stranger still if the party who failed to disclose his suspicions were liable in damages for the misconduct of the agent thereafter.'

> did not extend to telling the banks that their agent … was dishonest. If the obligation of disclosure incumbent upon parties to a contract of insurance could ever per se create the necessary proximity to give rise to a duty of care, a matter upon which I reserve my opinion, it is clear that the scope of any such duty would not extend to the disclosure of facts which are not material to the risk insured. It follows that the appellants' reliance on the duty of disclosure does not assist them to establish negligence on the part of [the underwriter].

The insured's contention that the existence of the duty of disclosure created the necessary proximity between insurers and insured to give rise to a duty of care on the part of the former to the latter could not therefore get off the ground. However, Lord Jauncey did not dismiss *in limine* the proposition that the existence of a duty of disclosure provided the necessary proximity on which to found a duty of care in tort.

The reasoning in *Banque Financière* was discussed by Rix LJ in *HIH Casualty and General Insurance Ltd & Ors v Chase Manhattan Bank & Ors.*[115] His Lordship recognised that the problem case so far as breaches of the duty of good faith were concerned arose when the insured was complaining of such a breach. He said:

> If there is a problem at all, it lies in the highly unusual case where the breach of good faith is on the other side, as in Banque Keyser, and it is the *assured* who is seeking a remedy. It is of course well established that the duty of good faith is mutual and reciprocal, as Lord Mansfield himself recognised in the seminal case of Carter v Boehm (1766) 3 Burr 1905 at 1909/1910 and as is now also recognised in section 17 of the MIA 1906. Where, then, the insurer is in breach, avoidance of the contract is perhaps unlikely to provide a satisfactory result for the assured, who would thus lose his insurance: but it is not possible to be confident about that, since examples of a breach by an insurer are so rare, and the usual example cited, for instance by Lord Mansfield and others, of the insurer taking a premium for a risk which he knows no longer exists, is one where avoidance and the recovery of the premium will entirely satisfy the assured. The fact remains that, save perhaps in a highly unusual, even unprecedented case, the duty of care adds nothing to the right of avoidance. Thus there is no need for a new remedy in the present case, where the current dispute is generated not by any lacuna in available remedies but by the insurers' concern to demonstrate that an exclusion clause has not covered all available heads of damage.

However, further to the abolition of avoidance, there is now a lacuna in the remedies available to the insured. A duty of care would thus make all the difference. Nor is it safe to assume that a remedy will only be needed for rare or exceptional cases.[116] As this book has argued, if insurers profile insureds using big data analytics, the duty of good faith disclosure should apply to all risk-related factors that insurers rely upon in proposing terms of cover: as insureds will not know what is being relied upon, and as some of those risk factors may not apply or may be incorrect such as to be risk-reducing, they ought to be disclosed even on Lord Jauncey's narrower formulation of insurers' duty of disclosure. Whether they are or not will, however, only be known if they are disclosed to the insured as the GDPR recognises. Indeed, Rix LJ conceded that there would be justification for a remedy in damages in a case where an insured had been

[115] [2001] 2 Lloyd's Rep 483.

[116] Even that is not a good argument since a remedy for breach of a common law right should issue in the exceptional case.

misled as to the basis on which the insurance was entered into, but did not press the point precisely because he thought the remedy would rarely be needed:

> From the point of view of an assured who has been caused by the insurer's negligence to enter a contract of insurance, the position is probably more complex, for if he had not been misled he might have been able to buy a better or more suitable policy in time: that is the example contemplated above of an assured for whom avoidance is not in itself a solution. It seems to me, however, that the case of such an assured is so rare, that it would be wrong to base any general decision upon it.[117]

If that assumption is falsified by insurers' increasing use of big data analytics, finding a duty of care for loss caused by the negligent use of those tools becomes – on Rix LJ's hypothesis – entirely plausible.

In broad terms, three tests have been used in deciding whether a defendant who has caused pure economic loss to a claimant owed him a duty of care in tort. The first is whether the defendant assumed responsibility for what he said and did vis-a-vis the claimant, or is to be treated by the law as having done so. The second is commonly known as the threefold test:[118] whether loss to the claimant was a reasonably foreseeable consequence of what the defendant did or failed to do; whether the relationship between the parties was one of sufficient proximity; and whether in all the circumstances it is fair, just and reasonable to impose a duty of care on the defendant towards the claimant (the test that underpinned the analysis of whether insurers could owe a duty of care in the *Banque Financière* litigation).[119] Third is the incremental test, based on the observation of Brennan J in *Sutherland Shire Council v Heyman*.[120] The inter-relationship between the three tests was discussed by Lord Bingham in *Customs and Excise Commissioners v Barclays Bank plc*.[121] However, in a trilogy of decisions in 2018 the Supreme Court has in effect killed off the threefold *Caparo* test for a duty of care. In *Michael v Chief Constable of South Wales Police*[122] Lord Toulson referred to Lord Bridge's warning in *Caparo* that the concepts of proximity and fairness 'were not susceptible of any definition which would make them useful as practical tests, but were little more than labels to attach to features of situations which the law

[117] His Lordship's proposed solution for the exceptional case was that the insured could look to his broker for a remedy where unsuitable cover had been purchased. However, where the basis upon which an insurer has unilaterally profiled a risk and offered terms on that basis, then without the duty of disclosure expanding to accommodate this change in insurance practice, those insureds who seek cover through a broker will be no better off: neither they, nor the broker would, without more, be able to call for that information. A consumer insured could do so in reliance on the right of access under the GDPR. But that right may not always or often be exercised; and again it will not assist a non-consumer insured.

[118] Said to have been established in *Smith v Eric S Bush* [1990] 1 AC 831 and *Caparo Industries plc v Dickman* [1990] 2 AC 605.

[119] What Kirby J in *Perre v Apand Pty Ltd* (1999) 198 CLR 180, para 259, labelled 'policy'.

[120] (1985) 157 CLR 424, 481.

[121] [2007] 1 AC 181 paras 4–8. His Lordship considered that assumption of responsibility (which was to be determined objectively) was 'a sufficient but not a necessary condition of liability, a first test which, if answered positively, may obviate the need for further inquiry'. Lord Bingham considered that the threefold *Caparo* test provided 'no straightforward' answer to the question of whether a duty was owed, and further considered that the incremental test was 'of little value as a test in itself, and is only helpful when used in combination with a test or principle which identifies the legally significant features of a situation'.

[122] [2015] UKSC 2.

recognised as giving rise to a duty of care'.[123] He observed: 'Paradoxically, this passage in Lord Bridge's speech has sometimes come to be treated as a blueprint for deciding cases, despite the pains which the author took to make clear that it was not intended to be any such thing.' As a consequence, a duty may now only be established either through an assumption of responsibility or by application of the incremental test.

Applying that test to a world in which insurers underwrite risk by reference to big data analytics, it is contended that a duty of care may well arise from insurer to insured. The basis upon which doubt has traditionally been expressed over whether insurers can owe a duty of care to the insured is the information asymmetry between the parties which has historically put insurers at a disadvantage. The leading textbook on the duty of good faith puts the point thus:

> There is a greater difficulty in imposing a duty of care on the insurer to be observed towards the insured than on the insured as it is more often the insurer who relies on the information given to him by the insured, rather than the reverse. Indeed it is more common for the insured to rely on his broker or insurance agent than the insurer himself.[124]

It is the thesis of this book that that asymmetry is rapidly and radically changing. The call for an expansion of insurers' common law duty of disclosure arises because of the various means by which insurers may profile an individual risk without recourse to the insured. Risk factors which might only be known to insurers and which, because of their reliance on those factors render them material to the risk (at least as perceived by insurers), are the basis for the terms on which cover is offered. In light of how risk may be profiled on a predictive and automated basis, the test of materiality should, as has already been contended, be sufficiently wide to require disclosure not just of matters which, from the perspective of the insured, reduce the risk but of matters which increase the risk from the perspective of insurers. Insofar as the insured may not be the provenance of much risk-related information, and where that information is no longer crossing a line, the insured may, without more, be unaware of what has been taken into account, why or the impact those matters have on the price and scope of the cover.

If there is an expansion in the duty such that insurers are obliged to disclose risk-related information to insureds, it is submitted that insurers should be required to discharge that duty with reasonable care. Insofar as consumer insureds have a right of access, a right to correct and a right to erase, those rights correspond to an overarching duty on insurers to process data not just transparently but with reasonable care and skill. Indeed an expanded duty of disclosure and a duty of care in tort go hand in hand in this further respect: if insurers are obliged to disclose what information they have sourced and considered relevant to the pricing of the risk, and insureds are

[123] At para 106. The point was reinforced in *Robinson v Chief Constable of West Yorkshire* [2018] UKSC 4, where Lord Reid then referred to Lord Toulson's 'landmark judgment' in *Michael* in which Lord Toulson had explained that 'the whole point of the *Caparo* case … was to repudiate the idea that there is a single test which can be applied in all cases in order to determine whether a duty of care exists, and instead to adopt an approach based, in the manner characteristic of the common law, on precedent, and on the development of the law incrementally and by analogy with established authorities.' These two judgments were referred to by Lord Wilson giving the leading judgment in *NRAM Ltd v Steel* [2018] UKSC 13.

[124] MacDonald-Eggers and Picken, *Good Faith and Insurance Contracts*, above n 85, para 16.157.

entitled to correct any errors revealed by that information, insurers are more likely to write risk on a sound basis. By involving the insured, the prospect of insurers becoming liable on the basis of a breach of a duty of care are commensurately reduced.[125]

The existence of a duty of care appears to be supported by the House of Lords decision in *South Australia Management Corporation v York Montague Ltd.*[126] In that case, which was concerned with the measure of damages resulting from the negligence of a property valuer, Lord Hoffman, giving the judgment of the court, distinguished the positions of a person who had undertaken a duty of providing information to another so that the recipient may decide upon a particular course of action and a person who has undertaken the duty of providing advice to another as to the course of action to be taken. In the latter case, the adviser as a matter of principle will be responsible for the foreseeable consequences of the wrong course being pursued, assuming of course he has failed to exercise reasonable care. In the former case, the giver of information will be responsible for the information being wrong. If an insurer is bound to disclose information, particularly where the purpose of that disclosure is to inform the insured's decision as to whether to enter a contract of insurance on the proposed terms or not, then it would seem to follow that such a duty should be discharged with reasonable care and skill. The position of a party to an insurance contract who is bound to accurately disclose material facts is the same as the person reliant on being provided with accurate information as explained by Lord Hoffman. This common law analysis is reinforced by the regulatory obligations that overlay consumer insurance.

In those circumstances, given the duty of disclosure to which insurers are subject, it is arguable that in the exercise of that duty – given the purposes for which it must be discharged – insurers assume a responsibility for the reliability of the information disclosed. The analogous regulatory duties of access and erasure reinforce the argument that insurers assume a responsibility to discharge its common law duties with reasonable care and skill. The position is *a fortiori* in respect of an expanded duty of disclosure. Alternatively, and notwithstanding the passing of the threefold *Caparo* test, if an insurer carelessly misrepresents to an insured that it had taken account only risk factors that in fact applied to the insured and/or which increased the risk and/or for which it had an actuarial basis for relying, it is suggested that an insured might yet recover his foreseeable losses as a result of entering the contract in reliance on those representations. Relying on the incremental approach, if the insured could in principle make a claim for negligent misrepresentation, he should also be able to recover for negligent non-disclosure of the risk factors that insurers took into account when proposing the cover and where those factors did not pertain to the insured and/or were not objectively material and/or were unsupported by any actuarial evidence where, had disclosure been made, the insured would have sought cover elsewhere or on better terms. There are, in addition, several scenarios where a remedy in damages might be necessary post-contractually: if insurers again rely on incorrect data in

[125] Much as the use of provisional, or minded-to decisions operate to try and reduce the risk of public law errors being made in public-law decision making.

[126] [1996] 3 All ER 365. This point is made forcefully by MacDonald-Eggers and Picken, *Good Faith and Insurance Contracts*, above n 85 at 16.158.

refusing a claim, where, having exercised reasonable care and skill they would have identified the error and accepted the claim, the insured ought, it is submitted, be entitled to recover his pecuniary losses from the refusal of cover. Finally, and again by analogy with the non-material damages provisions under s 13 of the DPA 1998 and now Article 82 of the GDPR, the courts might also consider the appropriateness of awards of damages for non-pecuniary losses; where dignitary harms have been caused by misuse of data that has resulted in a refusal of cover or discriminatory profiling, awards for distress should, perhaps, also be available at common law.

PART V

Conclusions

9

Conclusions

I. Summary of the Argument

As insurers acquire more and better information about certain individual risks, the duty of good faith disclosure will increasingly operate in a residual manner as regards the insured, who will be required to disclose only private knowledge of matters material to the risk. And then only insofar as a duty of disclosure is maintained on insureds at all. By contrast, the new data-driven information asymmetries will multiply the instances in which the duty will require disclosure by insurers. Specifically, an expanded duty of good faith disclosure ought to require insurers to explain all risk-related information relied upon, have an actuarial basis for the use of that information and identify which risk factors have a particular bearing on the price of a particular risk. This expanded duty of good faith will mitigate some (but not nearly all) of the consequences of the increasing segmentation of risk pools including the risks that: (i) an insured is included in the wrong risk pool; or (ii) the particular risk pool itself is founded on a misconception (for example, as to the relevance of a particular risk factor to the incidence of insured loss).

The use of big data analytics gives rise to the wider issue of access to insurance. As the segmentation of the risk pool accelerates, the price of cover will increasingly reflect the actual risk posed by particular individuals. In principle, that seems fair: insured A will no longer be required to subsidise insured B's unhealthy choices (for example). But the use of these tools will allow for the exploitation of vulnerable insureds if non-risk-related information enables insurers to offer the same cover at higher prices (price discrimination). More invidiously, it may also permit insurers to adopt a new range of risk proxies that lead to certain groups of insureds being penalised because of their membership of those groups; a combination of where someone shops, their credit rating, and who their Facebook friends are may lead to new forms of direct and indirect discrimination. And ultimately, society will have a more fundamental question to ask as to whether a solidarity- or mutuality-based approach is more appropriate for certain types of insurance in a big data age. Insurers' wider access to what is often deeply sensitive personal information raises the question of whether there are certain categories of information that insurers should not be permitted to take into account in underwriting decisions at all. Alternatively, even if insurers are permitted to access that information (which, beneficially, will enable more accurate actuarial assessment) will regulation be necessary to impose price-capping or generate new forms of cross-subsidy? The use of genetic data will provide the acid test. The distinction between choice and circumstance will guide us only so far. An insured has no control of his DNA but it is not completely irrelevant to the provision of life insurance to know that a particular insured has a single-gene early onset disorder that would, in pure economic terms, render that insured uninsurable or insurable at a price that most insureds would be unable to pay. In the UK insurers are monitoring the instances where they are required to provide cover and pay out in such circumstances. As the economics become clearer and the technology is more widely used, the pressure will grow to allow insurers to utilise this information – and insurers in the UK will argue that processing sensitive (including genetic) information is a substantial public interest for the purposes of para 20 of Schedule 1 to the DPA 2018. A pure market-based solution would be deeply unfair. Insurers may obtain explicit consent to access that data compatibly with the GDPR; but if they adopt a 'no disclosure, no cover' model, some individuals will, without more, be rendered uninsurable. Insofar as this deeply sensitive information is risk-related information, it is unlikely that insurers' duty of good faith would operate to constrain insurers from accessing or using such information. It will fall to regulators to develop controls that balance actuarial relevance against the wider social need to enable individuals to obtain affordable access to cover. What regulation is required will depend on how these developments play out. But regulation in some form seems inevitable.

II. Detailed Conclusions

A. Impact of Big Data on Duties of Disclosure by Insureds and Insurers

In *Carter v Boehm*, Lord Mansfield expounded the duty of good faith disclosure in such a way as to make clear that insurers could not expect to be wholly passive recipients of all matters material to the risk. They were expected to make inquiries to inform themselves about the nature of the risk, save that that duty did not extend to matters wholly within the private knowledge of the insured. Although the rationale for the duty remained the same throughout its common law development, the retrenchment in the nineteenth and twentieth centuries redrew the parties' respective disclosure obligations in a way that permitted insurers to become passive recipients of information about the risk. However, 250 years later, it might be considered that the law is in the process of restoring the division of responsibility in relation to the investigation and disclosure of risk adopted by Lord Mansfield. Two factors contribute to that restoration: (i) first, the reforms of 2012 and 2015 modify the duty of disclosure as it applies to consumer insureds and remove the harsher consequences of its breach (for all insureds); (ii) second, and perhaps more importantly, is the impact that insurers' use of big data will have on the question of whether there is an information asymmetry and if so in what direction it lies. Insurers' use of big data analytics vastly increases what they know or can be taken to know about the risk. It follows that the duty will come to have a commensurately reduced application in relation to the insured: it will be the unusual and unknowable aspects of the risk that (at least in the UK, business) insureds will still be obliged to disclose, matters that remain within their private knowledge. However, the use of those techniques raises the prospect that insurers may come, in many respects, to know as much and sometimes more than the insured. While it is of course true that an individual insured may well know many of the primary facts that are the subject of insurers' risk profiling, there is much that the insured will not know: the insured will not know what primary facts the insurers have mined nor, therefore, the relevance of those facts to the risk or their accuracy at the time at which they are accessed; the insured will not know what inferences or secondary facts that insurers have drawn from those primary facts or therefore what conclusions have been drawn about the level of risk; the insured will not know to what extent, if at all, insurers have sought to establish the accuracy of those primary risk factors or whether there is any actuarial basis for insurers' reliance on those factors and whether they relate to that individual or the wider cohort that exhibits those same factors. All of these matters are within the private knowledge of insurers. It is the thesis of this book that insofar as they are either objectively risk-related or have subjectively had an impact on insurers' assessment of the risk, they ought to be disclosed pursuant to the insurers' duty of good faith. Insurers are no longer passive recipients of information; they have embraced big data analytics to improve their competitiveness and in order to avoid adverse selection. Having done so, it is suggested that insurers' duty of good faith, in a big data age, must be expanded to require disclosure of (i) all factors that insurers have both accessed and taken into account when assessing an individual risk; (ii) all actuarial or other evidence demonstrating why those risk factors suggest a greater likelihood of insured loss; (iii) any evidence as to why insurers consider certain risk factors apply specifically to the individual insured (over and above any actuarial evidence that may support such reliance); and (iv) the relative impact each such risk factor has on the price and scope of the proposed cover (a duty that would not require insurers to show the specifics of a calculation or underlying proprietary information but merely that factors A, B and C are what increased the insured's premium significantly). It is not difficult to imagine that these details could be set out in an annex to any offer of insurance the same way that insurers are required by: (i) ICOBS 5 and 6 to establish an insured's needs and demands and set out a summary of the cover; and (ii) by Article 20 of the IDD to provide enhanced details of the scope of cover in a Product Information Document. These are regulatory requirements imposing informational duties on insurers in relation to the product. However, the information that ought to be disclosed pursuant to insurers' expanded duty of good faith is risk-related information. In addition, having provided such information pre-contractually (or prior to the determination of any claim) insurers must give the insured an opportunity to consider and correct that information; in addition, if the decision was taken on a fully automated basis, the insured should be able to ask an individual insurer or underwriter to reconsider the proposal in light of any further information or evidence the insured might provide in response to insurers' proposed use of the risk factors identified.

The reforms in the UK of 2012 and 2015 do not address insurers' duty of good faith disclosure. Plainly the law does not require insurers to use big data in the way they are increasingly using it. However, insofar as insurers' duty continues beyond the 2012 and 2015 reforms, the common law needs to grapple with the implications of those practices. In a world where insurers proactively seek out more and more information about individual risks and increasingly use complicated algorithms to assess the nature and extent of those risks, the law of insurance ought to require insurers to be transparent about the data that they have acquired for those purposes, and to permit insureds to correct any errors that would arise from the use of that data. This book has referred, in particular, to data law and the requirements of the GDPR as supporting and indeed encouraging such a development. There is no reason in principle why the common law cannot have regard to the specific rights and duties established under the GDPR as reflective of the more broadly applicable principles of transparency and fair dealing that mediate the relationship between service providers and their customers. Moreover, in circumstances where the duty of good faith exists without a remedy, now is the time for the courts to consider how insurance law ought to protect insureds from the use and abuse of big data analytics. There is a need for the common law to develop: as we saw in chapters six and seven, data law does not provide a complete suite of remedies for insureds in relation to insurers' use of big data: in particular, the GDPR only applies to consumer insureds and even then it is unlikely to require disclosure of risk-related information to the extent required by an appropriately expanded duty of good faith. It is plainly not being suggested that insurance law co-opts the entirety of the GDPR's framework within its compass. Rather, it is merely suggested that the fundamental rights of information and access can shed light on what an expanded duty of good faith requires of insurers who use big data analytics in insurance decisions. To that end, the EDPB observes that data subjects should be given information about their risk profile, for example, in which segments or categories they are placed.[1] Moreover, some of these rights are already envisaged within the context of insurance law as can be seen from the Concordat between the government and the insurance industry over the use of genetic data in underwriting: specifically, the Concordat gives customers the right to ask an insurer to provide information on whether, and if so, how, a predictive test result has contributed to an underwriting decision. It also confers a right of appeal against an underwriting decision and a right to have a complaint dealt with fairly. These rights mirror those conferred under the GDPR. Indeed transparency already plays its part in insurance law as a result of the transparency conditions that arise under s 17 of the IA 2015 should insurers wish to contract out of the protections afforded to non-consumer insureds under that Act. But transparency works both ways: if insurers want the benefit of contracting out, insureds should equally be given the information insurers hold to enable them to decide whether to contract at all, or to contract on more favourable terms where the proposed cover is shown to be based on inaccurate information or inferences.

Further support for the suggestion that the duty should be expanded to extend to business as well as consumer insureds arises from the fact that data law is expanding to confer data rights on legal persons: (i) the Committee of Ministers' Recommendation Rec(2002)9 on the protection of personal data collected and processed for insurance purposes said, as far back as 2002, that: 'Member States may extend the application of the principles set out in this Recommendation to the collection and processing of data relating to groups of persons, associations, foundations, companies, corporations and

[1] WP251, Guidelines on Automated individual decision-making and Profiling for the purposes of Regulation 2016/679, p 16.

any other bodies consisting directly or indirectly of individuals, whether or not such bodies possess legal personality';[2] (ii) the ePrivacy Regulation will extend data rights to legal persons.

The common law development of insurers' duty of good faith disclosure will occur incrementally. But the common law will have to go further and develop suitable remedies. For the same reasons set out above, and as amplified in chapter eight, relying on remedies under the FSMA 2000, the CRA 2015 and the GDPR will only cover consumer insureds and cannot be assumed to provide redress for all forms of loss that an insured might suffer as a result of a breach of the expanded insurers' duty of good faith. Those remedies will in any event not extend to business insureds for whom a refusal to, for example, pay a claim on an incorrect basis may have very serious financial consequences.

B. Insurers' Expanded Duty of Disclosure as a Means of Mitigating Incorrect Profiling

A wider issue arising out of insurers' use of big data relates to the relationship of the individual insured to wider groups of insureds constituted by reference to a new range of risk factors. The balance between knowledge and ignorance has traditionally been struck at the level of statistical knowledge about large groups. Big data analytics promises to enable insurers to profile an individual insured on the basis of a wider array of risk-related information that is personal to each insured. This not only allows insurers to more accurately write risk, but frees individual insureds from the tyranny of group profiling (at least for those who benefit from the more accurate – and lower – premiums). We saw how the atomisation of risk profiling had, as its corollary, the increased segmentation of risk pools. But insurance on some basic level depends on the pooling of risk – and premiums – to ensure that there is cover for those who in fact suffer insured loss. That will continue within and across the larger number of smaller risk pools. Insurers will continue to benefit from the law of large numbers across the wider range of risk pools. But the promise of big data will be undermined if new risk proxies are based on correlations that have not been actuarially established. Such proxies will, absent actuarial evidence, lead to individuals being profiled by reference to these new groups in a way that might be significantly more invidious than traditional, actuarially-based profiling: (i) first, insureds may be placed in the wrong risk pool; and (ii) second, the particular risk pool into which the insured is placed is itself wrong in conception (for example, where it is founded on risk factors that correlate with insured loss but where there is no proof, even in the aggregate, that such risks cause or materially

[2] Committee of Ministers' Recommendation Rec(2002)9 on the protection of personal data collected and processed for insurance purposes, para 2.4. It is interesting to observe, in 2018, that the Council of Europe was contemplating the consequences of risk profiling in 2002. In the same recommendation it refers at Recital (3) to: 'the fact that automated processing of personal data for insurance purposes is increasingly widespread, not only for the preparation, conclusion, implementation and termination of insurance, but also to facilitate rational and economic management of insurance and to fight against fraud'. https://www.coe.int/t/dg3/healthbioethic/texts_and_documents/Rec(2002)9E.pdf.

contribute to such loss). Insureds may continue to pay the wrong price but on the basis of potentially irrelevant or inaccurate information. The proposed expanded duty of good faith would meet this risk in part by requiring insurers to ensure that the individual insured is given the opportunity to show why the proposed cover is based on an inaccurate profile and would also require insurers to provide an actuarial basis for the new risk factors sought to be relied upon. This reflects the market rationale that in part justifies the duty: promoting accuracy in market transactions will ensure that those markets operate more efficiently. The duty, so expanded, thus operates to require insurers using big data to do so in a way that fulfils its promise. It is likely that big data will itself quickly develop evidence of relationships between risk proxies and insured loss in a manner akin to traditional, actuarially based underwriting. While not providing evidence in relation to any particular individual, it will provide a non-arbitrary basis upon which insurers might rely on newly established correlations. Yet even then, insureds should be permitted to contest the application of new risk proxies to them, particularly where there is a risk that some of the new risk factors are proxies for discrimination. That would not impose a materially greater burden on insurers than that which is required under the GDPR and ultimately, insurers can reject the insured's response and either repeat the proposed terms of cover or walk away.

C. Regulatory Consequences: Access to Insurance

But even if insurers use correct information in a non-discriminatory way, risk segmentation raises a wider question over access to insurance. Intuitively, insureds who choose to engage in more risky conduct or who live less risk-conscious lives ought to be responsible for those choices. Why should those who consciously get out and exercise subsidise those who do not? Connected devices enable the identification of those sub-categories of life and health insured. But this is complicated by a number of other social factors such as educational attainment and poverty: given the correlation between unhealthy lifestyles and low income the risks are clear. But although the line between choice and circumstances – and its practical application – is sometimes hard to draw, it is a reasonable starting point as to what information insurers might be entitled to access and rely upon in writing risk. Big data, and in particular connected devices not only enable insurers to more accurately identify insureds who make riskier choices; it is providing the means whereby insurers can reveal to those insureds the precise impact of those choices on the scope and cost of their cover. That information makes it more difficult for an insured to pray in aid those other social factors that might excuse (and thus mitigate) those choices. As to information pertaining to an insured's circumstances, should such information be available to insurers at all, even if the insured provides an explicit consent, and if so to what extent? In the UK, insurers can rely on age and disability as circumstances that are relevant to the scope and price of the cover that may be offered. The issue will really come to the fore over the use of genetic data: the types of information that insurers can access and rely upon has an important bearing on the extent to which certain matters should be the subject of solidarity-based insurance and which can safely be left to market-driven, mutuality-based insurance. And the answer to that question reflects, more broadly, the type of society that we want to live in. Should society permit risk-writing on the basis of genetic data, segmentation will accelerate and people will be priced out of, in particular, life cover through no fault of their own. As big data reveals the extent to which insurers are paying out on more than a statistically insignificant number of claims where there was a clear and obvious genetic indicator of risk, the pressure to use this data will grow. At that stage, society will have to decide whether to allow access at all, and if so, what mitigating measures might have to be put in place to ensure continued access.

III. The Future of Insurance in the Big Data Age

Insurance works because we are ignorant of our individual fates. It is the fact that any of us might turn out to be a bad risk that makes it sensible for everyone to insure against that chance. The pooling of individual risks that can only be known in the aggregate underlies the whole system. But there is a mismatch of aims between insurers and insured. Insureds want to avoid the consequences of misfortune; insurers want customers who avoid misfortune. The two aims are reconciled because both sides are operating behind a veil of ignorance. But big data is starting to lift the veil. Those who might have suspected they were better risks and needed less insurance are increasingly able to verify those suspicions. Those who know they are less risky prospects may not buy cover or, if they do, can insist on a good price. By the same token, big data identifies more accurately those who really do need the cover; those individuals will pay more not just so as to reflect their greater risk, but also to compensate from the loss of premium income from less risky insureds. A framework will have to be put in place to address these issues as and when they become more pronounced.

We have not reached 'peak data-profiling'; we are not even in the foothills. That is in part because, at least in the EU, insurers have been preparing for the implementation of the GDPR and considering its impact on how they might permissibly acquire and process data for the purposes of risk profiling, whether by solely automated means or otherwise. Moreover, insurers are, whether in partnership with tech companies or otherwise, working on the accuracy of their algorithms, something that will continue to improve as a result of competitive forces. As the John Hancock announcement in the US confirmed, the big data genie is well and truly out of the bottle and other insurers are bound to follow for fear of suffering the consequences of adverse selection.

The need for the common law to expand insurers' duty of good faith disclosure will be a necessary but insufficient condition of ensuring fairness and transparency in the provision of insurance in the big data age. If the issues identified in this book are to be properly addressed, there will also be an important role for regulators to play. In this regard, the Information Commissioner notes that detecting discriminatory decisions in hindsight will not be sufficient to comply with the accountability provisions of the GDPR. She observes that big data analysts will need to find ways to build discrimination detection into their machine learning systems to prevent such decisions being made in the first place.[3] This gives rise to the concept of transparency by design:[4] insurers

[3] ICO, para 117, GDPR, Recital (71).
[4] Which would operate in parallel to the general obligation of privacy by design under Art 25 of the GDPR.

should build algorithms and hold datasets on their insureds in such a way as to provide clarity on what information is held, how it is processed, and what impact it has on the scope of the proposed cover. In this regard, many academics have called for 'algorithmic audits' of any systems directly affecting the public.[5] This would include risk profiling systems. It is through the auditing of algorithms and their use that insurers' compliance with an expanded duty of disclosure could be ensured at a systemic or institutional level.[6] This dovetails with the accountability obligation imposed by Article 5 of the GDPR: such algorithmic audits may be the way in which insurers discharge that general obligation.[7] In addition, to avoid playing catch-up (an inherent problem in any system of regulation), regulators will themselves have to develop regulatory technology (or RegTech as it has been referred to) to enable them to understand how these technologies are being used by, in this case, insurers, and to diagnose improper uses or outcomes. Moreover, big data is not a matter for any single regulator. In the past competition regulators have sometimes considered questions relating to data and data acquisition to be a matter only for privacy regulators.[8] That was mistaken. A joined up regulatory response will be needed if the use of big data by commercial actors is to be fair and lawful. In the UK, the FCA, the ICO and the Equality and Human Rights Commission will have to increasingly engage with each other to develop integrated policy on the use and abuse of big data. In this way, regulators will be better prepared for the many and varied challenges that lie ahead.

[5] eg V Mayer-Schonberger and K Cukier, *Big Data: The essential guide to work life and learning in the age of insight* (London, John Murray, 2017) 178–82.

[6] And so Swedloff argues that regulators will have to audit insurers' classification systems looking at the 'data sets mined' by the algorithms, as well as the source codes and inferences embedded in the algorithm. These audits should focus on whether personal data is scrubbed from the data used to create the predictions, whether carriers are gathering inappropriate individual data and whether the data are suggesting inappropriate correlative predictions: R Swedloff, 'Rick Classification's (R)evolution', *Connecticut Insurance Law Journal*, Vol 21.1, 2014, 371.

[7] The accountability obligation is one of the significant enhancements under the GDPR as compared with the previous Data Protection Directive.

[8] As Stucke and Grunes point out: 'data-driven mergers … have the potential to lessen non-price competition in terms of the array of privacy protections offered to consumers. Likewise, monopolies' data-driven exclusionary practices can hamper innovative alternatives that afford consumers greater privacy protection.' M Stucke and P Grunes, *Big Data and Competition Policy* (Oxford, OUP, 2016) p 4. The European Commission thus appeared to err, in considering the Facebook/WhatsApp merger, in concluding that 'Any privacy-related concerns flowing from the increased concentration of data within the control of Facebook as a result of the Transaction do not fall within the scope of the EU competition law rules but within the scope of the EU data protection rules'. European Commission: Facebook/WhatsApp Case Comp/M.7217, Commission Decision C(2014) 7239 3 October 2014, para 70.

INDEX